EXPLORING PROFESSIONAL COOKING

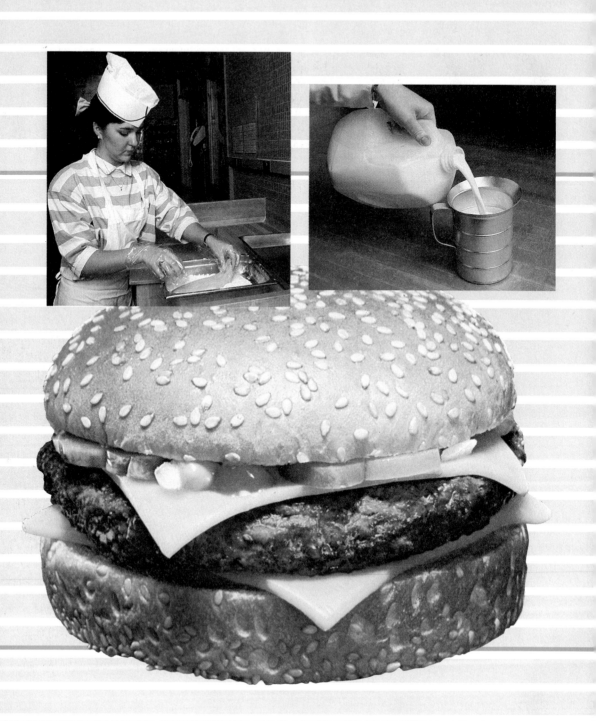

EXPLORING PROFESSIONAL COOKING

MARY FREY RAY and EVELYN JONES LEWIS

THIRD EDITION

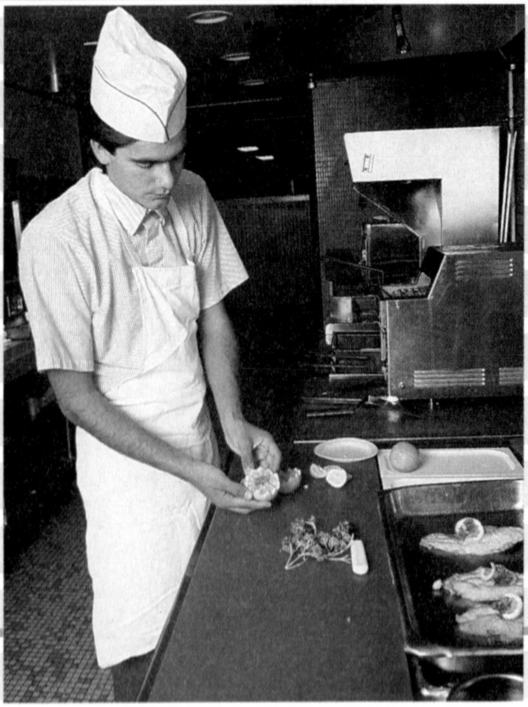

GLENCOE/ McGRAW-HILL
A Macmillan/ McGraw-Hill Company
Mission Hills, California

Send all inquiries to:
Glencoe Division, Macmillan/McGraw-Hill
809 West Detweiller Drive
Peoria, IL 61615-2190

ISBN 0-02-667950-7

4 5 6 7 8 9 10 92 91 90

photo credits

Special thanks to Janet Raymond for her drawings.

American Dairy Assn., 388
American Spice Assn., 260
Anchor Hocking Corp., 256
Aratex Services, 394
Atlantic Vocational Tech Center, 80, 399, 403
Bunn-O-Matic Corp., 119, 387
Burger King, 17, 336
California Olive Industry, 155
The Confectionary, 307, 308, 314, 316, 317, 318
Cres-Cor, 255, 403
Dudley-Anderson-Yutsy Public Relations, Inc., 154, 277, 334
Fleischmann's Yeast, 265, 269, 275
Florida Department of Citrus, 263
Florida Department of Natural Resources, 7, 213, 214, 215, 217
David Frazier, 42
R. T. French Company, 341
James R. Gaffney, 22, 159, 246, 247, 262, 278, 283, 307, 308, 312, 314, 316, 317, 318, 347, 373, 378
Gideco, Inc., 285
Groen, 133
Hamilton Beach, 105
Hearst Magazines Public Relations, 249
Heinz, 8
Hobart Commercial Equipment Division, 125, 130
Chuck Hofer, 168, 238, 288, 362
Impact Communications/Wendy Boersema, Photographer, 19, 24, 35, 46, 176, 177, 178, 223, 227, 229, 234, 237, 248, 251, 263, 264, 268, 270, 271, 297, 299, 301, 305, 319, 322, 329, 350, 368, 395, 396, 399
Joan of Arc Company, 21
Kentucky Fried Chicken, 342
Le Bakery, 262
Lewis & Neale, Inc., 206
Limestone Community High School, Linda Ragain, 12, 15, 20, 36, 48, 60, 84, 104, 122, 138, 152, 168, 182, 198, 210, 222, 238, 250, 276, 288, 306, 320, 330, 342, 362, 382, 394
Thomas J. Lipton, Inc., 167
McDonald's Corporation, 2, 321
Robert McElwee, 2, 3, 307, 326, 327, 346, 354, 355, 358, 390, 392, 399, 404
National Broiler Council, 25, 183
National Livestock and Meat Board, 10, 170, 191, 192, 328, 332, 337
National Marine Fisheries Services, 219, 331
National Pasta Assn., 245
National Pork Producers Council, 171, 174, 183, 331, 363
National Turkey Federation, 161
Nestlé Foods Corp., 289
New China, 347
Ocean Spray Cranberries, 14
Old Country Buffet, 152, 389
O'Leary's, 278, 283, 312
Oscar Mayer and Company, 151
George O. Pasquel Co., 129, 256, 257
Pekin Area Vocational Center, Becky Bagley, 2, 10, 54, 100, 106, 121, 123, 137, 179, 208, 324
Pelouze Scale, 113
Pepe Taco, 378, 380
Pepperidge Farm, Inc., 252
Brent Phelps, 233, 274
Purdue Memorial Union, 405
Rice Council, 9, 162, 199, 239, 241
Slater Associates/Image Gate, 31, 169, 185, 226, 253, 264, 282, 289, 290, 294, 381
Stephanie, 246-247
Rick Sullivan, 32
Sunkist Growers, 23
Swift & Company, 200, 204
Taco Bell, 374, 375
Texas Highways, 181, 364, 379
Toastmaster, 119, 120, 127, 131, 132
United Dairy Industry Assn., 26, 27
Victory Refrigerator Co., 135
Vulcan-Hart, 135, 333, 338
Waring Products, 120
Wear-Ever, 103, 105
Wendy's International, 363
Woodruff High School, 32
Ann Wright, 21, 188, 189, 203, 205, 209, 256, 258, 259, 277, 280, 284, 286, 287, 383, 403
Duane Zehr, 2, 6, 10, 12, 15, 20, 36, 48, 56, 60, 64, 84, 100, 104, 106, 121, 122, 123, 129, 137, 138, 152, 164-165, 176, 179, 182, 198, 208, 210, 222, 250, 257, 272-273, 276, 283, 293, 302-303, 306, 320, 324, 330, 342, 382, 394, 367, 371, 389

contents

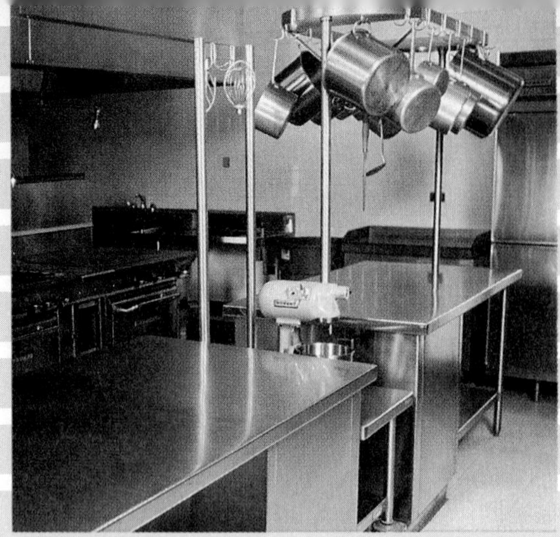

Unit 1

The Food Service Industry and You

The food service industry is bigger than you might imagine. It goes far beyond fast food restaurants and school lunch programs. In fact, it is one of the largest industries in this country, employing millions of people.

Up until now, you have probably seen only one side of food service operations. As a customer, you see the meals served and the people who serve them. But each meal depends on a large number of people behind the scenes. It is their planning, organization, and teamwork that result in the meals you eat.

You are about to learn what is involved behind the scenes of the food service industry. By the time you finish studying this book, you will have gained many of the basic skills needed by a professional cooking team member. You will then understand how food service operations work, both behind the scenes and over the counter. You should also have a better idea whether there's a career in food service that is right for you.

The food service industry is a people industry. Although the future will bring more specialized equipment to speed food preparation, it will not eliminate the need for food service workers. People enjoy having personal service and attention when eating out.

"Jim Lincoln slipped the burgers off the grill and onto the buns. He really enjoyed cooking out. "Lunch is ready everybody!" Ruthann, Tony, and Rosita gathered around and filled their plates. They were enjoying a picnic on one of the last days of summer before the school year began.

Jim finished his glass of lemonade and said, "I think I'll quit school and get a job at Sizzling Sam's. They pay minimum wage, and I hate school anyway."

"It's your life, I guess," Ruthann Harris responded, "but that sounds like a stupid idea to me. My cousin quit school and had a lot of trouble getting a job. I'm going to be trained to do a job I enjoy!"

"Like what?" asked Jim.

"Well, I really enjoyed my foods and nutrition class last year. So, I signed up for that new food service class this fall. You like to cook. Maybe you ought to think about adding that class to your fall schedule. You learn all about quantity cooking, meal planning, and how to work in a professional kitchen."

"I don't know." Jim seemed doubtful. "Do you think anybody else will be taking it?"

"I am," responded Tony di Franco as he reached for a second hamburger. "My uncle and cousin are both professional cooks, and I've always wanted to be one too. They said I should take some food service courses to see if I really like it."

"Hey, I'm taking it too!" Rosita Morales sounded surprised. "And so is David Smith. He's been working down at Graf's Bakery this summer and thinks he may want to be a baker when he gets out of school."

"And Kim Lee signed up, too," Ruthann added.

"Okay, okay! You convinced me! I just hope we all get into the same class!""

chapter 1

food service — the people industry

Set your goals

When you complete the study of this chapter, you should be able to . . .

- Define and correctly use the vocabulary terms.
- Identify the kinds of jobs available in food service.
- List the qualities employers look for in employees.
- Describe the advantages and disadvantages of food service work.

Build your vocabulary

back of the house
caterers
front of the house
institutions
nonprofit
registered dietitian

THE FOOD SERVICE INDUSTRY AT A GLANCE

Food service isn't just one of the largest industries in the country, it is also one of the best known. Every meal purchased and eaten away from home is part of the food service industry. That amounts to millions of meals each day.

Many of these meals are served in restaurants. Some people eat out daily — perhaps a quick breakfast on their way to work or lunch with friends. For others, eating out is a special occasion treat.

Restaurants come in all sizes and types. A lunch counter in a store may serve a very limited menu but draw customers because of its convenience. A cafe that specializes in homemade-type meals draws a different crowd. Its customers may include older adults, singles, and families. Fast food restaurants are noted for their quick meals of dependable quality and low prices. An elegant restaurant attracts those who don't mind spending more for high-quality food and plush surroundings. There are restaurants to fit any taste and price range.

Many food service establishments offer an appealing variety of breakfast foods.

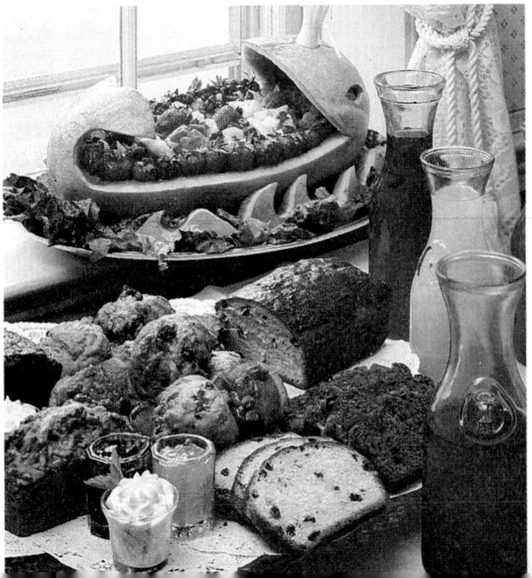

But food service includes more than restaurants. There are also many ***nonprofit*** food service operations. Unlike restaurants, these operations do not have to make a profit to stay in business. Their goal is to make good meals available at a reasonable price while covering their expenses. Many ***institutions*** such as schools, hospitals, and nursing homes have nonprofit food service operations.

Institutions also differ from restaurants in another way. Since most serve people who cannot choose to eat elsewhere, they must be careful to serve nutritious meals. In hospitals and nursing homes, people are often on special diets. Some, for example, may require meals low in salt. Others may be allowed only soft foods. It is the responsibility of the food service operation to prepare the proper food. A ***registered dietitian*** — a professional trained in nutrition — usually plans the meals for those on special diets.

Some companies provide food service facilities for their employees. These are often cafeterias where employees can choose their food and eat within an allotted meal break. These operations are usually nonprofit. In some cases, the company actually subsidizes (pays part of the cost of) the operation.

There are many other food service operations that do not fit any of these categories. The workers in some food service kitchens never see their customers. They may prepare meals for airline passengers, baked goods for restaurants, or food for vending machines. ***Caterers*** specialize in preparing food that will be served elsewhere. They provide food for banquets, parties, weddings, and similar special occasions.

This school cafeteria is an example of institutional food service.

THE PEOPLE OF FOOD SERVICE

More than 3.5 million people are employed in food service and that number continues to grow. Unlike some other industries, food service will remain a people industry. Better, more specialized equipment will speed preparation, but will not eliminate the need for workers. Part of the enjoyment of eating out is the personal attention and service provided by food service employees.

There are hundreds of different jobs in the food service industry. There are beginning jobs for those with no experience, intermediate jobs for those with some training and experience, and high-level management jobs that require years of training and work. In food service it is still possible to "work your way up" to a top job.

Restaurant-type food service operations are often divided into two parts for purposes of organization. Each part has its own staff.

The ***back of the house*** includes all the people who work behind the scenes. The storage area, kitchen, and dishwashing area are considered back of the house. Although customers rarely see the back-of-the-house staff, they are responsible for all the work that makes it possible to serve delicious food.

The ***front of the house*** is the part customers do see. It includes such areas as the dining room, waiting area, and rest rooms. The front of the house must be comfortable, attractive, and very clean. Front-of-the-house employees are the sales people of the operation. Their knowledge, friendliness, politeness, and skills help keep customers coming back.

In this book, you will learn most about back-of-the-house operations. However, you will probably have an opportunity to try out some front-of-the-house jobs as well. Remember, it takes the efforts of every employee to make food service run smoothly.

The pastry chef is a member of the back-of-the-house staff in a food service operation.

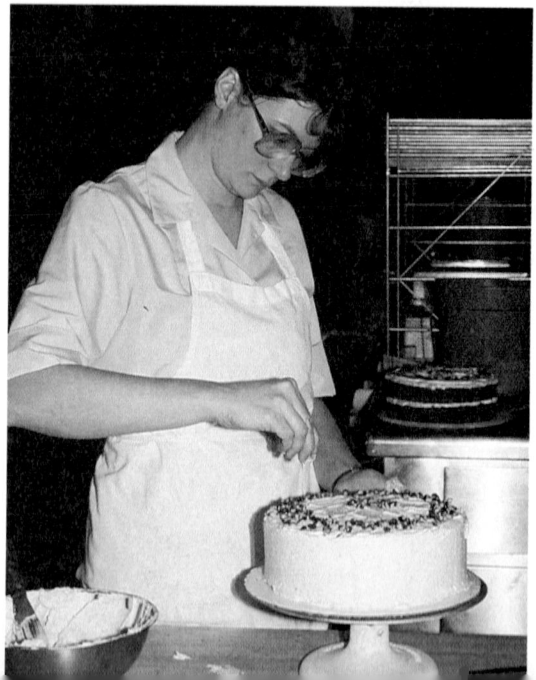

What Makes a Good Employee?

Those who hire people for food service jobs know what type of person makes a good employee. How many of these traits do you already have? Which do you need to work on?

- **Dependable.** Food service operations schedule only the minimum number of employees needed to work at a given time. An employee who is absent often or always late puts an extra burden on everyone else.

- **A team worker.** No job in food service is isolated. Everyone works as part of a team. If you are assigned to assemble tossed salads for lunch, you rely on the person responsible for preparing the lettuce and chopping the vegetables. If you are waiting on tables and have a few minutes to spare, you help out someone who is busy. This type of cooperation pays off for everyone.

- **Willing to learn.** Whether you are a new worker or an experienced one, every job is a learning experience. Employers want people who are anxious to learn and able to take criticism. They know these are the employees who will go far in food service.

- **Accurate.** Most food service operations must work very hard to make a profit or cover their expenses. Employees' mistakes mean wasted money and, often, unhappy customers. In the dining room, accuracy means writing down customers' orders clearly and adding up their checks accurately. In the kitchen, it means following the recipe exactly so food is not wasted. In the storeroom, it means checking orders to see the proper amount and type of food was delivered and storing it right to avoid spoilage. Operations with careless employees are often forced to close. Then, all the employees lose their jobs.

- **Clean and well-groomed.** Have you ever found a hair in your food when you were eating out? If so, you probably weren't sure you wanted to eat at that place again. Actually, employees who are not clean and neat can cause even more problems. They can actually spread disease to customers or other workers. Employers won't take a chance on hiring those who are not careful about their appearance.

Working as a member of a team is vital to the success of every food service establishment.

IS A FOOD SERVICE CAREER FOR YOU?

Right now you may just be thinking about a career in food service or you may already have decided on one. In either case, this course will be of help to you. You will learn about the many different types of jobs available in food service operations. You will also learn job skills. Some will be specific skills related to professional cooking. Other will help you be a better employee, whether you work in food service or some other occupation.

All jobs have both good points and drawbacks. Those in food service are no different. You should consider both if you are thinking about a food service career.

Advantages

It is not hard to find advantages to food service work. In almost every town there are places that serve food. These may be a drug store, hospital, nursing home, restaurant, fast food outlet, or school. Whatever they are, they represent job opportunities.

Here are some of the advantages:

- Work is readily available in almost any location.
- Wages and benefits for food service workers are improving.
- There is always a demand for new employees.
- Many part-time jobs are available.
- The need for food service workers is expected to continue to increase.
- With education and experience, you can advance to better jobs.

Disadvantages

What are the negatives of food service jobs? Of course, they vary from job to job. Here are some points that concern many food service workers:

- You often work under pressure. Can you work quickly and efficiently as orders pile up? Can you stay calm when a customer gets upset? Food service workers must be able to take problems and deadlines in stride.
- You may be expected to work at night or odd hours. Few food service workers have a regular 9:00 to 5:00 job. Food service operations need to be open when people want to eat.
- Most jobs require some Saturday, Sunday, and holiday work. These are the busiest times in restaurants. Many institutions are open every day of the year.
- Beginning jobs in food service usually offer low pay and few benefits. However, as you show a willingness to work and accept responsibility, you can advance rapidly to better paying jobs. Managers, chefs, and head cooks are usually very well paid.

A lot of on-the-job training takes place in the food service industry. A good food service worker will try his or her best at each job assignment.

SUMMARY

Millions of people daily eat away from home. Preparing and serving these meals is the job of food service. Food service means more than restaurants. Fast food chains, hospitals, and even caterers are part of the food service industry. Although the hours and pay are not always ideal, there are many beginning food service jobs available. Dependable workers who are willing to learn new skills can advance quickly in this profession.

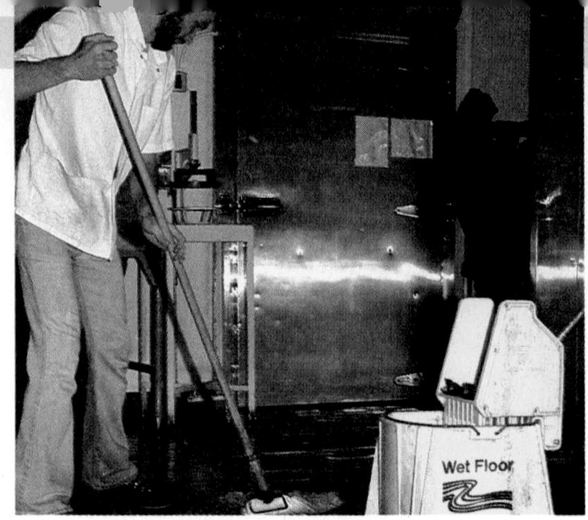

chapter recap

CHECK YOUR KNOWLEDGE

1. How does a nonprofit food service operation differ from a for-profit operation?
2. Name three types of institutions.
3. What is a registered dietitian?
4. What does a caterer do?
5. Describe the outlook for employment in the food service industry.
6. What parts of a restaurant are considered "back of the house"?
7. What are the traits of a good food service worker?
8. Give two examples of the importance of accuracy in food service.
9. Name the advantages of a food service job.
10. Describe four disadvantages of food service jobs.

EXTEND YOUR LEARNING

1. The *Dictionary of Occupational Titles* published by the U.S. Government is available in most libraries. Use the DOT to locate the occupational cluster that includes food service jobs. Read about and record the jobs that interest you.
2. Discuss front-of-the-house jobs and back-of-the-house jobs. List as many as possible in each category. Does each type have particular advantages and disadvantages?
3. Make a chart showing for profit and nonprofit food service operations in your area.

Unit 2

Mastering the Basics

When most students first consider entering a food service program, they usually are most interested in learning to cook. Cooking is fun and eating the food you cook is also enjoyable. However, food service is much more than cooking. If you are considering a career in food service, you must master certain basic skills.

A professional cook must know the nutritional quality of food. The first chapter in this unit introduces you to the basics of good nutrition.

The following four chapters are concerned with management. A professional cook must understand menu planning and its importance to food service. The menu serves as the backbone of every operation in the food service kitchen.

A professional cook must be able to prepare and serve large quantities of food without varying the quality. By following recipes exactly and measuring ingredients carefully, you will always be able to produce large amounts of high quality food.

Controlling costs must also be the concern of every professional cook. Cost control often determines the success or failure of food service operations.

Because a professional cook prepares food for others to eat, sanitation principles and safety rules are basics that you must master. The sanitation and safety of the food service customer is a professional cook's primary concern.

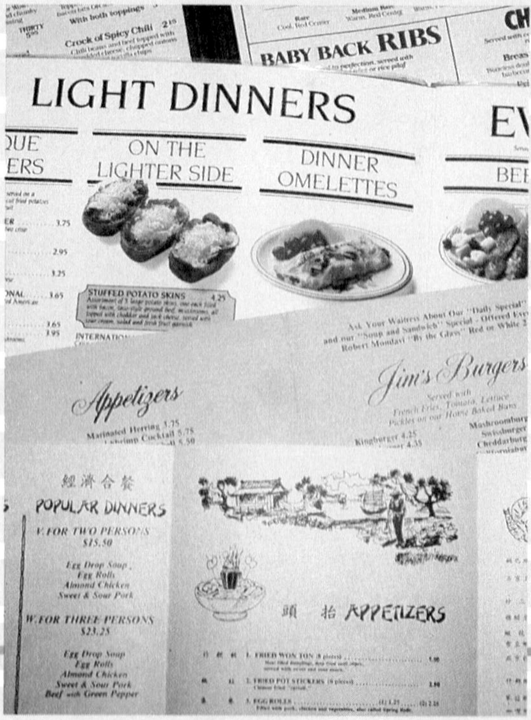

"Ruthann slipped into the seat next to Jim's. "How do you like the class so far?" she asked him.

"Better than I thought. Chef Robinson is okay! He really seems to know what he's talking about. But I don't know about this next chapter on nutrition. It sounds boring."

"When I took food and nutrition last year, a dietitian visited our class and showed us slides of children who had not been eating properly. This one little boy looked so awful! His legs were crooked and he had sores all over his body. Another slide showed this little girl with terrible teeth. Some of them were real skinny, but their bellies stuck out. The dietitian said the children all had diseases that were caused by not having enough of the right kinds of food to eat."

"Sounds depressing. Did any of the children in those pictures get better?"

"I don't know. The dietitian said they would always have problems. That boy's legs would never be totally straight, and that girl's teeth would stay that way. But the worst part is that their brains might even be damaged. Those children might not be able to learn things like we do."

Jim responded, "But if I'm just the cook, I can't decide what people eat. Why should I have to learn about vitamins and minerals?"

"So you can eat better yourself. No more pop and potato chips for breakfast!" Ruthann teased.

"I don't do that!" Jim looked hurt. "I think I'll ask Chef Robinson why he thinks it is important for a professional cook to study nutrition.""

chapter 2

nutrition

Set your goals

When you complete the study of this chapter, you should be able to . . .

- Define and correctly use the vocabulary terms.
- Describe how eating habits can affect your job performance.
- Explain how the body uses food.
- Describe the function of the six types of nutrients.

Build your vocabulary

calories
carbohydrates
fat-soluble vitamins
metabolism
nutrition
nutrients
protein
RDA
water-soluble vitamins

NUTRITION AND YOUR JOB PERFORMANCE

Nutrition is the study of the food you eat and the way the body uses it. ***Nutrients*** are the substances in food which help your body to:

- Grow.
- Repair and maintain itself.
- Regulate its processes.
- Make heat and energy.

The study of nutrition is important to you personally because it helps you make wise food choices in the food you eat. Whether you are studying, cheering on your teams, or working at a job, the energy you need comes from the food you eat. You will feel better, look better, and act better if your body is well-nourished with nutritious food. What you learn in this chapter, if you apply it to everyday living, may change your life.

Employers want workers who are both healthy and alert. People who are sick often disrupt work schedules and may pass on their illnesses to other workers. Employees who are not alert may forget what they are assigned to do. They also make mistakes easily — mistakes that can cause accidents or ruin food. People who have good nutrition are less likely to have health or alertness problems.

The study of nutrition is especially important in food service. People who prepare and serve meals have a responsibility to provide nutritious food choices. In institutions, the customers are "captive." They cannot eat elsewhere. The management is obliged to offer well-planned meals. The cooks must prepare the food carefully so the nutritional quality is preserved. Even in restaurants, the responsibility for good nutrition cannot be forgotten. The food service industry serves around 50,000,000 adults each day. It must accept some responsibility for their welfare.

By studying nutrition, you can select and prepare foods that promote good health. The next time you eat out, try to select nutritious items from the menu.

FOOD AND ENERGY

Your body is something like a car. The car gets the energy to run from the gasoline it burns. This process is called internal combustion because the fuel burns inside the engine to produce energy. The energy drives the pistons which turn the wheels.

Your body is also driven by the internal combustion process. The car burns gasoline, but your body burns food to give you energy, to keep you warm, make movement possible, build and repair cells, and keep your whole body working.

The process of turning food into energy inside the body is called ***metabolism***. Metabolism begins in the digestive system where food is broken down into its nutrients. The blood carries the nutrients to the cells where they are changed into energy.

Metabolism goes on day and night. Even when you are sleeping, energy is needed to keep your heart beating, your lungs expanding and contracting, your kidneys functioning and your brain working.

This is how you are different from a car. When you turn off the ignition the car stops, but your body is never completely at rest. The need for food to supply energy does vary with the body's activity, but it is always there.

Calories

Everybody has heard of ***calories***. Some say, "Calories make you fat." Others say, "Calories don't count." What is the true story of calories?

Calories are actually a measurement of the amount of energy produced when food is burned in the body. When you read that two tablespoons of sugar have 90 calories, it simply means, if you put two tablespoons of sugar on your cereal, your body will produce 90 calories of energy from it.

All foods have calories, some more, some less. When you eat more calories than your body can burn, the excess is stored on your body as fat. You might say that the fat on your body is your fuel tank. The fuel tank on your car has a definite capacity — it cannot get any bigger. But the fuel tank

Choosing nutritious snack foods can help prevent the storage of excess body fat.

Daily exercise burns calories, develops muscles, and keeps you fit.

on your body (the excess fat) gets bigger and bigger as you continue to eat more calories than you need. If you eat fewer calories than you burn up, the body uses up some of that fat and you lose weight. You can see that calories do count.

While the body needs some fat as insurance, it is easy to build up too much. And the longer you carry excess weight on your body, the harder it is to get rid of it. Fat is heavy, so your body builds up muscle and blood vessels to support it. They are part of the excess weight. The best plan is to learn to balance your body's energy needs with the foods you eat.

Exercise burns up calories. Jogging, bicycle riding, swimming, and walking are good for you. Exercise has other benefits as well. It helps develop muscles, and keep you fit. Plan to make some type of exercise part of your daily routine.

If you are concerned about losing weight, find a chart that tells how many calories various foods have. Some foods give you a lot of calories without nourishing the body. They are sometimes called "empty calorie foods." While such foods do not hurt you, they do not give your body much but calories. They can also fill you up and keep you from eating foods that do provide good nutrition. Most snack foods such as potato chips and candy are empty calorie foods. People who eat these foods regularly are more likely to be overweight. Make your calories count — for good nutrition!

THE FUNCTIONS OF FOOD

When gasoline is burned in a car, the force of the explosion moves the car. The only function of the gasoline is to make the car move.

The production of energy is the first function of food in the body. But it also does much more.

- **Food builds the body.** Once an automobile is built, its size never changes. You never see a small car grow into big, luxury car. But the human body begins as a microscopic egg and grows to a full-size man or woman.
- **Food repairs and maintains the body.** You don't expect gasoline to repair a smashed fender. Your body, however, uses its food not only for energy but also to repair itself. If you break a leg, the doctor can set it and perhaps put it in a cast. But the healing of the leg comes from the ability of the body to heal itself. The process depends on the food you eat.

You know that good maintenance is essential to keep a car in top running condition. Parts of the car do wear out. Your body maintains itself using the food you eat. For example, your body cells are constantly being worn down and must be replaced. Also the digestive juices are used up every day and must be remanufactured. These are examples of the constant maintenance of your body which must come from the food you eat.

If you forget to fill the gas tank of your car, it will soon come to a sputtering halt. If you forget to feed your body good, nourishing food, it cannot maintain its activity. You may feel sluggish, tired, and irritable. Perhaps you have noticed how "touchy" you become when you are hungry. Then after you have eaten, you are much less irritable. Food can make the difference.

- **Food regulates the body processes.** Sometimes you have to take the car to the garage because it isn't running quite right. Perhaps the carburetor needs adjusting or the spark plugs need replacing. Your body can regulate its own processes. For instance, it automatically accelerates if you need a sudden burst of energy. To do this, it needs the right kinds of food in the right amounts.

THE NUTRIENTS

Nutrients are the chemicals the body needs which are supplied by food. There are six types of nutrients which are essential for good health. These are proteins, carbohydrates, fats, minerals, vitamins, and water. The nutrients cooperate in nourishing the body. No one nutrient can do the job alone. Each is dependent upon the others.

Chicken is a good source of complete protein that helps to meet your body's nutrient needs.

Protein

Protein is perhaps the most important of the nutrients. It is absolutely essential for growth, repair, and maintenance of the body. It is found in every part of the body. In fact, scientists have not found any living substance that does not contain protein.

Not all proteins are of the same quality. Proteins from animal sources such as meat, eggs, and milk are "complete proteins." That is, they contribute everything the body needs to fulfill the function of protein. Proteins from grains, some vegetables, cereals, and breads are "incomplete" or "partially complete." Eating a variety of protein foods each day — including some that contain complete proteins — will meet your body's needs.

Carbohydrates

Carbohydrates are the nutrients found in starches and sugars. They provide most of the energy needed by the body. Many inexpensive foods such as bread and cereal are good sources of carbohydrates.

The chief function of carbohydrates is to provide heat and energy for the body's activities. They are also "protein sparers" because they take care of this basic need, and the protein can be used for the other functions of food. Foods high in protein are generally more expensive than those high in carbohydrates.

Besides starches and sugars, there is another carbohydrate — cellulose. You probably know it as fiber or roughage. Cellulose cannot be digested by the human body, but it does have an important function. It provides the bulk in the intestines necessary for the elimination of the body wastes. Foods such as fruits, vegetables, and whole-grain breads and cereals are excellent sources of cellulose.

Not all foods high in carbohydrates are nutrition bargains. Sugar, for example, is pure carbohydrate. It is the chief source of sweetening for foods like cakes, pies, and cookies. But sugar and most other sweets are high in calories but provide few other nutrients. Make sure your carbohydrate choices give you more nutrition. Eat vegetables, fruits, and whole-grain breads or cereals daily. Save sweets for a special treat.

This meal provides carbohydrates in the rice, beans, rolls, and pie being served. Which carbohydrates provide the most nutrition? Which ones provide the most calories?

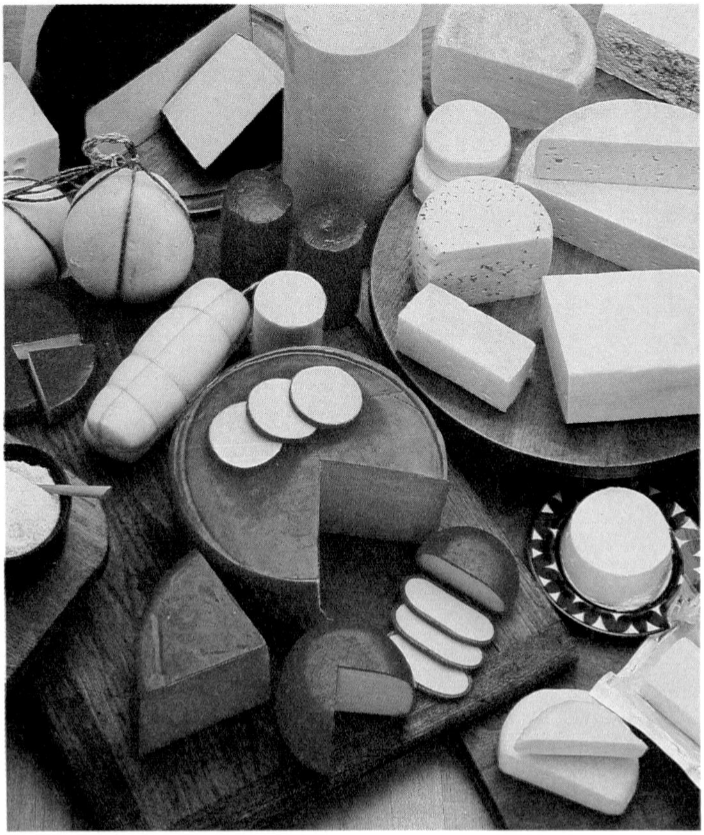

Tasting a variety of cheeses may be fun, but remember that cheese contains many hidden fats and calories.

Fats

Fats are another source of energy. Some fat can be easily seen such as the fat you cut off a piece of meat or the butter or margarine you spread on bread. But there is much hidden fat in food. Cakes, pies, fried foods, potato chips, mayonnaise, and nuts are some foods that contain large amounts of hidden fat.

Why should you be concerned about these sources of fat? Fat has many uses in the body. It supplies energy for the body's activities. Fat helps protect the body from sudden changes in outside temperature. Stored fat around the vital internal organs such as the kidneys help protect the organs from injury. Fat takes a long time to digest. It helps delay the return of hunger pains after eating. Fat adds much to the pleasure of eating since most people relish the flavor it gives to food.

However, eating fat foods, although pleasurable, adds many calories to a meal. Fats contain 2¼ times as many calories as the same amount of carbohydrates. There is also evidence that too much fat from animal sources increases the risk of health problems such as heart disease.

Minerals

The human body contains about five pounds of minerals. These minerals are important for regulating body processes. They also become part of the body itself in bones, teeth, tissues, and body fluids. Calcium and phosphorus are two of the most important minerals. However, there are many more that are also needed. The chart below describes functions and sources of the major minerals needed by the body.

Major Minerals

Mineral	Functions	Major Sources
Calcium	• Formation of bones and teeth. • Muscle contraction. • Heartbeat.	Dairy products, canned fish, greens
Phosphorus	• Formation of bones and teeth. • Metabolism.	Widespread in animal foods and whole-grain products
Sodium	• Maintain water balance.	Table salt, processed foods, many others
Potassium	• Heartbeat. • Depletion affects brain cells. • Metabolism of protein and carbohydrates.	Orange juice, bananas, potatoes, dried fruits
Iodine	• Regulates metabolic rate (rate body uses energy from food).	Seafood, iodized salt
Iron	• Formation of hemoglobin (the iron carrier of the blood).	Liver, other meats, eggs, dried beans, dried fruits, greens, whole-grain and enriched breads, and cereals
Magnesium	• Healthy nerves and skin. • Use of proteins and carbohydrates.	Organ meat, dried beans, whole-grain products

Vitamins

In order to burn gasoline in a car, the spark plugs must generate a spark that ignites the fuel. Vitamins are the spark plugs of the body. They make it possible for the food to perform its jobs. They also aid in metabolism.

Do you know people who take a vitamin pill each day? Vitamins are essential to good health, but most people who eat nutritious foods do not need vitamin pills. They get the vitamins they need in their food.

Water-Soluble Vitamins

Vitamins	Functions	Major Sources
Vitamin B_1 (thiamin)	• Promotes growth, appetite, muscle tone, nerve functions. • Helps body use carbohydrates.	Lean Pork, organ meats, nuts, oranges, dried beans and beans, enriched cereals, lamb
Vitamin B_2 (riboflavin)	• Releases energy from food. • Aids digestion of fats and protein.	Milk and milk products, organ meats, eggs, dark green greens
Vitamin B_3 (niacin)	• Essential for digestion of carbohydrates.	Whole-grain cereals, all protein foods
Vitamin B_6	• Adapts proteins and fats to body needs. • Helps form red blood cells.	Liver, meats, vegetables, whole-grain products
Vitamin B_{12}	• Formation of healthy red blood cells. • Promotes healthy nerves.	Meats, fish, eggs, dairy products
Pantothenic Acid	• Aids digestion.	Widespread in many foods.
Biotin	• Aids digestion.	Egg yolks, organ meats, peanuts
Folacin	• Helps form red blood cells.	Meats
Vitamin C (Ascorbic Acid)	• Works with calcium for strong bones and teeth. • Helps fight infection.	Citrus fruits, strawberries, broccoli

Fat-Soluble Vitamins

Vitamin	Functions	Major Sources
Vitamin A	• Keeps skin and eyes healthy. • Helps night vision. • Improves resistance to infection.	Fish oils, liver, yellow and green vegetables, yellow and orange fruits, milk, cheese, eggs
Vitamin D	• Promotes strong bones, teeth. • Improves use of calcium and phosphorous by the body.	Fish oils, fortified milk, sunshine
Vitamin E	• Protects unsaturated fats from oxidation.	Vegetable oil, whole-grain products
Vitamin K	• Needed for blood clotting.	Dark green vegetables

The special functions of vitamins are quite different than those of other nutrients. They do not provide energy like fats and carbohydrates or become part of the body like minerals. They do not provide the material for growth and repair as proteins do. Instead, they regulate the many chemical processes that keep the body functioning.

Each vitamin is known by a chemical name, a letter, or both. For example, vitamin B_3 is also known as niacin. The charts on pages 29 and 30 show the vitamins needed by the body, their food sources, and the functions they perform in the body.

Fat-Soluble and Water-Soluble Vitamins

Vitamins are often divided into two groups — those that dissolve in water and those that dissolve in fat. These are called ***water-soluble vitamins*** and ***fat-soluble vitamins***. This difference is important in both nutrition and cooking.

The body stores extra fat-soluble vitamins — vitamins A, D, E, and K — in body fat. That means the body can call on these vitamin reserves on days the foods you eat do not include enough of these vitamins. However, it also means that if you take in very large amounts of these vitamins (perhaps from too many vitamin pills), the body cannot get rid of the excess. Sickness or damage to the body can result. Extra water-soluble vitamins, however, are simply excreted with body wastes. Your body has no reserves of these, but neither will it be poisoned by an oversupply. Minerals are also water-soluble.

In cooking, special care must be taken to preserve water-soluble vitamins and minerals. Foods, especially vegetables, should not be soaked in water for any length of time. This allows the water-soluble vitamins in the food to dissolve in the water. Instead, vegetables should be cooked in a small amount of water for as short a time as possible to preserve their nutrients. Good cooks also find ways to use this cooking water with its valuable nutrients in other dishes instead of throwing it away. It can, for example, be added to soups, stews, and gravies for a nutrition and flavor boost.

Citrus fruits, cantaloupes, strawberries, spinach, and tomatoes are all good sources of vitamin C.

Vitamin C — A Closer Look

While all vitamins are important, vitamin C plays an especially important role in the body. That is why you often see it in advertisements for many foods. Unfortunately, not all such ads give accurate information.

Vitamin C is a water-soluble vitamin that is also known as ascorbic acid. Its discovery is an interesting story.

Back in the days of sailing ships when sailors were at sea for months, they were afflicted by a dread disease called scurvy. It caused the teeth to fall out, the skin to peel, and the muscles to become weak. Sometimes two-thirds of the sailors on a long voyage would die. In 1747, a British doctor discovered that if sailors were given fresh lime juice, they would not develop scurvy.

Many years later, the chemical in lime juice responsible for preventing scurvy was identified and named vitamin C or ascorbic acid. Today, scurvy is seldom seen, but the importance of vitamin C in the diet is recognized all over the world.

Vitamin C helps the cells work together by promoting the formation of a "cement" between them. It is essential in the building and repair of teeth and bones, and the maintenance of healthy gum tissue. It promotes the healing of wounds because it assists in the formation of strong scar tissue. It helps the body combat infection and fever. It reduces bruising.

Ascorbic acid has an important use in commercial food preparation. It prevents discoloring of cut fruits and vegetables and is frequently used in preparing them.

The best source of vitamin C are the citrus fruits such as oranges, grapefruit, lemons, and limes. Apples, cranberries, pineapples, tomatoes, and other fruits also contain vitamin C, but in smaller amounts. Vegetables can also make a contribution of vitamin C to the diet. Most of the deep green vegetables are good sources of vitamin C. Vitamin C is destroyed by heat so fruit and vegetables should be prepared with care.

Water is essential to life. Drinking plenty of water helps to regulate body temperature, aid digestion, and remove waste products.

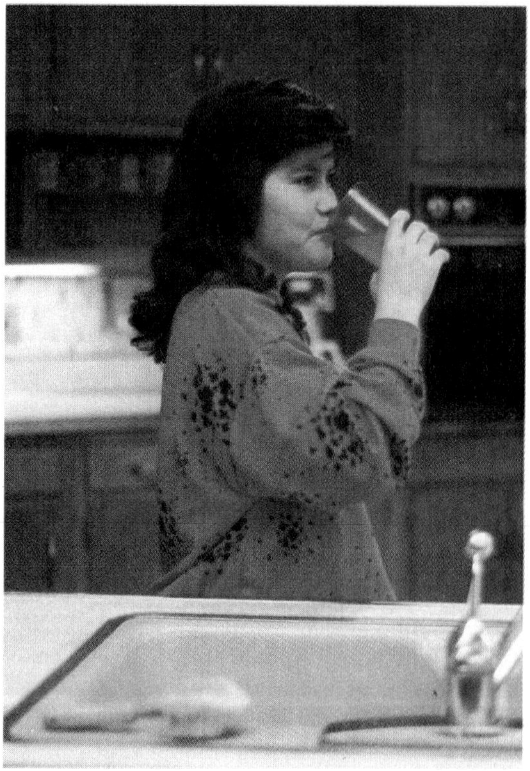

Water

Water is not a food, but it is essential to life. Perhaps you have read tales of prospectors for gold in the old West. The gold was so precious to them that they even threw away the water in their canteens so they could carry more gold. In crossing the hot, dry desert, they would gladly have given all their gold for one drink of water to quench their thirst.

The average-size adult weighs about 150 pounds. Of that 150 pounds, about 90 pounds are water. Water regulates all the body processes. As part of the blood, it carries most of the nutrients to the cells and removes the waste products. Water is part of the digestive fluids, such as the saliva that mixes with food when you chew. Virtually all foods contain some water.

Water also helps maintain the normal body temperature. When you exercise or get too warm, you perspire. This is actually a loss of water which must be replaced. The amount of water which you need is also influenced by the amount of salt you eat. Perhaps you have noticed how thirsty you feel after eating salty foods such as ham.

THE COMPUTER BRAIN

The human body is like an intricate machine whose activities are programmed by a computer — the brain. The computer brain directs the digestion of food so the nutrients are broken down into the form the body can use. They enter the bloodstream and are directed to the cells that need them to make energy or heat, for repairs, or for building or maintaining the body. In turn, the cells dispose of their waste products in the blood. They are carried to the proper organ for elimination. All this is directed by the computer brain.

FOOD HABITS

Your body reacts to poor eating habits much the same way a car reacts to poor quality gas. Do you have a hard time starting in the morning? Do you get tired in the middle of the morning? Does your body seem to go along in jerks instead of running smoothly? Maybe your poor eating habits are showing.

Your food choices are largely the result of habit. You have learned your eating habits from your family and your friends. After you finish studying this chapter, you may decide that some of your eating habits need changing. If you do decide this, don't expect to be bursting with energy and good health overnight. Remember, it took many years to make you as you are now. It will take awhile to undo the effects of poor eating habits. But the results will be a healthier and perhaps a longer life.

THE BASIC FOOD GROUPS AND THE RDA

You may wonder just how to tell if you are getting all the nutrients you need. There are several ways to tell, each providing a different degree of accuracy.

The most informal method is by thinking about your health and the way you feel. Do you have enough energy to get through the day with ease? Do you have any health problems, such as persistent dry skin or sore gums, that could be related to a poor diet? These may give you clues. But such health problems could also have other causes. It is possible, too, to eat poorly for some time before you notice the effect on your body.

Basic Food Groups

Food Group	Nutrients	Servings Per Day
Meat, Poultry, Fish, Beans Group	Protein, iron, riboflavin, niacin.	2
Milk-Cheese Group	Calcium, protein.	2 (4 for teens)
Fruit-Vegetable Group	Vitamin A, Vitamin C, iron, riboflavin.	4
Bread-Cereal Group	All whole grains enriched flours and products.	4
Fats-Sweets-Alcohol Group	Not needed. Eat only in moderation.	0

Using the basic food groups provides a better guide to good eating. This method divides foods into five groups:

- Meat-Poultry-Fish-Beans Group.
- Milk-Cheese Group.
- Fruit-Vegetable Group.
- Bread-Cereal Group.
- Fats-Sweets-Alcohol Group.

People in a particular age group just need to remember how many servings from each group they should eat daily. Teens, for example, should eat four servings daily from the Milk-Cheese, Fruit-Vegetable, and Bread-Cereal Groups. They need two servings daily from the Meat-Poultry-Fish-Beans Group. Foods from the Fats-Sweets-Alcohol Group are not needed for good health.

The food group method of diet planning is easy to use and remember. It does, however, have drawbacks. It does not mention calories although they are important to balancing weight. It also does not show different amounts for males and females, though males generally need more calories. It can also be difficult to classify some foods, like chili, which contain several foods into one food group.

Dietiticans — trained nutrition professionals — use a much more precise method of diet planning. It is based on the ***RDA*** or Recommended Dietary Allowances. The RDA is a chart developed by experts that estimates how much of each major nutrient a person of a given sex and age needs daily. Other charts are available which calculate the amount of nutrients in different foods. To check your diet against the RDA, you would first keep track of everything you ate for a period of time (such as a week). Next, you would check each of those foods to find out how much of each nutrient it contains. Then you would compare your totals for each nutrient against the RDA chart for your age and sex. While this method is much more complicated, it does give you a more accurate picture of the quality of your diet. Computer programs are available which make the process much easier. These also help dietitians plan meals for people with special dietary needs.

The five basic food groups are easy to use for diet planning. However, you must remember to also count the calories!

chapter recap

SUMMARY

Nutrition is the study of foods and the way the body uses them. The type of foods that are offered and the way they are prepared affect the nutrition of all who eat in food service establishments. Workers there should know the basic types of nutrients, the foods they are found in, and how to preserve them during food preparation and service. Knowledge of the basic food groups and use of the RDA charts help in planning good nutrition.

CHECK YOUR KNOWLEDGE

1. Give a brief definition of nutrition.
2. Give two reasons the study of nutrition should be important to you.
3. What is the process of metabolism?
4. What are calories? Why is it important to consider calories when making food choices?
5. Name the four functions of food in the body.
6. Name the energy nutrients.
7. Why is protein often considered the most important nutrient? Name three good sources of protein.
8. What is the difference between fat-soluble and water-soluble vitamins? How does it affect cooking?
9. Why is water, as well as food, needed for life?
10. What is the most accurate method of checking a diet for good nutrition?

EXTEND YOUR LEARNING

1. Discuss ways food service workers can help meet the nutritional needs of customers. In what ways are they limited?
2. Keep track of the "empty calorie foods" you eat for a three-day period. Figure out the total number of calories from these foods.
3. Use your library to find out what the experts say about using vitamin pills or other nutrient supplements. Write a paper summarizing your findings.

"Hey, Tony, look at this one!" Jim remarked as he held up a menu by the corner. It had several grease spots and a mustard stain among three columns of small print.

"Yuck!" exclaimed Ruthann. "I sure wouldn't want to eat in that place! If the menu looks that dirty, I wonder about the kitchen!"

"This one looks a lot more inviting," Tony agreed. "It even has colored pictures of some of the foods they serve."

"It's interesting," said Ruthann as she examined the two menus. "The breakfast menus in these two places are almost exactly the same! Eggs cooked in different ways, served with ham, bacon, or sausage. Tomato or orange juice and toast with everything. Why not pineapple juice or a fresh fruit bowl? I wonder how pizza would taste for breakfast?"

"Now that's Italian!" Tony joked. "Here's the menu from my uncle's restaurant." He held it at arms length and pretended to examine it critically. "I guess it looks pretty good."

"I don't recognize some of the food on it," Ruthann commented. "What's tortellini?"

"Tortellini is a pasta, made of little curled noodles with filling on the inside. It's really good."

"Sizzling Sam's is okay," Jim said, "if you like hamburgers. But there isn't much else on the menu. They don't even have fresh salads!"

"No enchiladas, either!" Ruthann held up a menu from the Casa Blanco Mexican Restaurante. "It was a good idea for Chef Robinson to bring in so many menus. It's interesting to compare them. I guess it's really important to serve food that customers like."

chapter 3

the menu

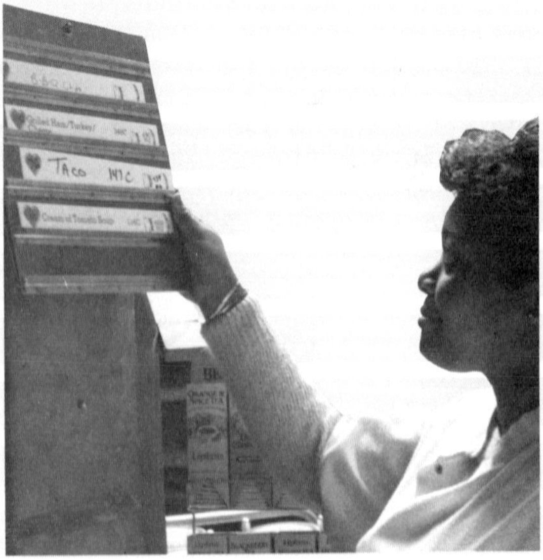

Set your goals

When you complete the study of this chapter, you should be able to . . .

- Define and correctly use the vocabulary terms.
- Identify the various kinds of menus and how they are used.
- Describe the influences on the type of menu offered.
- Write well-planned meal menus.

Build your vocabulary

a la carte	fixed menu
clip-ons	menu
cuisine	table d'hôte
cycle menu	tent cards

THE MENU

When you decide to eat out, how do you choose where to go? Several things probably influence your decision — location, price, whether you want a quick meal or a leisurely one. But the deciding factor is usually the restaurant's menu. ***Menu*** means more than the printed card the waiter or waitress hands you when you are seated. It also means the food choices the restaurant offers for each meal it serves. When you eat out, you want to go to a place that serves the kind of food you like.

Actually, the menu plays a far more important role in a food service operation than you might expect. It's the menu that determines:

- The supplies to be ordered.
- The workers needed and their skills.
- The kitchen equipment required.
- The type of customer the operation will attract.

Kinds of Menus

Although menus seem to vary widely, most can be grouped under two types, the fixed menu and the cycle menu. Each has a different purpose.

The Fixed Menu

Most restaurants have a ***fixed menu***. This means the same foods are served each day. Such menus often offer meals in two ways. The ***table d'hôte*** (TAHB-lah-DOTE) section features complete meals at a set price. Foods offered ***a la carte*** (AH-lah-CART) may be purchased separately. A hamburger platter that includes a burger, fries, salad, and a drink for $4.95 would be considered table d'hôte. If you chose each item separately — a hamburger for $2.25, fries for 75¢, salad for $1.75, and a drink for 75¢ — you ordered a la carte. The same foods ordered a la carte are usually more expensive than on the table d'hôte menu.

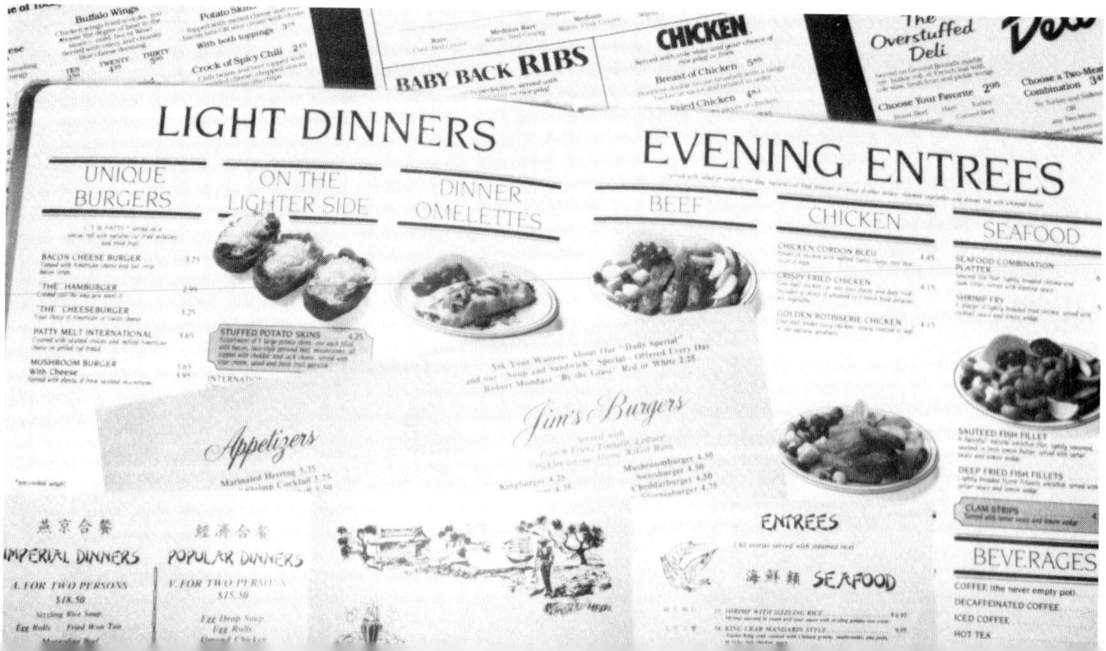

This array of menus shows you the variety of foods offered by different food service establishments. Because people have varying tastes, more and more restaurants are appearing to satisfy their selective taste buds.

The Cycle Menu

A ***cycle menu*** offers different food items each day for a set period of time (often a month or more). At the end of that time, the cycle begins again and the foods are repeated. Cycle menus are most often used in institutions such as hospitals and schools. Check the lunch menu at your school. Is it a cycle menu?

Influences on the Menu

The foods included on a menu are not just the chef's favorites. Menu planning is serious business. Some of the main influences include:

- **People to be served.** A cafe that serves lunches to office workers needs foods that can be prepared and served quickly. A nursing home will choose appealing foods that are easy to eat. Residents on special diets (such as low-fat or soft foods) may need separate menus.
- **Cost.** Most restaurants serve foods within a certain price range. That means some foods may be too high- or low-priced for a certain menu. Institutions do not try to make a profit, but they do work with a limited budget.
- **Type of cuisine.** ***Cuisine*** (kwee-ZEEN) is a particular style of cooking such as Italian, French, or Chinese. There's even American cuisine. The menu reflects the cuisine. Sometimes the menu is written in the language from which the cuisine came.
- **Equipment.** A menu may be limited by the equipment available in the kitchen. A fast food outlet could not produce a French menu because its kitchen does not have all the needed equipment.
- **Skill of workers.** The skills of the kitchen staff must match the menu. New, untrained workers cannot handle complicated dishes.
- **Cultural and regional differences.** People in different parts of the country prefer different foods. For instance, fried chicken, grits, black-eyed peas, and corn bread are favorites in the South. Many restaurants on the seacoast feature fresh seafood such as lobster in New England and Pacific salmon in Seattle. Restaurants in the Southwest often feature Mexican food.

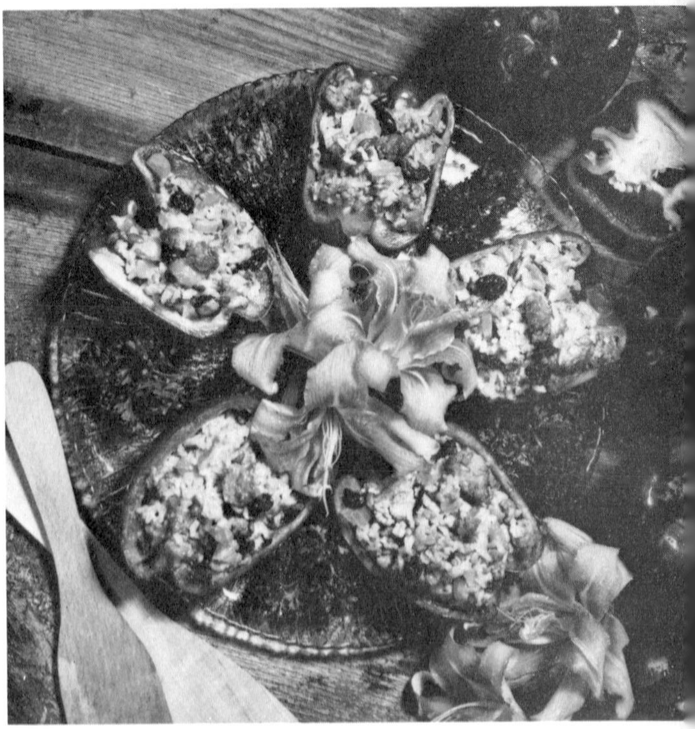

A restaurant with a menu that offers a variety of foods appeals to most people. Specialty dishes like this one are also crowd pleasers.

Who Decides the Menu?

In most food service establishments, someone in management plans the menu. In a chain restaurant, the menu may be decided in the main office. In a hospital, the chief dietitian or food service director makes the menu.

In a large food service establishment such as a hotel, an executive chef works with management to write the menu. The menu is of great importance to the kitchen staff because it determines the work of the day. A professional cook always checks the menu first when arriving for work.

MEAL PATTERNS

Meal patterns are the types and quantities of food eaten at different times of the day. In the United States, three meals generally are eaten — breakfast, lunch, and dinner. These three meals are served at fairly standard times during the day. However, between-meal snacks are very common. People vary greatly in the amount of food they eat. Food service menus reflect this variety. The chart on page 41 shows various eating patterns for breakfast, lunch, and dinner. Some operations specialize in light or heavy meals. However, most offer the customer some choice in the amount of food.

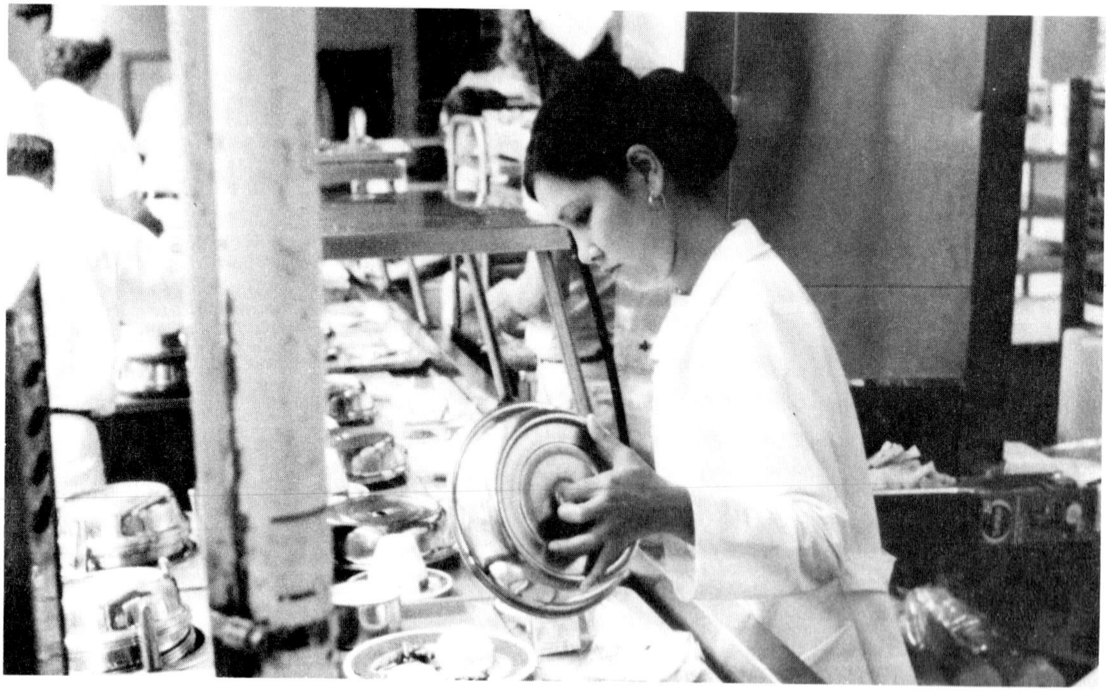

This dietitian is checking the amount of food on the plate as well as the execution of the planned menu.

Typical Meal Patterns

	Continental	Light	Medium	Heavy	Very Heavy	Notes
Breakfast	• Juice • Rolls • Beverage	• Fruit/juice • Egg/cereal • Toast • Beverage	• Fruit/juice • Egg • Bacon/ sausage • Toast • Beverage	• Fruit/juice • Cereal/ grits/fried potatoes • Egg Bacon/ sausage • Toast • Beverage		• Pancakes, Waffles, or French toast may be the main dish. • Sweet rolls may replace toast.
Lunch		• One main dish (salad or sand-wich) • Beverage	• Two main dishes (sandwich/ soup/salad) • Beverage	• Two main dishes • Dessert • Beverage	• One main dish • Vegetable • Salad • Bread/rolls • Dessert • Beverage	• Often a light meal. • In restau-rants, must have quick service be-cause customers have lim-ited time to eat.
Dinner		• Main dish (contains meat, fish, or poultry) • Two vegetables • Bread/rolls • Beverage	• Main dish • Two vegetables • Salad • Bread/rolls • Dessert • Beverage	• Appetizer • Main dish • Two vegetables • Salad • Bread/rolls • Dessert • Beverage	• Appetizer • Soup • Main dish • Two vegetables • Salad • Bread/rolls • Dessert • Beverage	• Usually heaviest meal of the day.

Snacks

Foods eaten between the main meals are considered snacks. The popularity of snacks has brought a new dimension to fast foods — the drive-in window. Although drive-ins are used for quick, on-the-run meals, they serve a steady stream of customers all day long. Many of the customers just want a snack. Coffee shops, lunch counters, and similar operations also benefit from between-meal customers. They provide a place for friends to meet, relax, and eat a light snack. Some institutions, such as hospitals, also operate snack counters for the convenience of workers and visitors.

Ice cream is this young athlete's snack selection for the day. It gives her one serving of milk, containing vitamins A and D, calcium, and phosphorus.

PRINCIPLES OF MENU PLANNING

How would you go about planning a successful menu? You have already learned some things to consider. Experts have devised a list of principles, or rules, to help insure success. You can use these principles to plan your own meals or a complicated menu for food service.

A Menu Should Offer Variety

Some restaurants specialize in one type of food such as fried fish or steak. Such restaurants may offer a very limited menu, perhaps one vegetable, salad, and beverages, with the main menu item. Customers do not expect a variety of foods at this type of restaurant. Many institutions have cycle menus which do not offer choices. In general, however, a food service operation should offer options so everyone can find some appealing foods on the menu. This variety can be achieved in many ways.

Besides offering a variety of foods, there should also be choices within each type of food. For example, different kinds of meat, such as beef, pork, and veal, will give variety. Offering a choice of several types of salads adds interest to a menu.

Color contrast makes food more appetizing and appealing. Think about the visual appeal of the finished meal as you plan the menu. A meal of broiled chicken, mashed potatoes, and cauliflower lacks appeal because it has little color contrast. A few changes will make the meal more appealing. Chicken with barbecue sauce, a baked potato split open with chives sprinkled on top, and carrots for a vegetable make the meal more colorful.

Foods can be prepared in different ways. Meats may be roasted, fried, or broiled. Potatoes may be baked, creamed, fried, or scalloped.

The menu should offer a variety of textures, flavors, and temperatures. Foods that are soft or crispy, spicy or bland, hot or chilled, all make a meal more interesting.

A Menu Should Be Balanced

A menu should offer the customers complete meals that are balanced in appearance, serving size, and nutrition.

As you read a menu, think about how the foods will appear on the serving plate. Plates are more attractive if there are three items. Traditionally, a meat or meat substitute, a starchy food such as potato or rice, and a vegetable are the three items. Today, however, many customers prefer two vegetables instead of a starchy food.

A scoop of chicken salad on a plate by itself would look bare. Nestle the scoop of salad in a lettuce cup, and it looks much more attractive. Adding a slice of tomato, a few olives, and a small sandwich or muffin gives even more appeal. The plate is balanced and attractive.

The serving size should also be in balance. Smart managers offer smaller portions for children and senior citizens. But these smaller portion must be arranged on the plate so they do not look skimpy.

A Menu Should Offer Good Nutrition

As explained in Chapter 2, those who prepare and serve food to institutions have a great nutritional responsibility. Those who eat in an institution usually cannot go to another place if the food does not please them. The menu planner is obligated to offer meals that are nutritious, appetizing, and well-prepared. Institutions such as hospitals and nursing homes must also offer a variety of special diets for patients with special needs.

The nutritional responsibility of restaurants is less well-defined. Many offer a good variety of nutritious foods including vegetables, salads, and fruits. It is up to the customer to make good choices. However, some restaurants include few nutritious foods on their menu. The goal of all food service operations should be to properly nourish the people they serve.

Another nutrition issue involves methods of food preparation. Careless cooking methods can lower the nutritional value of food.

For example, minerals and some vitamins dissolve in water. If fruits and vegetables are soaked for long periods before cooking, much of their nutrition is lost. Or if a cook adds baking soda when cooking green vegetables, the vegetables stay greener, but their vitamin C is destroyed. You can see why a professional cook needs to know about nutrition.

A Menu Should Be Flexible

Perhaps it would be better to say that the operation's management should be flexible. The menu must adapt to new situations. A change of workers in the kitchen, the purchase of a new piece of equipment, a delivery of food that fails to arrive may mean changes in the menu. Many restaurant menus include a "special of the day." This allows the chef to take advantage of inexpensive food items. It also adds variety.

A Menu Should Be Truthful

If a fresh fruit salad appears on the menu, it should not be made with canned fruit. "Homemade pie" should be prepared and baked in the food service kitchen. It should not be purchased already prepared. Customers do not often return to a restaurant that does not serve food as described in the menu.

THE MENU AS A SELLING TOOL

How the menu looks is important because it sets the tone for the restaurant. A long, elaborate menu tells the customer that the food service is rather formal. A menu hand written on a chalk board means the service and food will be casual. Each menu has a message.

This menu tells the customer that only salads are available.

Salads and Cold Platters

Served with Bread and Butter.

Chef's Julienne Salad 4.25
Crisp Salad Greens Topped with Julienned Ham, Turkey, Swiss and American Cheese, Garnished with Tomato Wedges and Egg Slices.

Fresh Spinach Salad (Seasonal Availability) 3.50
Chilled Fresh Spinach Leaves, Tossed with Fresh Mushrooms, Bacon Bits and Hard Boiled Egg—Your Choice of Dressing.

Stuffed Tuna Tomato 4.25
Tuna Salad Filling a Split Red Ripe Tomato Garnished with Egg Wedges.

Fresh Fruit Plate 4.50
Seasonal Fresh Fruits Served with Cottage Cheese or Sherbet.

The Board Menu

A menu written or printed on a board on the wall has the advantage of flexibility. A chalk board can be erased. A board with printed inserts can easily be changed. If the demand for a certain food has been heavy and it has all been served, it can be deleted from the menu and something else put in its place. A board menu's informality and flexibility make it perfect for certain types of food service such as cafeterias, fast foods, or restaurants on college campuses.

The Spoken Menu

Some restaurants use the spoken menu. After the customers are seated, the waiter or waitress tells what foods are available. Such a menu must be limited to three meals at the most. Even then, some customers find it difficult to remember the choices and prices. Often all the meals are priced the same to minimize confusion.

Some people like a spoken menu. They say it is friendly and increases conversation between the customer and the waiter or waitress. Others say that they do not have a chance to study the menu and make choices.

In some restaurants, the customer is handed a printed menu, but the waiter or waitress tells them what the specials of the day are. This allows for some friendly contact, but gives a customer more time to decide what to eat.

The Printed Menu

The printed menu is the first thing the customer sees when seated at the table or counter. It can set the tone for the whole meal.

Think about the various printed menus you have seen. Those that clearly state the food items available and their prices are easiest to use. The a la carte items should be listed separately from the table d'hote meals and the items should be grouped by type of food. On a good menu the price is given for each item. When the table d'hote meals are grouped together, it is easy to compare them. The foods that come with each meal should be listed clearly.

A table d'hote menu may list the foods included in the menu in a block such as this:

Soup of the day
Roast Beef
Baked Potato
Choice of Vegetable
Salad Bar
Beverage $8.95

Or it may be listed more formally like this:

Consomme
Roast Prime Rib of Beef
Duchesse Potatoes Fresh Broccoli
Garden Salad
Fresh Baked Rolls Coffee or Tea
$12.95

Printed menus may be made more flexible by including a separate list of the daily specials. If the specials are fastened to the regular menu, they are called ***clip-ons***. If they are printed on a stiff paper and folded so they stand up on the table, they are called ***tent cards***.

The printed menu should be absolutely clean. A dirty, finger-smudged menu will make the customer suspicious of the standards of cleanliness in the kitchen.

THE COMPUTER AND THE MENU

Menu planning, like many areas of food service, can be simplified by use of a computer. For instance, cycle menus can be put in the computer to be repeated at a set time. The food manager can make any needed changes and print the menu. The copies are distributed to the kitchen staff.

A hospital dietitian has many special diets to prepare. The computer can save hours of work. When the doctor prescribes a certain diet for a patient, that information can be entered into a computer in the nurses' station along with the patient's age, weight, and other vital statistics. Even the room number is entered. The dietitian can print a list of each patient who needs a particular type of diet. Menus and recipes for different types of special diets can also be entered in a computer.

In a restaurant, a chef can make good use of a computer. All the recipes commonly used can be entered in the computer's memory. If chickens are a good buy, management may instruct the chef to include a chicken dish on each day's menu. On command, the computer will print out a list of all recipes in its memory using chicken as the main ingredient. This is easier than the chef searching for written recipes for chicken. The chef can decide on a chicken dish to be prepared each day. The computer will print out the recipe for each.

This dietitian is about to print out a list of all the patients who are on a bland diet. She can then select special menus and recipes for these patients with the computer's assistance.

SUMMARY

The menu is the basis of a food service operation. The type of food served determines the supplies, workers, and equipment it needs, and the type of customers it will serve. There are two types of menus — fixed and cycle. Fixed menus, written or spoken, are used mostly in restaurants. Cycle menus are found in institutions. Regardless of the type, all menus should offer variety, balance, flexibility, truthfulness and good nutrition.

chapter recap

CHECK YOUR KNOWLEDGE

1. What four functions of the menu make it of first importance in food service?

2. What is table d'hote? What is a la carte?

3. What type of food service operation would use a cycle menu?

4. Who decides the menu in a fast food chain operation?

5. Name four factors that influence menu planning.

6. You are served a plate of cauliflower, mashed potatoes, and creamed chicken. What is wrong with this menu?

7. Why are menu planners in a nursing home obligated to serve nutritious menus?

8. A cook puts a pinch of soda in the green beans while cooking. When served, customers enjoy the bright green color. Why was the manager upset?

9. Name two ways the computer can help in menu planning.

10. Which type of written menu is easiest to change?

EXTEND YOUR LEARNING

1. Draw up a list of ten food service operations in your area. Include a variety of for profit and nonprofit operations. For each, determine whether the operation uses a fixed or cycle menu. How is the menu displayed — board, spoken, or printed? What type of customers is each operation trying to attract?

2. Discuss what regional or ethnic foods are featured in restaurants in your area.

3. Select pictures from magazines that show food arranged on a plate. Tell what principles of meal planning are shown.

"Standardize, standardize!" complained Jim. "All I hear is standard tools, standard recipes, standard measurements, standard this, standard that. Why can't I experiment a little? When I make hamburgers at home, I like to put in a dash of this and that. It makes it more fun."

"It also makes it more salty sometimes," commented Rosita. "I remember one time you made some we could hardly eat. That would be awful if it happened in a restaurant. Can't you see all the hamburgers sent back to the kitchen because they were so salty? You might even get fired."

"I guess so," replied Jim. "But my grandma is a great cook and she hardly ever looks at a recipe. She just sort of puts things together, and they always taste good. I'd like to cook that way instead of following a recipe exactly."

"How long has your grandma been cooking?" asked Rosita.

"Oh, a million years or so," said Jim. "I get your point. I need a lot of experience."

"Don't get mad," said Rosita. "From what Chef Robinson said, it's a matter of money. Suppose you were baking cakes for a banquet — like a hundred or so. Suppose all the cakes fell because you didn't measure all the ingredients accurately."

"Right!" said Jim. "Lots of money would be wasted. The cakes would have to be made all over again. Maybe the banquet wouldn't even be served on time."

"Remember what happened when we served dinner to the coaches?" asked Rosita. "We ran out of mashed potatoes because Tony didn't use the right size scoop. The first people he served got lots of potatoes, and there weren't any left for the last. Didn't you have to mix up some instant potatoes to finish the meal? Chef Robinson says he always keeps instant potatoes on hand for emergencies. So I guess he is right about standards. They are important for professional cooking."

chapter 4

standardization

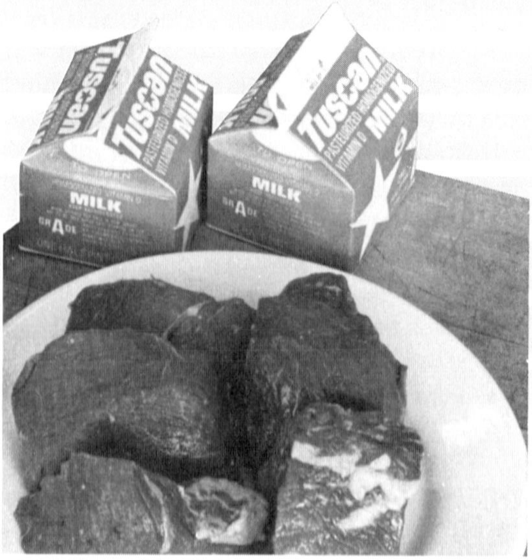

Set your goals

When you complete the study of this chapter, you should be able to . . .

- Define and correctly use the vocabulary terms.
- Explain the purposes of standardization.
- Identify the parts of a standardized recipe.
- Correctly increase or decrease recipes.
- Demonstrate correct measuring procedures.

Build your vocabulary

balance scale
desired yield
equivalents
mise en place
original yield
portion control
portion scale
spring scale
standardized recipes
thermostats
volume
yield

WHY STANDARDIZATION?

In food service the word "standardized" pops up often. Perhaps you have wondered why there is so much emphasis on following directions. The answer lies in the nature and purpose of food service operations.

Think about what might happen if a food service operation didn't care about standardization:

- In a college dormitory, the cafeteria runs out of the main menu item after only two-thirds of the students have been served. The manager discovers an employee is serving extra-large portions.
- A local restaurant hires a new cook and loses many of its regular customers. The cook adds a handful of this and a dab of that when preparing the dishes on the menu. Customers complain that their old favorites "just don't taste the same anymore."
- Preparation work for the noon meal in a nursing home is running behind schedule. An assistant cook decides to substitute gingerbread for the carrot cake on the menu. She knows the gingerbread can be prepared more quickly. She starts the batter, then sends to the storeroom for molasses. Word comes back that there is none.

In each case, an employee who failed to follow standardized procedure caused a major problem. When you are feeding hundreds of people, you can't afford such mistakes. They can cause delays, wasted food, or even accidents or broken equipment. Standardization is also a key to controlling costs — to keeping food service operations in business. You will read more about cost control in Chapter 5.

Standardization is essential to the success of every food service operation. It helps avoid major errors, wasted food, accidents, equipment breakdowns, and high costs.

In this chapter, you will learn about two areas where standardization is absolutely essential. Standardized recipes and procedures help make certain a dish tastes the same and serves the same number of people each time it is prepared. You will also learn the role computers are playing in standardization.

THE STANDARDIZED RECIPE

A recipe tells you how to make a certain food item. It is a formula for putting the ingredients together in the proper amounts and by the best method. To most people, the word "formula" is a scientific term. In food service, however, recipes are frequently called formulas.

In food service ***standardized recipes*** are used. That means the recipes have been carefully tested to give the quality and quantity of food each time the recipe is prepared. Standardized recipes, like the one on the next page, usually have the following parts:

Meat Loaf

Equipment: Bench mixer, Quart measure, Cutting board, Chef's knife, Portion scale, Measuring spoons, Measuring cups, Hook attachment, Loaf pans

Yield: 50 slices
Temperature: 350°F

Ingredients	Amount	Method
Bread slices	1 lb.	1. Crumble bread into bowl of bench mixer.
Milk	24 oz.	2. Pour milk over bread.
Chopped onion	1 c.	3. Chop onion, celery, and parsley. Add to bread mixture.
Chopped celery	1⅓ c.	4. Weigh beef and pork and add to mixture.
Ground beef	6 lb.	5. Add remaining ingredients to mixture and attach dough hook.
Ground pork	2 lb.	6. Mix on low speed for 3 minutes.
Salt	2 T.	7. Portion 3 lb. of meat loaf mixture into each of the five loaf pans.
Worcestershire sauce	2 T.	8. Bake 1 hr.
Chopped parsley	¼ c.	9. Remove from oven. Cut each meat loaf into 10 slices.
Eggs	7	

Serving size: 1 slice, ¾″ thick

Cost per serving: ____________

- **Yield.** The number of servings a recipe will provide if it is followed exactly is its ***yield***. Most standardized recipes for food service yield 25 servings, 50 servings, or even more.
- **Ingredients.** The ingredients needed for the recipe are listed in the order they are used. The description of each ingredient is very specific. It may say "Flour, hard wheat, sifted" or "Garlic, minced." Be sure to use the exact ingredient the recipe calls for.
- **Measurements.** The recipe tells exactly how much of each ingredient to use. Measurements may be given by weight (10 pounds), by volume (3 quarts), or by number (15 slices).
- **Mixing and cooking methods.** Over the years, experience has taught cooks that certain food preparation methods give the best results. A standardized recipe specifies the best method to use for a particular preparation.

- **Equipment.** A standardized recipe tells what equipment to use because the results usually depend upon them. Recipes, especially for baked products, are developed for certain size pans. A smaller or larger pan will give poor results.

- **Temperature.** Most foods require a specific temperature to cook properly. For cooking on top of the range, temperatures are usually described, such as "low heat," "simmer," or "boil.' Ovens and many electrical appliances have ***thermostats*** — devices which keep the temperature exactly where you need it. For deep-fat frying and candy-making you may need to use a thermometer to check the temperature of the food you are cooking.

- **Time.** Time is closely related to temperature control. Just as foods require specific temperatures, they also need a certain amount of time in which to cook properly. Standardized recipes give the proper cooking time.

There are many sources for standardized recipes. Most food service operations have their own files of recipes. Many excellent recipes come from companies that sell food and equipment to food service. These companies employ chefs and home economists to develop and test new recipes which they make available to food service operations.

Increasing and Decreasing Yield

Often the amount a recipe yields and the amount of food you need are not the same. In that case you must convert the recipe to the yield you want. To do this you must increase or decrease the amount of each ingredient by the same amount.

Start by finding the ***original yield*** — the amount the original recipe makes. Then decide on the ***desired yield*** — the amount of food you need. Use these numbers in this equation:

$$\frac{\textbf{desired yield}}{\textbf{original yield}} = \textbf{number to multiply by}$$

"Number to multiply by" means that you must multiply each original ingredient amount by this number to find your new ingredient amounts.

Here is an example. You have a recipe for pudding that makes 50 servings. You expect to serve 150 people. Your original yield is 50. Your desired yield is 150. That makes the equation:

$$150 \div 50 = 3$$

Now you know that you must multiply the amount of each ingredient in the recipe by 3. The recipe will then give you 150 servings of pudding.

Below you will find a chart of ***equivalents*** or equals. The chart will help you when increasing or decreasing yields by showing you which measurements equal each other.

Equivalents Chart

Volume Measures		
3 teapsoons	=	1 tablespoon
16 tablespoons	=	1 cup
8 fluid ounces	=	1 cup
2 cups	=	1 pint
2 pints	=	1 quart
4 quarts	=	1 gallon
8 pints	=	1 gallon
Weight Measures		
16 ounces	=	**1 pound**

Portioning

The standardized recipe tells the expected yield, but the actual yield of any recipe depends upon standardized portions. ***Portion control*** means making sure each serving is the same. Portions may be checked by weight on a ***portion scale***. This is a small scale that can usually weigh amounts up to one pound. Portions of meat are commonly checked on a portion scale. In many food service operations, meat is portioned accurately at the meat packers. For instance, steaks may be purchased in 5-, 6-, 10-, or 14-ounce portions.

Equal portions of such foods as mashed potatoes or soup may be assured by using scoops or ladles. These come in various sizes. Portions can also be measured by length and width, such as for a piece of cake.

Making sure each serving is the same size and the correct size is called portion control. It is a determining factor in the financial success of any food service business.

This cheesecake has been sliced for portion control. Notice how equal the portions appear.

STANDARDIZED METHODS

Using standardized recipes does not guarantee cooking success. You need to know how to follow the recipes correctly.

If you cook at home, you already know much that will help you in quantity cooking. But there are also many differences. In a food service operation, you must cook large quantities of food. Much of the equipment is quite different than home equipment. So are some of the ingredients. Most importantly, there are standardized ways for doing everything. This standardization insures the food will be good, safe to eat, and ready on time. In this section you will learn more about these standardized methods.

Measuring Techniques

In food service, accurate measurement begins with the first ingredient in a recipe and does not end until the food is served. Learn to measure accurately. It is a skill you will use every day.

You have already read that standardized recipes indicate ingredient measurements by volume, weight, or number. Some standardized recipes give both a volume and weight measurement for the same ingredient. If so, you may use either.

- **Volume measurement.** The term ***volume*** refers to the amount of space taken up by anything. In food service, volume is usually used to measure liquids, but not dry ingredients. (In home cooking, volume is also used for most dry ingredients.) Small amounts of dry ingredients, such as spices, are measured by volume.

Measuring cups are used in food service for volume measurement, but they are larger than those used at home. Most of the volume measures used in food service are made of metal. Measuring spoons are the same sizes as in the home. (See pages 111 and 112 for more information on measuring equipment.)

To measure liquids by volume, first choose a liquid volume measure that is the size needed, or larger. Place the cup on a level surface and fill with the liquid to the appropriate line. Since the cup is metal, you will not be able to look at the measurement on eye level. Therefore, try to fill the liquid exactly on the line so that your measurement will be most accurate.

To measure very small amounts of dry ingredients, use measuring spoons. Dip the spoon into the ingredient. Tap the spoon against the edge of the container to shake off the excess or scrape the flat edge of a knife across the spoon. This will give a level measurement.

Large amounts of dry ingredients can sometimes be measured by volume in dry measuring cups. Spoon the ingredient into the correct size cup. Draw the straight edge of a spatula or knife across the top of the cup.

- **Weight measurements.** In food service, most dry ingredients are measured by weight. It is the quickest, easiest, and most accurate way of measuring.

This liquid volume measure can hold up to one quart. Here milk is being poured into the measure on a level surface for accuracy. Notice the lip on the liquid measure to aid in pouring.

Two types of scales are used for measuring ingredients. The ***spring scale*** is much like a bathroom scale. You place the approximate amount of the ingredient on the scale and check the weight. Then add to or subtract from the amount on the scale until you have the exact amount you need. The ***balance scale*** works differently. It has a bar that connects two platforms. Weights that equal the measurement you need go on one platform. You add the ingredient to the container on the other platform until the two sides are balanced. Then you have the correct amount of the ingredient.

By weighing this meat on a spring scale, it can be portioned for sandwiches.

A balance scale tells this food service worker how much dough is needed to fill one sheet pan, which will yield 100 brownies.

Abbreviations

To save space, abbreviations are commonly used in recipes for measurement amounts. An abbreviation is a shortened form of a word. (In metric measurement, symbols are used.) In order to understand recipes, you need to know what these abbreviations and symbols mean. The chart below shows abbreviations and symbols commonly used in food preparation.

Common Abbreviations and Symbols

Weights and Measures	
Customary Abbreviations	Metric Symbols
t. or tsp. = teaspoon	g = gram
T. or tbsp. = tablespoon	kg = kilogram
C. or c. = cup	mL, ml = milliliter
pt. = pint	L = liter
qt. = quart	mm = millimeter
gal. = gallon	cm = centimeter
oz., ou. z. = ounce	
fl. oz. = fluid ounce	
lb., pd., # = pound	
pk. = peck	
bu. = bushel	
Temperature	
F = Fahrenheit	C = Celsius

The Metric and Customary Systems of Measurement

The system of measurement used in the United States — sometimes called the customary system — is different from that used in most other countries. In most of the world, the metric system of measurement is used instead. That means the units of measurement are not the same. Food is measured by grams, liters, and kilograms instead of ounces, quarts, and pounds.

You have probably noticed that most of the measurements in this book give both the customary amount and the metric amount. For example, it may say "Water boils at 212°F (100°C)." The amount of heat needed to make the water boil is the same. It is just that on the customary Fahrenheit thermometer, that amount of heat registers 212°. On the metric Celsius thermometer, it is equal to 100°.

This book gives only customary amounts in standardized recipes because the customary system is still used in most food service operations in the United States.

It is important to become familiar with the metric system. The United States will probably formally adopt that system in the future. And knowing the metric system will make it possible to use recipes that are written with metric measurements.

Some pieces of measuring equipment are marked in both customary and metric measurements.

Learning the Language

It only takes a look at a recipe to know that food preparation has its own language. "Chop" doesn't refer to cutting wood or a karate chop. In cooking it means to cut food into small pieces. When you work in a food service kitchen, you are expected to understand the recipe terms and follow them exactly. Review the food preparation terms below. Learn and practice any that are unfamiliar.

Food Preparation Terms

Bake — To cook in the oven with dry heat.
Beat — To mix ingredients by using a fast, circular motion.
Blend — To mix two or more ingredients together.
Boil — To cook in liquid in which the bubbles rise continuously, break on the surface rapidly, and give off steam (212°F or 100°C).
Chill — To place in the refrigerator until cold.
Chop — To cut food into small, irregularly shaped pieces.
Cook — To apply heat to food.
Cube — To cut into pieces about ½ in. (1.3 cm) square on all sides.
Cut-in — To cut fat into dry ingredients until the mixture is in very small pieces.
Dice — To cut into small pieces about ¼ in. (6 mm) square on all sides.
Dissolve — To make an ingredient disappear into a liquid so that it can no longer be seen or felt.
Drain — To pour off liquid.
Fold — To blend by hand by cutting down through a mixture, lifting it up, and folding it over with a spoon, spatula, or whip. In food service, the whip attachment on the mixer is usually used.
Freeze — To lower the temperature below 32°F (0°C).
Fry — To cook in hot fat.
Heat — To raise the temperature of food.
Mince — To chop into very, very small pieces.
Mix — To combine two or more ingredients so that they are evenly distributed.
Parboil — To boil in water until partially cooked.
Preheat — To heat a pan, broiler, or oven to the desired temperature before cooking the food.
Roast — To cook meat uncovered in the oven with dry heat.
Scald — To heat to just below the boiling point, just before bubbles start to form.
Simmer — To cook in liquid just below the boiling point (185°-210°F or 90°-95°C). The bubbles rise to the surface slowly.
Stir — To mix with a circular motion.
Whip — To beat rapidly using a whip, egg beater, or electric mixer.

Mise en place not only makes you a more efficient food service worker, but it also relieves you of a lot of extra stress while preparing food for the public.

Mise En Place

The French have a phrase that quickly becomes well known to every food service student. The term ***mise en place*** (MEES en PLASS) means set-up, or "don't start cooking until you have all the needed equipment assembled and all the ingredients ready." It means complete organization for efficiency before you begin. For mise en place follow these rules:

1. Assemble all ingredients and get them ready to use. Wash, chop, cut, or complete other pre-preparation as needed.
2. Get out all needed tools and equipment.
3. Arrange the tools in order of use.
4. Weigh or measure all ingredients.
5. Follow the sequence of steps outlined in the recipe.

THE COMPUTER AND STANDARDIZATION

Most large food service restaurants, chains, and institutions have found the computer useful in the standardization of recipes. After being tested, all recipes in general use are entered on the computer. On command, the computer can convert the recipe to the needed yield. The computer can also suggest substitute ingredients if a needed ingredient is not available.

Recipes can be printed and distributed to the cooks to use in the day's food preparation. The computer can save time and eliminate many costly mistakes.

SUMMARY

Standardization is vitally important in food service. Recipes are standardized so that food will always have the same quality and quantity. The utensils and equipment used to prepare food are standardized by size, as are the methods of preparation, the cooking time, and the temperature. Special care is taken to control portion size. Standardization is important for planning and for controlling costs and quality.

chapter recap

CHECK YOUR KNOWLEDGE

1. What does "standardized" mean in food service?

2. List the parts of a standardized recipe.

3. The recipe you are using will yield 25 servings. You need to make 100 servings. Write the equation and tell how you would determine correct ingredient amounts.

4. Name the three types of measurements included in standardized recipes.

5. What two types of scales are used to measure ingredients?

6. Why is it helpful to know metric measurements?

7. What piece of equipment would you use to measure each of the following ingredients — 3 c. milk, 3 T. salt, 1 lb. flour, 6 oz. hamburger?

8. Give the equivalents of the following measurements — 3 tsp., 16 T., 8 fl. oz., 16 oz.

9. Define the following cooking terms — bake, chop, dissolve, mince.

10. Give three examples of how the computer is useful in standardization of recipes.

EXTEND YOUR LEARNING

1. Check your classroom laboratory kitchen or the school cafeteria for standardization tools. List all of those you find and tell their purpose.

2. Investigate the metric system. Why is the United States one of the few countries in the world that does not use it as the official system of measurement?

3. Discuss the problems lack of standardization could cause in a food service operation.

"Ruthann stuck her head into the computer lab. "What are you doing here?" she asked Jim. "You're supposed to be eating lunch."

"Come here a minute," said Jim. "This computer stuff is fascinating! You know how I hate math, but with a computer it's fun!"

"What are you working on now?" Ruthann asked.

"It's a project for food service class. Chef Robinson thought I could really help our planning for the Awards Banquet next month by precosting the recipes."

"How do you do that?" asked Ruthann as she studied the recipe Jim was working on.

"First, I enter all the ingredients and their prices into the computer," Jim explained. "Even though flour comes in those huge sacks, the computer can figure the cost for as little as one cup! It's sure a lot faster than my brain!"

"How can I help?"

Jim handed her the recipe sheet and glanced at the clock. "Read off the ingredients for the Boston cream pie and the amount needed for each ingredient," instructed Jim. "After I get that information entered, we can let the computer figure out how much each pie will cost us. We ought to have just enough time before our next class.""

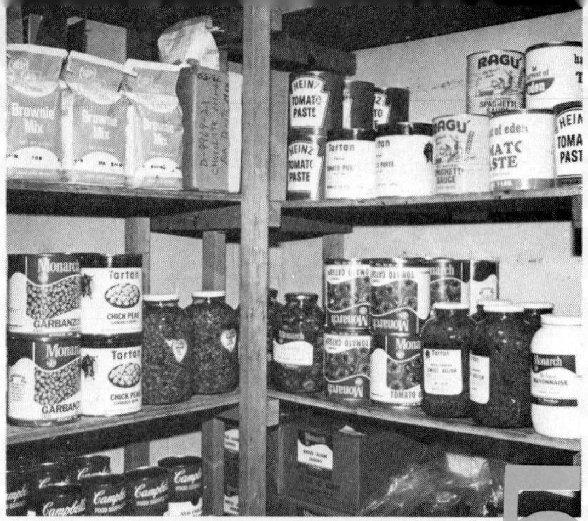

chapter 5

cost control

Set your goals

When you complete the study of this chapter, you should be able to . . .

- Define and correctly use the vocabulary terms.
- Complete purchase order forms.
- Receive, inventory, requisition, and issue food and supplies.
- Compute food costs.
- Identify and perform cost control measures.

Build your vocabulary

forecasting
inventory
invoice
management
mark up
precosting
purchase order
requisitions
specifications
stock rotation
vendor

MANAGEMENT AND COST CONTROL

Good management practices are essential to good service. The main step in operating a financially successful business is to practice strict cost control measures and maintain a good system of recordkeeping. Management must know what is to be purchased, when and in what amounts, and the best price available on each item. The work schedule must be planned with a conscious effort to increase productivity. Remember, effective controls are necessary for a profitable operation.

Everyone who earns a paycheck has to learn to live within that income. Managing your money to get the things you need and want is what cost control is all about.

Management means controlling and directing in order to get a job done correctly and within the allotted time. It may also refer to the person or people responsible for managing the operation. In most food service operations, several people make up the management team. Each person has different responsbilities, but the same goal — to make the operation run smoothly. These responsibilities include hiring, training, and supervising all the workers plus planning menus, and purchasing food. The management team will vary in number and responsibility, based on the size and organization of the food service operation. It is the management team that is primarily responsible for cost control in a food service operation, However, the storeroom clerk, the cooks in the kitchens, and maintenance personnel are also involved in cost control. Spoiled or wasted food, stealing of supplies, broken equipment, and lost time through accidents can all make costs soar out of control.

The manager is showing a new employee how much milkshake should fill each cup in order for both the customer and the restaurant to get their money's worth.

Labor Costs

Labor costs are an important concern in food service operations because they are such a large part of the entire operation's budget. Labor costs include such things as:

- Salaries.
- Vacation pay, holiday pay, sick pay.
- Employee uniforms and meals.
- Social security taxes.
- Worker's compensation insurance.
- Health and life insurance.

It is easy to see that workers play an important part in controlling labor costs. But labor costs mean more than salaries, vacations, and uniforms. Food service operations need employees who give "an honest day's work for an honest wage." Employees who talk when they should be working or take unnecessary sick days waste their employer's time and money. A good employee is one whose work is done cheerfully, accurately, and efficiently.

This food service worker wears a company uniform and receives a salary in addition to insurance benefits. All of these items are a part of labor costs.

Food Costs

Food costs include the actual cost of all foods used in the operation plus delivery and transportation costs. The type of food, its quality, and its availability are only some of the factors that affect food costs.

Precosting

Food service operations can't afford to guess at food costs. One way they control costs is by ***precosting*** the recipes to be used in the menu. Precosting means figuring the cost of each ingredient used in a recipe. A master recipe for each dish is filed in the purchasing department. A master recipe lists the following:

- The name of the product.
- The number of servings the recipe makes.
- Each ingredient and the amount needed.
- The purchase price per unit of each ingredient. (If flour is purchased in ten-pound sacks, the cost of one sack is entered.)
- The cost of each ingredient.
- The total cost of the recipe.
- The cost per serving.

The manager bases the selling price of the food on this precosting of the recipe. Therefore, the precosting must be accurate and up-to-date. A sample of a precosted recipe for Angel Food Cake is shown on page 64.

Precosted Recipe
Angel Food Cake

Method	Ingredients	Lb.	Oz.	Cost per Pound	Cost
1. Beat 5 minutes at high speed.	Egg White Vanilla	2	 1		
2. Blend together. Add gradually to ingredients in Step 1. Beat until mixture forms soft peaks.	Sugar Cream of tartar Salt	1	 ¼ ¼		
3. Sift and blend. Add to the ingredients in Step 2 and fold in.	Sugar Flour (cake)	1	 13		
Total Yield: 50 servings Each cake cuts 10 servings		**Total Cost:**			
Scaling Instructions: Five, 8 in. tube pans 15 oz. to pan		**Cost Per Serving:**			
Baking Temperature: 325°F. for 40 minutes					
Note: Be careful not to overbeat in Step 2. Fold in Step 3 until thoroughly mixed. Turn cake upside down on removing from oven. Cool before removing from pans.					

Angel food cake has a light, airy texture that is very appealing to the taste buds. It is often served with a fruit glaze or light icing to improve appearances.

Pricing

One of the most important functions of management is to determine the selling price of food. Most food service operations have a food cost percentage level. This means a specific percent of total sales is spent for food. This percentage differs among operations. It depends on whether the operation must make a profit and the type and quality of food that is purchased.

Some restaurants offer luxury services such as extra waiters or waitresses or tableside food preparation. The customer pays for these extras and a smaller percentage of the bill goes for food.

In an institution such as a nursing home, the main goal is to provide nourishing food at a low price. The food cost percentage level will be higher in such places.

Besides the food percentage cost, all operating costs must also be included in the price of meals. Operating costs include labor costs, rent or mortgage costs, insurance, taxes, nonfood supplies, as well as the expected profit. This figure is called the ***mark up***. Mark up — the cost of operating the business — is expressed as a percentage. A restaurant noted for its excellent service, gourmet menu, and expensive table settings will naturally have a much higher mark up than a family-style restaurant.

Sales Price

The sales price is based on the cost of the food and the mark up. It may be expressed in the simple formula:

food cost + mark up = sales price

A typical mark up would be 35% of the food cost. However, other points must also be considered:

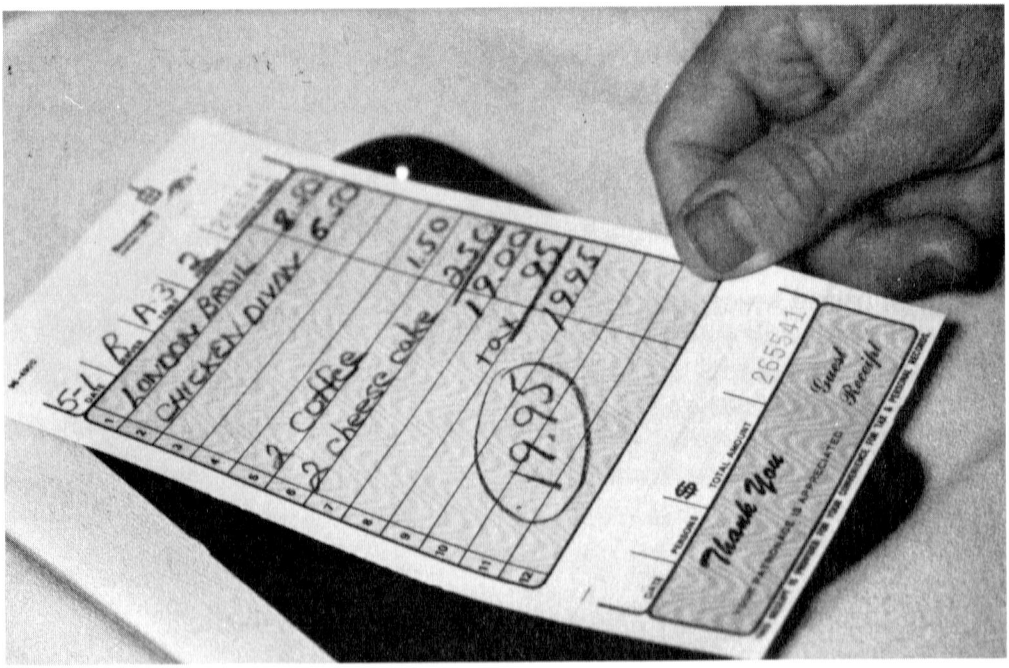

Can you guess what the mark up percentage is for the cheesecake on this customer's check?

• Prices must be in line with other food service operations which offer similar food and service. Competition is very keen in the food business. Customers are generally not willing to pay a higher price at one eating place if they can get the same quality food and service for less money at another.

• Not all foods give the same amount of profit. Many times higher profits on some foods make up for the lower profits on other foods. A high-profit is one that can be sold at a higher price in relation to its food cost. For instance, spaghetti is relatively inexpensive to produce. The mark up can be high, yet the price will seem reasonable to the customer. In planning complete meals, the manager will include a few low-profit foods and many high-profit foods. In this way, the overall mark up for the complete meal will cover the operating expenses and the expected profit of the business.

Quality Control

Quality control means setting standards to keep food quality consistently high. Standards of quality include:

- Use of quality ingredients.
- Use of standardized recipes.
- Following approved cooking procedures.
- Serving portions of the correct size.
- Keeping prepared foods fresh and safe to eat.
- Using leftovers in other meals.

PURCHASING FOOD

It is easy to see the importance of purchasing in controlling costs. The person responsible for buying food and other supplies — called a buyer, a steward, or a purchasing agent — must buy the right quality at the best possible price.

Think about your own family's food buying habits. If you carelessly choose overripe fruit or meat that is not fresh, the food will go to waste. If you do not pay attention to sales and the prices of different brands, your food costs will probably be much higher. Buyers for food service operations cannot afford to make such mistakes. They are often responsible for purchasing food for thousands of meals each week!

In a small business the owner, the manager, or the chef may do the buying. In a larger operation, it is a full-time job. The person in charge of purchasing is usually part of the management team.

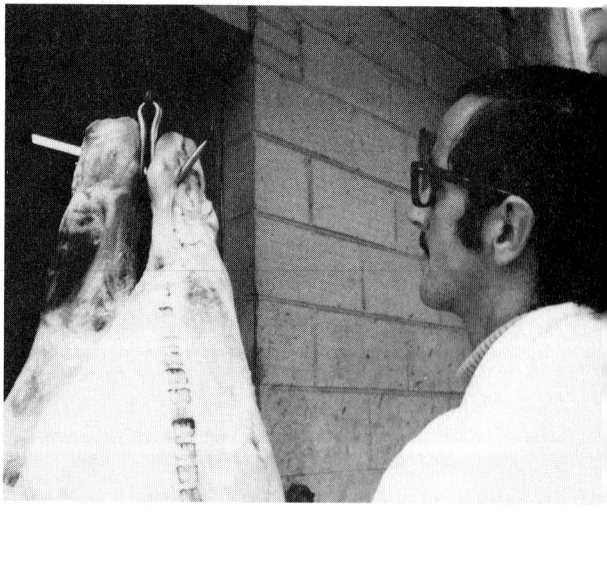

Meat is an expensive investment for any food service operation. This buyer carefully inspects the meat before agreeing on a selling price.

Steps in Purchasing

A buyer must have practical knowledge and experience in foods. It is the buyer's responsibility to work closely with the chef and production staff to make wise decisions about the food and supplies needed. Those decisions should include the following steps:

1. Determine what is needed by checking the master recipes and the supplies on hand.
2. Determine the quantity and quality needed for each item.
3. Obtain price quotations from several ***vendors***. A vendor is a seller of supplies.
4. Choose the best vendor for each item.
5. Order the supplies needed.
6. Receive and inspect all goods.
7. Check the ***invoice*** against the order to be sure it is accurate. The invoice is the list of goods delivered.
8. Complete all purchasing records.

THE PURCHASE ORDER

The ***purchase order*** (sometimes abbreviated P.O.) is a form the buyer fills out telling what products should be delivered. A separate purchase order must be written for each vendor. Staples such as flour and sugar may come from one vendor, meats from another, and produce from a third.

Filling Out the Purchase Order

Study the purchase order on page 68. Each purchase order is given a number. Then two copies of the purchase order are prepared giving the following information:

- Item needed.
- Quantity needed.
- The unit desired — the size and type of container used in packaging.
- Clear description of the item.
- Unit price per weight, measure, can, or package.
- Total price.
- Date and time of desired delivery.

A purchase order provides the vendor with needed information in written form. It serves as a guide for the storeroom clerk to know exactly what has been ordered and when to expect it. The storeroom clerk can tell immediately whether the shipment is late or if the correct amount of food has been delivered. The purchase order also verifies the prices on the invoice.

PURCHASE ORDER

ENERGIZER RESTAURANT
1701 N. Terrace Drive
Rainbow, TX

Date: ____________________ P.O.# ____________________

Ship Via: ____________________

Terms: ____________________

This number must appear on all delivery slips and invoices.

Vendor: ____

Address: ____

City: ____________________ State: ______________ Zip: ______________

Delivery Date: ____________________

Please furnish: Shipping charges: ____________________

Prepaid: ____________________

Quantity	Unit	Description	Unit Price	Total Amount

Approved: ____________________
Signature

Make all deliveries through rear entrance.

Specifications

Specifications are a definite statement of the standards expected for a particular product. They include information on wholesomeness, quality, type and size of container, count per unit of weight, and the total weight of an item ordered by the purchaser. Specifications help make certain the product the vendor delivers is exactly the product ordered.

Food specifications spell out the standards of excellence set by the food service establishment. Standards, of course, vary greatly from one place to another.

Specification Card for Milk

Number ______

Product Name ____________

Specifications
  Pasteurized
  Not more than 2% butterfat
  Meets State regulations
  Deliver in ½ gallon containers

Suggested Vendor __________

Address ____________

Price ______

The Specification Card

Specifications for products are kept on specification cards like the one at the left. These cards give the buyer all the information needed to prepare purchase orders. Specification cards are kept on file in the purchasing office. From time to time, the cards must be updated because prices and package sizes change. Specifications are concerned with the following information:

- **Wholesomeness.** Foods that are wholesome are safe to eat. Note on the sample specification card the word "pasteurized." This specifies that the milk supplied be heat-treated so all disease-causing bacteria are destroyed. The United States has rigid standards for the wholesomeness of food. All food shipped between states must meet standards set by the U.S. Department of Agriculture (USDA) and the Food and Drug Administration (FDA). Additional controls are often set by other federal, state, and local agencies.
- **Quality.** The USDA also sets standards of quality for many foods. Four USDA labels or shields that appear on meats and canned goods are shown below. The round seals guarantee wholesomeness. The shields indicate the quality of the food. A chart showing the common grades for different types of foods is on page 70. Remember that grades indicate quality, not wholesomeness. Foods of different grades are just as nutritious and safe to eat. Higher quality foods usually have better flavor and appearance. You will learn more about judging the quality of specific foods in other chapters.

USDA quality grades.

• **Containers.** The buyer must specify the kind and size of container for each product ordered. Milk, for example, is available in many different size containers. A school lunch program might order individual serving-size containers for student lunches. A family-style restaurant that serves milk by the glass might order by the gallon. As you work in a food service operation, you will learn what size containers are available. The chart on page 71 shows common can sizes. Sugar and flour can be ordered in 2-, 5-, 10-, 50-, or 100-pound sacks. Each food is different.

Common U.S. Grades

MEATS			
Product	**1st Grade**	**2nd Grade**	**3rd Grade**
Beef	USDA Prime	USDA Choice	USDA Good
Veal	USDA Prime	USDA Choice	USDA Good
Lamb	USDA Prime	USDA Choice	USDA Good
DAIRY PRODUCTS			
Product	**1st Grade**	**2nd Grade**	**3rd Grade**
Butter	U.S. Grade AA	U.S. Grade A	U.S. Grade B
Cheddar Cheese	U.S. Grade AA	U.S. Grade A	U.S. Grade B
Swiss Cheese	U.S. Grade A	U.S. Grade B	U.S. Grade C
Nonfat dry milk	U.S. Extra Grade	U.S. Standard Grade	
Cottage Cheese	No Grades — May be marked USDA Quality Approved		
POULTRY AND EGGS			
Product	**1st Grade**	**2nd Grade**	**3rd Grade**
Poultry	U.S. Grade A	U.S. Grade B	U.S. Grade C
Eggs	U.S. Grade AA Fresh Fancy Quality	U.S. Grade A	U.S. Grade B
PROCESSED FRUITS AND VEGETABLES AND RELATED PRODUCTS			
Product	**1st Grade**	**2nd Grade**	**3rd Grade**
	U.S. Grade A Fancy	U.S. Grade Choice or Extra Standard	U.S. Grade C Standard

CONSUMER DESCRIPTION			
INDUSTRY TERM	APPROX. NET WEIGHT OR FLUID MEASURE (Check Label)	APPROX. CUPS	PRINCIPAL PRODUCTS
Buffet	8 oz	1 CUP	Fruits, vegetables, *specialties for small families: 2 servings.
Picnic	10½ to 12 oz	1¼ CUPS	Mainly condensed soups. Some fruits, vegetables, meat, fish, *specialties: 3 servings.
12 oz (vacuum)	12 oz	1½ CUPS	Principally for vacuum pack corn: 3 to 4 servings.
No. 300	14 to 16 oz	1¾ CUPS	Pork and beans, baked beans, meat products, cranberry sauce, blueberries, *specialties: 3 to 4 servings.
No. 303	16 to 17 oz	2 CUPS	Principal size for fruits and vegetables. Some meat products, ready-to-serve soups, *specialties: 4 servings.
No. 2	1 lb 4 oz or 1 pt 2 fl oz	2½ CUPS	**Juices, ready-to-serve soups, some *specialties, pineapple, apple slices. No longer in popular use for most fruits and vegetables: 5 servings.
No. 2½	1 lb 13 oz	3½ CUPS	Fruits, some vegetables (pumpkin, sauerkraut, spinach and other greens, tomatoes): 7 servings.
No. 3 cyl or 46 fl oz	3 lb 3 oz or 1 qt 14 fl oz	5¾ CUPS	"Economy family size" **fruit and vegetable juices, pork and beans. Institutional size for condensed soups, some vegetables: 10 to 12 servings.
No. 10	6½ lb to 7 lb 5 oz	12-13 CUPS	Institutional size for fruits, vegetables and some other foods: 25 servings.
Meats, fish and seafood are almost entirely advertised and sold under weight terminology.			
Infant and junior foods come in small cans and jars suitable for the smaller servings used. Content is given on label.			

*Specialties — food combinations prepared by special manufacturer's recipe.

**Juices are now being packed in a number of other can sizes, including the 1-quart size.

STORING FOOD

Storing food properly is important to maintaining quality. It is also vital to cost control. Food that is not stored properly may become unusable.

Storeroom clerks, or receiving clerks as they are sometimes called, are in charge of the storeroom where all supplies are kept. The storeroom clerk must be accurate, trustworthy, and understand the duties of the job.

Storeroom clerks have certain general rules to follow, though these may differ according to the establishment. These rules cover deliveries, storing food, and keeping the storage area clean. There are also procedures to sending food to the kitchen and keeping track of supplies.

Inventory should be taken constantly in a food service operation. It plays a large part in cost control.

Receiving Procedures

When a vendor delivers supplies, two copies of the invoice and one copy of the purchase order are usually included with the order. The storeroom clerk checks each item on the purchase order against each item on the invoice. The weight, quantity, and quality of the items delivered must be carefully checked. If any item has been omitted or damaged, a note is made on both the purchase order and the invoice. If items do not meet the specifications, they are returned to the vendor. The clerk signs and dates the purchase order and an invoice with a ball-point pen, never a pencil. (See the sample invoice on page 73.) Goods received immediately become part of the ***inventory***. An inventory is an itemized list of food and supplies on hand.

Storage Procedures

Food should be stored in an orderly manner. Store similar items together. For instance, all cans should be stored together and grouped according to the kinds of food they contain. Canned fruits should be in one section, canned vegetables in another, and canned meats and fish in a third place. Odor-causing foods, such as onions, should be stored away from odor-absorbing foods, such as cheese.

A basic principle of storage is to use older supplies first. As new items are brought in, they should be placed on the back of the shelves and the old ones moved to the front. This is called ***stock rotation***. Nothing must spoil because of old age. Many storeroom clerks mark the date of arrival on cans, boxes, and bags. This helps the clerk rotate the stock.

INVOICE

No. ____________

LEWIS WHOLESALE GROCERY, INC.
1000 Park Place
Rainbow, TX 00123

P.O. No. ____________

Date: ____________

BILL TO: Energizer Restaurant
1701 Terrace Drive
Rainbow Town, FL 33311

Quantity	Unit	Item/Description	Unit Price	Total Price

All storage areas must be clean and free from insects and other pests. Refrigerators need a weekly cleaning. Spills should be wiped up immediately. Most operations follow a set schedule of cleaning for the storage area. Chapter 6 discusses sanitation in more detail.

Safety is another consideration in the storeroom. When possible, use your brains instead of your body. Store heavy articles on the bottom shelves and lighter items on higher shelves. Use a stepladder to reach the top shelves. Use a cart if you must move heavy items.

The food in a storeroom is worth thousands of dollars. It must be protected from theft. When the storage area is unattended, it should be locked and the keys kept by a responsible person.

An employee is removing some ketchup from the dry storage area of this pizza establishment.

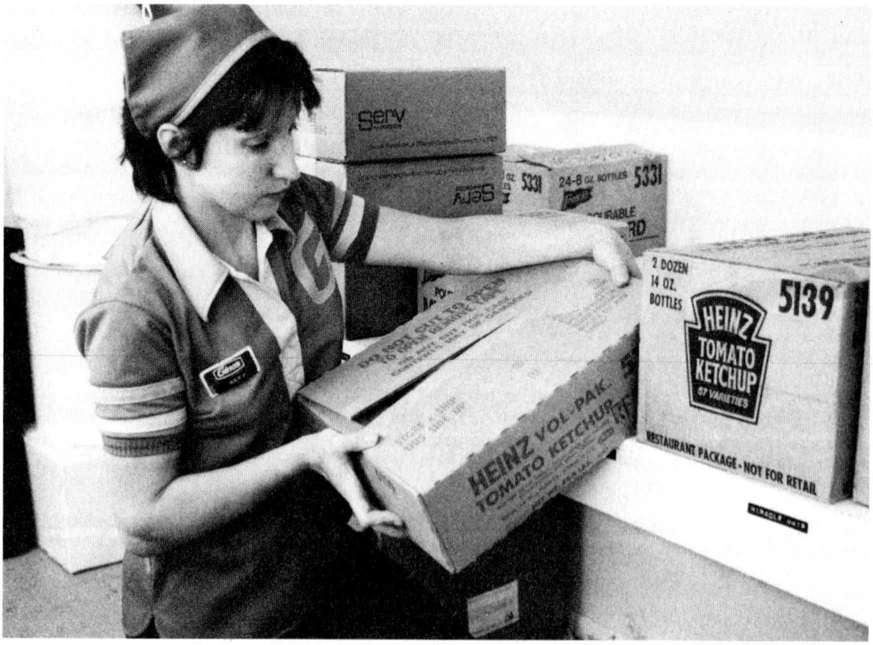

Kinds of Storage

Just as a home kitchen, a food service operation needs different kinds of storage. Some foods, such as crackers, keep best in a warm, dry area. Others, such as flour, need storage that is dry but cool. Most fresh fruits and vegetables keep best in cool, moist storage. Below freezing temperatures are required for ice cream and other frozen products.

Dry Storage

Dry storage areas should maintain a temperature of 55°-65°F (10°-20°C). A reliable thermometer is essential and it should be checked often. Foods requiring dry storage need to be placed on metal shelves at least 8 in. (20 cm) off the floor and 4 in. (10 cm) from the wall. This allows for adequate air circulation.

Place food containers upright on the shelves with their labels facing front. Store all nonfood supplies away from food items so no mix-up can occur.

Refrigerated Storage

Refrigerated storage must have a temperature of 38°-40°F (3°-5°C). Arrange food on the shelves so cold air can circulate freely. Do not store food on the floor of a walk-in refrigerator. Place foods such as butter, milk, cream, and cheese away from foods with strong odors. Dairy foods and eggs absorb odors and tastes easily. Many large establishments have specific storage areas for such foods. Large pieces of raw meat and poultry are stored loosely wrapped to allow free circulation of air.

Freezer Storage

Freezers must have temperatures between 0° and − 10°F (− 18° and − 23°C) in order to keep food solidly frozen. Food must be securely wrapped in heavy freezer paper, labeled, dated, and placed to allow air space between the items.

Some large operations have two freezer areas. One is a deep-freeze around − 10°F (− 23°C). The other is set at about 0°F (− 18°C). Items to be prepared within 24 hours are moved from the deep-freeze to the slightly warmer freezer. They will take less time to thaw for preparation and reduce the chance of spoilage. Ice cream is brought to the warmer freezer to thaw enough for service.

This employee is retrieving tomatoes from refrigerated storage. Foods stored here are for short-term use.

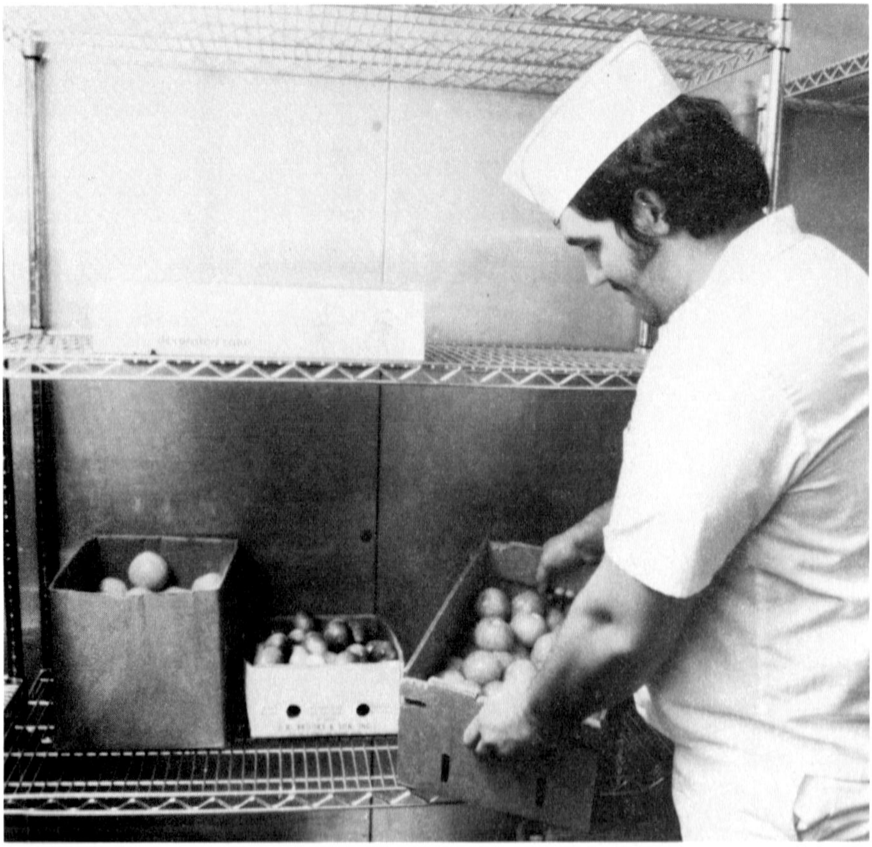

Issuing Food

How does food get from the storeroom to the kitchen? The storeroom clerk is usually responsible for issuing food to the kitchen. ***Requisitions***, written orders for food, are used within the operation to withdraw supplies from the storeroom. Requisitions may also be used to request the purchasing department to order certain supplies. A requisition is filled out in the kitchen and taken to the storeroom. It should list the date, the kitchen area that needs supplies, the supplies needed, the quantity, and the grade (quality). The kitchen supervisor signs the requisition.

The storeroom clerk fills the order and deducts the supplies from the inventory. The person who receives the supplies must sign for them. A sample requisition is shown on page 77.

PERPETUAL INVENTORY CARD

Name Rice (White long-grain) Brand China Rose

Supplier Lee Import Co Size 5 lb. sacks

Date Rec'd	Quantity Rec'd	Date Issued	Quantity Issued	On Hand	New Balance
3-26-85	10-5lb. sacks			1-5lb. sacks	17-5lb. sacks
		3-28-85	1-5lb. sack		16-5lb. sacks

An efficient inventory system helps a food service operation control costs and avoid supply shortages. Each establishment usually develops their own type of inventory system, either on inventory cards, sheets, or by computer.

Inventory Control

The inventory is a vital tool for management. It is the only way to keep track of what has been received, what has been used, and what must be ordered. The storeroom clerk is responsible for keeping an accurate inventory.

Perpetual Inventory

At the end of each day, the storeroom clerk checks the inventory. This is usually done by checking the records of filled requisitions and subtracting them from the previous inventory. When supplies are delivered during the day, they are added to the perpetual or constant inventory. If a computer is used in the storeroom, the delivery or filled requisition is automatically recorded and the inventory adjusted.

Monthly Inventory

The monthly inventory is an actual count of every item on the shelves of the storeroom. Even if a computer is used daily, the physical count checks on the accuracy of the computer count. Errors are always possible.

Two people usually take the inventory. One person calls out the items, the other records the information on an inventory form. This count should agree with the perpetual inventory. If it does not, the reason must be discovered. Maybe security needs to be tightened or perhaps the clerk's math skills are not what they should be.

The storeroom clerk must know basic math skills in order to keep accurate records. Without accurate records, management cannot know the cost of food and cannot determine the right selling price for it. A good system of inventory is the only way to control the use of supplies.

THE ENERGIZER RESTAURANT

Storeroom Requisition

____________________ **Station** ____________________ **Supervisor**

Quantity Requested	Unit	Description	Quantity Issued	Unit Cost	Total Cost

Monthly Inventory

Location ______________________ Date ______________________

Signature ______________________________

Quantity	Description	Unit	Unit Price	Total Cost

COOKING AND SERVING FOOD

Those who work in the kitchen and dining area of a food service operation are as important to cost control as the manager or buyer. Every worker is part of the cost control effort.

The Kitchen

Kitchen workers are responsible for correctly preparing large quantities of food each day. If that food is prepared incorrectly or the wrong food is cooked, the food is wasted. Food waste can be a major cost problem in food service. Here are some ways to control costs in the kitchen:

- **Remember time costs money.** Plan your work before you start. Make sure you have all the ingredients and equipment you need. That way you will work more quickly and efficiently.
- **Be sure you understand what to do.** If you are assigned to clean and slice carrots, you must know how many, whether to slice them lengthwise or across, and how large the finished slices should be. If you slice them in several different sizes, the pieces won't all cook in the same amount of time. It is important to do even the smallest job right.
- **Measure ingredients carefully.** Perhaps you are assigned to measure the ingredients for the spice cake that will be served in the cafeteria for lunch. You read the amount of buttermilk wrong and measure twice the amount the recipe calls for. The cakes turn out flat and soggy — all 15 of them that the recipe made. Since they must be thrown out, your mistake has cost the operation considerable money. In addition, a substitute dessert must quickly be prepared.
- **Control portion size.** Giving each customer the same size serving not only keeps customers happy, it also controls costs. Standardized recipes indicate both the number and size of portions the recipe makes. The management team uses the information to decide how much food should be prepared. If the portion — serving — given to customers is larger than the recipe specifies, the kitchen may run out of food before everyone is served. If the portion is smaller than it should be, there may be leftovers that go to waste.

The Dining Room

Those who work in the dining room have a different role in cost control. Waiters and waitresses are responsible for taking customers' orders and relaying them to the kitchen. In many operations, the orders are written and handed in to the kitchen. If the order is wrong or written sloppily, the customer may receive the wrong meal. This wastes food and makes the customer unhappy.

Dining room workers also handle money. This requires good math skills and special care. It is important to correctly

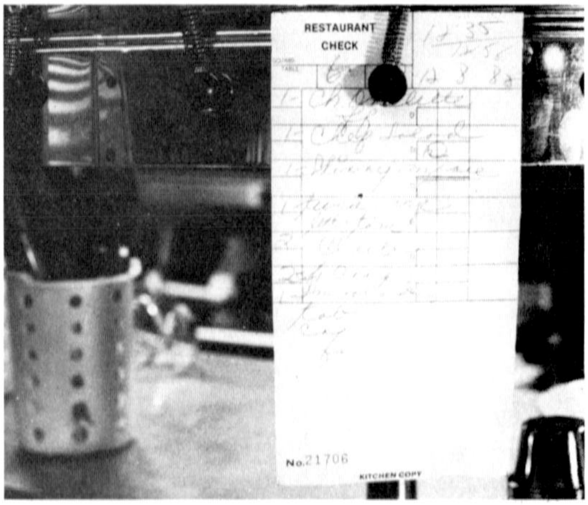

Waiters and waitresses must be careful to take orders correctly and write legibly. An incorrect order wastes food — which costs money.

enter the cost of each item ordered on the customer's check. Then the cost of all the items must be totalled correctly. Finally, the customer's payment must be taken and correct change given. Any errors can cause loss of money and customers.

COMPUTERS AND COST CONTROL

Computer technology is being used a great deal in the larger food service operations. The computer is especially useful in cost control because:

- It is fast and accurate for computing food costs, operating costs, mark ups, and sales prices.
- It keeps up-to-date inventory records, automatically adding and substracting items upon command.
- It records customers' choices on every item on the menu, thus giving management a record of the item's popularity. This is a basis for dropping unpopular items.
- It records purchase orders and compares invoices with purchase orders.
- It precosts standardized recipes.
- It keeps records of specifications and displays such records on command.
- It gives management a constant supply of information. This helps solve such problems as slow table turnover in the dining room and low productivity in the kitchen. It analyzes changing food costs, and customer food check control, slow sales, and other factors that make food service a complicated retail business.

The Computer and Purchasing

The purchasing department finds many uses for the computer. The specifications for all food used in the master recipes are entered in the computer. When the purchasing department makes out the purchase order, the specifications for each item are printed on the purchase order.

When the order is received, the storekeeper enters it in the computer. The computer compares the invoice with the purchase order, notes any differences and adds the items received to the inventory. The date, amount, description, price, invoice number, and name and address of the vendor are all part of the computer record. Purchase of new equipment is recorded in the same manner as food, except warranty information is included.

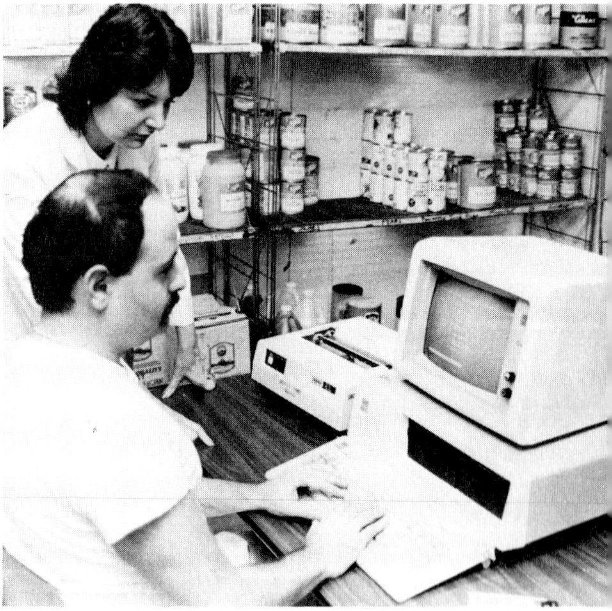

Computers are essential to the efficient food service operation of today. They save countless hours of paperwork for cost control and make inventory an easy task.

The Computer and Labor Costs

The computer is also useful in controlling labor costs. Personnel records of all employees can be maintained and updated as needed.

Payroll records on each employee, hours and days worked, days off, vacation time, sick leave, and tardiness are accurately recorded.

The Computer and Control of Food Cost

With a computer, menus are easily altered. Changes can be made at will with additions, deletions, and other pertinent information. This information is needed for ***forecasting*** — projecting the number of meals to be served on a given day.

Master standardized recipes are kept on file for all menu items in the purchasing department. The recipes are also on file in the computer in the kitchens. All recipes to be prepared on a particular day are printed and distributed to the cooks.

Inventory items received, issued, or lost through theft are recorded. When a computer is used to handle this function in the storeroom, each item is usually given a stock number. The requisition would then include the stock number as well as the name of the item. When the requisition is filled, the withdrawal is entered in the computer which automatically adjusts the inventory. On page 82 is a stock withdrawal form used in Disney World. Note the detailed information which is done by computer.

The Computer and The Control of Income

Sales are recorded by item, price, and number of portions. A complete analysis of sales for the day is available by category. The computer shows the number and cost of portions served.

Transactions needed for efficient business operations, records, and reports can be maintained by the computerized cash register. It also adjusts for sales price updates and makes current price changes. The computerized cash register is also able to denote cash drawer receipts, sales tax, credit, or checks received, as well as special functions.

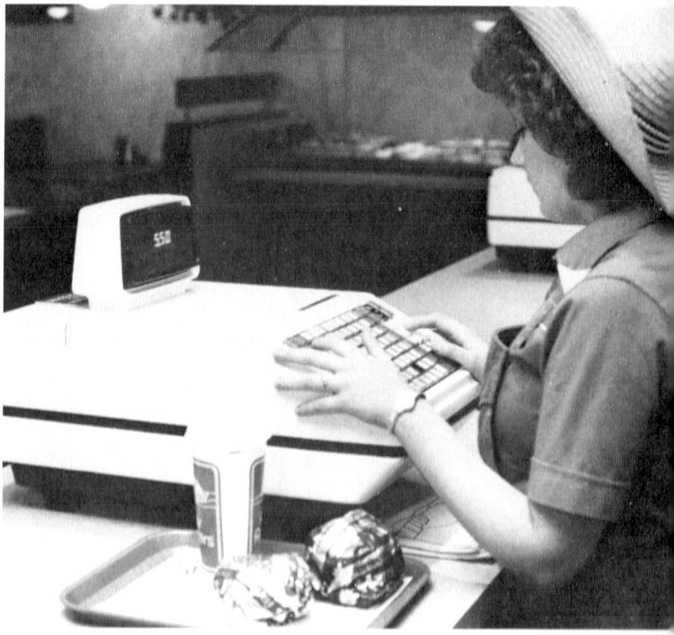

Computerized cash registers relieve employees of the burden of making correct change. They also speed up register close-outs at the end of the day.

FOOD STOCK WITHDRAWAL

PAGE 2 OF 4

TO: WAREHOUSE

PLEASE PRINT

FREEZER #2

DATE REQUIRED

TC 4 8   FROM: DEPT/LOC PLACING ORDER   LOC. NO.   ORIGIN   SUB   REVENUE AND COST CONTROL

INVENTORY DIVISION 0 1

QUANTITY ORDERED	QUANTITY DELIVERED	STOCK NUMBER	U/M	DESCRIPTION	QUANTITY ORDERED	QUANTITY DELIVERED	STOCK NUMBER	U/M	DESCRIPTION
		02-110001	CS	CHICKEN BRD. 3 PIECE			03-130003	LB	SNAPPER FILLET BRAZIL 7oz
		02-110002	LB	CHICKEN DRUMS RAW			03-130005	LB	COD TAILS REW 5oz
		02-110003	CS	CHICKEN BREAST BRD. 4oz			03-130008	LB	SCROD 8oz
		02-110005	LB	CHICKEN TENDERS BREADED			03-130009	LB	ANGLER WHITE FISH
		02-110006	LB	CHICKEN TENDERS RAW			03-130010	LB	COD BREADED SQUARE 4oz
		02-110007	LB	CHICKEN MEAT DICED			03-130011	LB	COD FINGER RAW 1.5oz
		02-110008	CS	CHICKEN BRD. 2 PIECE			03-130017	LB	SCALLOP SEA RAW 40/50
		02-110010	LB	CHICKEN BREAST BNLS 5oz			03-130018	LB	SALMON STEAK 6oz
		02-110011	LB	CHICKEN GIZZARDS			03-130020	LB	SOLE DOVER 16-20oz
		02-110012	LB	CHICKEN BACKS			03-130021	LB	SOLE FILLET 5-7oz
		02-110015	CS	CHICKEN SPLIT 12oz			03-130023	LB	TURBOT BLOCK
		02-110017	LB	CHICKEN THIGH 3.5oz			03-130024	LB	SNAPPER FILLET FLA.
		02-110018	EA	CORNISH HEN 20oz			03-130025	LB	SEATROUT FILLET 4-6oz
		02-110019	PTN	CHICKEN CORDON BLUE 7oz			03-130033	LB	KINGFISH SMOKED 2#
		02-110020	LB	CHICKEN WHOLE SHELL 21/2#			03-130037	LB	TROUT RAINBOW 5oz
		02-110021	CS	CHICKEN QUARTER 6oz			03-130043	LB	TURBOT BREADED 8oz
		02-110023	LB	CHICKEN LEG PRECOOKED			03-136007	LB	GROUPER 6-8oz
		02-110024	LB	CHICKEN WHOLE STEWING 5/6			03-136009	LB	SALMON NOVA SLICED (LOX)
		02-110025	LB	CHICKEN BREAST FRENCH 10z			03-140001	LB	SHRIMP GRN.HDLS U-8
		02-110026	LB	CHICKEN MEAT RAW DRK/LHT			03-140002	LB	CRABCLAW STONE 6/8
		02-116006	LB	CHICKEN LIVERS			03-140004	LB	SHRIMP BREADED 16/20
		02-116009	LB	CHICKEN SPLIT 16oz			03-140005	LB	SHRIMP ROCK SPLIT 50/60

REQUESTED BY	PICKED BY	DELIVERED BY	RECEIVED BY

WDW 234 L2 R-4

SUMMARY

Food service managers are responsible for controlling costs. Labor and food costs are the main items managers can control. Although some labor costs cannot be changed, managers can see that employees do their jobs efficiently and without wasting time. They can control the cost of food by using techniques like portion control and quality control. Computers can play an important role in food service cost control.

chapter recap

CHECK YOUR KNOWLEDGE

1. List the factors influencing cost control.
2. What is a perpetual inventory?
3. What information does the food specification card give? What is its purpose?
4. What information does a master recipe give?
5. List the items included in labor costs.
6. What is stock rotation?
7. What does quality control mean?
8. List the steps used in purchasing.
9. What are the four major ways in which portions are controlled?
10. How are requisitions used?

EXTEND YOUR LEARNING

1. As a class project, plan a menu for a faculty luncheon to serve 20 people. Write the purchase order, figure the cost per plate, and set a price. Make a work schedule and decide on the seating arrangement.
2. Use the section in the chapter on "Storage Procedures" to check all storage areas in your classroom. Is the present system correct? What changes might be made?
3. Discuss the importance of inventory control. Make a list of security, delivery, and storage problems that could affect your classroom. Come up with solutions.

"Hey, Ruthann," Jim called as he caught up with the group of students walking toward the food service classroom. "How are you feeling?"

"Better today, Jim, but I sure was sick for awhile! Dad even had to take me and Mom to the hospital. A lot of other folks from the church were brought there, too."

Jim showed Ruthann the newspaper he was carrying. The headline read: **63 STRICKEN WITH FOOD POISONING AT CHURCH SUPPER: HEALTH DEPARTMENT BLAMES TURKEY.** "I guess you didn't know you would be making news by just going to eat at a church supper! According to the paper, the Health Department ran tests on all of the food served at the church supper. The turkey was loaded with salmonella!"

"Salmonella?" Rosita asked. "What's that? Sounds like a fish or something!"

"The paper says it's a bacteria," explained Jim. "I'll bet we'll hear more about it when we study safety and sanitation."

"How did they know it was in the turkey, anyway?" Rosita asked.

Ruthann answered, "This man came from the Health Department while we were still at the hospital. He wanted to know exactly what we had eaten that day, and what time we had eaten it. I guess they figured out it was something we ate at the church supper."

"Say, Ruthann. Why don't you tell the class about your experience?" Jim suggested.

"Okay," said Ruthann. "Maybe it will keep someone else from getting sick. It's funny. That turkey tasted so good. I never dreamed it was spoiled."

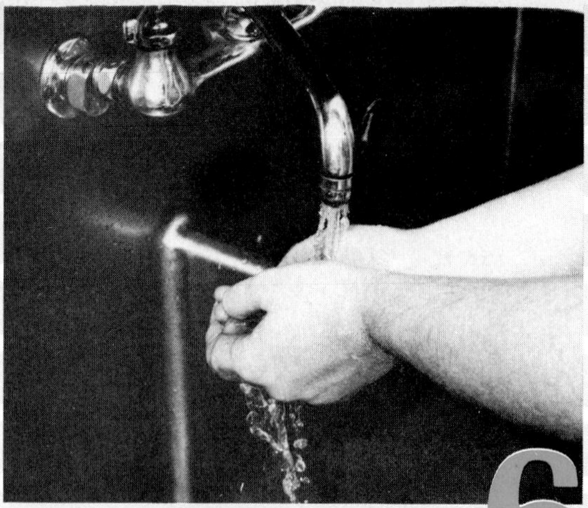

chapter 6

sanitation and safety

Set your goals

When you complete the study of this chapter, you should be able to . . .

- Define and correctly use the vocabulary terms.
- Identify causes of food-borne illnesses and ways to prevent them.
- Practice correct sanitation and safety procedures.
- Demonstrate first aid practices.

Build your vocabulary

bacteria
botulism
contaminate
first aid
flammable
hazard
microorganisms
salmonella
sanitation
sanitize
staph
sterilizing
toxins

YOUR #1 JOB

Serving tasty food is not the only job of food service operations. It is equally important to safeguard the health and safety of employees and customers. If standards of health and safety are not followed, injury, illness, and even death can occur. The information in this chapter is essential for food service workers. Learn it well and practice it daily.

SANITATION

Sanitation in food service is the science of maintaining a clean and germ-free environment for food production. This is important so that the food served customers will not cause illness.

For food service employees, sanitation must become a way of life. They are responsible for the health and well-being of the customers who eat the food they prepare.

If your goal is to become a good food service worker, you must understand how food becomes contaminated. To ***contaminate*** food means to allow it to become dirty or harmful to eat. Sickness caused by food contamination is called food-borne illness. By developing habits of keeping equipment, kitchens, and food clean, and by taking pride in your personal cleanliness and appearance, sanitation will become a way of life for you.

Most work surfaces in a food service kitchen are made of stainless steel. They must be constantly cleaned and sanitized to avoid possible contamination of food.

Bacteria

To most people, cleanliness means a kitchen looks clean. The range is wiped off. The work counters shine. The sink is scrubbed. However, a kitchen that looks clean may not be *really* clean. It can still contaminate food.

Most surfaces are covered with thousands of ***microorganisms***. These are living cells so small that they can be seen only with a microscope. The only way to be sure that microorganisms have been destroyed is to ***sanitize*** all surfaces. That is what sanitize means — to clean with a product that kills all microorganisms. In this chapter you will read about the most common microorganisms that contaminates food.

The most common source of food contamination is ***bacteria***, simple one-celled microorganisms. Actually, not all bacteria are harmful. Helpful bacteria are used in making cheese, buttermilk, and yogurt. Harmful bacteria, however, cause illness, infection, and even death.

Understanding bacteria makes it easier to keep them under control. Here are some points to remember:

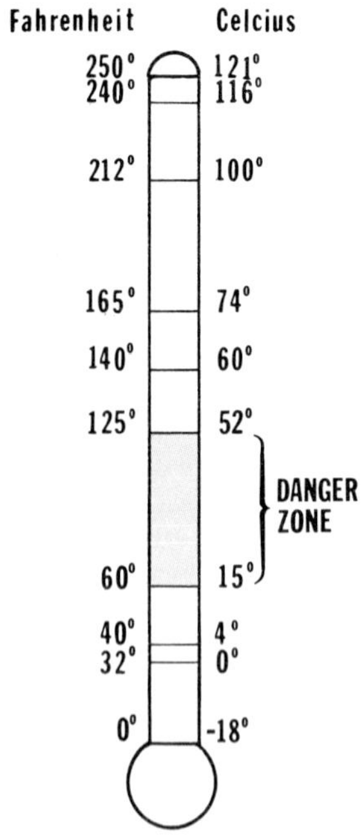

• **Bacteria need food, moisture, and warmth to live and grow.** Bacteria grow best on foods that contain both proteins and fats. Meat, poultry, fish, milk, and eggs are particularly at risk. Bacteria grow best at room temperatures, between 60°F and 125°F (15°C and 52°C). Refrigerating or freezing foods slows the growth of bacteria. Boiling temperatures kill most bacteria.

• **Most bacteria require oxygen to live.** Store food in airtight containers. This cuts down on available oxygen.

• **Bacteria can grow and reproduce very rapidly.** Bacteria reproduce by dividing in half. Each of these two new cells then divide making four, and so on. The process is fast and continuous. In just three hours, one bacterium can become 500. You can see that food that has been contaminated by just a few harmful bacteria can become spoiled in a very short time.

• **Bacteria are easily moved from place to place.** They move by hitchhiking. They hitch rides on anything or anyone — people, dirt, rats, mice, bugs, even the air. A bug crawling across the counter leaves a trail of bacteria. These enter food that is placed on the counter. Workers who forget to wash their hands carry bacteria into the food they prepare. A dirty mixer will mix bacteria into the food. A sneezing or coughing worker will infect the food with cold-causing bacteria.

• **Harmful bacteria can make you sick.** These bacteria produce ***toxins*** — poisonous substances. With some bacteria, the toxin is produced inside your body after you eat the food. It can be difficult to detect that such foods are spoiled. With other bacteria, the toxin is produced before you eat the food. These foods usually smell and look spoiled. Never use food you think may be spoiled.

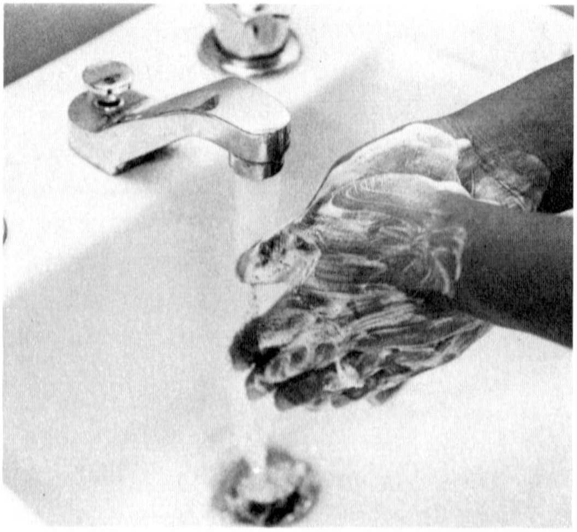

A thorough washing of the hands, using soap and water, is essential to sanitation. Hands should be washed before beginning any task in a food service kitchen, as well as after visits to the restroom.

There are four kinds of bacteria that cause special problems in food service:

Salmonella (sal-muh-NELL-uh) is a bacteria found in the intestines of animals and humans. It is present in most raw foods. Salmonella can be killed by proper cooking. Careful cleaning of hands and food preparation surfaces keeps salmonella from spreading.

Staphylococcus (staf-uh-low-KAH-kus) or ***staph*** bacteria come from humans. These bacteria are present on skin, in your mouth and throat and in some sores. Staph germs are resistant to heat. Workers must be clean and healthy to avoid spreading staph.

Clostridium perfringens (clah-STRID-ee-um per-FRIN-jens) bacteria grows on meat that is not kept hot enough or cold enough. If equipment temperatures are not set correctly, this bacteria can grow.

Clostridium botulinum (clah-STRID-ee-um botch-a-LIE-num) bacteria is one of the earth's most deadly poisons. This bacteria causes ***botulism***, a disease which paralyzes the muscles. Victims often die because they can't use their muscles to breathe. These bacteria usually grow in places without air. Canned foods that were not heated properly when processed are a good source for growth. Bulging, leaking cans probably have these bacteria. Never open such a can. Even one taste can cause death. Tell your supervisor if you find such a can so it can be disposed of properly.

- **Bacteria cannot stand extreme temperatures.** They grow fastest at warm temperatures between 60° and 100°F (15° to 38°C). Contaminated food that stands at room temperature for several hours can make a person very ill because of bacterial growth.

Below 60°F (15°C) bacteria are less active. However, even when frozen, bacteria do not die. You can see why refrigeration is so important in food storage. It slows the rate of bacterial growth so food "keeps" longer.

As temperatures get warmer, bacteria become more active. However, when the temperature reaches 108°F (42°C) some bacteria begin to die. Others can withstand even boiling temperatures for a short time.

Sources of Contamination

There are many sources of microorganisms that contaminate food. The largest single source is human beings. Other sources are animals, insects, equipment, and the general enviroment.

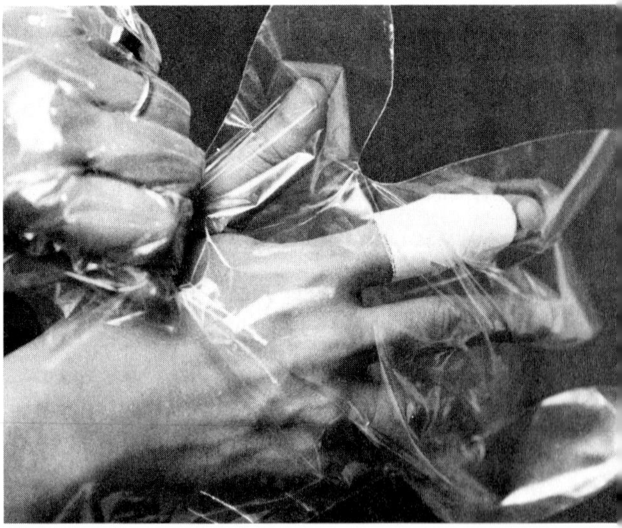

Even a small cut can be a source for contamination. Therefore, cuts should be bandaged properly and a plastic glove worn over the hand to prevent spread of bacteria.

The Food Service Workers

Food workers can control the spread of microorganisms into food. They are in close contact with the food to be served to the customers. Earlier in this chapter, you read that sanitation is a "way of life" which you need to develop. The chart on this page should help you.

In handling food and utensils follow these rules:

- Touch only the handles of serving and eating utensils.
- Handle tableware properly. Do not touch the rims of glasses or cups. Do not put your fingers inside plates, bowls, and other tableware.
- Use tongs or disposable plastic gloves when serving ice or preparing food which will not be cooked.
- Use a clean spoon each time you taste food. Do not put the tasting spoon back in the food or use your fingers for tasting.
- Use a scraper to remove leftover food from plates.

This is the WRONG way to pick up glasses. Your hands should never touch the rim of glasses or cups.

Personal Habits Affect Sanitation

Cleanliness

- Wear a clean uniform or apron daily.
- Wear a hair restraint — hair net or cap — to keep hair out of food.
- Bathe and wash hair frequently.
- Keep fingernails short, clean, and free from polish.
- Wash hands before preparing food and especially after smoking, eating, or using the toilet.
- Do not wear rings on your fingers.
- Keep hands away from mouth, nose, and hair while handling food.
- Do not chew gum or smoke in kitchens or serving areas.

Health

- Wear rubber gloves if you have an open cut, boil, or rash on your hands. Wear gloves even if you are wearing a bandage.
- Avoid using handkerchiefs. Use disposable tissues and throw them away promptly. Wash hands after use.
- Do no work when you are ill. Even a slight cold can easily spread to other workers and to customers.

This is the WRONG way to taste test your cooking. Never taste from the stirring spoon and never stand over the pot or pan when tasting.

Pests, The Uninvited Customers

Pests such as flies, roaches, rats, and mice are another source of contamination. Any sign of these pests is considered a serious health problem.

Flies go anywhere and eat anything. They will eat garbage and sewage as well as expensive steak. Their strong sense of smell attracts them to toilets, garbage cans, spilled food, or open cans. They always breed near the places they are seen. Flies are filthy and dangerous because they carry germs from dirty places to clean food. Serious diseases such as tuberculosis, typhoid fever, and dysentery are often spread by flies.

Roaches are another filthy pest. They are often brought into the kitchen accidentally on boxes. Once there, they find a cozy home in a warm place such as under the refrigerator, close to the hot water pipes, or under the sink. Roaches do not like the light, so they usually appear only at night when they come out to eat. As they crawl over counters, they leave their droppings. Roaches carry all kinds of disease-causing bacteria.

Insecticides are used to exterminate roaches and flies. Because some insecticides are poisonous, they should be approved by the local board of health before being used. Screens on all doors and windows will keep out most such pests.

Rodents such as rats and mice are found in great numbers throughout the world. They can gnaw through wooden doors, soft cement walls, screens, and boxes. Complete control is too big a job for a single person or business. Tell your supervisor immediately if you see any sign of these pests. An exterminator can be called to help control them. Here are some ways to protect the kitchens and storage areas from rodents:

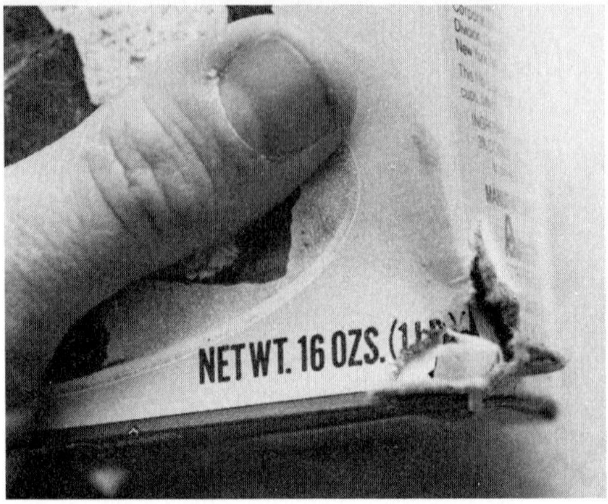

A rodent has made his way into this box of cake flour. Signs like this should be reported immediately.

- Store food in metal or heavy plastic containers with rounded corners and tight covers. Make sure no food is spilled around them. Rats and mice will not stay long where there is no food supply.
- See that the building is rat- and mouseproof. Inspect the outside regularly for signs of entry such as gnawed holes. Keep doors and windows closed at all times. Remember, rodents can climb.
- Watch for signs of rats and mice inside the building. They come out at night when everyone has gone, but they leave telltale droppings wherever they go. Look for signs of gnawing on food containers.
- Use traps and poisons carefully so they do not contaminate food.
- Practice "good housekeeping" so that no food supply is available to attract pests. Keep things clean. Wipe off the counters. Wipe up any spilled, moist food and liquids. Sweep up any dry food that has been spilled. Refrigerate food or store it in covered containers before leaving for the night. Garbage and refuse should be kept in tightly covered containers.

Tools and Equipment

Earlier you read that a kitchen that looks clean may still contaminate food. Tools, utensils, and equipment need to be washed and then sanitized — that extra step beyond cleaning. Special chemical compounds called sanitizers are used to destroy harmful microorganisms.

Follow these rules for washing and sanitizing tools, utensils, and equipment:

1. Soak them in a mild detergent and water if any food is stuck. This will save much scrubbing.
2. Wash inside and out using a stiff brush, a wire brush, or a pot scrubber.
3. Wash with warm, sudsy water and rinse under hot water.
4. Sanitize by rinsing in water to which sanitizer has been added.
5. Store in clean place, hanging from a rack or upside down on a clean shelf.

Once this pot is scrubbed thoroughly with a brush and warm sudsy water, it should be rinsed with hot water and sanitized with a sanitizing agent.

The Environment

Keeping the environment clean is part of good housekeeping. The air is always filled with bacteria, some good, some bad. Sweeping the floor when food is being prepared or served can spread bacteria to the food. Major cleanup should be done after food has been prepared and served, and all food and cooking tools have been put away.

Keep kitchen and dining areas clean by removing any waste food that accumulates in cracks and corners. Use clean cloths for cleaning jobs. Bacteria grow in greasy or sour cloths and sponges.

Cleanliness also includes the garbage area. After garbage has been emptied, scrub the cans and allow them to air dry. Line garbage cans with plastic bags to keep them clean. Make sure they are always tightly covered. Many food service operations have a refrigerated garbage area to slow growth of microorganisms.

Lining garbage cans with plastic bags helps to keep them clean.

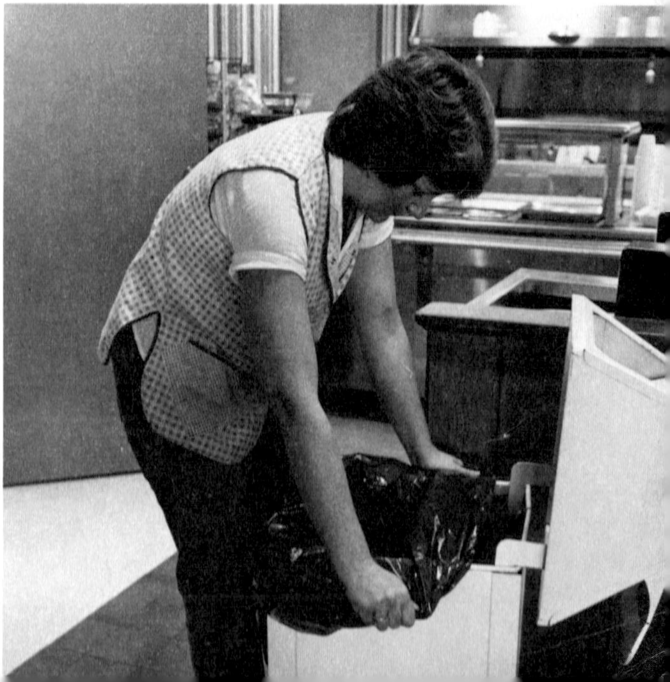

Here are some other sources of contamination:

- Sprays and insecticides used in growing crops can harm humans. Before serving fruits and vegetables, wash them thoroughly in running water.

- Store chemicals such as pesticides, detergents, and sanitizers well away from food. Label all such chemicals plainly.

- Solid objects in food can be very dangerous. Screws, pieces of glass, bugs, and worms are just a few of the many foreign objects that are occasionally found in food. They get into food only through carelessness.

Controlling Growth of Bacteria

Besides preventing contamination of food, bacteria growth can also be controlled by storing foods at the correct temperature and by heating properly during cooking and serving.

Temperature Control in Storage

Temperature control is a critical factor in preventing the growth of microorganisms during the handling and storage of food.

Many dry foods do not need refrigeration but should be kept cool. Dry food storage is for those foods which do not grow bacteria in their normal state. Examples of such foods are sugar, salt, flour, cereals, rice and grain products, dried beans and peas, canned and bottled foods, fats and oils.

Nevertheless, temperature control is as crucial in controlling bacteria growth in dry food storage as in any other type of storage. A reliable thermometer should be kept in the storeroom at all times so that a temperature of 55°-65°F (10°-20°C) is maintained.

Even in refrigerators, milk sours, meat becomes slimy, and cheese molds. Check refrigerators often to see they are between 35°-38°F (2°-3°C). Remember the danger zone starts at 40°F (4°C).

Most frozen food kept at 0°F (18°C) can be safely stored for at least six months. Never refreeze foods that have thawed. While frozen foods are thawing, bacterial growth begins again. The bacterial count after thawing will be much higher than it was when the food was frozen. Remember how quickly bacteria can grow! If the frozen food is thawed, refrozen, and then thawed again, it may be seriously contaminated. Cook frozen food after thawing.

Cooling and Storing Food

- Cool food slightly before storing in the refrigerator or freezer. Place large containers of food in cold water until cool. Remember that the center of the food takes longer to cool.
- Do not refreeze food that has thawed.
- Allow airspace around food in the refrigerator or freezer to promote quick cooling.
- Cold is drying. All food should be tightly covered.
- Refrigerators and freezers are coldest at the bottom.
- Clean refrigerators and freezers regularly.

Heating

Since most microorganisms die at temperatures above 140°F (60°C), prolonged boiling will kill all but the most heat-resistant kind. Temperatures above boiling will sterilize food completely. ***Sterilizing*** means killing all microorganisms.

Sterilized food will not spoil unless it is recontaminated. In the story at the beginning of this chapter, Ruthann was made sick from eating turkey. When the turkey was taken from the oven, all the harmful bacteria had been killed by the heat of the oven. However, the cutting board had not been properly sanitized. It was infected with salmonella bacteria. The salmonella entered the turkey when it was sliced. As the turkey cooled, the bacteria grew and grew and grew.

The time between preparation and serving should be as short as possible. Be sure the temperature in the center of the food does not fall below 140°F (60°C). You can test the temperature with a cooking thermometer. Keeping food at the proper temperature is also very important in the control of microorganisms.

To control growth of microorganisms, remember these points:

- Heat leftover food thoroughly. Use a thermometer to check the temperature in the center of the food.
- Do not hold food in a warm place for a long time before serving.
- Chill all food that should be refrigerated promptly.

SAFETY

Food service workers work with dangerous equipment and work under potentially hazardous conditions. A ***hazard*** is any risk or danger. Safety rules are written and enforced for the protection of the worker. A safe operation depends largely upon employees who are informed about safety rules and practice them daily.

A steam table is often used to keep food warm while serving. However, it should be removed promptly when serving is complete. This will prevent the food from becoming contaminated.

Responsibilities of Management

Safety begins with a clean, orderly workplace. Responsible management will make the workplace as safe a place as possible by providing the following:

- A structurally sound building with adequate wiring kept in good repair.
- Electrical equipment properly grounded and in good condition for use with necessary safety devices. Grounded equipment has a special plug which allows electricity to go into the ground. These plugs have three prongs on them instead of two.
- Adequate lighting.
- Nonslip floors.
- Well-planned and marked traffic lanes.
- Clearly marked exits.
- Approved fire extinguishers easily accessible.

Responsibilities of Workers

Workers are also responsible for on-the-job safety. They should develop a professional attitude toward work. "Horse-play" at work, carelessness in handling equipment or food, or disobeying safety rules is unprofessional and dangerous.

Carelessness causes accidents. If you forget safety precautions, you may lose working hours because of injury. Your employer will lose money, and you may even cause injury to a fellow worker. On a team, everyone must follow the same rules.

Avoiding Accidents

Food service work can be dangerous. Falls, cuts, burns, strains, shocks and even fires can occur unless safety rules are constantly practiced.

Falls

Studies of accidents in food service show that most injuries are caused by falls. Observing a few simple rules will help avoid most accidents of this type. The chart below gives guidelines for preventing falls.

Avoiding Falls

- Walk, do not run.
- Keep floor clean and dry. A wet floor is slippery, so wipe up any spills immediately. Sprinkle salt on any spots that are still slippery until the floor can be thoroughly washed.
- Wear low-heeled comfortable shoes with rubber soles. These grip the floor well.
- Keep floor mats flat to prevent stumbling. Wrinkled mats or ones with curled corners can cause falls.
- Keep work areas and traffic lanes clear. Electrical cords should not extend across traffic lanes. Put mops and brooms away promptly. Never leave boxes or crates in the aisles.
- Use correct door to enter or exit the kitchen.
- Look where you are going.
- Use a stepladder, never a chair or table, if you need to reach something on a high shelf.

Strains

A strain is a feeling of stiffness or soreness from using muscles too long or the wrong way. Strains usually occur in the lower back — the weakest point of the spinal column. In food service, strains are often caused by lifting heavy loads incorrectly. Once your back has been strained or weakened, it can easily be injured again.

- You can prevent back strain by lifting with your strong leg muscles. When you must lift a heavy object, squat with knees bent, feet apart, and back straight. With your arms straight, get a firm grip on the load. Stand up keeping your back straight. Make your leg muscles do the work. Do not twist or bend.
- Set objects down by using the same method in reverse. Ask for help if the object is too heavy. Use a cart to carry heavy objects any distance.
- Check methods of storage. Heavy articles should be stored on the bottom shelves.

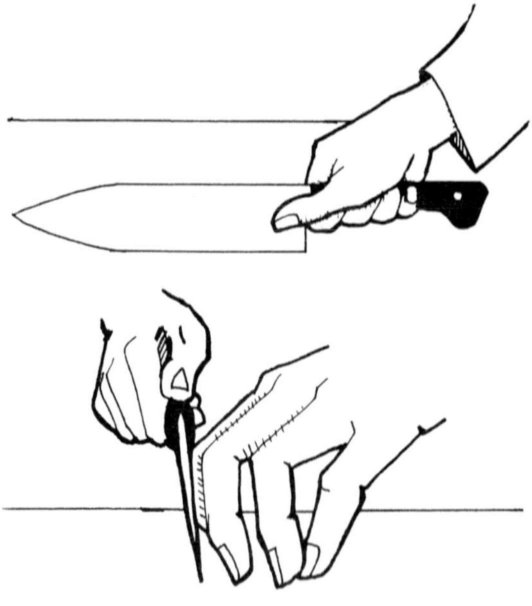

Cuts

Food service workers handle dangerous tools and equipment daily to cut, mix, chop, slice, and grate. Workers should know how to use them correctly in order to avoid cuts.

Cuts often result from the improper use of knives. A sharp knife is safer than a dull one because it will cut food more easily and with less pressure. The following ideas will help you use knives safely:

- Use the correct knife for the job.
- Use the knife correctly.
- Use a cutting board. Place a damp cloth under the board to prevent slipping.
- Always cut away from your body.
- Use knives only for cutting food. It is dangerous to use them for prying lids, opening cans, cutting string or paper, or sharpening pencils.
- If you drop a knife, let it fall. Never try to catch it in midair.
- Place dirty knives on the counter in plain sight. Never put them in the dishwater where they are hidden.
- Clean knives carefully with the cutting edge away from your fingers.
- Store knives correctly with the blades protected in a rack or slots in a drawer.

Care should also be taken when handling other tools and equipment. Peelers, graters, slicers, blenders, and mixers can all cause cuts if not used correctly. Learn how to operate and clean all equipment before using it.

Learn to hold a knife properly by gripping the handle firmly. Curl your fingers like a claw to keep them away from the edge of the blade. Knife safety is extremely important in food service.

Even the dishes used to serve customers can cut you if they are broken. Sweep up broken glass promptly. Pick up glass splinters with a damp paper towel and discard. If a glass is broken in dishwater, drain the water, and then remove the pieces. Do not "fish" for the broken pieces in the water.

Even a small cut can be serious in food service. Most cuts require a bandage to protect them. If you need a bandage on your hand, you must wear a plastic glove. This prevents contamination of the food you are preparing.

Shocks

Shocks are caused by touching an exposed electrical wire or electrical equipment which has not been grounded properly. Shock can vary from a slight tingle to a rocking jolt. A very severe shock can cause death. Protect yourself against shocks by following these rules:

- Check the condition of electrical cords on equipment. When disconnecting a cord, pull it by the plug. Never give it a yank. You may loosen the wires and get a shock.
- Never handle electrical equipment with wet hands or while standing in water.
- Wear rubber-soled shoes to prevent shocks. Rubber does not conduct electricity. Tennis shoes or sneakers are not wise, however, because they do not protect your feet against spilled hot food.
- Be sure an appliance is turned off before plugging it into an outlet.

Burns

Although cooking involves handling hot food and equipment, a little care can prevent most burns.

- Protect your hands by using hot pads. Use thick, dry hot pads which will not conduct heat quickly. When reaching into an oven, protect the back of your hands by pulling the rack out. Use a mitt.
- Protect yourself from steam burns. Always tilt the lid of a pot away from you to let the steam escape. Be sure all steam is gone from a pressure cooker before opening the lid. Wet hot pads can also cause steam burns.
- Hot fat can cause very painful burns. Never put cold or wet food into hot fat because it will cause the fat to splatter. It may also cause the hot fat to boil over and perhaps catch fire.
- Keep handles on pans turned away from the front of the range so the pan cannot be tipped over easily.
- Wear close-fitting clothes. Keep long hair tied back and do not wear dangling jewelry. Loose sleeves and jewelry can catch the handle of a pan and turn it over. Loose sleeves and hair can also catch fire.
- Avoid filling containers more than half full. They will be less likely to spill when carried.
- Get help when moving heavy pans of hot fat.
- Warn others when you are walking with hot food.
- Keep flammable materials such as towels away from open flames. ***Flammable*** materials are ones that catch fire easily.

Preventing Fires

- Do not overheat fat. A flash fire may result.
- Do not fill the fryer too full.
- Never leave hot fat unattended.
- If oil or fat spills, wipe it up with a paper towel and clean the surface with warm water and detergent.
- After cooking with grease, fat or oil, clean accumulated grease from range hoods, grills, and deep fat fryers. Use warm water and detergent.
- Check electrical equipment and extension cords frequently. Faulty wiring and fraying cords can cause electrical fires.
- Relight pilot lights on ranges only after cleaning all accumulated gas from the room. This will prevent explosion and resulting fire.

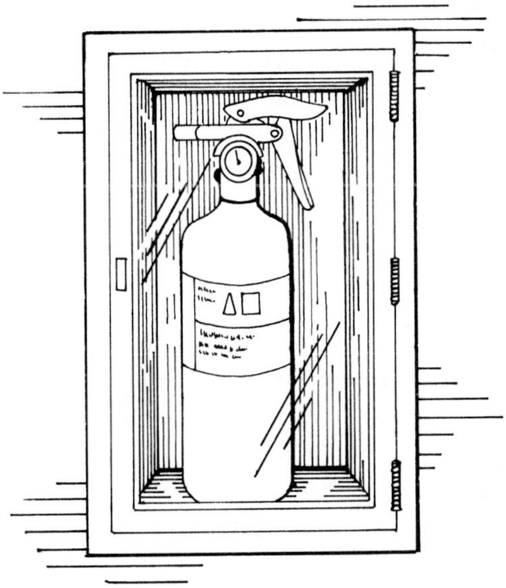

A chemical fire extinguisher should be nearby the hot station in a food service establishment. Fire extinguishers should also be located throughout the serving area for customer safety.

Fires

There are several types of fires that can start in a food service operation. Paper, wood, or fabric catch fire easily. Grease, oil, and fat can also burn. Even electrical equipment or wiring can cause a fire if it is damaged.

Fires are one of the greatest hazards in food service. They spread quickly and can injure or kill both employees and customers. A fire can also put a food service operation out of business. The chart at the left tells how you can help prevent a food service fire.

If a fire did happen would you know what to do? You will if you plan ahead.

Begin by locating the fire extinguishers in the kitchen. Many fire extinguishers can be used on all three types of fires — paper, grease, and electrical. Check to make sure *before* there's a fire. The illustration on page 98 shows how to use a fire extinguisher.

What if a fire extinguisher is not available? You may be able to stop a *small* paper or grease fire without one. For a paper, fabric, or wood fire, use water or a damp towel. Never use water on a grease fire. On grease, use baking soda to smother the flames.

Fires spread quickly. As soon as you spot one, alert others to the problem. Call the fire department immediately. Be sure you know where all exits are located. If the fire spreads, help customers from the building and stay outside. If the air is smoky, crawl to safety. The smoke will be lighter near the floor.

Paper, cloth, wood, rubber, and many plastics cause fires needing a water-type extinguisher labeled A. Oils, gasoline, some paints, lacquers, grease, cleaning solvents, and other flammable liquids cause fires requiring an extinguisher labeled B. Wiring, fuse boxes, energized electrical equipment, and other electrical sources cause fires using a chemical extinguisher labeled C. Fire extinguishers labeled ABC will cover all of the types of fires discussed.

Every food service worker should be trained in the proper use of the fire extinguisher used at their place of employment.

Enforcing Sanitation and Safety

Many federal, state, and local agencies work to protect health and safety in food service. The Department of Health, Education and Welfare (HEW), the Public Health Service (PHS), and the Food and Drug Administration (FDA) have all worked to set up guidelines in these areas. The FDA also works with state and local governments and tests contaminated food.

The National Sanitation Foundation (NSF) is an independent organization which works with industry and government. It sets standards for the construction and operation of food service equipment. The NSF also sponsors educational and sanitation programs nationally.

OSHA, the Occupational Safety and Health Administration, is a government agency in charge of the health and safety of workers. This agency has the power to enforce the standards of safety it has developed. OSHA also conducts research and provides information, education and training for employers and safety inspectors.

Setting the Rules of Safety

In addition to these national organizations, individual states, communities, and food service establishments may also set and enforce additional regulations.

An inspection report, similar to the one on page 99, checks safety as well as sanitary standards. The inspector has the right to close down a food service operation that does not pass inspection. In actual practice, a warning is usually issued and the management is given a certain amount of time to correct the errors.

FOOD ESTABLISHMENT INSPECTION REPORT

PERMIT NO.	ORIG. TRANS DATE	TYPE	ESTABLISHMENT NAME	
ADDRESS		CITY	ZIP	HEALTH CNTR
OWNER NAME		ADDRESS		
OPERATOR NAME		ADDRESS		

RATING SCORE ☐☐☐ STAT ☐ WATER SUPPLY ☐ 1. Public ☐ 2. Private SEWER DISPOSAL ☐ 1. Public ☐ 2. Private

PURPOSE ☐ 1. Routine ☐ 2. Follow-up ☐ 3. Complaint ☐ 4. Investigation

PERMITTED ☐ 1. Yes ☐ 2. No OWNER OPERATOR CERTIFIED ☐ 1. Yes ☐ 2. No

	Description
	Food
	Source: sound condition, no spoilage
	Original container; properly labeled
	Food Protection
	Potentially hazardous food meets temperature requirements during storage, preparation, display, service, transportation
	Facilities to maintain product temperature
	Thermometers provided and conspicuous
	Potentially hazardous food properly thawed
	Unwrapped & potentially hazardous food not re-served
	Food protection during storage, preparation, display, service, transportation
	Handling of food (ice) minimized
	In use, food (ice) dispensing utensils properly stored
	Personnel
	Personnel with infections restricted
	Hands washed & clean, good hygienic practices
	Clean clothes, hair restraints
	Food Equipment and Utensils
	Food (ice) contact surfaces: designed, constructed, maintained, installed, located
	Non-food contact surfaces: designed, constructed, maintained, installed, located
	Dishwashing facilities: designed, constructed, maintained, installed, located, operated
	Accurate thermometers, chemical test kits provided
	Pre-flushed, scraped, soaked
	Wash, rinse water: clean, proper temperature
	Sanitization rinse: clean, temperature, concentration exposure time: equipment, utensils sanitized
	Wiping cloths: clean, use restricted
	Food-contact surfaces of equipment & utensils clean, free of abrasives, detergents
	Non-food contact surfaces of equipment & utensils clean
	Storage, handling of clean equipment/utensils
	Single-service articles, storage, dispensing
	No re-use of single service articles
	Water
	Water source, safe: hot & cold under pressure

	Description
	Sewage
	Sewer and waste disposal
	Plumbing
	Installed, maintained
	Cross-connection, back siphonage, backflow
	Toilet and Handwashing
	Number, convenient, accessible, designed, installed
	Toilet rooms enclosed, self-closing doors, fixtures good repair, clean; hand cleaner, sanitary towels/tissues/ hand-drying devices, provided, proper waste receptacles
	Garbage and Refuse Disposal
	Containers or receptacles, covered: adequate number insect/rodent proof, frequency, clean
	Outside storage area enclosures properly constructed, clean: controlled incineration
	Insect, Rodent, Animal Control
	Presence of insects/rodents — outer openings protected, no birds, turtles, other animals
	Floors, Walls and Ceilings
	Floors, constructed, drained, clean, good repair, covering installation, dustless cleaning methods
	Walls, ceiling, attached equipment: constructed, good repair, clean surfaces, dustless cleaning methods
	Lighting
	Lighting provided as required, fixtures shielded
	Ventilation
	Rooms and equipment — vented as required
	Dressing Rooms
	Rooms clean, lockers provided, facilities clean, located
	Other Operations
	Toxic items properly stored, labeled, used
	Premises maintained free of litter, unnecessary articles, cleaning maintenance equipment properly stored. Authorized personnel
	Complete separation from living/sleeping quarters. Laundry
	Clean, soiled linen properly stored

Remarks

___

First Aid

When someone is injured, first aid is needed immediately. ***First aid*** is on-the-spot help for injuries. Sometimes this is the only help that is needed. Other times, first aid is given until trained medical help arrives.

If you need to give first aid, remain calm. Decide if expert help such as a doctor or ambulance is needed. Know where the first aid kit is at work and be familiar with its contents *before* you need to use it. Taking a first aid course from the American Red Cross would be extremely helpful. The chart on page 101 may help you when you must administer first aid.

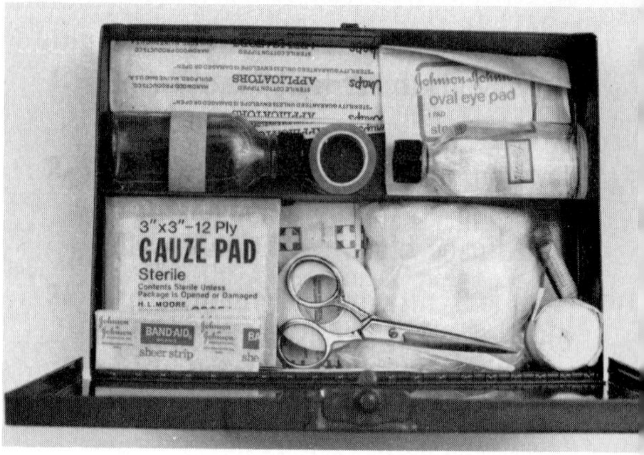

A first aid kit should always be located in the food service kitchen. Do not administer first aid if you are not trained.

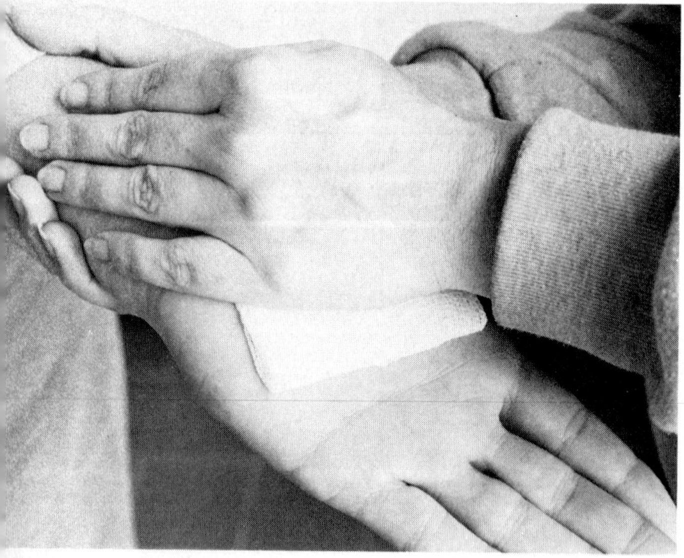

Burns are treated by gently applying a dry, sterile bandage. Get medical attention immediately!

Persons suffering from shock should be laying down, with their feet elevated higher than their head. Keep the person warm and call for medical assistance.

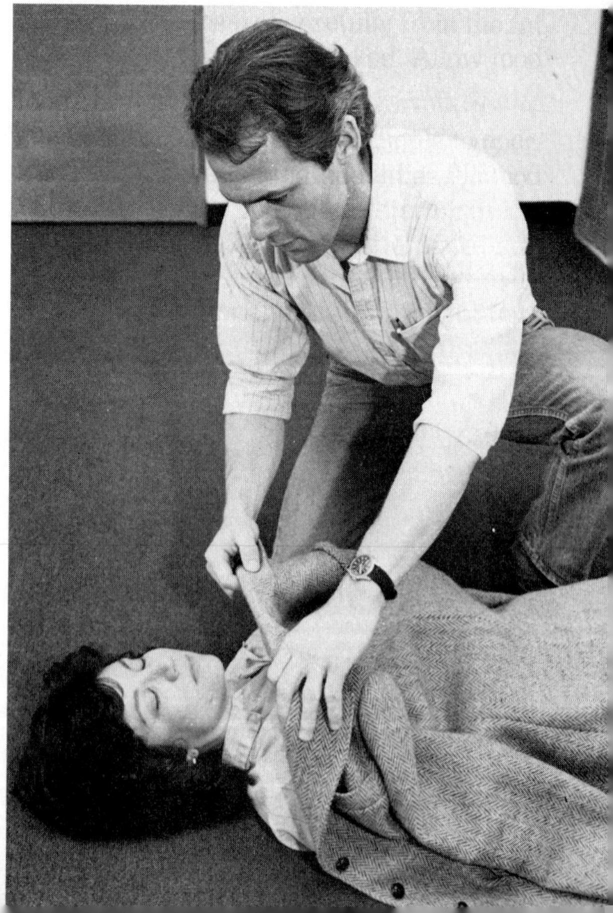

First Aid

Type of Injury	Symptoms	Treatment
Choking	Object stuck in throat May not be able to speak or cough Unconsciousness may occur.	If person can speak, do not interfere with his/her own attempts to remove object. If person cannot speak, give four hard slaps on back between shoulder blades. If this does not work, begin using Heimlich maneuver. If unconscious, apply artificial respiration, then back blows and Heimlich maneuver.
Poisoning **Swallowed**	May feel ill, vomit or be unconscious	Unless person has swallowed an acid or alkali substance, induce vomiting. First aid kit should contain medicine for this. If acid or alkali is swallowed, person should drink milk to dilute. If unconscious, apply artificial respiration. Call for medical help.
Inhaled	May have difficulty breathing or be unconscious.	Remove person to fresh air. If unconscious, apply artificial respiration. Call for medical help.
Severe Burns	Large blistered areas of skin or skin badly burned and grayish white	A dry, sterile bandage This type of burn is life-threatening. Get medical help immediately.
Smoke inhalation	May have difficulty breathing or may not be breathing	Get person to safe area. If not breathing, begin artificial respiration. Call for medical help.
Shock from serious injury	Shallow breathing cold, moist skin weakness Thirst Unconsciousness Usually not breathing	Have person lie down. Elevate feet higher than head. Loosen clothing, keep person warm. If unconscious, do not give any liquids as choking could occur. Do not touch person if still in contact with electricity. Try to turn off electrical current. If you can't use rope or dry broom handle.

SUMMARY

Many government agencies set safety and sanitation standards for food service because food service operations affect the lives of many people. Food service workers should practice good personal hygiene and follow all safety and sanitation guidelines. This will help prevent injuries, illnesses, or even deaths. Following sanitation and safety rules carefully is one of the most important jobs of the food service worker.

chapter recap

CHECK YOUR KNOWLEDGE

1. Why is sanitation important in food service?
2. What are microorganisms?
3. What four types of bacteria cause problems in food service?
4. What does sterilizing mean?
5. What precautions must be taken to control the growth of microorganisms?
6. What is a hazard?
7. How can food service workers help prevent falls?
8. How can strains be avoided when lifting heavy objects?
9. What three types of fires occur most often in a food service kitchen?
10. What is first aid?

EXTEND YOUR LEARNING

1. Number four sterile agar plates 1 to 4. Contaminate each as follows:
   #1 — Place a strand of hair on top.
   #2 — Make fingerprints on top.
   #3 — Sneeze or cough on the surface.
   #4 — Place a cube of bread on top.
   Allow the plates to incubate at room temperature from three to five days. Check the growth on each and report your results.
2. Discuss factors that affect a safe work environment. Make a checklist and check your lab kitchen. How does it measure up? What improvements could be made?

Unit 3

Organizing for Efficiency

Have you ever wondered how the workers in a busy restaurant can prepare and serve hundreds of meals in such a short time? The key to such efficiency is good organizational skills. Without them, food service operations would fail to meet deadlines, please customers, and stay in business.

Organization starts with having the right equipment for the job. In your kitchen at home, you probably have some basic tools and equipment. But professional cooks know that several sets of tools are needed to run a food service operation. That way tasks like peeling potatoes can be finished quickly by more than one person.

A professional cook also knows that expensive, specialized equipment can actually save money. It often reduces the amount of time needed for a particular task. This unit deals with many of the specialized tools and equipment used in food service.

The final chapter in this unit explains how food service kitchens are organized to promote efficiency. Professional kitchens are divided into sections, or stations. Each station is responsible for specific types of tasks. The workers in each station have all the necessary tools, equipment, and work space required for the task assigned to that area. By dividing tasks, a professional cooking team can produce more food in less time.

One Saturday morning, Jim picked up Ruthann at her home. They were going to the beach for a picnic.

"I hope you don't mind, " he said, "but I have to stop at the hardware store to get a special size screwdriver."

"That's okay," replied Ruthann. "There's lots of stuff to look at in a hardware store."

After buying the screwdriver Jim found Ruthann in the houseware section. "Look at all these knives, Jim," she said. "There's a knife for just about every kitchen job. Here's a knife just for boning, and a French knife for chopping. They are expensive, too. We don't have nearly this many knives at home."

"Neither do we," said Jim. "Look how well they are made. See how the metal runs clear to the end of the handle? It's riveted, too, so the blade can't come loose."

"These are stainless steel," commented Ruthann. "Didn't Chef Robinson say stainless steel doesn't rust and always looks nice, but it doesn't hold a sharp edge? Here's a case with high carbon steel. Isn't that the kind most chefs use?"

"Yes," said Jim. "but look at the price! They cost even more than the stainless steel ones. If I'm ever a chef, I'm going to have my own set of knives."

"My dad has lots of tools in his workshop. He must have one for just about every job," said Ruthann. "I said something to him about the tools in the kitchen, and he was surprised. I don't think he had ever considered the knives, mixing spoons, and measuring equipment as tools. But they really are, you know."

"Chef Robinson calls them 'Tools of the Trade'," said Jim.

"Here's a spring scale," said Ruthann. "Until I studied food service, I never thought of measuring ingredients by weight. But I can see that weighing is much more accurate when you are working with large quantities."

"It's getting late," reminded Jim. "David and Kim will think we forgot about the picnic. Let's get chicken this time instead of hamburger. It's cheaper, and I'd like to try barbecuing one."

"Great," said Ruthann, "Let's go!"

chapter 7

tools and small equipment

Set your goals

When you complete the study of this chapter, you should be able to . . .

- Define and correctly use the vocabulary terms.
- Identify tools and small equipment used in food service.
- Select, use and care for tools and small equipment correctly.

Build your vocabulary

conduct
equipment
gauge
grind
purees
serrated
tang
tempered
tools

THE FOOD SERVICE WORKER AND EQUIPMENT

The job of cooking, like most jobs, requires equipment. Correct use of this equipment makes workers more productive and efficient — more valuable employees.

In food service, the term ***tools*** means hand-held items used for food preparation, cooking, and serving. Containers used for mixing, cooking, or storing food are also considered tools. The word "utensils" is often used in place of the word "tools." Appliances such as refrigerators, mixers, and fryers are usually referred to as ***equipment***.

Food service kitchens include everything from small paring knives to large walk-in refrigerators. Kitchen workers must be able to identify each piece of equipment and know how to use it safely and efficiently.

Modern technology continues to develop more specialized and efficient equipment. This equipment helps reduce labor costs, the major expense in food service. However, the equipment itself is very expensive. It is essential that workers who use it be thoroughly trained in its use and care.

Hand tools are fairly simple to use. But to use them skillfully requires not just knowledge, but also lots of practice. You will become faster and more efficient at using hand tools the more you work with them. Food preparation and cooking equipment is as safe as the person who uses it. Learn about the equipment before you use it. If you have a question while you are working, ask. Equipment can be dangerous. It is also expensive to repair. If a machine is not operating correctly, turn it off immediately and report the problem to your teacher or supervisor.

Materials

Tools and equipment are made of different materials, each having advantages and disadvantages. Some of the factors influencing which materials are used include:

- Durability.
- Price.
- Ability to ***conduct***, or transfer, heat.
- Ease of use and cleaning.
- In metal, the ***gauge***, or thickness.

The chart on page 107 shows some of the most common materials found in food service kitchens.

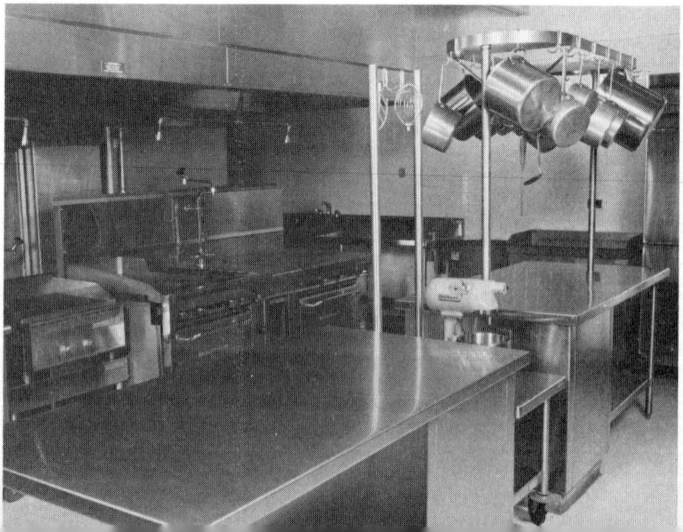

As you can see in this food service kitchen, many of the tools and pieces of small equipment are made of stainless steel. Notice that the work areas are also stainless steel. They are easy to clean, rustproof, and stainproof.

Materials for Tools and Utensils

Material	Advantages	Disadvantages	Notes
Stainless steel	• Rustproof. • Stainproof. • Easy to clean.	• Heavy to handle. • May heat unevenly.	• May be purchased in many gauges.
Aluminum	• Inexpensive.	• Turns dark when used with alkali-containing vegetables. • Reacts chemically with acids in food. • Dishwasher detergent will darken and stain.	• Light gauge will dent easily. • Cleans with mild soap and steel wool.
Copper	• Excellent conductor of heat.	• Expensive • Soft metal. • When heated will form a poison — copper oxide — which may react with food.	• Usually used as coating on bottom of aluminum or stainless steel utensils.
Cast iron	• Distributes heat evenly. • Holds heat for long period of time.	• Rusts easily. • Difficult to clean . • Food sticks to it easily.	• Wash in hot water and dry well. • May coat with salt-free oil to prevent rust.
Re-tinned iron	• Inexpensive. • Shiny appearance. • Fairly durable.	• Tin coat wears off exposing iron underneath to rust.	• Do not scour.
Plastics and hard rubber	• Won't dull knives. • Sanitary.	• Surfaces become scratched. • Brittle plastic cracks easily. • Hard rubber dries out and cracks.	• Wash in warm, soapy water rinse thoroughly and air dry. • Do not store near heat. • Used widely for cutting boards, in serving and storing food.
Wood	• Often preferred for rolling pins and baking tables.	• Porous. • Absorbent • Hard to sanitize.	• Wash with warm, soapy water and air dry. • Sanitize with chlorine. • Not allowed by some local food service codes.

TOOLS

Although food service operations usually prepare large quantities of food, a surprising amount of the work is performed by hand. You are probably familiar with many of the hand tools used. Some, though, are larger or different than those found in a home kitchen. Basic tools are described here. Some specialized tools will be introduced in other chapters.

Knives

Knives are among the most important tools in the kitchen. They are used for tasks such as cutting, chopping, and slicing. Many chefs even have their own personal set of knives. They take them to their job for their personal use.

Knives in food service operations get hard use. That is why they must be of good quality. A knife is made of three parts, the blade, the tang, and the handle.

- **Blade.** The blade of the knife should be made of ***tempered***, high-carbon, steel. Tempered steel has been heat-treated so it is very hard, yet flexible. It can be sharpened to a very sharp edge and hold it.

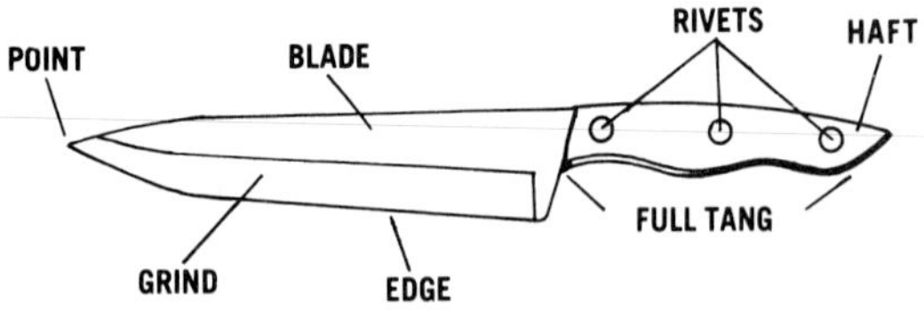

Stainless steel knives are popular because they are stain resistant, but they are much harder to sharpen.

Grind refers to the finished shape of the knife edge. The knives pictured on page 109 have different types of grinds. The cutting edge of a knife may be ground so that it is flat, saber, concave, or hollow.

Flat and saber grinds have thicker blades. They are ideal for such heavy-duty jobs as chopping, cutting big chunks of raw meat, or cutting soft bones. Flat and saber grinds need frequent sharpening.

Concave and hollow grinds have a thin cutting edge which becomes thinner as the knives are sharpened. Blades with these cutting edges are used to perform lighter jobs such as slicing, cutting, and chopping light food. These grinds also require less frequent sharpening.

Blades may have straight or ***serrated*** edges. Serrated means having sawlike notches on the edge. Serrated edges are used when a sawing motion is needed, such as for cutting fresh bread or cake.

- **Tang.** The ***tang*** is the part of the blade that is attached to the handle. For safety, the tang should extend the full length of the handle. Look for rivets that fasten the tang securely to the handle.
- **Handle.** Handles may be made of several different materials. Plastic and hard rubber are usually used in food service instead of wood. These materials resist heat and moisture and are slip-proof for safety.

There are many kinds of knives, each with a specialized use. Select the right knife for a particular job. The correct knife makes the task much easier.

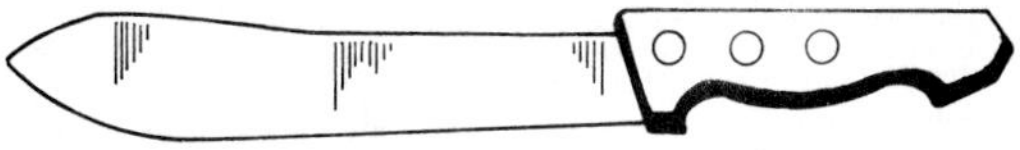

Butcher Knife
Used to divide raw meat, poultry, or fish into sections. Has a heavy blade and a saber or flat grind.

French or Chef's Knife
Used to chop, dice, or mince food and to slice warm meat. Has a long, triangular blade with a concave or hollow grind. It is the knife used most often.

Boning Knife
Used to fillet fish, cut apart poultry, and remove raw meat from the bone. Has a thin, light blade with a concave or hollow grind.

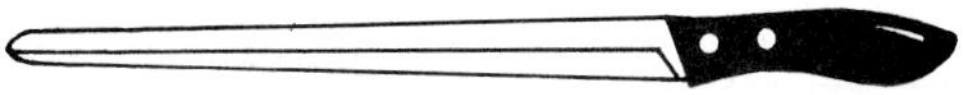

Slicing Knife
Used to slice roasts, hams, and thick, solid cuts of meat. The long, thin blade has a concave or hollow grind.

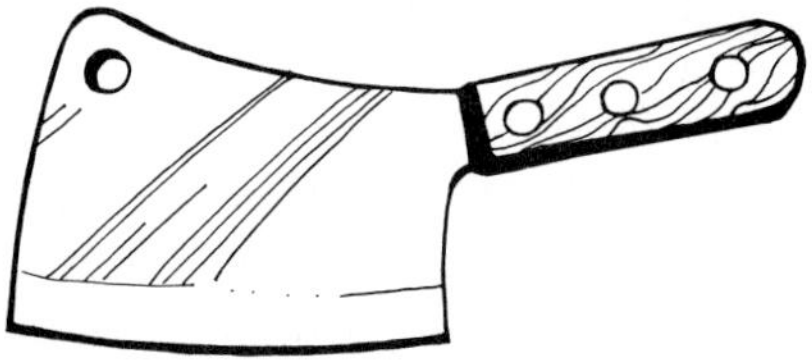

Cleaver
Used to chop through bones. The heavy blade has a flat or saber grind.

Fruit and Salad Knife
Used to prepare salad greens, vegetables, and fruits. Has a concave- or hollow-ground blade.

Citrus Knife
Used to section citrus fruit. The blade is two-sided and serrated. The tip is rounded to fit the round shape of citrus fruit.

Paring Knife
Used to core, peel, pare, and section fruits and vegetables. The blade is short with a concave or hollow grind.

Sharpening Steel
Used constantly to keep knives very sharp. Made of specially hardened steel with a wooden or plastic handle.

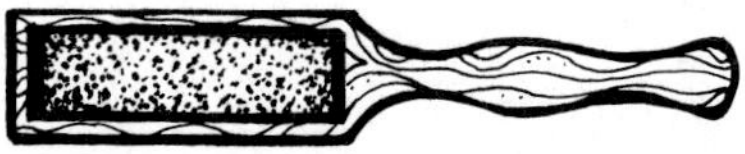

Sharpening Stone
Used to sharpen short knives such as paring knives. Made of soft stone, slanted on each side, and set in a plastic or wooden handle.

Flat Spatula
Used to level off ingredients when measuring and to spread frostings and sandwich fillings. The metal blade is flexible, with a rounded tip and no sharp edge.

Stirring, Lifting, and Turning Tools

Tools for stirring, lifting, or turning are made of stainless steel, plastic, or wood depending upon the intended use. Their handles are usually heat-resistant. Hang such tools conveniently from a rack or place in a drawer near where they will be used.

Spoons

Used for stirring and mixing. Made of stainless steel (or hardwood if food service regulations permit). Solid spoons are used to stir, to spoon liquids over foods, and to lift food and liquid out of pots. Slotted and perforated spoons are used to lift foods, such as vegetables, out of the liquid in which they were cooked.

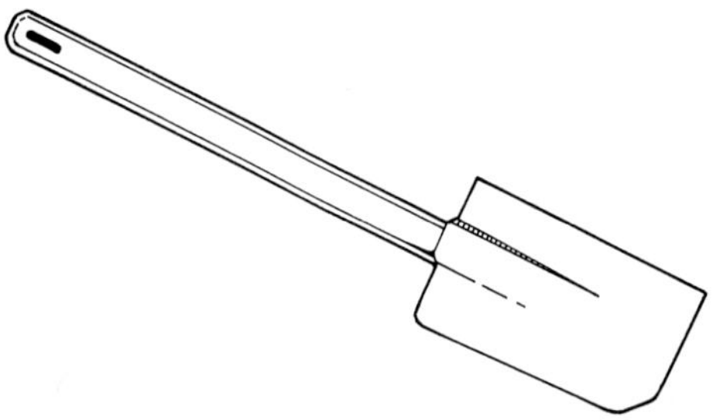

Rubber Spatulas or Scrapers

Used for all scraping jobs. Plate scrapers have a short handle. Those used for scraping out bowls have long handles. The blades are made of plastic or rubber.

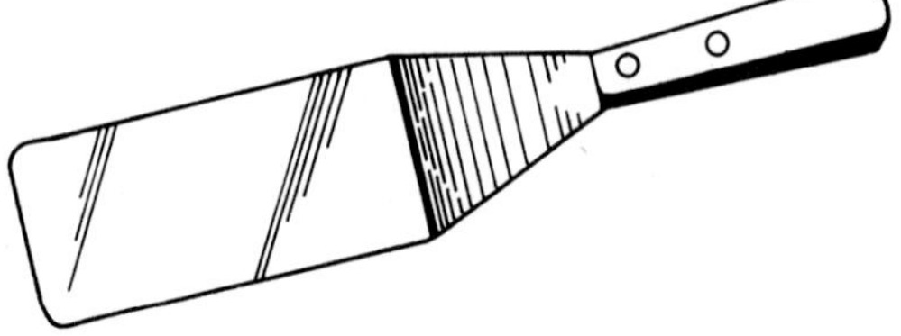

Turners

Used to turn foods such as meat and pancakes during cooking. Turners are made of stainless steel. Turners with a thin, flexible blade are also referred to as offset spatulas.

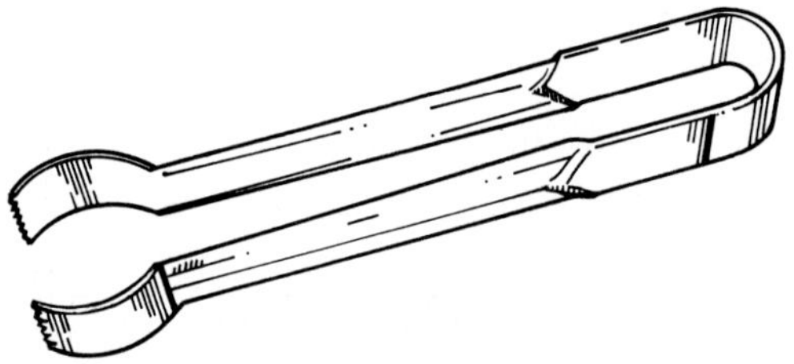

Tongs

Used to turn steaks, bacon, or chops while broiling and to remove corn and other vegetables from hot liquid. Also used in serving. Tongs are made of metal.

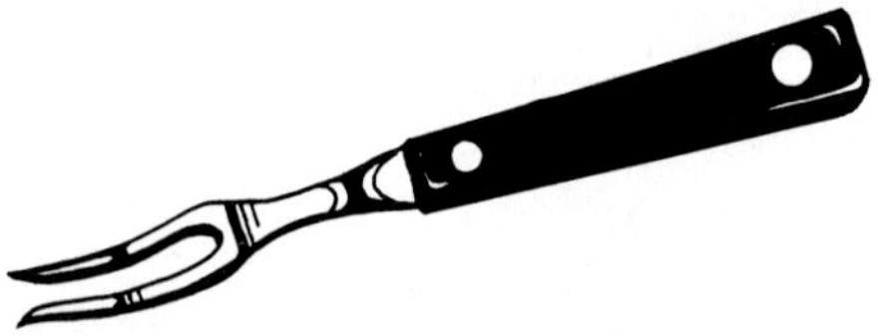

Kitchen Fork

Used to hold meats while slicing and to turn solid pieces of meat while browning or cooking. This large, two-pronged fork is made of stainless steel with a long, heat-resistant handle.

Beating and Whipping Tools

Large electric mixers (described in Chapter 8) are used for most beating and whipping jobs. For hand beating and whipping and for some mixing jobs, wire whips are used.

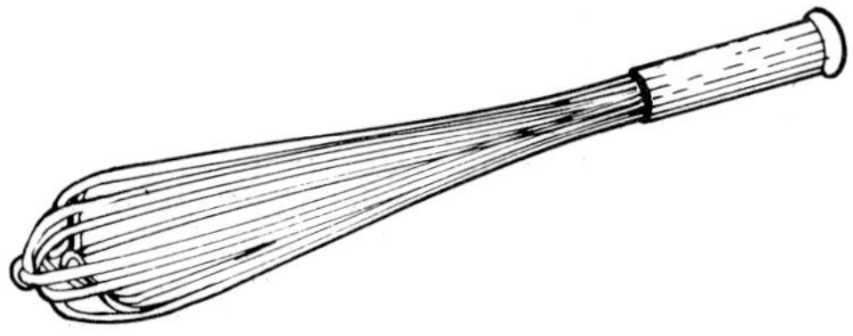

Piano Wire or Balloon Whip
Used for whipping eggs or batter and for blending thinner mixtures such as gravy. Made of flexible, looped wires which are fastened to the handle.

Heavy Wire or French Whip
Used for general mixing, stirring, and beating heavy liquids. Made of looped, heavy wires fastened into the handle.

Measuring Tools — Volume

Measuring tools are among the most important items found in any kitchen since good cooking depends upon accurate measurement. Review pages 53-56 for information on how to measure.

Measuring Spoons
Used to measure very small amounts of ingredients. A set of customary measuring spoons includes four sizes: ¼ teaspoon, ½ teaspoon, 1 teaspoon, and 1 tablespoon. A set of small metric measures include 1 milliliter, 5 milliliter, 15 milliliter, and 25 milliliter sizes.

Dry Measuring Cups
Used to measure dry ingredients. A customary set includes ¼ cup, ⅓ cup, ½ cup, and 1 cup sizes. A set of metric measures includes 50 milliliter, 125 milliliter, and 250 milliliter sizes. Dry measuring cups are usually made of metal.

Liquid Measuring Cups
Used to measure liquids. Measurements are marked on the sides of the cups. These are available in different sizes and in customary or metric. Most have a lip for pouring liquids easily.

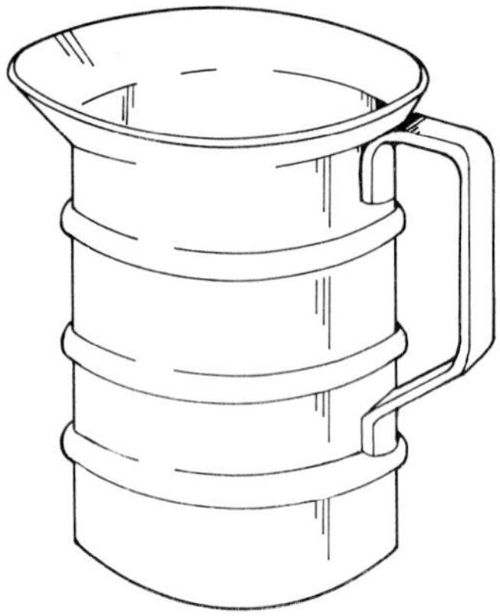

Large Volume Measures
Used to measure larger amounts of ingredients by volume. Made of aluminum or stainless steel with amounts marked by ridges. Available in several sizes.

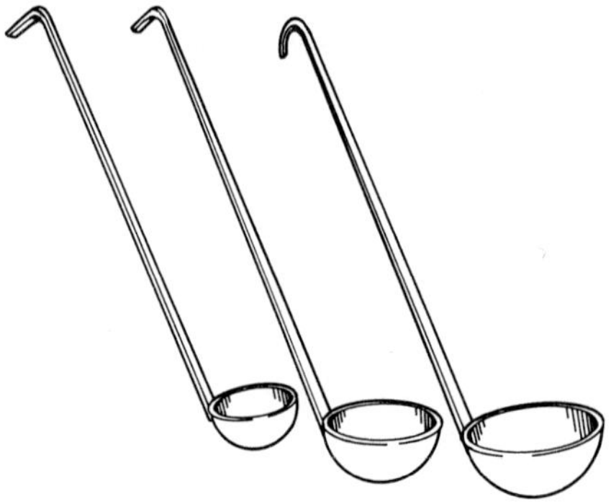

Ladles
Used for measuring and portioning liquids. They come in different sizes. The size is marked on the handle.

Scoops
Used to measure servings of foods such as ice cream and mashed potatoes. Made of stainless steel, usually with a plastic handle. Most have a level on the side to scrape the food out of the bowl of the scoop. Scoops are numbered according to size. The larger the number, the smaller the amount it holds.

Measuring Tools — Weight

In food service, most ingredients are measured by weight instead of volume. Weight measurements are more accurate. The scales used to measure ingredients are precision instruments and must be handled carefully.

Spring Scale
Used for weighing dry ingredients. Spring scales may not be absolutely accurate.

Portion Scale
Used to weigh food in order to maintain an equal serving size.

Balance or Baker's Scale
Used for accurately weighing dry ingredients, batters, and mixes.

Some tools are difficult to classify under any one particular use. However, these tools are used often in most food service kitchens.

Peelers

Used to scrape vegetables such as carrots and potatoes and to peel fruit such as apples. The best ones are made of stainless steel with a sharp, double-edged, swivel blade.

Utility Scissors

Used to snip parsley, cut pastry, and many other jobs. Utility scissors have heavy, straight blades.

Funnels

Used to fill jars with liquid. Made in various sizes of stainless steel, aluminum, or plastic.

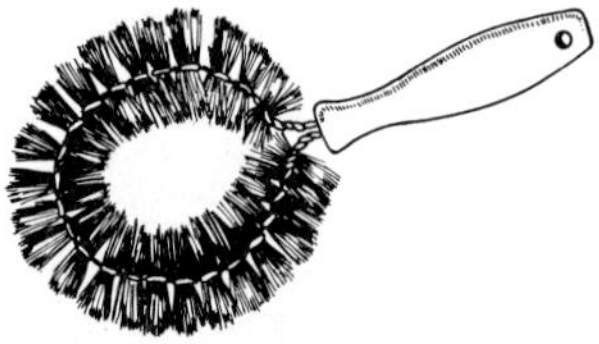

Brushes

Used for cleaning vegetables and utensils or equipment with hard-to-reach parts. Also used for small basting jobs. Their size and shape depend on their purpose. This is a vegetable brush.

Cook's Fork

Used for deep stock pots and turning heavy meats. It is made of stainless steel with a long, heat-resistant handle.

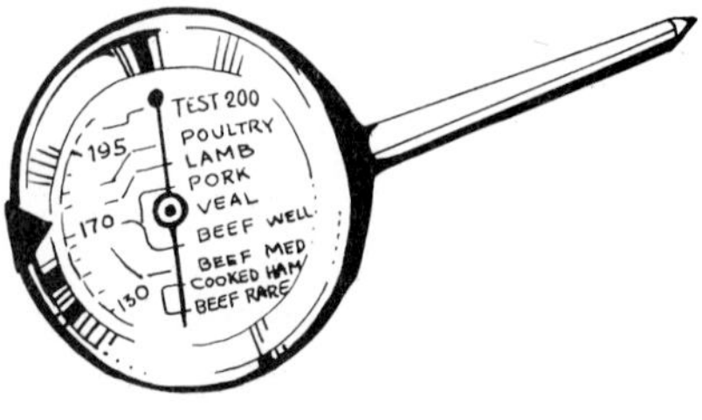

Thermometers

Used to check the temperature of ovens, refrigerators, or freezers; the internal temperature of roasting meat; or the temperature of hot fat.

Dredges

Used for shaking flour, salt, and pepper on meat, poultry, or fish. Dredges are made of stainless steel or aluminum and look like large salt shakers.

Skimmer

Used to remove scum from broth. The perforated, shallow bowl allows the liquid to flow back into the pot. It is made of stainless steel.

Apple Corer

Used to pare the skin and cut the core from apples. It is made of stainless steel with serrated edges.

Cookware

Good cookware distributes heat evenly and quickly. It does not develop hot spots that burn the food being cooked. As you read earlier in this chapter, even heating depends on the type of metal and its gauge.

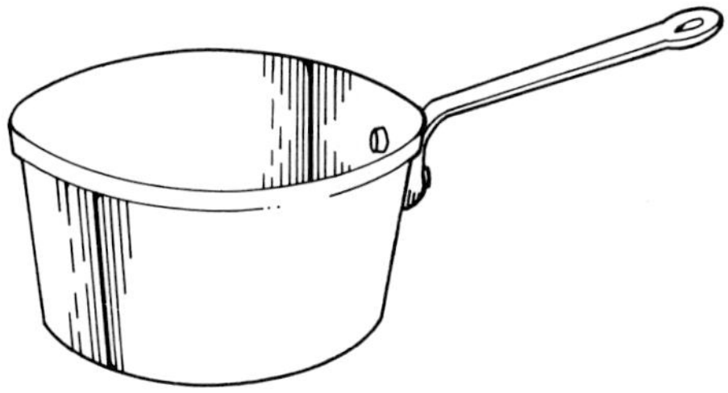

Saucepans
Used for cooking small amounts of food. The sides are straight with rounded corners and no seams. Saucepans have a handle, a lid, and come in various sizes.

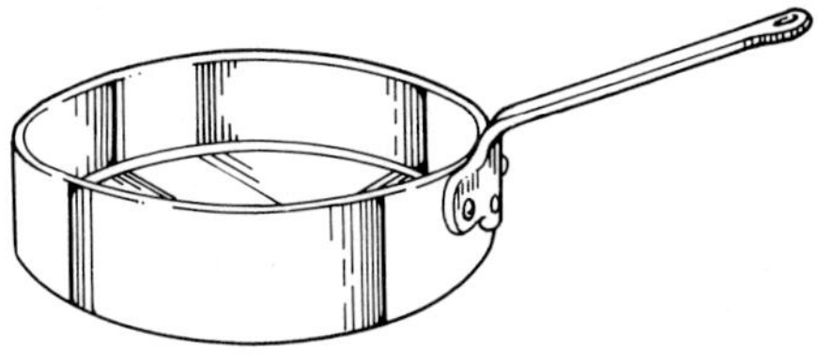

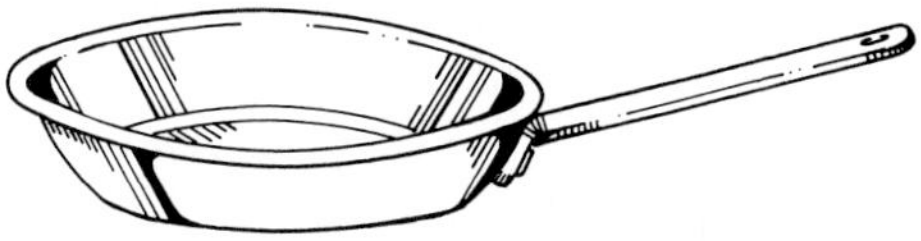

Frying Pans
Used for cooking food in a small amount of fat. Sometimes fry pans are called skillets or saute pans. They are made of heavy gauge aluminum, stainless steel, or cast iron.

Double Boilers
Used when temperatures must be kept below boiling or for keeping food warm without overcooking. They consist of two sections. The lower section holds water and the upper pan the food. They are made of stainless steel or aluminum and always have a lid.

Stock Pots
Used for soups, stews, chili, spaghetti, and corn on the cob. Stock pots are made of heavy gauge aluminum or stainless steel. They have deep, straight sides, two handles, and a lid.

Bakeware

Food service operations use a variety of bakeware. They are needed both for general food preparation and for baking desserts, breads, and other specialty items.

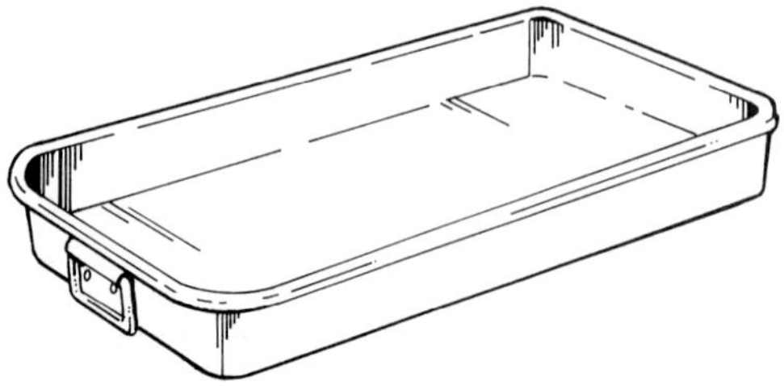

Utility Baking Pan
Used for many types of food such as cakes, gelatin salads, and macaroni and cheese. Made of stainless steel or aluminum.

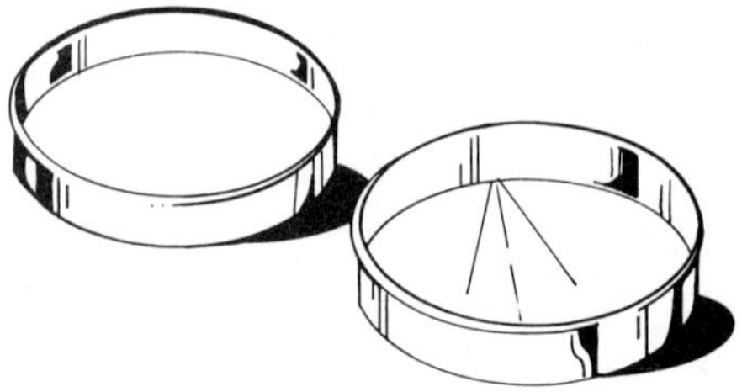

Cake Pans
Used for cakes and coffee cakes. Cakes pans are round, square, or rectangular and made of light- or medium-gauge aluminum or stainless steel. They come in various sizes.

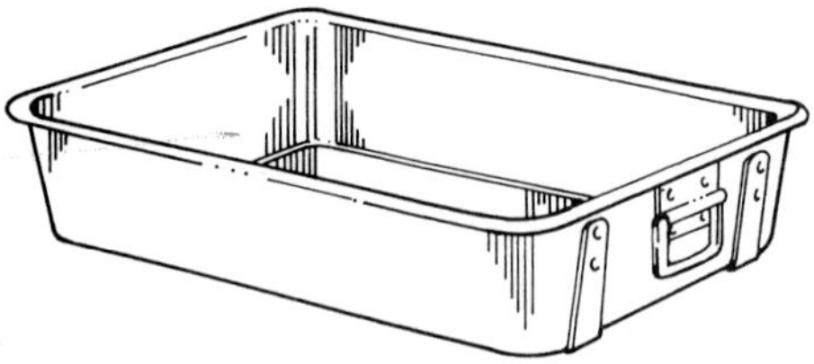

Roasting Pans
Used for roasting meat and poultry. Made of heavy gauge stainless steel or aluminum. Most have a lid and a rack in the bottom to keep the food out of the cooking juices. They are deeper than a utility baking pan.

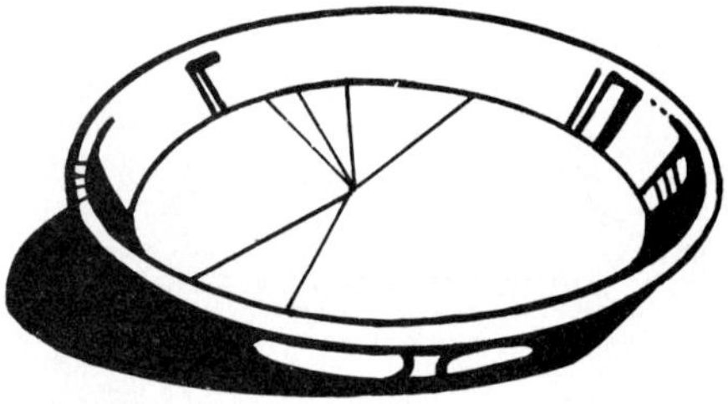

Pie Pans
Used for baking pies. They are round and made of re-tinned iron, aluminum, stainless steel, or aluminum foil. Pie pans are available in several sizes.

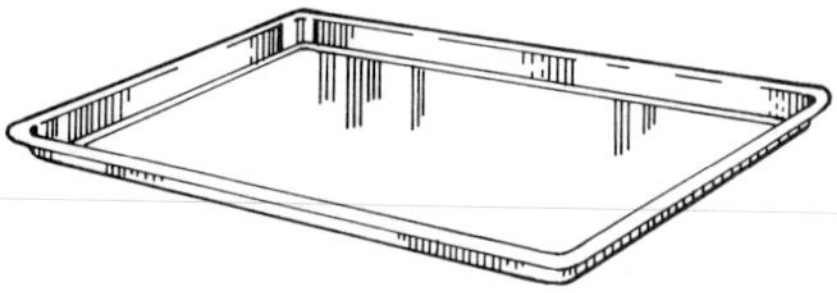

Bun or Sheet Pans
Used for cookies, rolls, biscuits, sheet cakes and some quick breads. Made of aluminum or stainless with 1 in. (3 cm) sides.

Other Tools

Like tools, there are many utensils in food service kitchens that are used in several areas and for a variety of jobs. Some of the most common are described here.

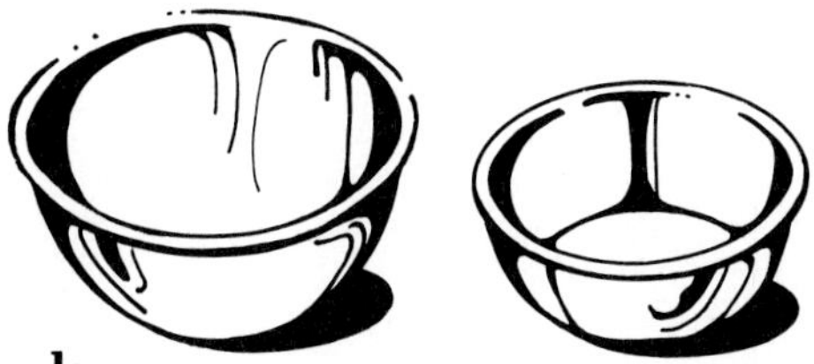

Bowls

Used for mixing and combining ingredients. In food service, bowls are made of stainless steel.

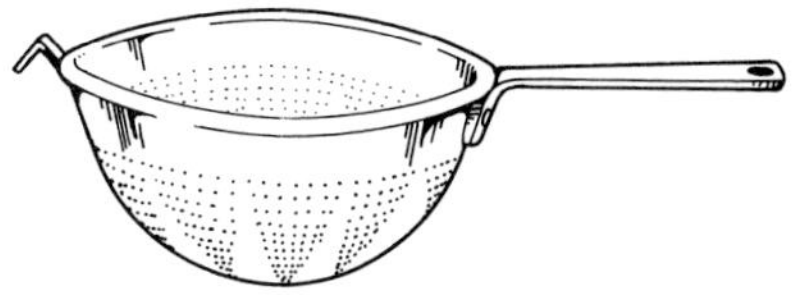

Strainer

Used to strain food which is too small to strain in a colander. Made of aluminum, stainless steel, or wire mesh. Strainers are available in many sizes.

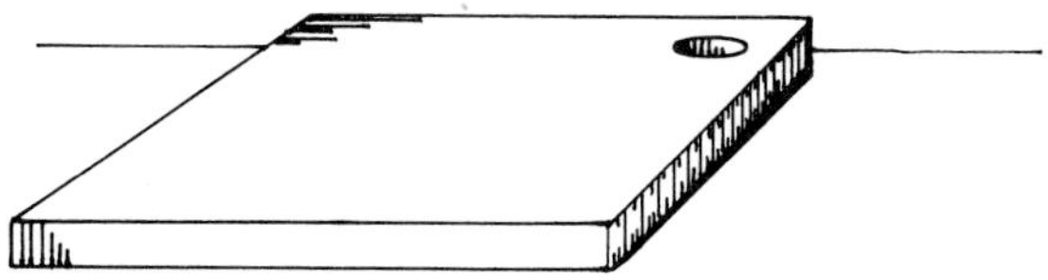

Cutting Board

Used for chopping, slicing, and cutting all kinds of foods. Plastic cutting boards are more sanitary than those made of hardwood.

Colander

Used to rinse and drain salad greens, vegetables, and fruit. They are also used to drain many cooked foods. Colanders are made of aluminum or stainless steel. They have a perforated bowl attached to a base with loop handles.

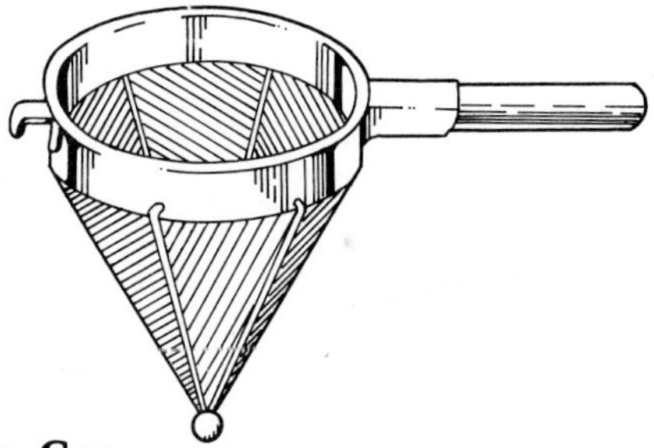

China Cap

Used for straining sauces and gravies and for making ***purees*** — thick pastes of vegetables, fruits, or dried beans or peas. (Purees are often used to make thick soups). The china cap has a cone-shaped, stainless steel, mesh bowl with a long handle and a hook so it can hang on the side of the pot. It also has a wooden mallet shaped to fit the cone for forcing food through the mesh.

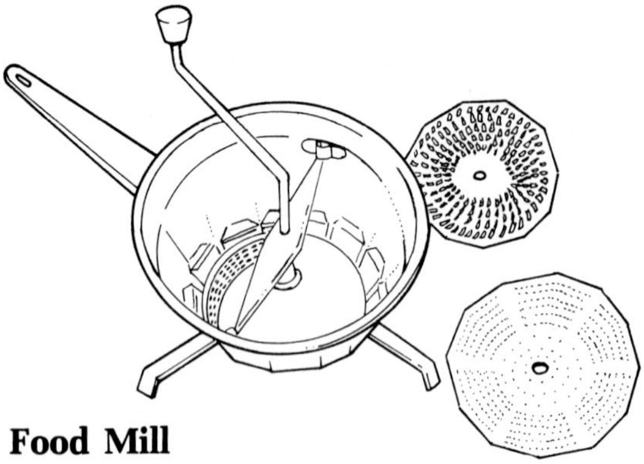

Food Mill
Used for mashing, straining, and pureeing. Usually made of re-tinned iron. The food mill has a revolving piece of metal with a handle on the top to push the food through the mesh.

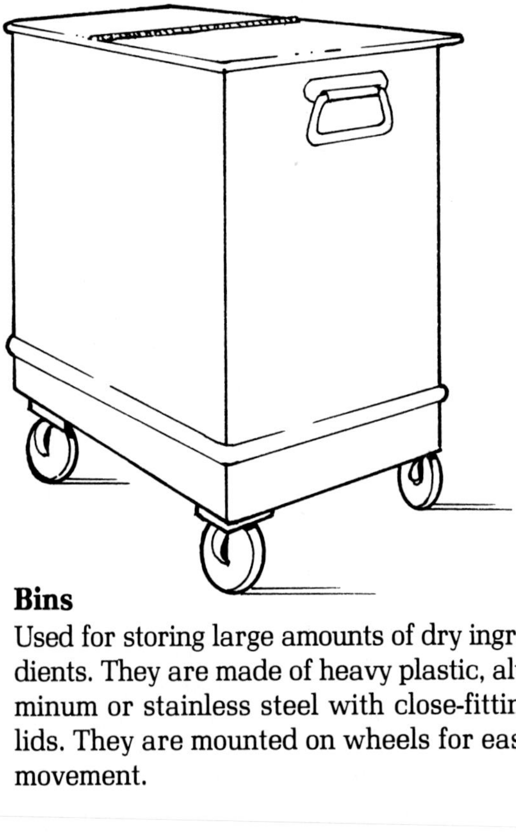

Bins
Used for storing large amounts of dry ingredients. They are made of heavy plastic, aluminum or stainless steel with close-fitting lids. They are mounted on wheels for easy movement.

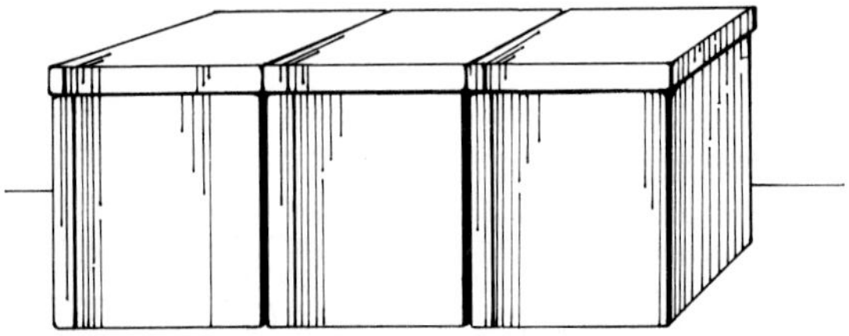

Canisters
Used for storing spices and small amounts of other dry ingredients. Canisters are made of aluminum, chrome-plated steel, or heavy plastic. They must have tight lids to keep out insects and rodents.

SMALL EQUIPMENT

There are many useful pieces of small equipment used in food service kitchens. Some do many jobs, others are specialized. Coffee makers, waffle bakers, blenders, and toasters are just a few of these helpful appliances.

Coffee Makers

Coffee makers are widely used in food service establishments. There are many different types, makes, and models, but each does the same job — making fresh tasting, hot coffee available at all times. Most coffee makers are automatic. Large urns that make 32 or more cups at a time are still used, especially in hospitals, but they are being replaced in restaurants by coffee makers that filter coffee directly into glass serving containers.

Waffle Bakers

These have only one use — to make waffles. Waffle bakers are heavy duty and are made of chromed steel on the outside. They have two grids with expandable hinges on the inside. The grids should never be washed. Just brush out the crumbs and wipe with a paper towel.

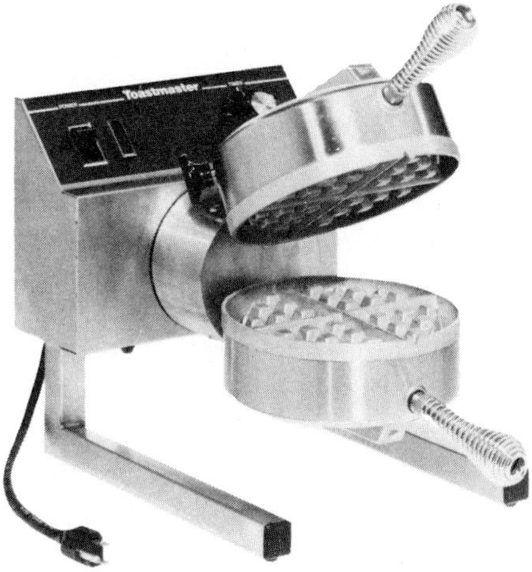

Blenders

Blenders are used to chop, blend, mix, puree, and liquify all kinds of food. Some containers, especially in food service, are made of stainless steel. There are also containers of heavy-duty plastic. Because all blenders do not do the same jobs, and because they also vary in the amount of power and speed, read and follow the manufacturer's guide. Blenders should be cleaned thoroughly after each use.

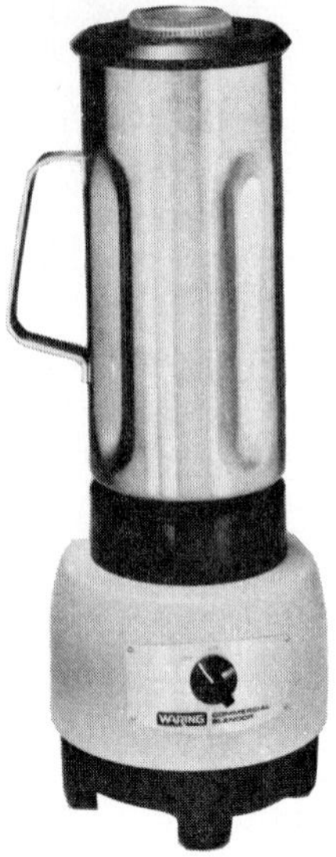

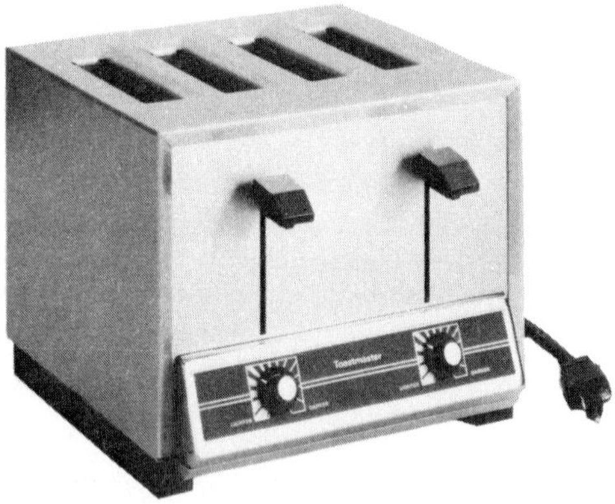

Toasters

Toasters are used for toasting bread, pre-baked waffles, English muffins, buns, and other items. They are usually made of chrome-plated steel with a crumb tray underneath. Conveyor toasters are used in fast food operations where large amounts of buns must be toasted at the same time.

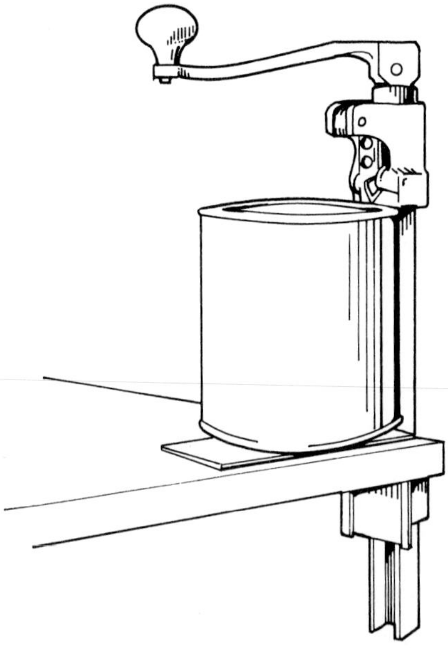

Can Openers

These vary from the small home size can openers to the large institutional size ones. Heavy-duty can openers are often bolted conveniently to the side of a workbench. They must be cleaned daily. Remove the shank, or vertical part, out of the base of bench-type can openers and soak in a hot detergent solution. Scrub the shank with a brush, rinse, dry, and replace it in the base. Blades should be wiped with a damp sudsy cloth. From time to time, check the blade for nicks. Small hand-held can openers can be washed by hand in warm, soapy water and dried carefully.

SUMMARY

Work in the food service kitchen depends on the use of special tools and equipment. Tools are hand-held instruments such as knives or items such as pans and pots for cooking or serving. Equipment means appliances run by electricity or gas. Food service workers must be able to recognize each item, use it skillfully, and care for it properly.

chapter recap

CHECK YOUR KNOWLEDGE

1. Which three kinds of knives are used most often in food service?
2. What tool is used to sharpen knives?
3. List three tools used to lift, turn, and stir food.
4. Name the three types of scales commonly used in food service.
5. How should tools be cleaned and stored?
6. What factors are most important to consider when selecting pots and pans for cooking?
7. List three advantages of having aluminum cookware and bakeware.
8. How should knives be stored?
9. Name three measuring tools used in food service.
10. What is the main use of brushes in food service?

EXTEND YOUR LEARNING

1. Visit a kitchen store or hardware store and a food service equipment company. (If there is no food service supplier nearby, use a catalog from one.) Compare the price of ten commercial tools with those for a home kitchen. What accounts for the differences?
2. Use this chapter to identify the following groups of tools in your classroom kitchen:
   - Cutting tools
   - Measuring tools
   - Serving tools
   - Portioning tools
   - Turning and lifting tools

"Hey, Tony," said Jim, "I liked your report on the way they use computers at Disney World. How'd you get to see so much?"

"You know my Uncle Marco, the one who is a professional cook?" replied Tony. "His son is my cousin Ricky. He's also a cook, but he works at Disney World. Uncle Marco took me along when he went to visit Ricky. Ricky showed us everything."

"What were the kitchens like?" asked Jim. "Lots of big equipment, I'll bet."

"You wouldn't believe it!" exclaimed Tony. "You know how we all like pizza? Well, in the kitchen there's a machine that makes 14,000 pizzas every three hours. And they are all sold the same day they are made! Three workers run the whole thing. One stands at the beginning and places baked pizza shells on a conveyor belt. They go underneath a tall machine. You can see a sheet of pizza sauce flowing down on the crust. Then they move along the belt where another machine covers them with grated cheese. As they come out of the machine, a worker covers them with a sheet of waxed paper cut to the same size as the pizza. Another worker packs them in boxes to go out to the restaurants where they are sold. We ate one later in one of the fast food cafeterias. They cook the pizzas there and add toppings like sausage and mushrooms."

"I'd sure like to see that!" said Jim. "What else do they have?"

"There were a lot of special machines in addition to the ones you see in most commercial kitchens. One hundred fifty restaurants are serviced by the one big kitchen I saw."

"You should tell the whole class about your trip," said Jim.

"I will." said Tony. "Chef Robinson wants me to share my experience when we study the chapter on large equipment."

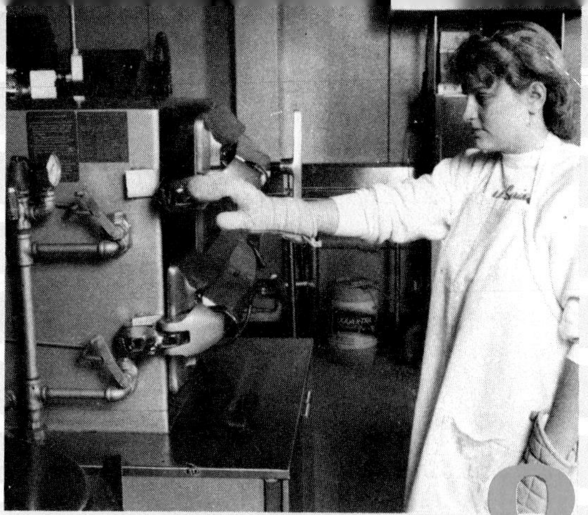

chapter 8

large equipment

Set your goals

When you complete the study of this chapter, you should be able to . . .

- Define and correctly use the vocabulary terms.
- Identify and safely operate major food service equipment.
- Clean and maintain food service equipment.
- Select the best equipment for the task.

Build your vocabulary

compartment steamer	open top range
convection oven	overhead broiler
deck oven	pilot light
flat top range	salamander
griddle top range	steam-jacketed kettle

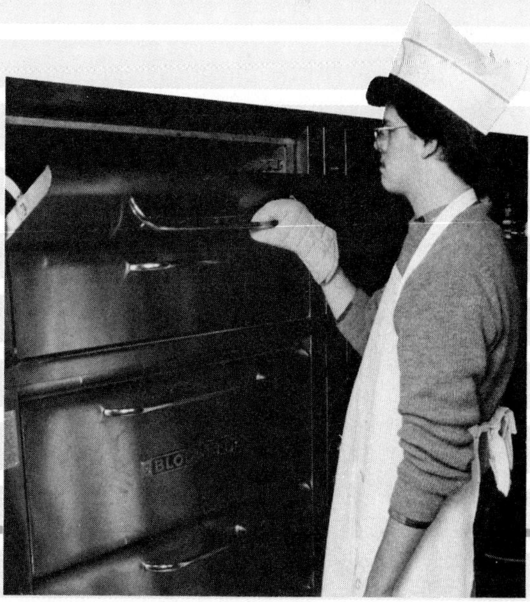

LARGE EQUIPMENT FOR FOOD SERVICE OPERATIONS

In the last chapter, you learned about many of the small tools and equipment used in food preparation. Food service operations also use many large pieces of equipment, sometimes called appliances. These speed efficient preparation, cooking, serving, and cleaning. Many types of equipment not found in your kitchen at home are used daily in large food service operations. Those most commonly used are discussed in this chapter. You will learn what they look like, how to use them, and how to care for them properly.

There are also some general points to remember about power-driven equipment:

- Each manufacturer's equipment has slightly different features. It is important to study the operating manual for each item before attempting to operate it. Your teacher or supervisor will show you how to operate the equipment correctly.
- All equipment needs to be cleaned after each use and thoroughly cleaned each week. Most large equipment has parts that can be removed for cleaning. Check the operating manual.
- If at any time a machine is not working properly, turn it off and notify your teacher or supervisor. Broken equipment can be dangerous.
- Even machines that are working right can cause injuries if not used properly. Avoid clothing that might catch in machines and keep your hair tied back. Remember that operating directions are written to assure safe operation. Never take shortcuts.

FOOD PREPARATION EQUIPMENT

In a food service operation, large amounts of food must be prepared quickly. Having the right equipment can save hours of time and workers' salaries. Of course, the equipment an operation needs depends upon the food it serves. A fast food restaurant that specializes in fried chicken will need several fryers. A lunch counter that serves mainly cold sandwiches probably won't have one at all.

Mixers

The mixers used in food service vary greatly in size. A small table model may be fine for occasional mixing jobs. But many operations need the larger bench model or the giant floor model. Mixers are used for everything from mixing salad dressings in the pantry station to preparing huge batches of bread dough in the bakery.

Most mixers have a variety of attachments. The most common are the paddle, the whip, and the dough hook. The paddle is used for general mixing like cake batters. The whip is used to add air to light mixtures such as eggs and whipping cream. The dough hook mixes heavy doughs such as bread dough. A chopping attachment is also available. It can grate, shred, or slice vegetables and cheeses.

Using the Mixer

1. Select the correct attachment for the job.
2. Make sure the bowl and mixing attachment are firmly in place.

3. Raise the bowl to the proper height. The attachment should not touch the bowl.
4. Set the machine to low speed before turning it on. Move to the desired speed gradually.
5. Turn the mixer off before changing speeds, attachments, or scraping down the bowl.

A commercial bench mixer.

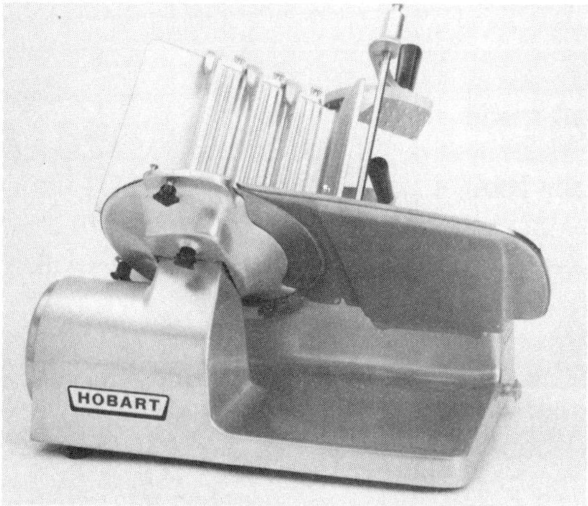

A manual slicer.

CARE AND CLEANING

- Remove the attachment and the bowl. Wash in hot, soapy water. Dry thoroughly.
- Store attachments where they will not be damaged or dropped.
- After unplugging the mixer, wipe it off with a damp cloth.

safety tip . . .

Do not place your hand or any other object into the mixer while it is operating. Always shut off the motor first.

Slicers

Slicers are used in food service to slice foods quickly and accurately to the thickness desired. This not only speeds preparation, but also helps control portion size. Each slice will be exactly the same size as the last.

Food slicers are either automatic or manual. The automatic model moves the food across the cutting blade automatically. The manual model must be moved by hand. In both cases, the food is placed on the food carriage, moved across the cutting blade, and falls onto the receiving tray.

Using the Slicer

1. Be sure the machine is properly assembled. Check the instruction manual.
2. Plug in the cord after making sure your hands are dry.
3. Adjust the blade control indicator to the appropriate thickness.
4. Place the food to be sliced on the food carriage.
5. Start the motor.
6. Use the food holder or guide to press the food against the blade. On a manual machine, push with a smooth, even motion.
7. Turn off the machine after you have cut 3-4 slices. Check the thickness of the slices and adjust the blade control indicator, if needed. Continue slicing required amount.
8. Return the blade control indicator to zero, turn the machine off, and unplug the cord.

safety tip . . .

The blade of the slicer is extremely sharp. Never hold the food in position with your hands. Never operate the machine without the blade guard in place. Use special care when cleaning the blade.

CARE AND CLEANING

- Make certain the machine is turned off and unplugged. The blade control indicator should be set at zero.
- Take the machine apart as directed in the instruction manual. The food carriage and blade guard can be washed in the sink with hot, soapy water. Rinse each part and allow to air dry.
- Wipe off the other machine parts that can't be removed with a damp, soapy cloth. (Be extremely careful around the sharp blade.) Rinse with a damp cloth and dry. Replace the blade guard immediately. A sanitizing solution is often used on the blade.
- Replace all parts and cover the machine.

COOKING EQUIPMENT

Most foods require cooking as part of their preparation. But much of cooking equipment used in a food service kitchen bears little resemblance to that in your kitchen at home. It is sized to cook large batches of food at a time. Much of it is also designed for very specialized tasks.

Ranges

Ranges provide heat for surface cooking. Those used in food service are built for constant use. Some are powered by electricity, others by gas.

Ranges have a variety of heat levels. The cook must learn to select the right amount of heat for each cooking job.

A commercial flat top range.

Several types of ranges are used in food service operations. ***Flat top ranges*** have burners set underneath a solid top. ***Griddle top ranges*** are similar but are used to cook foods like eggs, pancakes, and hamburgers directly on the range top. ***Open top ranges*** have exposed burners, usually six. The temperature of each burner is controlled with a separate thermostat. A drip pan beneath the burners catches any spills.

Using the Range.

1. Locate the position of the burners on flat top and griddle top ranges.
2. Use only the burners needed.
3. Burners have several heat levels. Do not use more heat than necessary.
4. Follow the safety precautions discussed in Chapter 6 to avoid fires and burns.

CARE AND CLEANING

- Allow the range to cool completely before cleaning.
- Wipe up spills as they occur. Clean the range thoroughly once a day.
- To clean the flat top range, first loosen any burned food with a scraper. Clean the range top with a detergent solution but avoid using too much water. Clean the rest of the outside, rinse, and wipe dry.
- The griddle top range must be cleaned carefully, but never washed. After each use, polish the top with a special griddle cloth or stone until the surface shines. Polish with the grain of the metal to avoid scratching the top. Wash the rest of the unit with warm, soapy water then rinse and dry. Finally, recondition the top by coating it with a thin layer of oil. Heat the top to 400°F (200°C) then wipe clean. Repeat until the top has a smooth, slick finish.
- To clean the open top range, remove the grids and drip pan. Soak in hot, soapy water, rinse, dry, and replace. While these parts are soaking, wash, rinse, and dry the rest of the range. Gas ranges usually have a ***pilot light***. (A pilot light is a flame that burns continuously and lights the burner when the control is turned on). After cleaning, check to see that all pilot lights are lit and burning with a blue (not yellow) flame.

safety tip . . .

Be careful not to use water near electrical wiring or switches to avoid electrical shocks.

Conventional and Convection Ovens

Several types of ovens are used in food service. The conventional oven cooks by heating the air in an enclosed space. Many ranges and broilers include a conventional oven, but the oven unit may also be a separate piece of equipment. A ***deck oven*** (also called a stack oven) has a series of shelves, one on top of the other. Each shelf has its own door and temperature control. The food is cooked directly on the deck, or floor, of each section, giving the oven its name.

A ***convection oven*** contains a fan which circulates the hot air in the oven. It cooks food more quickly at lower temperatures. The racks in a convection oven can be placed close together so more food can be cooked in the same amount of space.

Using Conventional and Convection Ovens

1. Set the temperature, turn on the oven, and preheat to the desired temperature. (Remember, lower temperatures are used in convection ovens.)

A convection oven.

2. Load the oven. In a conventional oven, pans should be at least 2 in. (5 cm) away from each other and the sides of the oven.
3. On a conventional oven, keep the vent control closed to prevent heat from escaping. This conserves energy.
4. Set a timer for the estimated cooking time.

CARE AND CLEANING

- Let the oven cool completely before cleaning.
- Remove any burned-on food with an oven scraper or wire brush.
- Take out shelves. Wash in hot, soapy water, then rinse and allow to air dry.
- Brush crumbs from the inside of the oven. Wash the inside with clean water and dry with a soft cloth. Use an oven cleaner to remove spilled, stuck-on foods.
- Wipe the outside of the unit with warm, soapy water. Rinse and polish with a soft cloth.

Microwave Ovens

Microwave ovens were used in food service kitchens before they were available for home use. They add a great deal of flexibility to food preparation. Food can be prepared ahead of time and frozen or refrigerated. Then it is quickly heated in the microwave oven when needed. Some operations such as snack bars purchase foods that are already prepared, divided into individual portions, and frozen. When a customer orders, the food is heated in the microwave oven and served. Even in full-service kitchens, the microwave oven is a useful piece of equipment.

Microwave ovens cook very differently than conventional or convection ovens. The oven produces invisible waves of energy called microwaves. Microwave energy causes food molecules to vibrate against each other, producing friction. The friction creates heat and cooks the food.

Microwave cooking calls for somewhat different methods than with other ovens. First, microwaves cannot pass through metal so containers for cooking cannot be made of metal. Glass, ceramic, plastic, or paper containers are used instead. Second, the microwaves do not hit all spots in the oven evenly so food must often be stirred or turned during the cooking period. Third, the amount of power rather than the temperature is controlled during cooking. Fourth, the microwave oven cooks much faster than a conventional one. Be sure to use times intended for microwave cooking.

Using the Microwave Oven

1. Place the food in a microwave-safe container.
2. Arrange the food in the oven in a circular pattern. Foods generally cook most slowly in the center of the oven.
3. Close the door tightly. Choose the correct power level and set the timer.
4. About halfway through the cooking period you may wish to stop the oven and rearrange or stir the food. This promotes more even cooking.
5. Allow the food to stand a few minutes after the power goes off. Cooking continues during this standing time.
6. Although the containers for food do not heat up as quickly as in a conventional oven, they can become too warm to touch. Use hotpads when removing food from the oven.

CARE AND CLEANING

- Let the oven cool completely before cleaning.
- Wipe up any food spills after each use.
- Wipe the inside and outside of the oven with warm, soapy water. Rinse and wipe dry.
- If the oven contains an air filter, clean weekly.
- Check to see that the door of the oven seals tightly. Do not use a microwave oven with a loose or damaged door. Microwave leakage is dangerous.

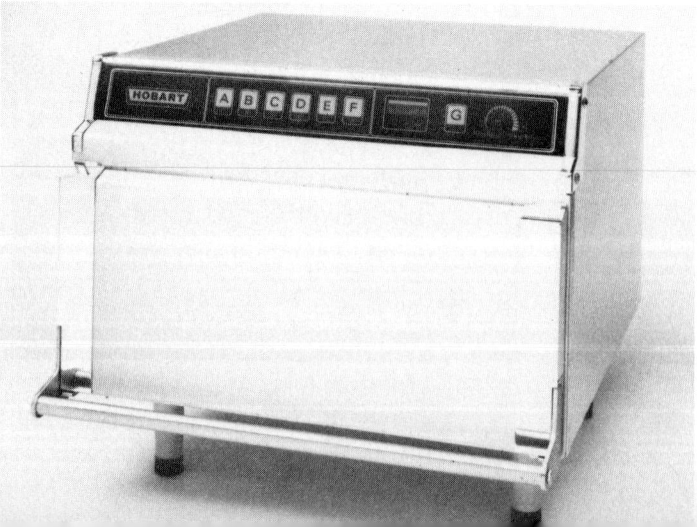

A small commercial microwave oven.

Infrared Ovens

Infrared ovens are used to thaw large amounts of frozen food in a short period of time. (Microwave ovens can be used to thaw small amounts.) Infrared ovens generate intense heat from quartz units. The heat is so intense and the process so fast that little flavor or moisture is lost. Follow the manufacturer's directions for operation.

Broilers and Grills

Broilers are used to cook food with intense heat from above. The food is placed directly on a grid below the heat. A grid level is used to control the distance from the food to the heat source.

There are three common types of broilers. The ***overhead broiler*** is a self-contained unit with a warming oven above the broiler grid. There is usually another oven or storage space below the broiler. The ***salamander*** is a small broiler unit often located above another cooking unit such as the range.

Grills should not be confused with broilers, although they are also used for broiling. The heat source for grills is below the grid that holds the food. (Broilers, remember, have their heat source above the food.) Grills are used for foods that cook quickly, such as hamburgers.

Using Broilers and Grills

1. Adjust the grid on the broiler to the correct distance from the heat.
2. Preheat the unit.
3. Distribute the food evenly on the cooking grid.
4. Check the grid during cooking. Excess grease or fat from the food could cause a grease fire.
5. Cook the meat on one side for half of the total cooking time.
6. Turn the food and cook on the other side until done.

CARE AND CLEANING

- Remove the grids and soak in hot, soapy water. Scrub with a wire brush to remove all food. Rinse, dry, and oil lightly.
- Wash the drip pans and replace.
- Scrape grease and burned food particles from the unit. Empty the grease trap, wash, and replace.

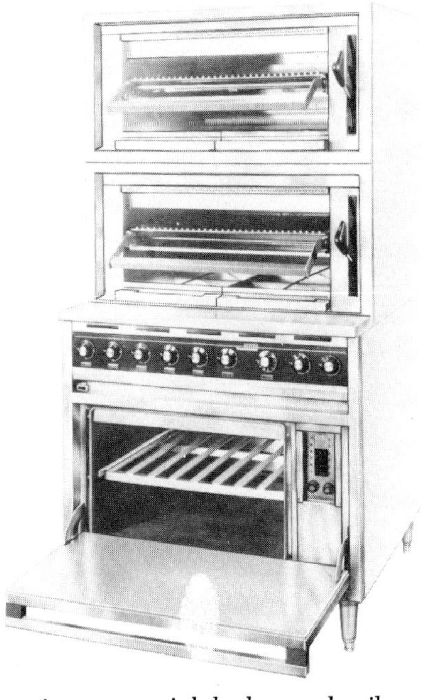

A commercial deck oven broiler.

Fryers

Fryers come in many types and sizes. The best ones have an automatic filtering system for the oil so it can be reused. Conventional fryers maintain the oil at a constant temperature. Automatic fryers lift the food from the fat at a preset time. (You may have seen these used in fast food restaurants for cooking fries.) Pressure fryers heat fat under pressure. This shortens the cooking time and helps keep the fat in good condition. The most modern fryers are computerized.

Fryers must be constructed of heavy metal to withstand the high temperatures of frying. Very accurate thermostats are also essential to control the temperature of the fat.

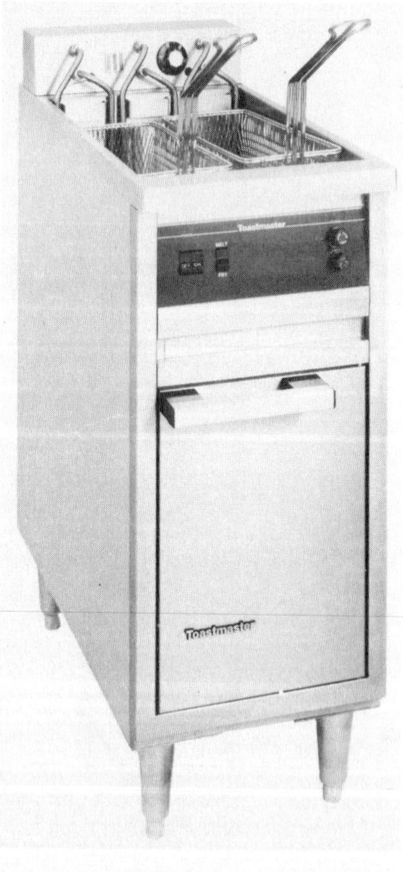

A commercial deep-fat fryer.

Using the Fryer

1. Check to see that the drain valve is closed.
2. Place the fat in the kettle of the fryer to the level indicated. Do not overfill — flash fires could result.
3. Turn the fryer on with the thermostat set to 250°F (120°C). Wait until the fat melts, about ten minutes.
4. Heat the fat to the desired temperature.
5. Drain any water from the food to be cooked. Wet food will cause the hot grease to spatter.
6. Place the food in the fryer basket. Lower the basket slowly into the hot fat.
7. Lift the basket carefully from the fat when the food is cooked. Allow food to drain.

Computerized fryers are simple to operate. Press the button that identifies the food to be cooked. The computer determines the quantity and the proper temperature and cooking time. The basket automatically lowers itself when the fat is the right temperature. When the food has cooked the required time, the basket automatically rises and drains.

CARE AND CLEANING

- Turn the unit off and allow the fat to become cool, but not solid.
- If the fat is to be reused, strain it through a filter into a clean, dry container. Open the drain when the container and filter are in place. Close it when all the fat has been removed.
- If the kettle is not removable, fill it with water and detergent. Boil for 15-20 minutes.
- Drain (open drain valve) and rinse with clear water to remove all detergent.
- Dry the kettle and baskets.

Steam-Jacketed Kettles

In food service operations, steam is often used to cook foods because it cooks quickly with minimum loss of flavor, nutrients, and color. One of the most common pieces of equipment in large production kitchens is the ***steam-jacketed kettle***. It consists of two stainless steel containers, one inside the other. Steam is pumped between the two containers, heating the inner one which contains the food. The steam does not touch the food.

Steam-jacketed kettles come in two basic types. The tilting or trunnion kettle can be tilted for easy emptying by turning a wheel or pushing a lever. The nontilting type has a drain and spout on the bottom for removing food.

safety tip . . .

Special caution is necessary when operating steam equipment. Remember that steam burns.

A non-tilting steam-jacketed kettle.

A tilting (trunnion) kettle.

Using the Steam-Jacketed Kettle

1. Be sure the kettle is in an upright position.
2. Add the food to be cooked to the kettle.
3. Turn on the boiler and wait for the pressure to reach the proper level.
4. Open the water valve. (If water must be added, follow the manufacturer's directions.)
5. Check the safety valve.
6. Turn on the switch or burner valve.
7. Adjust to the proper temperature and pressure.
8. When food is done, turn off the steam valve. When opening the kettle, tilt the lid so the opening is away from your face. Remove the hot food carefully.
9. Fill the kettle with water until it is cleaned. This will loosen food stuck to the inside of the kettle.

CARE AND CLEANING

- Allow the kettle to cool before cleaning.
- Drain the water from the kettle. On nontilting kettles, remove the drain screen.
- Add warm water and detergent to the kettle. Scrub well with a brush, inside and out.
- Drain the kettle. On nontilting kettles, clean the spout well with a bottle brush.
- Fill the kettle partially full of clean water. Rinse well. Drain.
- Dry the inside and outside of kettle well. Replace the drain screen. Leave the lid open.

Compartment Steamers

Compartment steamers cook by circulating steam around food held in pans or baskets. Unlike the steam-jacketed kettle, the steam comes in direct contact with the food. The compartment steamer can be used to prepare meat, fish, poultry, fruits, and vegetables.

Using the Compartment Steamer

1. Preheat the steamer. Close and seal doors by using the door wheels.
2. Open the door and put in the food to be cooked.
3. Close and seal the door.
4. Pull out the steam control valve. If steam leaks around the door, tighten it a bit more.
5. As the steam starts, you will hear a hissing noise. When the hissing stops and correct pressure is reached, begin timing the cooking.
6. When cooking time is up, push in the steam control valve.
7. Be sure to allow the pressure to return to zero before attempting to open the door. Then open the door slightly to allow any remaining steam to escape.
8. Remove the hot food carefully.

CARE AND CLEANING

- Clean the compartment steamer after each use.
- Allow the unit to cool completely.
- Drain all water from the compartments.
- Remove the shelves. Wash and rinse them at the sink. Allow to air dry.
- Wash the interior of the compartments and doors with water and a mild detergent. Rinse and wipe dry. Wash, rinse, and dry the exterior.
- Check the seals (gaskets) around the doors to be sure they are clean and in good condition.
- Check to be certain the drains are clean.
- Replace the shelves.
- Leave the doors slightly open when the unit is not in use.

A compartment steamer.

FOOD HOLDING AND SERVING EQUIPMENT

In food service, many foods must be kept cold or frozen between the time of purchase and preparation. Once food is prepared, it must be held at safe temperatures until time for serving. Special equipment is used for both of these jobs.

Refrigerators and Freezers

Refrigerators and freezers are insulated boxes equipped with refrigeration units to maintain low temperatures. Unlike appli-

A roll-in commercial refrigerator.

ances for the home kitchen, the refrigerator and freezer are separate units in food service kitchens.

There are three basic types of refrigerators — reach-in, roll-in, and walk-in. Walk-in and roll-in types are really small refrigerated rooms. They are located close to the section of the kitchen where they are most used. Reach-in types are smaller.

Freezers are used to hold food for long periods of time. All frozen foods must be wrapped well in airtight wrapping, labeled, and dated. Food that is not well-wrapped dries out and becomes unusable. This is called freezer burn.

CARE AND CLEANING

- Maintain a regular schedule for cleaning refrigerators. Wash the interior of reach-in refrigerators with a solution of baking soda and water. Wipe the outside daily with a damp cloth. Clean roll-in and walk-in refrigerators as directed by your supervisor.

- Freezers must also be cleaned regularly. To clean, disconnect the freezer and move all food to another cold storage area. Clean the interior with a solution of baking soda and water. Wipe the outside with a damp cloth. Replace the food and reconnect the unit's electricity.

DISHWASHING EQUIPMENT

Food service operations use large equipment to prepare, cook, and serve food. Equipment is also needed to clean all the tools, utensils, and serving dishes that have been used. Most food service operations use a dishwasher for this job.

Dishwashers

Mechanical dishwashing in food service is not only sanitary, but also cost effective. Health codes in many communities require mechanical dishwashing for food service operations. There are two common types of dishwashers.

The single tank machine has doors that must be raised to put in the racks of dishes. The doors are lowered when the washing cycle starts. Some single tank machines have a conveyor belt that moves the dishes slowly through the washing cycle.

The multiple tank machine has no racks. The dishes are placed directly on a conveyor belt. The wash cycle is continuous as long as the machine is on, thus providing a continuous stream of clean dishes. The dishes must be removed from the belt as they emerge from the machine. At least one worker is needed at each end of the machine.

1. Scrape all dishes and sort according to size and type.
2. Rinse the dishes.
3. Place the dishes in the racks or on the conveyor belt.
4. Put through the wash, rinse, sanitize, and dry cycles.
5. Remove the clean dishes and store.
6. Clean the machine following the manufacturer's instructions.

SUMMARY

Food service kitchens contain many pieces of large specialized equipment. Some are larger versions of equipment used in the home. Mixers, ranges, and refrigerators are used in food service, but have been adapted for quantity food preparation. Other equipment is found only in food service. Steamers and fryers are examples. It is important to follow instructions when using equipment.

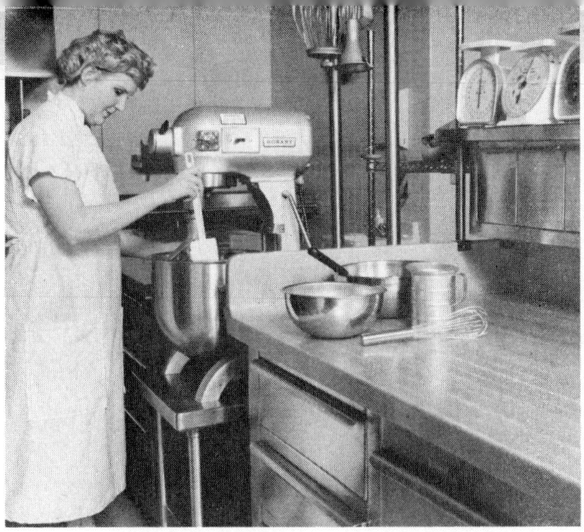

chapter recap

CHECK YOUR KNOWLEDGE

1. List jobs that can be accomplished using a mixer with attachments.
2. What precautions must be taken when cleaning the food slicer?
3. What are three types of ranges used in food service?
4. What is the griddle top range used for?
5. List three ovens used in food service.
6. What is the difference between a conventional and a convection oven?
7. Why must fryers have accurate thermostats?
8. What type of cooking containers cannot be used in microwave ovens?
9. What are three types of refrigerators used in food service? How do they differ?
10. What are two advantages of washing dishes by machine?

EXTEND YOUR LEARNING

1. Find out what type of mixer is in your classroom kitchen. What attachments does it have? Check the instruction book for recommendations on the use of each attachment and make a chart for the classroom.
2. Choose one piece of major kitchen equipment to learn more about. Check the instruction book to familiarize yourself with its use. Learn the proper care procedure. Demonstrate what you have learned for the class.
3. Discuss the differences between the conventional oven, convection oven, and microwave oven.

"Wasn't that a great field trip we took today?" asked Jim.

"Super!" agreed Ruthann. "I never thought an office building had a cafeteria. It even had a separate restaurant. I suppose there must be lots of people working in that building."

"Imagine serving 1200 people every day," said Jim. "What an operation, and that executive chef runs the whole thing! From his office windows, he can see everything that's going on. He's got a big job. I'll bet he makes a lot of money."

"I'm sure he must," said Ruthann. "He has a lot of responsibility. I was impressed by the kitchen, weren't you? All that stainless steel looked so shiny and polished!"

"Just like Chef Robinson told us," said Jim, "the kitchen was divided into stations. I watched the salad station. The salads were being assembled so fast, and beautifully. I never thought much about the looks of food before I started this class. They had the neatest refrigerator. When the salads were all assembled, the worker put them on a cart and wheeled them to the refrigerator. When she took us around to the cafeteria, there was a door to the refrigerator there, too. The counter worker was putting the salads on top of chipped ice on the serving counters. Pretty efficient, I thought. What did you see?"

"I checked the storage," said Ruthann. "There were huge walk-in supply closets. One, for dry storage, had controlled humidity. There were two freezers. The storeroom clerk explained that one was way below zero for longterm storage. The other was a little above zero for the food that would be used within 24 hours."

"I never saw such big equipment," said Jim. "No wonder they can feed so many people so fast. What an example of organized production! Everyone seemed to know just what to do."

"Jim, you sound so excited," remarked Ruthann. "Do you really think you might want to go into food service?"

"Maybe," answered Jim slowly. "I'm not sure I'm smart enough to get to the top, but I'd like to fit in somewhere."

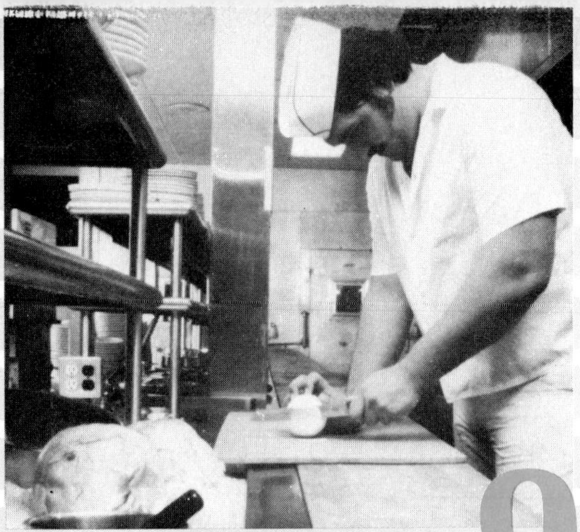

chapter 9

working in stations

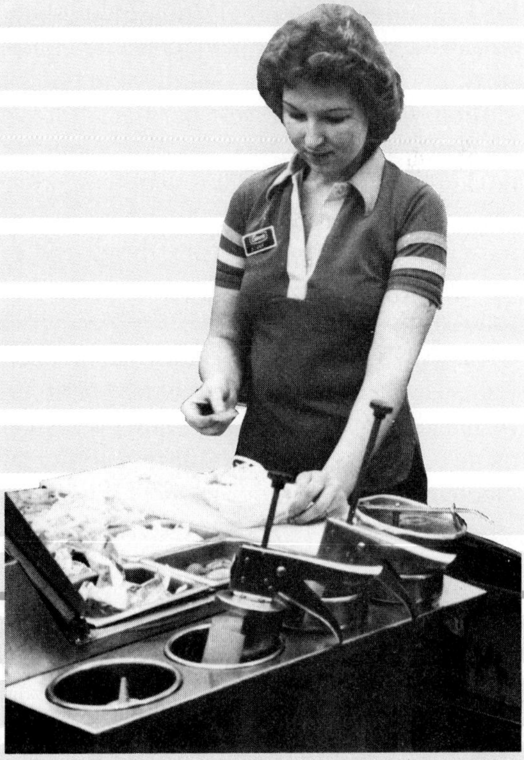

Set your goals

When you complete the study of this chapter, you should be able to . . .

- Define and correctly use the vocabulary terms.
- List and identify the stations used in the kitchen.
- Use work flow and work simplification techniques.
- Make time and production schedules.

Build your vocabulary

pre-preparation	time schedule
production schedule	work flow
teamwork	work simplification
time management	work stations

THE FOOD SERVICE KITCHEN

A food service kitchen is designed for efficient food production, not for beauty. For this reason, color is not a factor in the design. When you enter a well-planned food service kitchen, you see stainless steel counters and equipment, and tile floors with floor drains. These materials are used because they are easy to clean and withstand hard use. A convenient kitchen helps cooks prepare large amounts of food efficiently.

WORK STATIONS

Food service kitchens are very large, and are divided into work areas according to the type of food to be prepared. These work areas are commonly called ***work stations***. A work station is simply a specific work area where a particular kind of food is prepared or a specific job is done.

Cold foods, for instance, are produced in the pantry or salad station. Salads and sandwiches need the same tools and equipment for preparations. Usually, the pantry station will be near refrigerated storage but not a range. If food needs cooking as part of the preparation, it is sent to another station. For example, a grilled cheese and ham sandwich might be first prepared in the pantry station and then sent to the hot food station for grilling.

Each station should contain the needed utensils and have sufficient work counters. It should have all necessary equipment such as mixers and ranges. Water and sufficient electrical outlets must be available.

Kinds of Stations

Not every food service operation has the same number or type of work stations. A restaurant that serves only pizza will have only one station. However, a fine restaurant with a complicated menu would need many. An institution such as a school might need only these four stations:

- Salad station.
- Hot station.
- Bake station.
- Short-order or fast foods station.

Even the bake station might not be needed. Many operations purchase ready-to-eat baked goods. The number and type of work stations depends on the food being prepared. Check your school cafeteria. How many stations does it have?

The following chapters will help you develop beginning skills by explaining the jobs done in each station.

- Chapters 10 and 11: The Pantry Station
- Chapters 12 to 16: The Hot Station
- Chapters 17 to 21: The Bake Station
- Chapters 22 to 26: Fast Food Techniques

Organizing Work

If you were observing in a food service kitchen, you would notice that each worker has a definite job to do. One might be assigned to peel potatoes and scrape carrots. These tasks are part of ***pre-preparation***, or getting the food ready for final preparation or cooking. In the bake station one worker might be mixing piecrust, another rolling the dough, and a third might be making the filling.

When you prepare food in class, you will also be assigned a definite job. It may be a job in management, pre-preparation, cooking, or clean-up. Each job is important. The jobs will be rotated so you will have a chance to do each one.

The workers in each station work as a team. They cooperate to get the job done in the easiest, fastest way while maintaining quality. They know that others depend on them to do their job well. They assist others in their station if extra help is needed. ***Teamwork*** means working together for a common purpose.

There is also cooperation among the stations. It would not do for the steaks to be done before the salad is ready. Workers in one station must be willing to lend a hand if workers in another station are struggling to get a job done on time.

The work load is divided evenly among the workers according to the special abilities and talents of each. No one job is more important than any other.

Teamwork is essential in a successful food service operation. Some tasks are made much easier when they are shared.

Work Flow

In food service, several people often work together on one dish. The work is most efficient when it moves smoothly from right to left or from left to right. This is called ***work flow***. The placement of the major pieces of equipment, such as the range or the refrigerator, usually dictate the direction of work flow.

If you are working in a laboratory which was not designed for teaching quantity cooking, you may have to adapt a U-shaped kitchen to the needs of a work station. Such a "unit kitchen" usually has double sinks in the middle with counters on either side. Cupboards are above and below the counters. There usually is a range, but no refrigerator. The sketch on page 142 shows how to adapt one such unit kitchen to a pantry or salad station. You can readily see that the work flow should be from right to left. That is because the refrigerator where the salads will be stored is on the left. As shown in the diagram, the work counter to the right of the sink becomes the pre-preparation area. The sink will be the clean-up area. Preparation of the salads will take place to the left of the sink. Then the salads will be placed on a tray or a cart and taken to the refrigerator.

However, if the same kitchen were to be adapted to the hot station, the work flow would have to proceed from the left to the right because of the position of the range. This is shown in the diagram.

Now contrast the diagrams below with an actual salad station in a food service kitchen. The station has four refrigerators. Two are service refrigerators with doors in the front and the back so the salads can be placed in the front and removed from the back for service. Two are for storage to hold the ingredients to be prepared. Needed utensils and tools are hanging from a rack above the counters for easy access without stooping. There are single drawers under the counters to hold knives, mixing spoons, and other needed tools, but no under-counter cupboards.

Arrangement of Tools and Utensils

In Chapters 7 and 8, you studied the tools and equipment needed to do the job of food preparation in each station. The way these items are arranged has much to do with the ease with which you can work.

First check to be sure you have all the items you need. Remember the term "mise en place"? This is a reminder to be completely organized before beginning to cook.

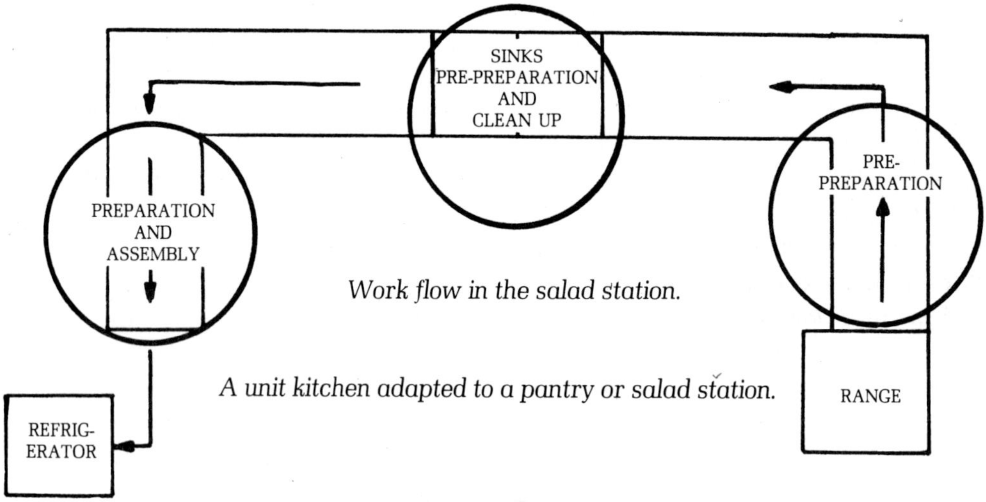

A unit kitchen adapted to a pantry or salad station.

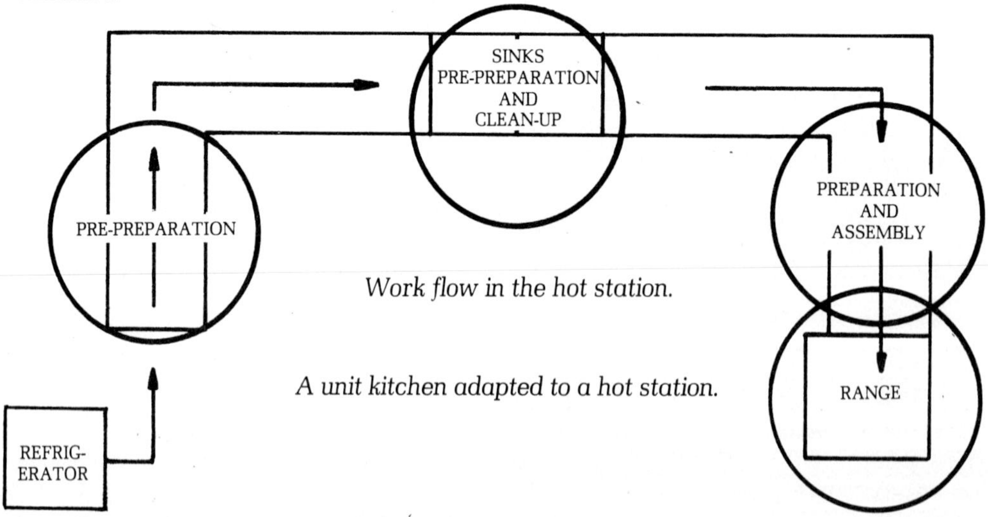

A unit kitchen adapted to a hot station.

Once you have started the job of food production, you will waste time if you stop to find a particular tool. Consider carefully where the items will be used and place them accordingly.

Following these principles of placement should prove helpful to you:

- Have a definite place for everything and be sure it is kept where it belongs.

- Consider where the worker will be standing and locate everything possible within arms reach.

- Tools which are used constantly should be placed closest to the worker. Those used less often can be placed farther away. Tools which are seldom used can be stored.

Work Simplication

Doing a job in the easiest, simplest, and quickest way possible is called ***work simplification***. You work more efficiently by eliminating unnecessary steps and wasted motions. For instance, you can mix a cake batter by hand. But using an electric mixer is easier, simpler, and quicker.

Another example is using the microwave oven. When cooking a large number of steaks for a banquet, the steaks are quickly browned in a very hot broiler. They are still very red inside. They can be finished quickly in the microwave oven to the correct degree of doneness desired by each customer.

Here are some keys to work simplification:

- **Use both hands equally.** Most people are either right-handed or left-handed, but practice using both hands. It will seem awkward at first, but gets easier with practice. For instance, some rolls are made by rolling the dough with the palms of the hand on the board. Why not roll two rolls at once using both hands?

- **Use tools or equipment which will do the job most efficiently.** For example, using the shredder attachment on the mixer is quicker than shredding cabbage with a knife.

- **Develop a smooth rhythm of work.** Arrange materials and equipment for a steady flow of work. Place tools close to the hand that will pick them up. Continuous motion is efficient; starting and stopping wastes time. When chopping onions for example, sweep the chopped onions into the waiting container with the knife used for chopping.

If you have the opportunity, watch the way short-order cooks work. There are many ways to recognize good short-order cooks, but one of the best is to watch their fast, flexible hands. Without any lost motions, they put hamburgers on the grill, flip them expertly, toast the buns, add the desired relishes, and serve on a plate — usually in only a few minutes.

Maintain Order

Order is absolutely essential to efficiency. Whenever possible, wash and put away tools, and equipment as you work. Work counters must be kept clean and free of clutter. The old saying, "A place for everything and everything in its place" is particularly true in food service. Workers must cope with a tight time schedule for food production.

TIME MANAGEMENT

If the service of a meal at home is late, no great harm is done. However, in food service, it may be disastrous for the business. Food must be appetizing and service must be prompt or the customers will not return.

Time management involves judging the time needed to prepare and cook each food and learning how to use that time most efficiently. Each food takes a different amount of time to prepare. For instance, a cake will bake in 35-40 minutes, muffins in 25 minutes, and biscuits in 12 to 15 minutes. Although you must allow for the difference in baking time, you must also consider any additional preparation which may be needed. Cakes take longer to mix than muffins or biscuits. Muffins and biscuits are served hot from the oven but cakes must cool before frosting.

Many foods require a long time to prepare. When you study the chapter on yeast rolls, you will find they take three to four hours to prepare. However, you can use part of this time to do other jobs.

Timing also involves the use of equipment. For instance, suppose both biscuits and baked custards are scheduled to be made in the bake station. Biscuits are baked at 450°F (230°C) for 12 to 15 minutes, but baked custard needs one hour at 325°F (160°C). You can see if you have only one oven to use, you must bake the custard first and then the biscuits since both require different temperatures. Also consider that the custard needs to cool before serving, but biscuits are served hot.

Until you get that experience in time management, you need a written schedule which will specify the correct sequence and the time needed for preparing food. This is called a ***time schedule***. It is a plan for the best use of the time needed to complete the job. It will help you develop self-confidence and also make clear the exact responsibilities of each worker.

When making up a time schedule, start with the recipe for the food you will be preparing. A standardized recipe often tells how long various steps take. It will also list the jobs to be done and the order of doing them. However, it cannot give you the time needed for every job because your experience and skill will affect the timing. One person may be able to chop onions in two minutes. Another may take five minutes.

Here are some principles that may help you organize your time schedule:

1. Check the recipe and note the estimated time for preparation.
2. Estimate the time needed for each step of pre-preparation. At first you will be slow. As you develop skill in handling food and using equipment, you will work faster. Time yourself and try to improve your speed for each job.
3. Work back from the serving time. See page 145 for a time schedule for serving biscuits at noon.

Time Schedule

Time Schedule for *Bake Station* Date *10/6/91*

Product *Biscuits*

Time of Serving *12 noon* *Frances Roach, head cook*

Job	Time Needed	Time for Completion
Pre-preparation	20 min.	11:30
Mix and cut biscuits	10 min.	11:40
Preheat oven	10 min.	11:40
Biscuits in oven	12-15 min.	11:55
Service	3-5 min.	12:00

Regardless of the job assignment, a time schedule must be followed in order to meet customer demand. This worker is preparing a deli tray scheduled for an 11:00 a.m. pickup.

PRODUCTION SCHEDULE

In each work station, one worker is the head cook. The head cook makes out the ***production schedule*** to be turned in to the executive cook or the manager after the preparation is completed. The production schedule tells you exactly what is expected of you. It is a clear record of the following:

- The food to be prepared.
- The quantity.
- The actual yield.
- The worker responsible for the preparation.
- The time for completion (the deadline).
- The cost. (This part is filled in by the manager or executive chef.)

Study the sample production schedule on page 147.

The manager of this operation is checking the progress of today's production schedule. The workers are responsible for 200 egg salad sandwiches and 300 tuna salads.

Production Schedule

Date 10/6/91

Station Bake Station

Item	Quantity Needed	Actual Yield	Completion Time	Cost	Cook
Biscuits	25	48	12:00	.05 (each)	Frances
Custard	25	25	1:30	.12 (per serving)	Cindy

THE COMPUTER IN THE SERVICE AND WORK STATIONS

Many large food service operations have computer terminals in the work stations. They are connected to the terminals in the service areas in the dining room. They provide an easy, accurate way to keep track of the food ordered in the dining room and the completion of that order in the kitchen.

Using computer technology in the work stations makes a more efficient operation. It also helps the management provide the best possible customer service.

In restaurants without computers, the waiter or waitress writes down the order and calls it out in the kitchen or brings it to the kitchen to be filled.

In the computer-run restaurant, the waiter or waitress enters the order on the dining room computer. Instantly, the computer terminal in the work stations displays the order, the number of the waiter/waitress, the time the order was placed, and the price. When the dish is completed, the kitchen worker presses a key on the computer. This information instantly shows up on the ready-to-serve screen in the kitchen and on the terminal in the service station in the dining room.

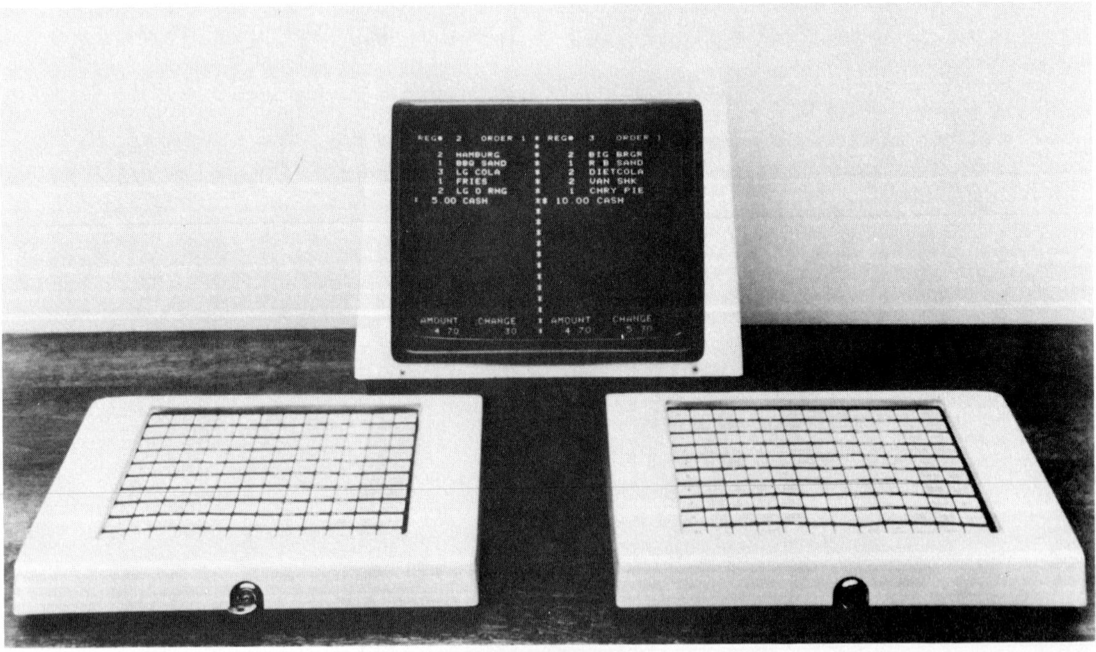

As you can see, this computer system will make a restaurant more efficient. It lists the orders taken as well as the cost of the meal. It also shows a cashier how much change should be given to the customer.

Kitchens usually have a checker at the entrance from the kitchen to the dining room. All orders must be checked for accuracy before they are served. The computer simplifies the checker's job and keeps accurate records of the food ordered each day. It also gives an accounting of the day's sales.

Use of the computer allows the workers to receive orders for the food to be prepared and to send responses without leaving the work station. This greatly reduces kitchen noise and traffic.

The introduction of the computer has brought about the greatest change in the organization of food service in the past few years. The changes began in the large chains, but soon they will reach into the smallest family-run restaurants. Any person who is interested in a career in food service should learn the basics of computer use.

Restaurants on the computerized ordering system find that their waiters and waitresses have more time to check the accuracy and presentation of their orders. They are also inclined to spend more time attending to the needs of the customer, which tends to make the customer visit the restaurant again.

SUMMARY

To increase efficiency, the food service kitchen is divided into work stations. Each station prepares a different type of food. Within a station, tools and equipment are arranged so work will flow smoothly. Using methods of work simplification and maintaining order help station efficiency. Time and production schedules are also helpful. Computers aid in scheduling and in efficient food production.

chapter recap

CHECK YOUR KNOWLEDGE

1. What is a work station?
2. What is pre-preparation?
3. What does teamwork among food service workers mean? Give an example.
4. In the work station in which you are preparing hamburgers, the grill is to the right of the sink, and the refrigerator is to the left. In which direction is the work flow?
5. In a work station, where will you find the pots and pans?
6. What does "mise en place" mean?
7. What is work simplification? Give an example.
8. Explain how to organize a time schedule.
9. Who makes out the production schedule?
10. How can a computer help link service and preparation areas?

EXTEND YOUR LEARNING

1. Study the work stations in your own classroom. Draw a diagram of each one and indicate the work flow. Use the diagrams in this chapter to help you. Make suggestions to improve the work flow and simplify the work.
2. Evaluate the placement of small and large equipment in your laboratory based on the principles in this chapter. Can you make suggestions for improvement?
3. Check several fast food restaurants in your area. How many use a computer for placing the orders rather than calling them in to the kitchen?

Unit 4

The Pantry Station

In a professional kitchen, the pantry station is responsible for preparing foods that are served cold. The pantry station is sometimes called the salad station or the cold food station because salads and sandwiches are the most common dishes prepared there. In some food service operations, hot and cold beverages are also prepared at the pantry station. You will learn about beverages in Unit 7.

Workers at the pantry station are especially skillful with their hands. Much of the preparation involved depends on their efficient use of hand tools. Pantry workers also need an eye for design. Salad and sandwich plates must look as good as they taste.

It is important for the pantry station to be located near refrigerated storage. Many of the ingredients used at the station, such as fresh fruits, vegetables, and dairy products, must be kept cold. Foods prepared in the pantry are often made ahead of time and refrigerated until serving time.

Preparing salads and sandwiches also requires a lot of counter space, storage areas for small equipment, and sinks for cleaning ingredients. Foods prepared by pantry workers add spark and color to food service meals. These members of the professional cooking team have a right to be proud of their skills.

"It was nice of your mom and dad to invite me to dinner Ruthann," said Jim as they walked toward the salad bar.

"Dad says you are so enthusiastic about food service that he thought you should see this buffet!"

"Wow!" said Jim starting down the salad line. "I've never seen so much stuff on a salad bar before! I could eat my whole meal here!"

"Lots of people do," Ruthann agreed. "But the hot foods are great too."

Jim heaped lettuce onto the chilled plate. "Look at all these dressings! And all labeled too! Poppy seed. Garlic. Italian. Blue cheese. Thousand Island. House dressing. Wonder what they put in it?" questioned Jim.

"I think there's bacon in it, and buttermilk," Ruthann said. "Come on, we're holding up the line."

Jim spread the house dressing on his lettuce. "Look at all the extras you can add! Onions, green peppers, two kinds of cheese, tomatoes, and croutons!"

"Try some alfalfa sprouts Jim," offered Ruthann. "Don't look so doubtful! They're crunchy, and good for you too."

"Okay, I'll try anything once," Jim said. "Garbanzo beans, sunflower seeds, beets . . . I guess I'll just take a bit of everything. Cottage cheese, marinated herring. I love it! I guess I'll have to come back later for the dessert salads."

"If you put any more on that plate," Ruthann laughed, "you won't be able to carry it back to the table!"

"I guess you're right!" Jim laughed. "Let's go eat!"

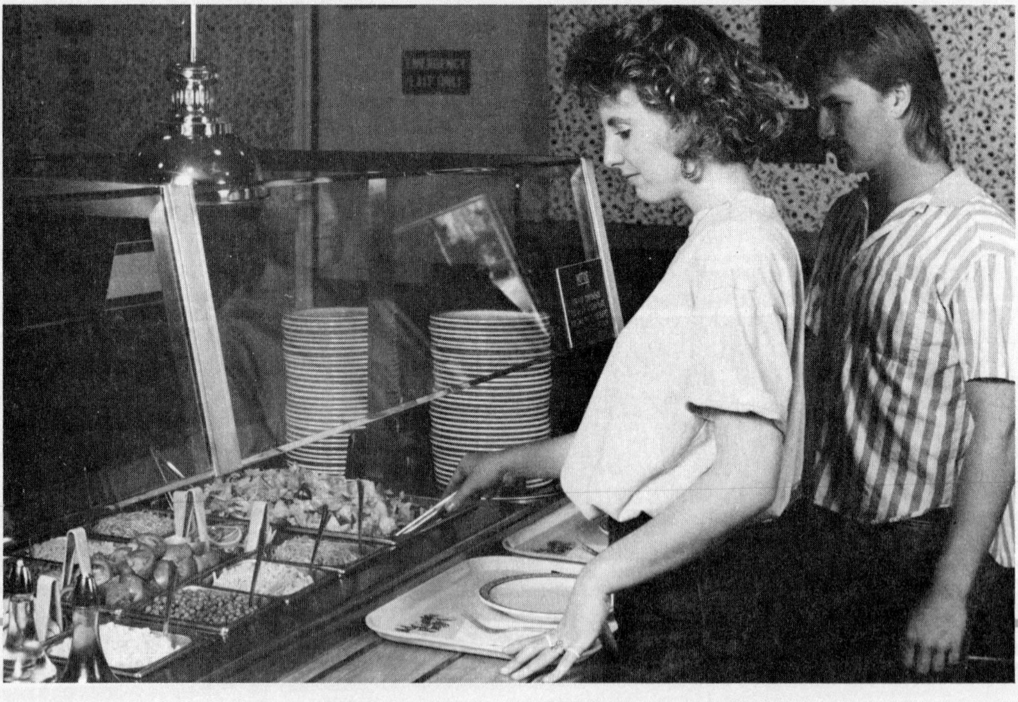

chapter 10

salads and salad dressings

Set your goals

When you complete the study of this chapter, you should be able to . . .

- Define and correctly use the vocabulary terms.
- Identify the parts of a salad.
- Describe and identify common salad greens.
- Prepare and serve a variety of salads that meet standards of excellence.
- Set up a production line for making salads.

Build your vocabulary

binder	flavor enhancer
body	garnish
congealed salads	gel
consistency	plating
emulsion	underliner

WHAT IS A SALAD?

A famous salad was born in a Mexican restaurant near the border of the United States and Mexico. The restaurant was run by a man named Caesar. One evening, Caesar's had an unexpected crowd of tourists from the United States. When Caesar ran out of the prepared food, he concocted a salad from the ingredients he had on hand — greens, croutons, cheese, eggs, and seasonings. He made the salad in front of the customers, tossing the salad and adding the seasonings with a great flourish. His supreme showmanship saved the evening, and he went down in the history of salad making. The salad he made was christened "Caesar's Salad", and that's what it is called to this day.

While not all salads have such colorful beginnings, salads are becoming increasingly popular. Much of this popularity comes from customers' interest in health and diet. Salads are generally high in vitamins and minerals, but relatively low in calories. They are an important part of the trend toward lighter eating.

A salad should be a beautiful picture framed by the edge of the plate. It is created by the salad cook just as an artist creates a picture by using a variety of colors, forms, and textures.

Kinds of Salads

Salads are usually grouped according to their place on the menu. A salad may be an appetizer, an accompaniment to the meal, the main dish, or a dessert.

- An appetizer salad is served at the beginning of a meal. It should be small, flavorful, and crisp. Its purpose is to stimulate the appetite. Shrimp or lobster salad, fruit cocktail, or a small tossed salad are examples of appetizer salads.

- An accompaniment salad is served along with the main course of the meal. Recently, the trend is to serve the accompaniment salad first in place of an appetizer. The salad is served on a separate plate or in a bowl. It is larger than the appetizer salad, but still light and attractive. It frequently takes the place of a vegetable in the meal. Tossed salad, cole slaw, and fruit salad are frequently served as accompaniment salads.

- A main dish salad is the main course of the meal. It should be filling and generous in size. Chicken or egg salad, a fruit plate with cottage cheese, or a chef's salad are some main dish salads.

- A dessert salad is served at the end of the meal. It should be sweet and rich. Gelatin fruit salad, and fruit mixed with nuts and whipped cream are examples.

This accompaniment salad consists of spinach, tomatoes, mushrooms, and avocados. It will substitute for the vegetable in the meal.

All salads should meet these guidelines:

- **Color.** Colors in a well-prepared salad are carefully chosen. Either several shades of the same color or contrasting colors are used.

- **Flavor.** Well-prepared salads are flavorful and zesty — never bland. The flavor may come from the ingredients of the salad or the salad dressing. Mild-flavored salads need a tangy dressing. However, a salad such as chicken, which has a definite flavor of it's own, needs a mild dressing.

- **Texture.** Salads whould have a variety of textures. Some of the ingredients should be crunchy, some crisp, some soft. A salad made of nuts, celery, and chopped carrots would be tiresome to chew. If the same ingredients are placed in a soft gelatin, however, the resulting salad would be quite enjoyable.

- **Compatibility.** This means that the ingredients go well together. Appearance, taste, and texture must all be compatible with each other, with the dressing, and with the rest of the meal. Use a light salad with a heavy main course. Use a heavy salad with a light main course.

- **Appearance.** Arranging the food on the plate — called ***plating*** — is an important step. A well-prepared salad looks neat. The ingredients are drained well before being put on the plate. The salad dressing is on top the salad, not dripping all over the plate. In food service, the salad may be served separately in a bowl or alongside on a small plate. It should never be placed on the main plate with a hot entree.

The salad bar is an alternative to the prepared salad. Customers enjoy salad bars because they can concoct their own salads from a variety of ingredients. Food service operators find salad bars profitable because they save the labor cost of making and serving individual salads. Most salad bars offer fresh greens, vegetables, and a choice of dressings. Many also offer a variety of prepared gelatin, pasta, and vegetable salads and several types of fruit.

A salad of broccoli, tomatoes, black olives, cauliflower and zucchini offers a variety of colors and textures. The ingredients are compatible, flavorful, and attractive in appearance.

PARTS OF A SALAD

A salad consists of four parts, the base, the body, the dressing, and the garnish. You will see these four parts in the drawing on page 156.

Base of the Salad

In food service, the base of the salad is often called the ***underliner***. It is usually some kind of greens such as lettuce. The underliner is placed on the plate first. It keeps the salad from looking bare and adds contrast of color and texture.

There are many kinds of greens used as the base of a salad. The one rule is that the base must appear fresh and green. The chart below and on page 157 tells the characteristics of common salad greens.

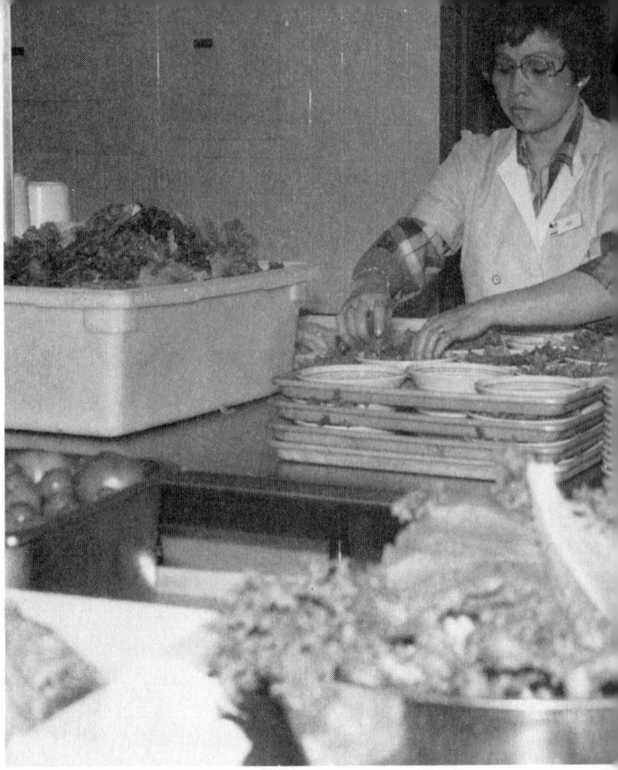

Salads should have a fresh, green underliner. What kind of salad greens is this food service worker using as a base?

Common Salad Greens

	Type	Description
	**Head or Iceberg** Lettuce	• Most familiar and popular salad green. • Crisp, compact head with green leaves and mild flavor. • Should be firm, free of brown spots and streaks, never bitter in taste. • May serve alone, with other greens, or as a base for other salads.
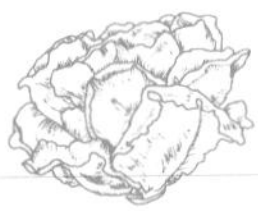	**Boston Lettuce** (butterhead)	• Very tender, mild tasting, fragile texture which wilts easily. • Loosely packed, round head, with easily separated leaves. Outer leaves are deep green, inner leaves are yellow green. • Heads should be springy and crisp, the leaves free of brown spots or streaks.

	**Bibb Lettuce**	• Sweet, mild, slightly spicy flavor. • Small, deep green heads and tender, fragile, crisp leaves. • Expensive but highly prized for its taste.
	**Leaf Lettuce**	• Long, green leaves which do not form a head. • Used as a base for salads and in sandwiches because the leaves are flat.
	**Romaine (cos)**	• Cylinder shaped with flat, crisp, deep green leaves. • Strong, but not bitter, flavor. • Used frequently in food service because the leaves are tender and mild in flavor and do not wilt.
	**Escarole**	• Broad, thick, dark green leaves with yellow edges. • Leaves have bitter taste, so use in combination with other greens.
	**Endive**	• Attractive, green, curly leaves. • Slightly bitter taste.
	**Watercress**	• Small, round leaves on thin stalks. • Mild, peppery taste. • Very perishable. • Frequently used as a garnish.
	**Spinach**	• Tender, deep green leaves. • Sharp flavor. • Avoid large, bitter leaves. • Good used with meat, eggs.

Body of Salad

The major part of the salad is called the ***body***. This is the part that gives the salad its name, such as lettuce, fruit, or chicken salad. The ingredients that form the body may be vegetables, fruits, or protein such as fish or meat. Frequently, a combination of different ingredients is used.

Vegetables

Most salads include one or more vegetables. Vegetables add to a salad's appearance, texture, and flavor. Raw or cooked, fresh, frozen, canned, or dried, vegetables can be used in salad. Since appearance is so important in a salad, only the highest quality vegetables should be used. They should be firm, colorful, and free from blemishes.

Raw vegetables for salad making are chosen for their color, texture, and flavor. For instance, red radishes add color as well as crunchy texture and spicy flavor. Tomatoes have an orange-red color, a soft texture, and a distinctive flavor.

Some salads call for cooked vegetables. Frozen, fresh, or canned may be used. See Chapter 15 for more information on cooking vegetables.

Fruits

Ripe fruits always make popular, colorful, and eye-appealing salads. Fresh, canned, or dried fruits are all possible choices. Frozen fruits become mushy when defrosted so they are rarely used in salads.

Small fruits, like berries, may be served whole. Larger fruits are usually halved or sliced before serving. When melons are used as in a mixed fruit salad, they are often shaped into balls. These are made with a tool called a melon baller.

Like vegetables, only the highest quality fruits should be used in salads. This insures good color, form, and flavor.

Meats, Fish, and Poultry

Meat, poultry, or fish are used to make main dish salads. They are used alone or in combination with vegetables and fruits, and served on a base of greens.

Ham is perhaps the most popular meat used for salads. Its smoky, salty taste and firm texture make it useful as the basis for ham salad or sliced in thin strips to top a chef's salad. Frequently, cold cuts such as bologna (baloney) and other sausages are used in salads because of their flavor. Sliced, rare roast beef adds distinction to a salad plate.

Fish and seafood salads always sell well because they are both colorful and tasty. Tuna, salmon, crab, shrimp, and lobster are the most popular. Canned fish is used often because it loses little flavor in canning and is acceptable for salads even in the best restaurants. Only the top grades should be used for salads.

Chicken and turkey make tasty and popular main dish salads. The thinly sliced white meat may be arranged on the salad plate with other ingredients. Or, the poultry may be coarsely cut into pieces, mixed with celery, onion, mayonnaise, and other ingredients for a salad plate or sandwich.

Eggs

The bright yellow color of hard-cooked eggs is very attractive in a salad. Chopped eggs add color and flavor to potato salad while sliced eggs brighten tuna fish salad. Stuffed eggs can be part of a main salad plate.

As you may recall, the quality of eggs is designated by letter. Grade AA is the top grade and should be used for salads. Eggs are also graded for size. For stuffing or slicing, the larger sizes are most attractive. For chopping, the less expensive small eggs may be used.

Cheese

Cheeses can be used as the base of a salad or a topping. They add flavor, texture, and color. Cheeses are also high in protein.

Cottage cheese is popular as a salad base. It has a delicate, sweet cream flavor that combines well with other ingredients.

Hard cheeses are usually shredded, cut in cubes or strips, or crumbled for use in salads. Cheddar, Swiss, and blue cheese are popular, but many varieties can be included.

Gelatin

Gelatin is the ingredient that turns liquid into a jelly-like substance. Both plain and flavored gelatin are available. Gelatin salads — sometime called ***congealed salads*** — are colorful and tasty. They are also a useful way to turn leftovers into appealing dishes.

Flavor Enhancers

A ***flavor enhancer*** is an ingredient added to a salad or any other dish to develop the taste. Flavor enhancers blend with the ingredients and do not dominate the flavor. The best known enhancer is salt. Food is flat without salt, but too much salt can make the food inedible.

Monosodium glutamate is a flavor enhancer sold under various brand names. It blends with the body of a salad, making it more tasty, but not adding any flavor of its own. It contains much salt, so the cook should be very careful in using it. Monosodium glutamate can cause allergic reactions in some people.

There are many other flavor enhancers. Bacon bits, spices, and herbs are among the most common ones. Check some salad recipes and see if you can identify the flavor enhancers.

Salad Dressings

The salad dressing is the third part of the salad. Some type of dressing is used on almost every kind of salad to add flavor and taste appeal.

There are three basic types of salad dressings: the oil, water, and vinegar type; the mayonnaise type; and the boiled type. These types take their name from the base of the dressing. Addition of other ingredients gives many variations on these basic types.

- **Oil, water, and vinegar dressings.** These may be very thin or rather thick, but they are always pourable. The creamy dressings contain gelatin or egg which acts as a ***binder*** to prevent the oil from separating from the vinegar and water. (You may remember from science that oil and water do not normally stay mixed.)

- **Mayonnaise dressings.** This type of dressing also has an oil base, but it is spoonable. Egg and gelatin are again used as a binder. They help make an ***emulsion***. An emulsion is a mixture of liquids which do not separate from each other.

- **Cooked dressings.** Cooked dressings contain no oil. They are thickened with egg, cornstarch, or flour. Some commercial salad dressings are a blend of cooked dressing and mayonnaise.

At a salad bar you will usually find a good selection of dressings.

Selection of Dressing

The flavor and ***consistency*** of the dressing should be compatible with the kind of salad. Consistency refers to the thickness or thinness and the smoothness of the dressing. Here are some general principles to follow in selecting a dressing:

- Salads with a strong flavor need a mild dressing.
- Salads with a mild-flavored body need a highly seasoned dressing.
- Sweet salads need a sweet dressing.
- The color and appearance of the dressing should make the salad more attractive.

Garnish

The fourth part of the salad is the ***garnish***. A garnish is an edible decoration that brings color, texture, or flavor to the dish. A salad is usually so colorful that it needs little garnish. It is best to use a colorful ingredient that is already part of the salad as the garnish. For instance, a tossed salad will usually have tomatoes and green pepper in the body. A slice of tomato and two thin strips of green pepper would make an appropriate garnish. However, potato salad is rather colorless. A cherry tomato and a sprig of parsley on top each serving makes it more attractive.

Garnishes for dishes other than salads are often prepared in the pantry. The chart on page 161 lists some possible salad garnishes by color.

PREPARATION OF SALADS

Salads require much pre-preparation before the final salad is ready to be put together. Since some ingredients may require cooking or chilling, timing of pre-preparation is an important factor when making salads.

Preparation of the Greens

1. Since greens grow close to the ground, they require careful washing and cleaning. Discard any parts which are bruised or discolored.
2. For loose-leaf greens such as leaf lettuce, romaine and endive, fill a sink with cold water. Place the leaves in the water, separate and gently swish them in the water. Lift the leaves into a colander, and drain water from sink. Rinse any sand or dirt down the drain and refill the sink. Repeat the process until all dirt is removed. Do not allow the greens to soak. Drain well.
3. For greens in heads, hold the head with both hands. Hit the bottom hard against the counter top. This will loosen the core. Remove the core with your fingers. Run cold water through the core hole to rinse the head thoroughly. Drain by turning the core hole down again so water can run out of it.
4. To store, place greens in large container and cover with damp cloth, or place loosely in a plastic bag. Refrigerate.

Garnishes for Salads

Sweet Salads	Tart or Piquant Salads
Red Whole cherries Whole, sliced strawberries Whole raspberries Pomegranate seeds Red-colored coconut Sugared grapes Currant jelly Sliced Delicious apple **White** Grated coconut Marshmallow **Other** Whole or chopped nuts Stuffed prunes or dates Sugared grapes **Yellow-orange** Stuffed apricots Sliced oranges Pineapple fans or fingers Melon balls **Green** Cherries Watercress Mint Sugared green grapes	**Red** Sliced or julienne beets Red pepper slices or rings Sliced or julienne pimiento Stuffed olives Plain radishes Whole cherry tomatoes Tomato slices or wedges Salmon roe **White** Celery curls or sticks Cottage cheese Swiss cheese — sliced, shredded, grated, or julienne Crumbled blue or Roquefort cheese Mushrooms **Yellow-orange** Sliced or chopped eggs Carrot curls or sticks Cheddar cheese — sliced, shredded, grated, or julienne Lemon slices **Other** Ripe olives Caviar **Green** Cucumber slices or curls Green pepper rings or strips Mint jelly Green olives Parsley Whole or sliced green onions Pickles

Salads are often garnished with meats, eggs, and tomatoes.

Preparing the Body of the Salad

The most important part of the salad is the body. It is the main source of nutrition in the salad. The body of the salad usually takes the most time to prepare. Care should be taken to make the body of the salad as attractive as possible.

Vegetables

Wash and trim the vegetables. Some vegetables, such as celery, need to be scrubbed with a brush. Others, such as carrots, must be scraped using the vegetable peeler.

Most raw vegetables are sliced, diced, or chopped to make them easier to eat. Always chop, dice, or slice on a wooden or plastic board, never on metal. The illustration below shows how to hold and use a chef's knife.

If greens are used in the body of the salad, it is better to tear them than cut them with a knife. Cutting can bruise greens, causing brown streaks to develop. If head lettuce is to be served as a wedge, use a sharp salad knife to cut it.

This food service worker demonstrates the correct way to use a chef's knife when chopping green pepper. Notice the position of her hands. She is also using a cutting board.

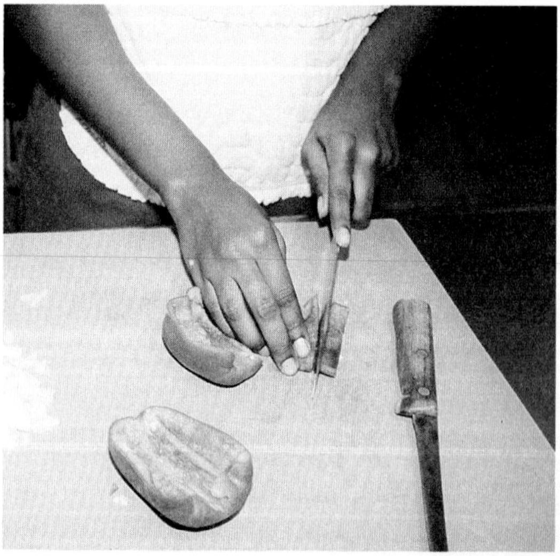

Fruits

Most fruits are sprayed with insecticides as they grow. Therefore they must be washed thoroughly. Discard any bruised or spoiled fruit.

Some fruits, such as apples and peaches, darken after they have been peeled and sliced. To prevent this, sprinkle them with lemon or lime juice or dip in an ascorbic acid (vitamin C) solution.

Adding sugar will also help prevent darkening, but it will also draw out the juices. Too much sugar will make a salad too juicy and will disguise the natural sweetness of the fruit.

Some fresh fruits may be purchased partially prepared. Oranges, for example, are purchased in slices or sections. This costs more but saves time-consuming pre-preparation.

The body of this curried strata salad contains apples, raisins, celery, green onions, rice, and fish.

Chicken Salad

Equipment: Stock pots, Tongs, Cutting board, Two-tine fork, Boning knife, Chef's knife, Bowls, Measuring cups, Quart measure, Measuring spoons, Wire whip, Kitchen spoon, No. 10 scoop

Yield: 50 servings

Ingredients	Amount	Method
Chicken	8 lb. (approx.)	1. Boil and cube chicken. You need 4 qt. of cubed chicken.
Eggs	12	2. Boil and dice eggs.
Celery	4 lb. (approx.)	3. Dice celery.
Pickle relish	2 c.	4. Add eggs, celery, and pickle relish to chicken.
Mayonnaise	1 qt.	5. In a separate bowl blend mayonnaise, sour cream, salt and lemon juice using a wire whip.
Sour cream	3 c.	6. Pour mayonnaise mixture into chicken mixture.
Salt	1 T.	7. Mix well using a kitchen spoon. Refrigerate until needed in a covered container.
Lemon juice	½ c.	

Serving size: One No. 10 scoop

Cost per serving: ______

Meat, Fish, and Poultry

Meat, fish, and poultry are usually chopped, ground, or cut into strips or cubes for use in salads. Keep the size of the pieces about the same. The "On the Job" feature on pages 164-165 tells how to set up assembly-line production of chicken salad.

safety tip . . .

Keep cutting boards sanitized so bacteria on the board is not transferred from one food to another.

On the Job

Making Chicken Salad

Assignment: Four workers are to prepare 125 chicken salads garnished with quartered, hard-cooked eggs and tomato wedges. The underliner will be lettuce cups. This assignment can be accomplished most efficiently by setting up a production line.

Check the Recipe

The recipe for Chicken Salad is on page 163. You will need to adjust the yield from 50 portions to 125 portions. (See page 52 to review this procedure.) Rewrite the list of ingredients with the new amounts for 125 servings. You also need to determine the amount of eggs, tomatoes, and lettuce needed.

Check Yourself

Before you begin work, make sure you are ready:

- Confine your hair with a hairnet, cap, or band.
- Wash your hands thoroughly.
- Put on a clean apron.
- Use plastic gloves for preparing the ingredients and assembling the salads.

Assemble the Equipment

- Equipment indicated in the recipe
- Stock pot for boiling eggs
- Cutting board
- Sharp vegetable knife
- Covered containers for ingredients
- No. 10 scoop for measuring 4 oz. portions of chicken salad
- Chilled salad plates
- Cart for the completed salads

Prepare the Ingredients

Worker #1 — Prepare the lettuce cups.
Worker #2 — Assemble chilled salad plates, the cart, a No. 10 scoop, and the chicken salad.
Worker #3 — Hard-cook the eggs, chill, and quarter them.
Worker #4 — Prepare the tomato wedges.

Follow this Procedure

Step 1. Use a clean, uncluttered counter or table for salad assembly. Set up the work flow from left to right.

Step 2. ▲ Worker #1 picks up the salad plate, arranges the underliner, and passes the plate to the next worker.

Step 3. ▲ Worker #2 places a No. 10 scoop of chicken salad on top of the underliner, and passes the plate to the next worker.

Step 4. ▲ Worker #3 adds two egg quarters and passes the plate to the next worker.

Step 5. ▲ Worker #4 adds two tomato wedges and checks the plating of each salad before placing it on the cart.

One Person Salad Assembly

If you are assigned to assemble salads alone, you would set up the production line in the same manner. Then, fill a rectangular serving tray with chilled salad plates. Using both hands, arrange the underliners on all the plates on the tray. Starting with the plate in the upper left-hand corner, portion a No. 10 scoop of chicken salad in the center of the lettuce cup. Work from left to right and top to bottom portioning the salad. Next, use both hands to add two egg quarters to each salad. Then add two tomato wedges in the same manner. Check the plating of each salad. Move the completed salads onto the cart. Refill your tray with chilled salad plates and repeat the procedure until all the salads are assembled.

Eggs

Have you ever wondered why hard-cooked eggs sometimes have a greenish ring around the yolk? The were cooked incorrectly. Here's how to make perfect hard-cooked eggs:

1. Have eggs at room temperature. Bring water in pan to a boil. Use enough water to cover the eggs.
2. Carefully lower the eggs into the boiling water. Reduce the heat to simmer. Cook 20 minutes.
3. Cool eggs immediately under cold running water. This prevents overcooking and greenish yolks.
4. Shell eggs immediately when cool. Start at the large end, peeling under cold, running water. If the shell seems to stick, carefully slip a teaspoon between the shell and the white of the egg.

Hard-cooked eggs are used in several ways in salads. They may be halved for salad plates. Grated eggs are often found in salad bars. Eggs can also be sliced to use as a garnish. A hand tool called an egg slicer simplies this job.

✓ standards ✓

Salads

Appearance

✓ Looks neat.

✓ Does not cover edge of plate.

✓ Color combinations pleasing.

Flavor

✓ Flavorful and zesty, not bland.

✓ Dressing complements body.

Texture

✓ Includes a variety of textures.

Gelatin

The key to successful gelatin is proper preparation. Be sure to dissolve the gelatin completely. Flavored gelatin is dissolved in boiling water. Unflavored gelatin must be soaked in cold water before it is dissolved in boiling liquid.

After the gelatin is dissolved, it is chilled. As the gelatin cools, it gradually becomes thick and then becomes a ***gel***. A gel is a jelly-like solid. Solid foods such as shredded carrots, cabbage, or fruits are added to gelatin after it starts to thicken. The thickened gelatin will keep the solids mixed throughout. Solids mixed in at the liquid stage will sink to the bottom or float to the top.

Remember that gelatin softens and reliquifies at room temperature. That means gelatin salads and desserts must be kept refrigerated until they are served. Gelatin salads served in salad bars should be kept on a bed of ice.

The appearance of gelatin salads and desserts is greatly enhanced when they are prepared in beautiful molds. Individual molds, made of metal, come in many different shapes. Gelatin salads are often made in a utility pan with 2 in. (5 cm) sides. This saves time and allows the salads to be easily portioned for serving.

chapter recap

SUMMARY

Tasty, nutritious, and generally low in calories, salads are a popular item on many food service menus. Green salads are most familiar, but salads are also made of poultry, meat, fish, dairy products, and fruit. Salad dressings and garnishes add flavor and appeal to salads. Salad ingredients require careful pre-preparation to preserve their nutritional value and to maintain an attractive finished product.

CHECK YOUR KNOWLEDGE

1. Name the four types of salads.
2. What factors should be considered when preparing a salad?
3. What are the parts of a salad?
4. What is an underliner? Why does a salad have one?
5. Name three foods that might be part of the body of a salad.
6. What is a flavor enhancer? Name two.
7. Name the three main types of salad dressings.
8. Name three ways of keeping prepared fruits from darkening. Which is best?
9. Why should gelatin be allowed to thicken before adding other ingredients?

EXTEND YOUR LEARNING

1. Assemble five kinds of commercial salad dressings. Using bits of lettuce as dippers, taste each one. Describe the flavor, texture, and color of each. Which would you use on the following salads: fresh fruit, tomato-cucumber, tuna fish, tossed greens, lime and pear gelatin, cottage cheese and peach, three bean?
2. Go to the produce department of a large supermarket. List each type of green available. Record the price of each.
3. Find and copy a recipe for salad that includes a good source of protein.

"Hey, Jim, do me a favor," said Ruthann. "What's up?" Jim asked.

"You know my Aunt Mary? She's in charge of her church's Christmas bazaar. Besides great handcrafts, they always sell sandwiches, cake, and coffee."

"Aha! I knew it!" said Jim. "She found out we're taking food service. What does she want us to do?"

Ruthann said, "Make sandwiches for them. They'll have everything ready. All we have to do is make chicken salad and ham sandwiches."

"How many?" demanded Jim. "Four hundred, to be ready by eleven o'clock Saturday morning," said Ruthann.

"What!" yelled Jim. "Are they nuts? How could we make 400 sandwiches by eleven o'clock?"

"Wait a minute," said Ruthann. "Just calm down! Rosita said she would help, and she thinks Tony will, too. Chef Robinson thinks we could do it using an assembly line."

"Okay," said Jim. "Let's find Tony. If he'll help, we can do it."

At seven o'clock Saturday morning, Jim, Ruthann, Rosita, and Tony met at the church.

"Let's check the supplies," said Tony. "Ruthann, you and Rosita get out everything we'll need for the sandwiches."

Jim checked the bread. "There are 40 loaves with 20 slices to the loaf. We'll make 200 chicken salad and 200 ham. That should do it."

"Okay," called Rosita. "We have everything out, and the counter has been scrubbed. Let's set up."

"I'll put the spread on the bread," said Ruthann.

Rosita said, "I'll be the filler. I'll use this scoop to measure the chicken salad."

"That leaves me to cut, wrap, and stack," said Tony. "Jim, you can go for supplies and stack sandwiches in the refrigerator. Let's wash our hands, put on these plastic gloves, and get to work."

By eleven o'clock all the sandwiches were being sold to the crowd.

"This was fun," said Jim as he stuffed a ham sandwich in his mouth. "Let's tell Chef Robinson about it on Monday."

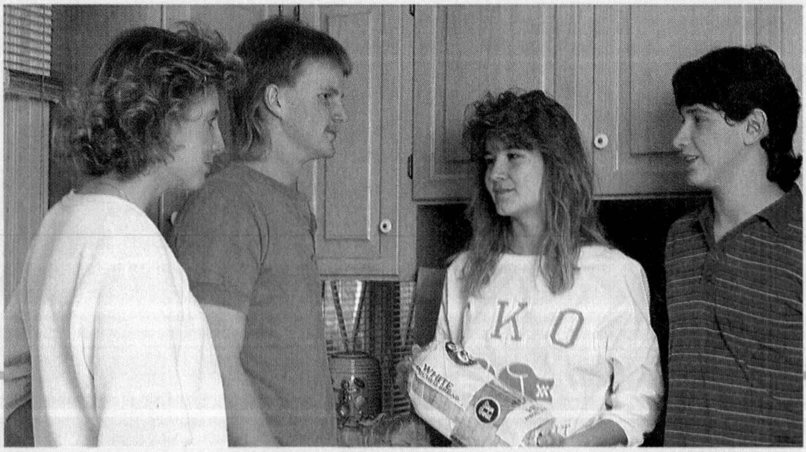

chapter 11

sandwiches

Set your goals

When you complete the study of this chapter, you should be able to . . .

- Define and correctly use the vocabulary terms.
- Identify and describe the various kinds of sandwiches.
- Prepare and serve a variety of sandwiches.
- Set up a production line for making sandwiches in quantity.

Build your vocabulary

canape
club sandwich
hors d'oeuvres
open-faced sandwich
pita bread
production line
shaved
short-order cook
spread
tortillas

SANDWICHES — FAMILIAR FAVORITES

Sandwiches have been popular since 1702 when in England the Earl of Sandwich put a slice of meat between two slices of bread and served it to his guests. They were delighted. The name of the earl will be remembered as long as sandwiches are eaten.

Sandwiches are one of the most popular foods sold in food service because they are quick, filling, and easy to eat. Sandwiches seem to be standard lunchbox fare for both adults and children.

A hamburger is probably the most familiar sandwich you can make. It is also one of America's favorite foods.

KINDS OF SANDWICHES

Sandwiches may be served either hot or cold. Their temperature depends upon the ingredients used and the preference of the customers.

Hot Sandwiches

Hors d'oeuvre (or-DURV) is a French word for a small bit of tasty food served before dinner. It often is a small, hot sandwich.

More filling hot sandwiches, such as beef, chicken, and pork in gravy, are usually prepared in the hot station. These sandwiches are popular and an excellent way to use up leftovers.

Grilled sandwiches, such as hamburgers and grilled cheese, are often prepared by the ***short-order cook***. The short-order cook is in charge of preparing quick foods. This cook may also prepare other quick foods that do not need grilling.

Barbecued beef and pork sandwiches are frequently a specialty of a restaurant featuring "open pit barbecue". They are very popular. You will study more about hot sandwiches in Unit 7, Fast Food Techniques.

Cold Sandwiches

Cold sandwiches may be grouped into five basic types:

- A ***canape*** (CAN-a-PAY) is a small, eye-appealing sandwich served before the first course, usually at dinner.
- A regular sandwich is made with a filling between two slices of bread.
- An ***open-faced sandwich*** consists of one slice of bread with a filling and an attractive garnish.
- A decker sandwich is made with at least three slices of bread and two types of filling. A decker sandwich made with ham and turkey is called a ***club sandwich***.
- A specialty sandwich is usually a filling placed in a crusty roll. It is often given an attention-getting name such as hoagie, submarine, or hero.

BREAD

Bread is an ingredient in all sandwiches. The bread must be fresh-tasting. But bread that is too fresh is not firm enough for sandwich making. It is best to use bread about 24 hours old.

Sandwich bread comes in an oblong loaf with a flat top. Each slice is the same size. The crust should be golden brown and the texture firm and velvety.

Kinds of Breads

For years, white bread has been most popular for sandwiches. But many people are now more health conscious. Other types of bread are more flavorful and provide more nutrition than white. Whole wheat, rye, and oatmeal are gaining popularity. Soft yeast rolls are used for hot dog and hamburger buns. Recently, crusty yeast rolls have become popular for specialty sandwiches.

Sweet breads have a more cake-like texture and taste. Boston brown bread, nut bread, and fruit breads make tasty, small sandwiches. Flavored butters and jams are often used as fillings. They are frequently served with a sweet salad for lunch.

Two other types of breads are also showing up on menus. ***Pita bread***, sometimes called pocket bread, originated in the Near East. It is a thin, soft, yeast bread which becomes hollow in the center when baked. This "pocket" can be filled to form a sandwich. ***Tortillas*** are thin, pancake-like breads originally from Mexico and Cuba. The tortilla may be soft with a filling rolled in it, or it may be fried crisp in a folded shape to hold the filling.

Pork pocket sandwiches are made by filling pita bread with salad greens, sprouts, pork, cheese, and red peppers.

Storing Bread

Bread should be refrigerated until used. Refrigeration makes the bread easier to handle. If the bread and the filling are both cold when the sandwich is made, it will stay fresh longer.

Bread freezes well. If freezer space is available, bread may be bought in quantity and frozen until needed.

SANDWICH SPREADS

A ***spread*** is a thin coating of butter, margarine, or mayonnaise on bread which makes it more flavorful and moist. Spreads also help keep the filling from soaking into the bread.

The most common spread is softened butter or margarine. These spreads should be soft enough to be spread easily, but never melted. Melted spreads soak into the bread. Sometimes spreads are whipped with an electric mixer or wire whip. Whipping smooths the spread and beats air into it so it goes further. Plain butter may be mixed with a tasty ingredient such as sharp cheese, anchovies, sardines, mustard, horseradish, or spices such as curry. These flavored butters are often used in making canapes.

Another common spread is mayonnaise. It should be added as close to serving time as possible. If applied too soon, the bread will become soggy. In food service, a small cup of mayonnaise is often served along with the sandwich if the customer requests it.

SANDWICH FILLINGS

The filling is the ingredient or ingredients placed on the slice of bread to make a sandwich. Fillings may be dry or moist.

The term "dry" refers to such ingredients as sliced meats, poultry, and cheese. "Dry" does not mean a dry-tasting sandwich, but merely separates this type of filling from the moist fillings which contain mayonnaise. For example, chicken may be sliced and served as a "dry" sandwich, or it may be finely chopped and mixed with chopped celery, onion, seasonings, and mayonnaise for a moist sandwich.

A salad sandwich, such as tuna salad, usually contains a good source of protein such as meat, fish, poultry, cheese, or eggs. Other flavorful ingredients are mixed with the main ingredient along with mayonnaise and seasonings. A flat leaf of lettuce may be added to the sandwich for color and crispness. See the recipe for Tuna Salad Sandwich Filling on page 173.

Salad sandwiches are popular for lunch because they are tasty and are a complete meal in themselves. These sandwiches should meet the same standards as a salad for taste, texture, and appearance.

Tuna Salad Sandwich Filling

Equipment: Can opener, Scales, Bowl, Cutting board, Chef's knife, Measuring cups, Rubber spatula, Kitchen spoon, No. 20 scoop

Yield: 50 servings

Ingredients	Amount	Method
Tuna	3 lb. 2 oz.	1. Drain and flake tuna.
Celery	3 c.	2. Chop celery finely.
Pickles	1½ c.	3. Chop pickles finely.
Mustard, prepared	3 T.	4. Combine celery and pickles with tuna using a kitchen spoon.
Lemon juice	2 T.	5. Add mustard, lemon juice, and salad dressing.
Salad dressing	3½ c.	6. Mix thoroughly. Refrigerate until needed in a covered container.

Serving size: One No. 24 scoop

Cost per serving: ________________

Tuna salad can be eaten as is, or become the filling for a delicious sandwich full of flavor and nutrition.

Variations of Sandwiches

Dry or moist, hot or cold, sandwiches may be served in many different ways. Here are several different ways of preparing a cheese sandwich:

- For a "dry" sandwich, place sliced cheese between two slices of bread spread with mustard butter.

- For a toasted cheese sandwich, place sliced cheese on one slice of bread. Toast until the cheese starts to melt. Then cover the cheese with another slice of bread and toast the whole sandwich on both sides.

- The same sandwich may be placed on the grill and browned on one side and then the other. Press the sandwich together with a turner as it cooks. This makes a grilled cheese sandwich.

- For another variation, place sliced cheese on a slice of bread and then place in the broiler to melt. This open-faced sandwich may also be topped with tomato, olives, or bacon.

- The cheese may be chopped, mixed with pickle, celery, and salad dressing for a moist sandwich. It can be served cold or heated in the oven.

- Sliced cheese may also be used along with other sandwich fillings such as sliced meats.

ACCOMPANIMENTS FOR SANDWICHES

A sandwich served alone on a plate looks bare. To improve its appearance, something should accompany the sandwich.

A simple garnish such as a pickle, olives, sliced tomatoes, carrot sticks would add color and appeal. Use a bit of leaf lettuce underneath the garnish. Sometimes, an olive and sliced pickle are held on top of the sandwich with a frilled toothpick.

Open-faced sandwiches require more elaborate garnishes. Stuffed olives may be sliced and placed on top. Chopped bacon with green pepper strips can be used. Radish roses and carrot curls also add interest to the sandwich plate.

Tortilla chips and a pickle have been used to garnish this porkburger.

Potato chips or corn chips may be placed alongside the sandwich. They add crunchiness, flavor, and eating enjoyment.

A small scoop of salad such as potato salad or cole slaw on a bed of lettuce, makes the sandwich plate more attractive and appealing.

SANDWICH PRODUCTION

Sandwiches are put together using a ***production line***. With a production line large numbers of identical items, such as sandwiches and salads, can be assembled quickly. Tools and ingredients are arranged on a clean, uncluttered surface in the order that they will be used. Either one person, or several workers then use the production line to produce a large quantity of one food item.

In the production of sandwiches, as in all foods, sanitation is essential. Sandwiches involve much handwork, so particular care is needed. Sanitation means a clean, sanitized work area, tools, and utensils. It means fresh, cold ingredients. Sanitation means clean workers with clean personal habits. Plastic gloves are often worn for hand work. Sanitation also means storing sandwiches in the refrigerator until they are served.

Meat or cheese used for a dry filling should be sliced very thin or even ***shaved***. Shaved meat is very, very thin. Many slices of thin or shaved meat are better than a single, thick slice. They make a more tasty sandwich and one that is easier to eat. It is also more economical. Many thin slices give the illusion of more meat or cheese in the sandwich. Meat should be well-trimmed of fat. The same amount — measured by weight or number of slices — is used in each sandwich. A thin slice of tomato or onion and a lettuce leaf are often placed on top of the filling. These add flavor, moisture, and crunchiness to the sandwich. Mustard, horseradish, ketchup, or mayonnaise may be offered alongside.

Salad sandwiches can be made from fish, chicken, turkey, ham, eggs, or cheese. Chop the ingredients finely, but do not mince. Chopped celery, onion, pickle, and cucumber may be added for flavor and crunchiness. Mayonnaise is used to bind the ingredients together and to add flavor. Sometimes spices and herbs are also added. Be sure to make the filling the right consistency. It must be moist, but not soggy. If lettuce is used, place it on top of the filling. Use a scoop to make sure the same amount of filling is added to each sandwich.

✓ standards ✓

Sandwiches

Appearance

- ✓ Looks neat.
- ✓ Attractively garnished and served.
- ✓ Appropriate amount of filling.

Flavor

- ✓ Pleasing combination of flavors.

Texture

- ✓ Made with fresh bread and fresh ingredients.
- ✓ Moist, but not drippy.

On the Job

Making Tuna Salad Sandwiches

Assignment: Working by yourself, you are to make 175 tuna salad and lettuce sandwiches on white bread. The spread will be mayonnaise and the garnish is a green stuffed olive and a black olive on a toothpick stuck in the center of each sandwich half. Potato chips will accompany each sandwich. You will add the potato chips and the garnish just before the sandwiches are served.

Check the Recipe

The recipe for Tuna Salad Sandwich Filling is on page 173. You will need to adjust the yield from 50 servings to 175 servings. (See page 52 to review this procedure.) Rewrite the list of ingredients with the new amounts for 175 servings. You also need to determine the amount of bread, lettuce, spread, olives, and potato chips needed.

Check Yourself

Before you begin work, make sure you are ready:

- Confine your hair with a hairnet, cap, or band.
- Wash your hands thoroughly.
- Put on a clean apron.
- Use plastic gloves for preparing the ingredients and assembling the sandwiches.

Assemble the Equipment

- Equipment indicated in the recipe
- Containers for spread, filling, lettuce, and garnish
- Sharp knife
- Two metal spatulas
- No. 24 scoop
- Trays
- Toothpicks
- Plastic wrap

Prepare the Ingredients

- Refrigerate the bread overnight.
- Prepare the filling according to the recipe. Place in a covered container and refrigerate until ready to make the sandwiches.
- Wash lettuce leaves and precut to the size of the sandwich. Place in plastic bags and refrigerate.
- Chill olives.

Follow this Procedure

Step 1. Use a clean, uncluttered counter or table for sandwich assembly. Set up the work flow from left to right.

Step 2. Remove the bread from the refrigerator, one loaf at a time. Cut the wrapper at the middle of the loaf. Remove half the bread and take off the wrapper. Place the other half, face side down, beside the tray.

Step 3. ▲ Using both hands, lay out 20 slices of bread in a 5-slice by 4-slice rectangle, as shown.

Step 4. Place the spread, the filling, and the lettuce to the right of the bread. Also lay out two metal spatulas and a No. 24 scoop. Place a tray covered with plastic wrap to the right of the ingredients.

Step 5. ▲ Dip one spatula into the spread. Beginning with the slice of bread on the right that is farthest away from you, spread the mayonnaise evenly on each slice using one continuous motion.

Step 6. ▲ Place a scoop of filling on each slice of bread in the second and fourth rows. Spread the filling evenly with the second spatula using one continuous motion.

Step 7. ▲ Place the precut lettuce on top of the filling.

Step 8. ▲ Working from top to bottom, cover the filling slices with another slice of bread. Use both hands so you can cover two sandwiches at once.

Step 9. Stack the sandwiches in twos. Cut through each stack diagonally, from corner to corner. Use a sawing motion. Do not press down on the sandwiches as you cut.

Step 10. Place the sandwiches on the tray to the right and cover with plastic wrap. Refrigerate. Repeat this procedure until all the sandwiches are made. Shortly before serving time, assemble the olive garnishes. Place each sandwich on a plate, add garnish and potato chips.

TIME MANAGEMENT

As in making salads, pre-preparation of the ingredients for sandwiches can be done hours before assembly time. There are a few exceptions, however. Meat and cheese will dry out if sliced too far ahead of time. It is better to slice them just before making the sandwiches.

For greater speed, you must learn to use both hands for setting out the bread on the counter and for putting the sandwich together. At first, you may find this a little awkward, but with practice you will soon be proficient with both hands.

Freshness is one of the most desirable qualities for sandwiches. Whenever possible, sandwiches should be served as soon as they are prepared. However, in mass production, this is not possible. Sandwiches may be wrapped in individual plastic or waxed paper bags.

In food service, large quantities of sandwiches are prepared at one time and stored for later use.

"Dry" sandwiches can be made well ahead of time and frozen. Be sure they are wrapped securely to prevent drying. However, no fresh greens can be used because greens lose their crispness when frozen. Sandwiches which have been frozen cannot be refrozen after they have been thawed.

Timing is important when producing large quantities of food. All of these sandwiches should be browned to the same degree of doneness.

STORING SANDWICHES

If prepared sandwiches are to be stored for a short time, stack them on a tray. Then cover them with waxed paper and a clean, damp towel. Do not put the towel directly on the sandwiches. Kitchen towels are not sterile even if they are clean. By protecting the sandwiches with a piece of waxed paper, they will not be contaminated.

For short-term storage, sandwiches are placed on lined trays, covered with wax paper, and then with a cloth before being refrigerated.

For long-term storage, sandwiches are wrapped individually in plastic and then placed on lined trays for refrigerated storage.

SUMMARY

Sandwiches can be served either hot or cold. They may be made using different kinds of breads and fillings. Depending on the type of filling, a sandwich can be a light snack or an entire meal. Accompaniments should add balance and variety to the sandwich. When making large numbers of sandwiches, a production line must be set up to increase efficiency.

chapter recap

CHECK YOUR KNOWLEDGE

1. What are hors d'oeuvres?
2. What is the title of the cook who prepares grilled sandwiches?
3. Name and describe the five types of cold sandwiches.
4. List at least three types of bread, other than white, that can be used in sandwiches.
5. Why should sandwich bread be refrigerated before use?
6. What is a spread? Name two common spreads.
7. Explain the difference between dry and moist fillings. Give two examples of each.
8. Suggest four accompaniments for sandwiches.
9. Explain why plastic gloves should be worn when making sandwiches.
10. What is the purpose of setting up a production line for making sandwiches in quantity?

EXTEND YOUR LEARNING

1. Search magazines for pictures of unusual sandwiches. Make them into a poster.
2. Visit a delicatessan or the deli department of a large supermarket. List the sandwich fillings available. Find out which is the most popular.
3. Check your school lunch menus for the types of sandwiches offered during one month. Mark each sandwich on your list as "moist" or "dry" according to the type of filling.

Unit 5

The Hot Station

Many people choose to eat at a particular restaurant because of the main dishes served. Main dishes include meats, poultry, fish, vegetables, cereals, and pasta. These foods are all prepared in the hot station. Since most breakfasts, lunches, and dinners include at least one of these foods, the hot station is often called the heart of the food service kitchen.

Most food service students enjoy working in the hot station. As you learn to prepare these foods, you will learn many important principles of professional cooking as well as how to use, care for, and maintain commercial food service equipment. The principles you learn will apply to the foods prepared in other parts of the food service kitchen.

A professional cook is always concerned with the sanitation and safety aspects of working with commercial equipment. You will learn to respect and appreciate the equipment used in the hot station because of the time and effort saved by its use.

Even though all food service operations do not use every station described in this book, the hot station can be found in most food service establishments. The heart of the kitchen will help you to become the professional cook that has a great future in the food service industry.

"Jim and Ruthann were on a picnic with Rosita, Tony, David, and Kim. As usual, Jim was going to cook hamburgers. He built a fire in the grill and watched the flames flare up.

"Hurry up, Jim!" exclaimed Ruthann. "We're starved. Let's get the hamburgers started."

"Hey," said Jim, "remember what Chef Robinson said about slow cooking meat? If it's okay with all of you, I thought we'd try it out."

"Okay," said Tony, "what did you have in mind?"

"Here are the hamburger patties," said Jim. "I've made twelve hamburgers as close to the same size as I could. I'll cook six right away. Then we can cook the others when the charcoal is only glowing, not flaming. Let's see which ones really are best."

"Good idea, Jim," said Kim. "But let's get started!"

As the hamburgers began to cook, the flames leaped higher because the fat was dripping into the charcoal. When they were brown on one side, Jim flipped them over. The flames flared again. Soon they were brown and ready for the buns.

Jim passed out papers and pencils. He said, "Keep track of what you put on the hamburger so you can make the next one the same way. Also grade the hamburger after you have eaten it on appearance, taste, and juiciness."

"Give me those onions," said David. "I love onions! Ketchup too."

By the time everyone had finished and graded the hamburgers, the flames had died down and the coals were glowing red. Jim raised the grill above the coals and put on the second batch of hamburgers. He had a small bottle of water close at hand.

"What's that for, Jim?" asked Ruthann.

"My dad told me that if the grease makes the coals flame up, to douse them with just a little water," answered Jim. "I don't want to put the fire out."

The hamburgers took about twice as long to cook. When they were browned on both sides, Jim put them in the buns.

"These hamburgers are delicious, Jim," said Rosita. "Let's tell Chef Robinson about our experiment in the morning.""

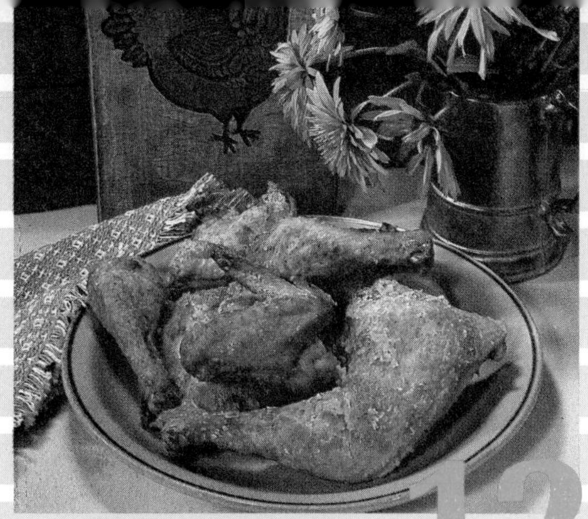

chapter 12

meats

Set your goals

When you complete the study of this chapter, you should be able to . . .

- Define and correctly use the vocabulary terms.
- Identify the factors that affect meat selection.
- Select and store meat correctly.
- Prepare meat using appropriate cooking methods.

Build your vocabulary

coagulation	grading
connective tissue	internal temperature
convenience food	marbling
cured	marinating
dredged	scoring
entree	wholesale cuts
fabricated cuts	

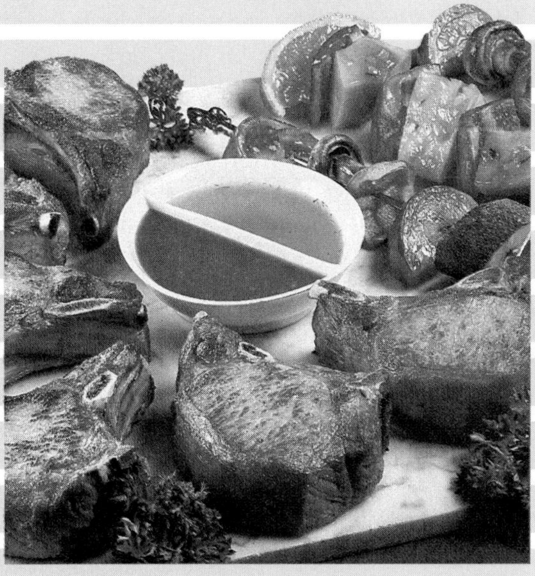

THE ENTREE

In food service, the main course of the meal is called the ***entree*** (AHN-tray), a French word meaning "of great importance." Vegetables, especially potatoes, as well as the meat are considered a vital part of the entree. Although it is customary to think of meat as the main course of a meal, the entree might be a salad, an egg dish, or even a sandwich.

In the broadest sense, the term "meat" includes poultry, fish, and seafood. In this chapter, however, it will be used to refer to beef, pork, veal, and lamb. Poultry, fish, and seafood are discussed in the next two chapters.

The Popularity of Meat

Beef, which comes from cattle, is the most popular meat in this country. Veal is the meat of very young cattle which are still milkfed. Pork — the meat from hogs — is second to beef in popularity. Lamb, which comes from young sheep, is becoming a more popular meat choice. Mutton, however, which comes from mature sheep has a strong flavor. It is rarely served in food service.

Meat is a basic part of the American diet. Each person consumes an average of about 100 lbs. (46 kg) of meat per year. That is about 3¾ oz. (106 g) per day. Meat is nutritious as well as satisfying. It contributes protein, carbohydrates, fats, vitamins, and minerals to the diet. Most full-service food service operations offer a variety of meat dishes daily.

The Cost of Meat

Meat is the single most expensive item on the food service menu. It may account for over 50 percent of the total meal cost. Because so much of the food dollar is spent for meat, food service managers choose meat items very carefully. Good cooks handle and prepare meat with care. They know that wasted meat is an expense an operation cannot afford.

Meat prices are generally set by demand. The very tender cuts, such as steak, are in demand and therefore expensive. Less tender cuts, such as stew meat, cost less.

SELECTING MEAT

Those responsible for purchasing meat for a food service operation have a big responsibility. They must know enough about meat to purchase the best quality for the lowest price. They must know the muscle and bone structure of meat animals and be able to identify cuts of meat by shape, appearance, and location on the animal carcass. If one cut is unavailable or too expensive, they must know what can be substituted.

The Structure of Meat

The structure of meat influences tenderness, juiciness, and flavor. Meat is composed of muscle, connective tissue, fat, and bone.

Muscle, the lean part of the meat, is made up of fibers. The fibers in muscles which are very active — those from the animal's legs for example — become longer and larger. Meat from these areas is less tender. Meat from muscles which receive little exercise, such as the back, are more tender.

Connective tissue is the white, stringy substance that binds the muscle fibers together and connects the muscles to the bone. The amount of connective tissue also affects the tenderness of the meat. The more connective tissue, the less tender the meat.

Fat appears in layers on the outside of the meat and also as small flecks throughout the muscle. These small flecks of fat are called ***marbling***. Meat that has many flecks of fat within the muscles is said to be well marbled. Fat adds flavor, juiciness, and aroma. It melts and browns during the cooking process.

Bones are not eaten but they do add flavor to stocks, gravies, and soups. When choosing meat, it is important to remember that bones add weight. Since meat is sold by weight, very bony cuts are usually not a bargain.

The structure of meat often determines the quality selected. This display of meat shows a good distribution of muscle, connective tissue, fat, and bone.

Wholesomeness

All meat which is shipped between states must be inspected and approved by the USDA as safe to eat. This guarantee of wholesomeness is indicated by a round, purple stamp like the one below. This stamp is rolled directly on the outside of the meat. Many states also have their own meat inspection for meat produced and used within the state.

Quality

Grading — determining quality — is not required by law. However, many suppliers carry only graded meat. That way buyers for food service operations can order meat without actually inspecting it but be assured of receiving the quality they expect.

Meat that has been graded is stamped with a shield like the one shown on page 69. The three most common grades of meat are prime, choice, and good. Prime meat is used in some expensive restaurants. Many institutional kitchens use meat that is graded good.

Quality grading is based on the age of the animal; the texture, firmness, and color of the meat; and the amount of marbling. Remember these are quality grades. They do not refer to wholesomeness. A piece of good grade meat will be less tender and flavorful than a piece of prime meat. But both are equally wholesome and nutritious.

How can you recognize quality in meat? It takes practice, but here is what to look for:

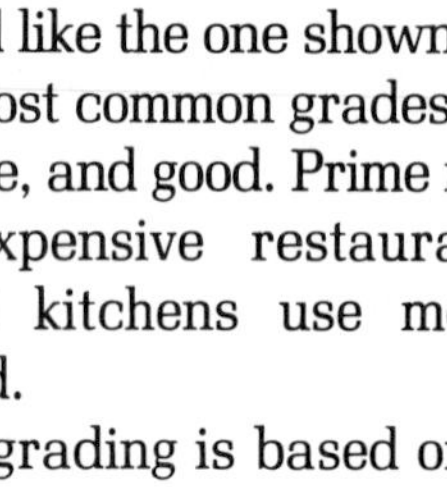

- **Beef**. Quality beef is bright red in color with firm, white fat on the outside and marbling throughout the muscle and along the connective tissue. The muscle portion is velvety and fine-grained. The bones are white and hard with just a bit of red in the center.

- **Veal**. Veal is pink with very little fat. The bones are soft and slightly red in the center. Veal has a great deal of connective tissue because the muscles are not yet fully developed.

- **Pork**. Pork may be fresh or ***cured***. (Ham and bacon are examples of cured meats.) Cured meat is treated with ingredients such as salt, sugar, and nitrites or nitrates. These give the meat a distinctive flavor and retard spoilage. Fresh pork is grayish-pink in color with a great deal of soft, creamy-white fat. The bones are fairly hard and slightly red. Cured pork is bright pink in color. Both fresh and cured pork may also be smoked for flavor. Unlike other meats, pork is not graded. It comes from young animals that vary little in quality.

- **Lamb**. Lamb is deep red with brittle, white fat and soft, reddish bones. As the animal ages, the meat darkens and the bones harden and loose their reddish color.

Cuts of Meat

Knowing about cuts of meat is important for both the food buyer and the cook. The buyer is concerned about quality and price — both related to the part of the animal the meat comes from. The cook must prepare the meat in a way that preserves or enhances its tenderness. Not all cooking methods are suitable for all cuts of meat. And both the buyer and cook need to know what cuts can be substituted for one another.

Just what are cuts? They are the large or small pieces of meat into which a carcass is divided. The carcass is first cut into several large sections called primal or ***wholesale cuts***. Each wholesale cut is then divided into smaller sections — roasts, steaks, and so on. In meat to be sold to food service operations, these smaller sections are called ***fabricated cuts*** because they are cut to a specific serving size. They are ready to cook and each cut weighs exactly the same amount. (Remember portion control?)

Most food service meat suppliers follow a standard set of specifications known as the Institution Meat Purchase Specifications (IMPS). Each cut is precisely described and numbered. This simplifies the job of ordering meats. Cuts can be ordered by name and number and do not have to be described.

One way you can learn to recognize cuts of meat is by checking the size and shape of the bone. There are four basic bones shapes — round; long, thin, and flat; curved and thin; and shaped like a T. The chart below shows these bones, tells what part of the body the bone comes from and whether the cut is usually tender or less tender. Which bones are in your favorite meats?

Bones Identify Meat

Bone Shape	Location on Animal	Quality of Meat	Examples of Cuts
Round 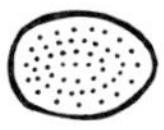	Arm or leg	Flavorful, less tender	Round steak Arm roast Shank
Long, thin, flat 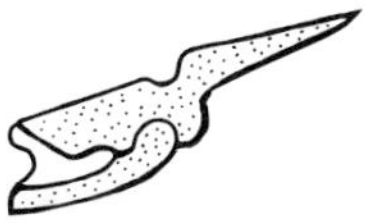	Top or arm (blade) Top of leg (sirloin)	More tender	Sirloin steak Pork chops
Curved, thin 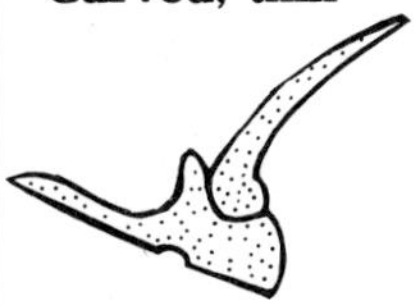	Ribs	Tender	Rib roast Spareribs
T-bone 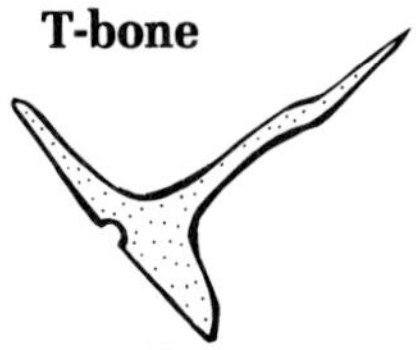	Loin	Most tender	T-bone steak Club steak Porterhouse steak

Prime Rib

Pork Chops

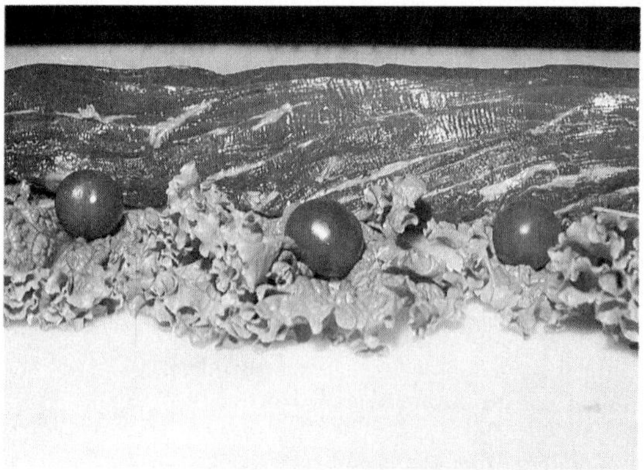

Beef Tenderloin

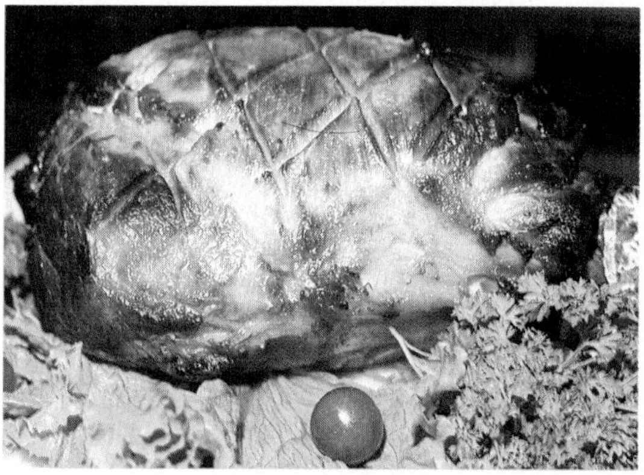

Ham

Veal

Lamb

STORING UNCOOKED MEAT

Even the highest quality meat can be ruined by improper storage. Since meat is so expensive, it must be handled and stored in a sanitary manner. Follow these guidelines when storing meat:

- **Fresh meat**. Wrap loosely to allow air to circulate freely. Refrigerate at 32°-36°F (0°-2°C). Avoid contamination by keeping storage areas, work areas, and tools clean and germ-free.

- **Frozen meat**. Wrap meat tightly with freezer wrap to prevent freezer burn. Freezer burn causes meat to dry out and gives it a slightly cooked appearance. The meat loses flavor and tenderness. Store frozen meat at 0°F (– 18°C). Thaw as needed by placing in the refrigerator. Never thaw meat at room temperature.

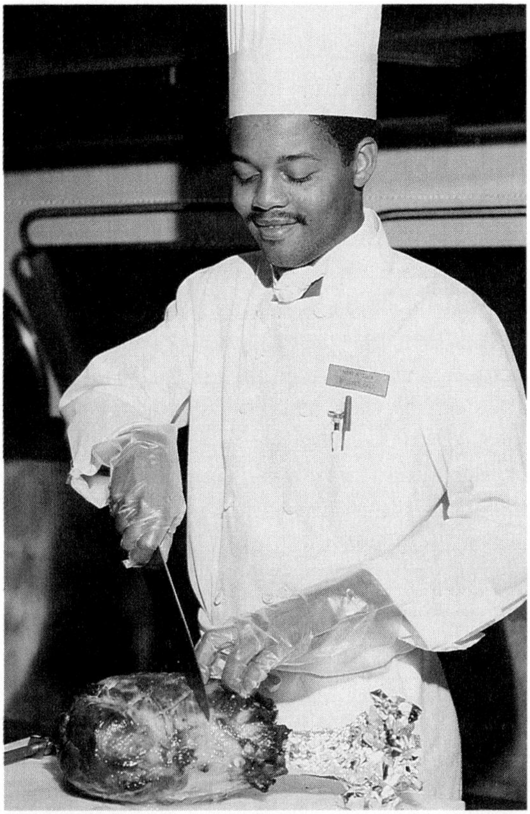

This chef is scoring a tender cut of meat after it has been cooked in order to add eye appeal to his buffet table.

PREPARING MEAT

Meat usually requires very little pre-preparation for cooking. However, several steps can be taken to increase the tenderness of less tender cuts.

The tough, connective tissue in meat can be broken down physically by cutting, grinding, scoring, or pounding. For instance, hamburger meat is made from less tender cuts of meat which have been tenderized by grinding. Cube steaks are tenderized by ***scoring***. The meat is cut with shallow gashes in a diamond pattern. This cuts through the long fibers and makes the meat more tender. So called "Swiss steak" is tenderized by another method — pounding with a mallet. This process breaks down fibers and connective tissues.

Meat may be tenderized chemically by the use of a powdered or liquid tenderizers. The tenderizer breaks down the connective tissues. However, the tenderizing action is not uniform because it cannot penetrate much below the surface of the meat. Pricking the meat with a fork helps the tenderizer to penetrate more deeply.

A process called ***marinating*** uses acid foods such as tomatoes, vinegar, lemons, or limes to break down the connective tissues of the meat. The meat is soaked in the marinating mixture for several hours before cooking. Marinating also adds flavor. The well-known German dish sauerbraten is an example of marinating.

The Principles of Protein Cooking

Cooking develops the flavor, enhances the appearance, and softens meats. This makes them tastier and easier to chew. However, cooking too long or incorrectly makes meat hard, dry, and unappetizing.

Meat is a protein food. If you understand the principles of protein cooking, you can apply them to cooking any type of protein food. Successful protein cooking depends upon cooking slowly at a low temperature until the food is just done. Never overcook.

When heated, protein gradually becomes firm. This is called ***coagulation***. The degree of firmness depends upon the amount of heat and the length of cooking time. You probably have noticed that an egg gradually hardens as it cooks. Eggs are also protein foods. If an egg is cooked slowly at low heat, it remains tender. If it is cooked quickly at high heat, it becomes tough and hard.

Meat reacts the same way. If meat is cooked at a low temperature, the hardening of the protein (the muscle tissues) and the loss of juices are kept at a minimum. Thus, tender, juicy meat with good flavor is produced. High heat will toughen or harden the meat muscle. Keep this in mind whether you are roasting, stewing, or frying meat.

Choice of Cooking Method

There is more to cooking meat than deciding on a particular cut. The cooking method must also be considered. Several factors influence the choice of method:

- **The amount of muscle, fat, and connective tissue.** The more connective tissue, the longer the cooking time. Choose a method for tougher cuts that uses long, slow cooking.

- **The kind of meat.** Pork must be cooked well done. Beef may be rare (still red in the center), medium (pink in the center), or well done (completely cooked all the way through). Veal, because of the great amount of connective tissue, must be well done. Lamb is sometimes served medium, but most people prefer it well done.

- **The tenderness desired.** Some cooking methods can make less tender cuts more tender.

- **The appearance desired.** For instance, does the meat need to be brown and crisp on the outside?

Methods of Cooking

As you have learned, cuts of meat with round bones are less tender. Cuts with long, thin, flat bones; curved bones; or T-bones are naturally more tender. This is because of the amount of connective tissue. Natural tenderness dictates the way meat should be cooked. There are two general categories of cooking meats — with dry heat or with moist heat.

Dry Heat Cooking

Dry heat means cooking the meat uncovered without any added moisture. This method of cooking should be used only for naturally tender cuts of meat with little connective tissue. Meats which have been tenderized (as described earlier) may also be cooked with dry heat. Roasting, grilling, broiling, and frying are all dry heat methods.

• **Roasting**. Cooking by dry heat in an oven is called roasting. The meat (usually a roast) is placed on a rack in a shallow roasting pan. This keeps the meat above the natural juices that drip into the roasting pan. The meat is always placed on the rack fat side up so that, as the fat melts, it keeps the meat juicy. The meat is cooked uncovered.

To roast means the same as to bake. For some reason, beef, veal, lamb, and fresh pork are roasted, but ham is baked. Actually, the same method of cooking is used for all.

Roast meat should be brown and crisp on the outside but juicy and tender on the inside. In order to meet these standards, the temperature of the oven must be strictly controlled. Tests conducted by the National Live Stock and Meat Board prove that roasts cooked at a low temperature are more tender, flavorful, and juicy. They yield more servings because the meat shrinks less during cooking. Temperatures for roasting range from 250°-325°F (120°-160°C). A good rule to remember is that larger the cut of meat, the lower the temperature.

This perfectly prepared roast was cooked at a low temperature to ensure tenderness, flavor, and adequate juices. It will also yield the maximum number of servings for a roast of its size.

It is difficult to judge the degree of doneness of thick cuts of meat from their appearance. A meat thermometer is used to find the ***internal temperature***, the temperature inside the meat. The thermometer is placed in the middle of the thickest part of the meat (but not touching a bone). The temperature will indicate the degree of doneness of the meat. For example, rare roast beef has an internal temperature of 140°F (60°C), while well-done beef has a temperature of 170°F (80°C).

The timetable on page 193 shows the time it takes to raise the internal temperature of meat to different degrees of doneness. This is helpful when deciding how long meat needs to cook.

The temperature of the oven, the weight of the meat, and the amount of fat and bone all affect the cooking time. Solid pieces of meat take longer to roast than meat with bone because the bone helps conduct the heat into the inside of the meat.

In food service, beef is roasted to the barely rare stage because it is easier to adapt rare meat to customers' orders. That is, if a customer orders medium or well-done roast beef, one serving can be quickly broiled to the desired stage. The cooking may also be completed in the microwave oven in a very short time.

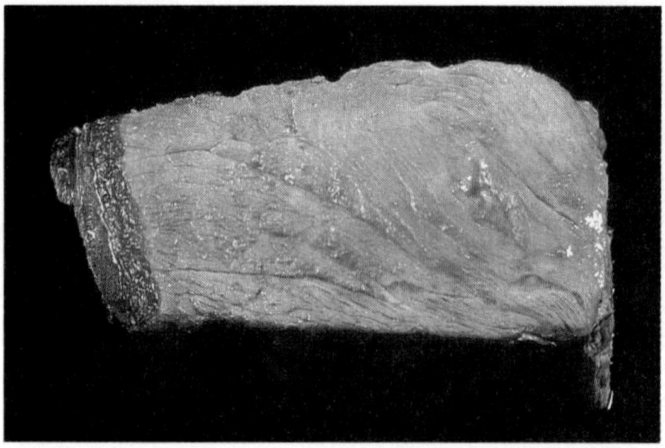

Beef cooked to the rare stage of doneness.

Beef cooked to the medium stage of doneness.

Beef cooked to the well-done stage.

Timetable For Roasting Meats*

Kind and Cut of Meat	Ready-To-Cook Weight (pounds)	Approximate Roasting Time at 325°F. (hours)	Internal Temperature of Meat When Done (°F.)
Beef			
Standing ribs			
Rare	6-8	2-2½	140
Medium	6-8	2½-3	160
Well done	6-8	3⅓-4½	170
Rolled rib			
Rare	4-6	2-3	140
Medium	4-6	2½-3¼	160
Well done	4-6	3-4	170
Rolled rump	5	3-3¼	160-170
Sirloin tip	3	2-2¼	160-170
Veal			
Leg	5-8	2½-3½	170-180
Loin	5	3	170-180
Rolled shoulder	3-5	3-3½	170-180
Lamb			
Leg	6-7	3¼-4	180
Shoulder	3-6	2¼-3¼	180
Rolled shoulder	3-5	2½-3	180
Pork, fresh			
Loin	3-5	3-4	185
Shoulder	5-8	3½-5	185
Ham, whole	10-14	5½-6	185
Ham, half	6	4	185
Spareribs	3	2	185
Pork, cured			
Ham, whole	12-16	3½-4½	160
Ham, half	6	2½	160
Picnic shoulder	6	3½	170

*From FOOD: The Yearbook of Agriculture, U.S. Department of Agriculture.

• **Grilling**. For grilling, the meat is placed on a hot pan or directly on the solid surface of a grill or griddle. Usually no additional fat is added for cooking.

Grilled meats are served most often in fast food restaurants. Steaks and hamburgers are the most popular items. See Chapter 22 for specific information on grilling.

• **Broiling**. Broiling is very similar to grilling. The difference is that the food is placed on an open grid and is cooked by direct heat. (Most home ranges include a broiler so you may be familiar with this method.) Broiling not only cooks meat, but also gives it an appealing brown crust.

Broiling is another method that is used extensively in fast food operations. Chapter 23 gives directions for broiling meat.

• **Frying**. Frying — cooking food in fat — is sometimes considered a dry heat method of cooking. Chapter 24 explains how to fry meat.

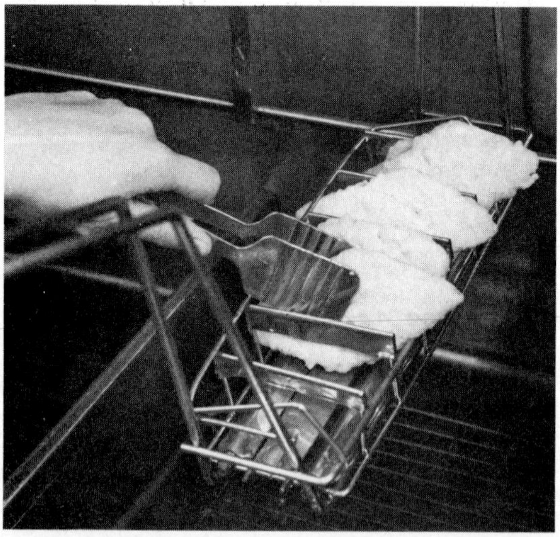

These fish fillets have just been deep-fat fried.

Moist Heat Cooking

Moist heat cooking is any method in which meat is cooked in a covered container either in the oven or on top the range. Moist heat is used to cook less tender cuts of meat. Liquid is usually added, but the meat is sometimes just cooked in its natural juices. There are two methods of cooking with moist heat — braising and stewing.

• **Braising**. Braising combines moisture with long, slow cooking in a covered pot. This combination breaks down the connective tissue and tenderizes less tender cuts of meat. It also provides a flavorful gravy. Braised meat should be well browned, juicy, flavorful, and tender. It should be well done, but not falling apart.

Braised meat may be cooked in the oven or on top the range. Oven braising requires a heavy roasting pan with a cover. On top the range, a Dutch oven (a round, heavy pan with a tight lid) is used.

Follow these general directions for braising meat:

1. Brown the meat in a heavy skillet or frying pan using a little fat to keep the meat from sticking. Browning helps develop the flavor and color.
2. Add the seasonings and cover tightly.
3. Cook very slowly at a low temperature. Most chefs prefer 300°F (150°C). The meat can be cooked in its natural juices, or a small amount of liquid may be added.
4. Depending on the size and thickness of the cut, allow 25-30 minutes cooking time per pound of meat.

safety tip . . .

When checking the meat during cooking, be sure to open the lid toward the back, away from your face. Steam builds up during cooking and can burn you.

- **Stewing**. Less tender cuts of meat may also be stewed. Stewing is the process of cooking slowly in enough liquid to cover it. Beef, veal, and lamb are often served as a stew.

To stew meat, follow these steps:

1. Cut the meat into uniform-size pieces.
2. Meat is then ***dredged*** — coated with seasoned flour.
3. Brown the meat on all sides in a heavy skillet with a little fat. Browning is not necessary, but it does add color and flavor.
4. Cover the meat with liquid and simmer — cook just below the boiling point — until tender. (Boiling would toughen the protein in the meat.)
5. When the meat is tender, the cooking liquid can be thickened into gravy.

Determining Doneness

When cooking meat, determining the degree of doneness is important for success. It is also difficult for a beginner. Experience is the key.

When using a moist heat method, meat is done when the connective tissues are soft and tender. A fork should pierce the meat with little resistance. When using a dry heat method of cooking, determining doneness is more difficult. Here are some suggestions:

- The meat thermometer is the most accurate method of testing doneness. You can depend on it.
- The color changes as the meat cooks. Beef and lamb will turn from red to pink to brown.
- Pork and veal are cooked to well done. There should be no hint of pink in the meat.

Using a meat thermometer to determine doneness is the most accurate method when cooking with dry heat.

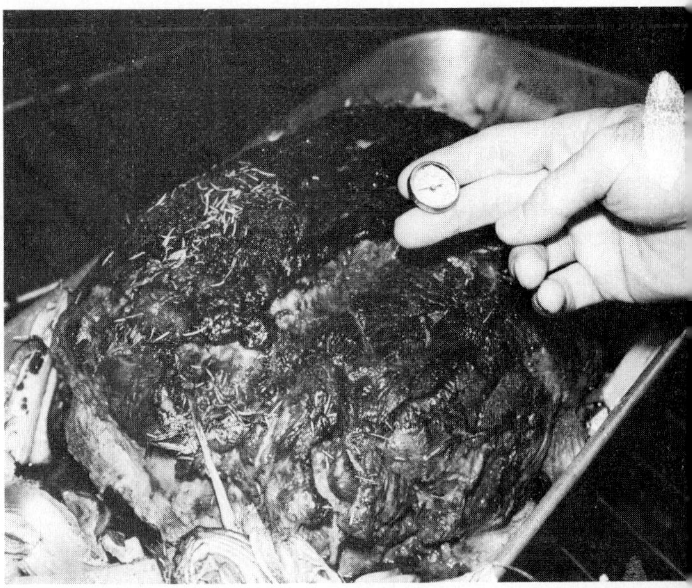

CARE OF COOKED MEATS

Cooked meats require special handling. The temperature the meat is held at between cooking and serving is critical. It must be hot enough to prevent growth of bacteria but not hot enough to dry out the meat. Ovens, steam tables, and heat lamps (infrared lamps) are some of the food service equipment used to keep meat warm.

When storing cooked meat for future use, wrap it tightly to keep in juices and prevent dryness. Refrigerate and use promptly.

Although raw meat may never be refrozen, cooked meat can be. Wrap it tightly in a moisture-proof wrapping and put it in the freezer. Be sure to mark the package with the contents, amount, and date. Frozen, cooked meats should be used as soon as possible.

CONVENIENCE FORMS OF MEAT

In food service, the choice of meat is considered the key to menu planning. Convenience food items simplify the planning and preparation in many operations.

A ***convenience food*** is any food item that simplifies preparation. This includes anything from packaged dry sauce mixes to completely prepared frozen entrees. Convenience foods are available in two forms — partially prepared and completely prepared. You must add something to a partially prepared convenience food, such as water or a fresh food item. A frozen entree, however, needs only to be heated for service.

The USDA requires that strict quality standards be followed by manufacturers of convenience foods. This assurance of quality and the ease of use has stimulated the use of convenience foods at home and in food service. It is often difficult to distinguish a convenience food from one made from a favorite recipe.

Even hamburgers can be purchased as a convenience food by a food service operation.

SUMMARY

Meat is the most popular meal entree. It is also the most expensive menu item, so it must be chosen and cooked carefully. Meat is inspected for wholesomeness and graded for quality. Depending on its tenderness, it can be cooked using a dry or moist heat method. Beef, pork, veal, and lamb are all used in food service menus.

chapter recap

CHECK YOUR KNOWLEDGE

1. Define the term "marbling."

2. What does the federal inspection stamp on large cuts of meat guarantee?

3. What are the three most common grades of meat? Which is the highest?

4. List the four bone shapes generally found in meat and give an example of a cut for each of these shapes.

5. Name four dry heat methods of cooking. Are these suitable for tender or less tender cuts?

6. Describe how to correctly place a meat thermometer in a cut of meat.

7. List and briefly describe the moist heat methods of cooking.

8. What is "marinating" and what is its purpose?

9. Briefly explain how cooked meats must be cared for.

10. Define the term "convenience food" and give two examples.

EXTEND YOUR LEARNING

1. Visit the meat department in a supermarket. Find a cut of beef that would be cooked by a dry heat method and one that would be cooked by a moist heat method. Write down the name of each cut and its price per pound. Do the same for pork and veal or lamb. Make a chart of your findings.

2. Discuss how braising differs from stewing. Give an example of each method.

3. In the supermarket find flavoring packets for meats. For three, list the type of flavoring, its purpose, the ingredients, and the price. Do you think such flavorings are worth the cost? Explain.

"Mmm, Thanksgiving's almost here," said Ruthann. "I can almost smell that delicious turkey cooking. Mom is defrosting a frozen turkey in our refrigerator right now. She bought a 18-pound hen turkey because Aunt Mary and her family are coming for Thanksgiving dinner. There will really be a full table."

"There will only be three of us at my house for dinner," said Jim. "We're getting a small turkey because Mom doesn't like leftovers. Of course, I could take care of the leftovers with no problem!"

"I can remember eating leftover turkey and stuffing at your house," he continued. "Your mom's stuffing is almost as good as the turkey. How does she make it?"

Ruthann explained, "It's very moist and has onions, eggs, raisins, and even sweet potatoes in it."

"Every family has a favorite stuffing," said Jim. "Rosita's family uses cornbread in theirs. In our family we make a dry stuffing with celery and onions. I once had oyster stuffing at Grandma's, but I didn't like it at all."

"Did you see the turkey we're going to cook in class?" asked Ruthann. "It must weigh 40 pounds. Chef Robinson said it is a tom turkey and will take at least three days to thaw in the refrigerator. We're going to cook it on Tuesday and serve it on Wednesday to the teachers and some guests."

"He also said we're cooking the stuffing outside the turkey," said Jim. "The turkey cooks faster and is easier to slice. Besides, I just learned that stuffing inside a turkey can spoil as the turkey cools. You have to be really careful about food poisoning in food service."

chapter 13

poultry

Set your goals

When you complete the study of this chapter, you should be able to . . .

- Define and correctly use the vocabulary terms.
- Identify the factors in quality grading of fresh poultry.
- Handle and store poultry correctly.
- Identify and prepare various kinds of poultry.

Build your vocabulary

basting	giblets
disjointed	mirepoix
fricassee	skewers
game	truss

KINDS OF POULTRY

The term "poultry" includes a variety of domestic birds used for food. Chickens and turkeys are the most common types. Ducks and geese are served mainly in fine restaurants. Wild birds used for food are called ***game***.

Poultry is important in food service for several reasons:

- It is generally less expensive than red meat. This keeps food costs down.
- It is nutritious. Poultry is high in protein, vitamins, and minerals. Chicken and turkey are lower in fat than red meat.
- Poultry can be used in a wide variety of recipes. It can, for example, be roasted, fried, baked, or used in casseroles.
- Poultry is liked by most people. This makes it a popular menu item.

Chickens and turkeys have both white and dark meat. The white meat, which comes from the breast, cooks faster, has less fat, and is more tender because it has less connective tissue. The dark meat is juicier and some consider it more flavorful. In general, more people prefer white meat. Sometimes restaurants charge more for chicken dinners with all white meat. Ducks and geese have only dark meat.

Broiled Cornish hens are often served in food service establishments because each hen equals one portion.

Types of Poultry

Types	Description	Cooking and Serving
Chicken		
Broiler	• 8-12 Weeks old, either sex • 1-1½ lb. (.5-1.2 kg) • Very little fat	• Fried, broiled, roasted • Cut in half to serve
Fryer	• 14-20 weeks old, either sex • 2½-3½ lb. (1.2-1.6 kg) • Meaty with some fat under skin	• Roasted, fried • Quartered or cut in smaller serving pieces
Roaster	• 5-9 months old, either sex • Over 3½ lb. (1.6 kg) • Very meaty, excellent layer of fat under skin	• Roasted, braised • Cut in serving-size pieces
Capon	• 7-10 months old, desexed • Male bird • 4-7 lb. (1.8-3 kg) • Well-developed, much fat • High proportion of white meat	• Roasted • Cut in serving-size pieces
Stewing Hen	• Mature female • 3-7 lb. (1.3-2.7 kg) • Less tender, well-developed flavor	• Braised, stewed • Cooked whole • Usually cut in chunks for chicken dishes
Turkeys		
Broiler	• Young, either sex • Little fat	• Broiled, roasted • Quartered to serve
Roaster	• Hens (female) — 8-15 lb. (3.6-7 kg) • Toms (male) — 18-30 lb. (8.2-13.6 kg)	• Roasted • Cut in serving pieces after cooking
Ducks		
Ducklings	• 8-12 weeks old, either sex 2-4 lb. (.9-1.8 kg)	• Roasted • Quartered
Geese	• young — under six months, 4-10 lb. (1.8-5 kg) • older — 10-18 lb. (4.5-812kg)	• Roasted • Rarely used in food service because of strong taste

SELECTING POULTRY

Poultry is usually classified and selected according to the intended method of cooking. The chart on page 201 describes the various types available and how they may be cooked.

Age and sex are the most important factors affecting the tenderness and flavor of poultry. Older birds are less tender but more flavorful than younger birds. They must be cooked by a moist heat method to improve tenderness.

As with meat, federal regulations require that all poultry shipped between states must be inspected for wholesomeness and approved. This approval may appear as a metal disc clipped to the wing, a paper tag stuck to the bird, or a label on the poultry package.

As shown in the chart on page 70, federal grades for poultry are U.S. Grades A, B, and C. There are five factors considered in the quality grading of poultry:

- **Shape**. The general form, shape, and body contour.
- **Flesh**. Plump, firm-looking flesh.
- **Cleanliness**. Free from pin feathers and down. Pin feathers are small feathers which must be removed before cooking.
- **Condition**. Free from tears, cuts, bruises, blemishes, or defects such as broken bones.

STORING POULTRY

Poultry is extremely perishable — it spoils easily. Fresh poultry should be delivered packed in ice. It must be stored immediately in the refrigerator in its original wrapper. Cook fresh poultry within 24 hours of purchase.

Frozen poultry should be thawed in the refrigerator. A large bird will take about two days to thaw. If it is still slightly frozen, thawing may be completed under cold, running water. Never set poultry on the counter to thaw at room temperature. Cook immediately after thawing. Never refreeze uncooked poultry that has thawed.

PREPARING POULTRY

The basic principles for cooking meat also apply to cooking poultry. High heat applied for long periods of time toughens protein foods. Long, slow cooking produces a tender, juicy product, especially if moisture is added. Like meat, poultry can be cooked using either dry or moist heat.

Dry Heat Cooking

Young birds are small and tender. This makes them suitable for dry heat methods of preparation. Two of the most common dry heat methods — broiling and deep-fat frying — are discussed in detail in Chapters 21 and 24. Roasting and oven frying are explained here.

Roasting

Roasted poultry should be juicy, tender, and cooked until well done. It should not, however, be cooked so long that the meat falls off the bones.

In a roasting bird, the neck and ***giblets*** often come wrapped in a paper bag in the breast cavity. The giblets are the edible internal organs such as the heart, liver, and gizzard. Remove the paper bag. Place the giblets in water and cook until tender. They are often added to stuffing or to soup stock.

Follow these general steps when roasting poultry:

1. Wash the bird thoroughly under running water. Drain well.
2. Oil the skin to protect against drying and promote browning.
3. Season the inside of the bird with salt and pepper.
4. ***Truss*** the bird. Trussing means to tie the wings and legs close to the body so that the body is compact. Trussing keeps the bird in shape during roasting and prevents the legs and wings from drying out.
5. Place the bird breast-side up on a rack in a shallow roasting pan. Do not add water or cover the pan.
6. Insert a meat thermometer where the thigh joins the body. Be sure the pointed tip does not touch a bone.
7. Roast in a 250°-325°F (120°-160°C) oven. (The larger the bird, the lower the temperature.) Roast to an internal temperature on the meat thermometer of 185°F (85°C).

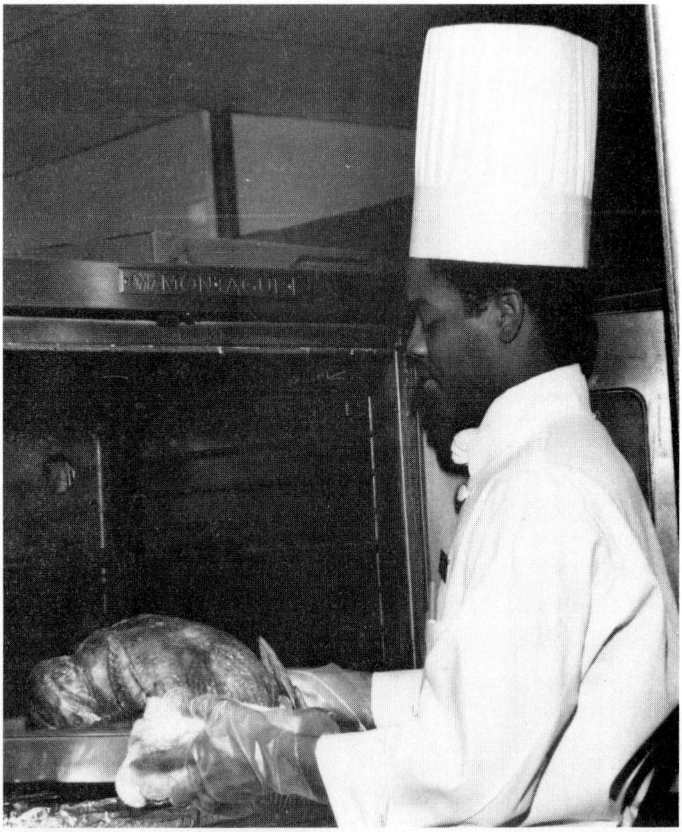

This chef roasted his turkey so it will be juicy and tender, yet well done. His customers will enjoy each slice taken from the buffet.

• **Stuffing**. Stuffing — sometimes called dressing — is a favorite side dish with roast poultry. In home cooking, the stuffing is usually placed inside the bird before roasting. In food service, however, the stuffing is more often cooked separately. The bird is stuffed only when it will be served whole.

There are many varieties of stuffings, but all have the same three main ingredients — a starchy base, fat, and seasonings. The starchy base is usually bread, although rice or potatoes are sometimes used. Fat in stuffings can be butter, margarine, poultry fat, meat drippings, or salt pork. They are used to add richness and flavor. Seasonings may include salt, spices, or herbs. Other flavorings such as onions, celery, mushrooms, oysters, chestnuts, sausage, or fruits may also be used.

Stuffings may be dry or moist. Dry stuffings are made from slightly stale bread which has been torn or cut into small pieces and mixed with melted fat and seasonings. Dry stuffings should be light, never soggy.

Moist stuffings are made of diced bread with eggs, liquid, and seasonings. The liquid may come from the giblets, vegetable juices, milk, or water. Too much liquid will make the stuffing soggy. The eggs add lightness.

If the stuffing is made ahead of time, it should be refrigerated until just before cooking. Stuffing is highly perishable, especially the moist type. Never allow it to stand at room temperature.

If the stuffing is to be cooked in the bird, season the inside of the bird first. Spoon the stuffing lightly into both the body and the breast cavities. Don't pack too tightly. The stuffing will expand as it cooks. Close the cavities with ***skewers***. Skewers are long, stainless steel pins used to hold food together during cooking. A string may be laced around the skewers to hold the cavity closed. Truss the bird and roast. A stuffed bird takes longer to cook than an unstuffed one.

A roasted Long Island duckling has been stuffed with a moist herb and rice mixture.

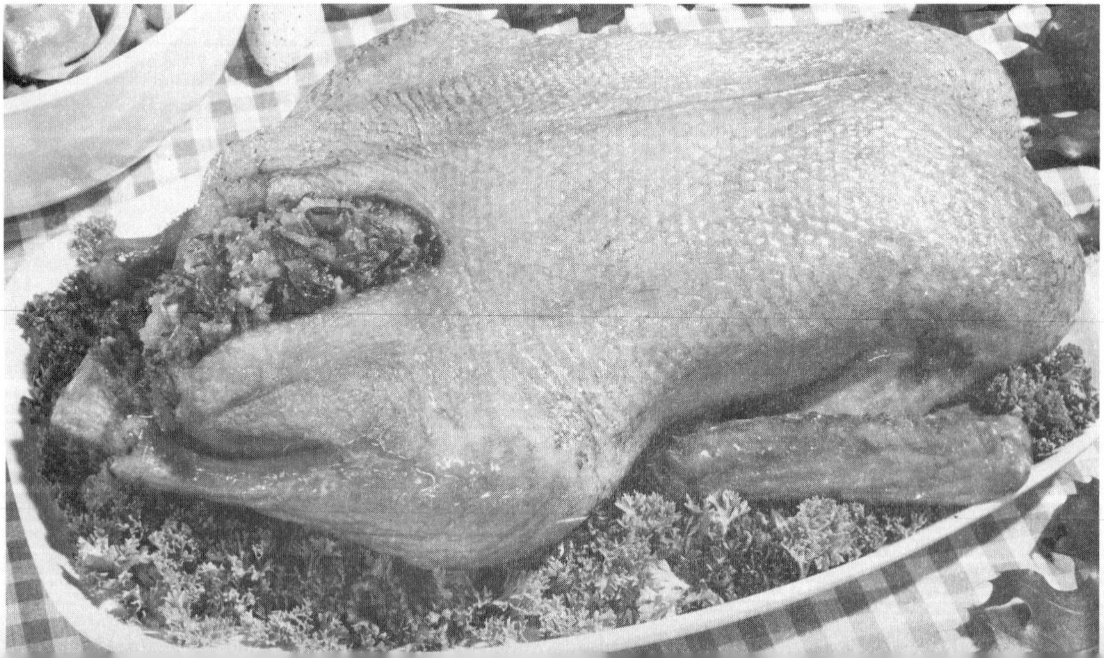

• **Basting**. Occasionally spooning the juices and fat over the bird or meat as it roasts is called ***basting***. Poultry with very little fat tends to dry out as it cooks. It helps to oil the skin before roasting to protect against drying. Some cooks like to place the bird breast-side down at first and turn it halfway through the cooking period to eliminate most basting.

Oven Frying

One of the easiest and most delicious ways to prepare poultry, especially chicken, is by oven frying. Oven frying is done by using a light coating of seasoned breading mix on the chicken and pouring a small amount of fat over the chicken which aids in the browning. The chicken is not as crisp as when deep-fat fried, but it browns nicely, is tender and juicy, and does not require turning or constant watching. This is an excellent method to use when a large quantity of food is needed. The recipe for Oven-Fried Chicken is on page 206.

Basting a turkey will keep it from drying out by oiling the skin. Can you think of other poultry recipes that call for basting?

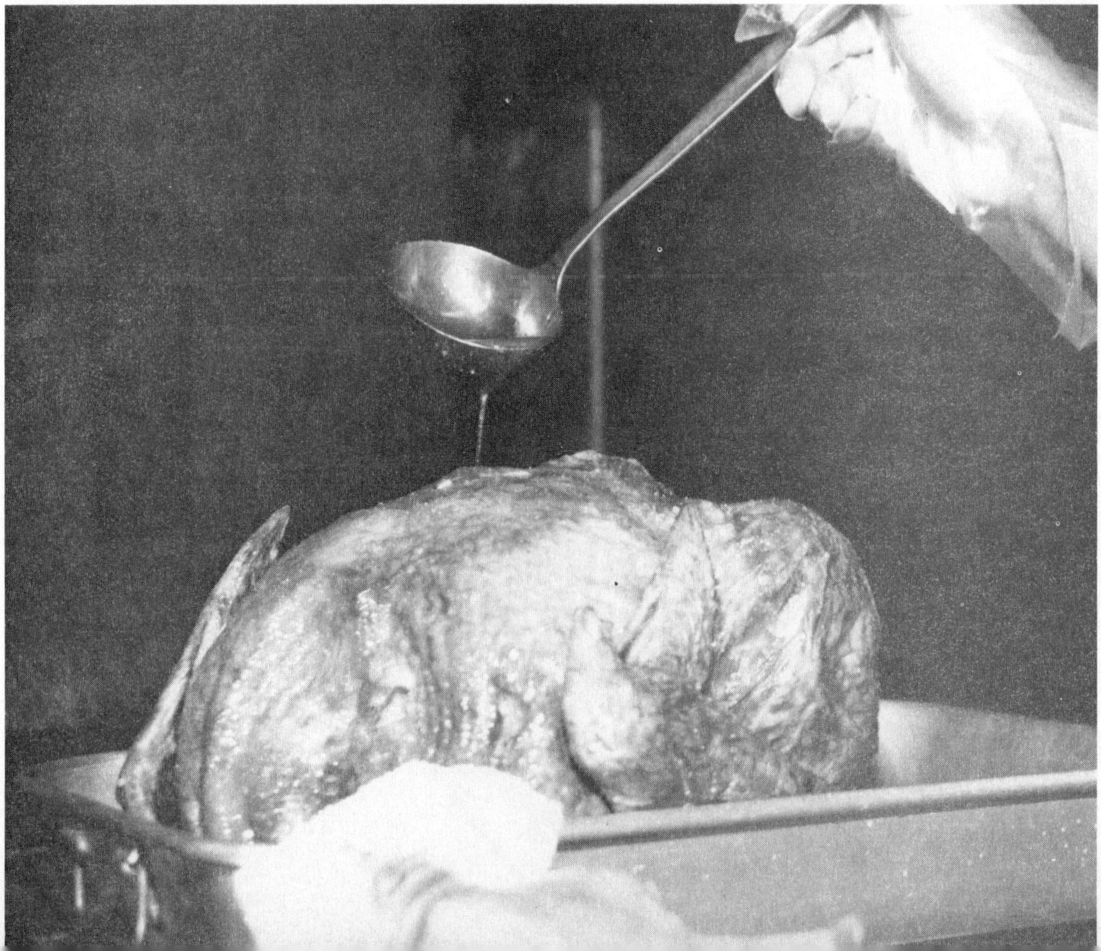

Oven-Fried Chicken

Equipment: Small bowls, Measuring cups, Measuring spoons, Colander, Paper towels, Baking Pans, Rubber Spatula, Tongs

Yield: 50 Servings
Temperature: 325°F

Ingredients	Amount	Method
Frying chickens	50 quarters	1. Use a wire whip to blend salad oil, lemon juice, and seasonings in a small bowl.
Salad oil	1½ c.	2. Wash chicken quarters and dry with paper toweling.
Lemon juice	½ c.	3. Place chicken in baking pans.
Salt	2 T.	4. Pour oil mixture over the chicken.
Pepper	1½ t.	5. Turn each quarter over twice to coat with the oil mixture.
Poultry Seasoning	1 T.	6. Marinate for 15 minutes.
Cornflake crumbs	2 c.	7. Drain off the oil mixture.
		8. Place cornflake crumbs in a bowl.
		9. Dip each quarter in the crumbs.
		10. Place the quarters in baking pans, skin side up. Sides should not touch.
		11. Sprinkle any remaining cornflake crumbs on top of the chicken.
		12. Bake for 1½ hrs.

Serving size: One chicken quarter

Cost per serving: ________________

Oven-fried chicken browns easily and has a delightful flavor.

Moist Heat Cooking

Older birds are more flavorful, but are also less tender than young birds. Slow, moist heat helps tenderize such birds. Roasters and stewing hens are most often cooked this way.

Braising

Poultry is braised in much the same way as meat. It is browned in hot fat then cooked slowly over low heat with a small amount of liquid. When cooked in this manner, it is sometimes called smothered, broasted, or chicken Maryland. Since this is a moist method of cooking, the birds may be slightly older than those used for roasting.

Poultry for braising may be halved, quartered, or ***disjointed*** — cut into pieces. The parts are dredged in seasoned flour, bread crumbs, rolled cornflakes, or a coating mix. They are browned in hot fat on all sides and arranged in a heavy pan. A small amount of liquid is added and the pan is tightly covered.

The cooking may be finished on top the range or in the oven. A low temperature is used. The cooking time depends on the age and size of the bird.

One dish prepared by braising is Chicken Fricasse. ***Fricasse*** (frik-a-SEE) means to serve meat in its own gravy. The chicken parts are browned as for braising then placed in a heavy roasting pan. A small amount of liquid is added, such as canned soup, milk, or vegetable juices. The pan is tightly covered and the poultry cooked over low heat until very tender. The cooking juices are thickened into a gravy that is served with the chicken.

The age of a chicken determine its class. Shown here are a Cornish game hen (left), a roaster (center), and a broiler or fryer (right).

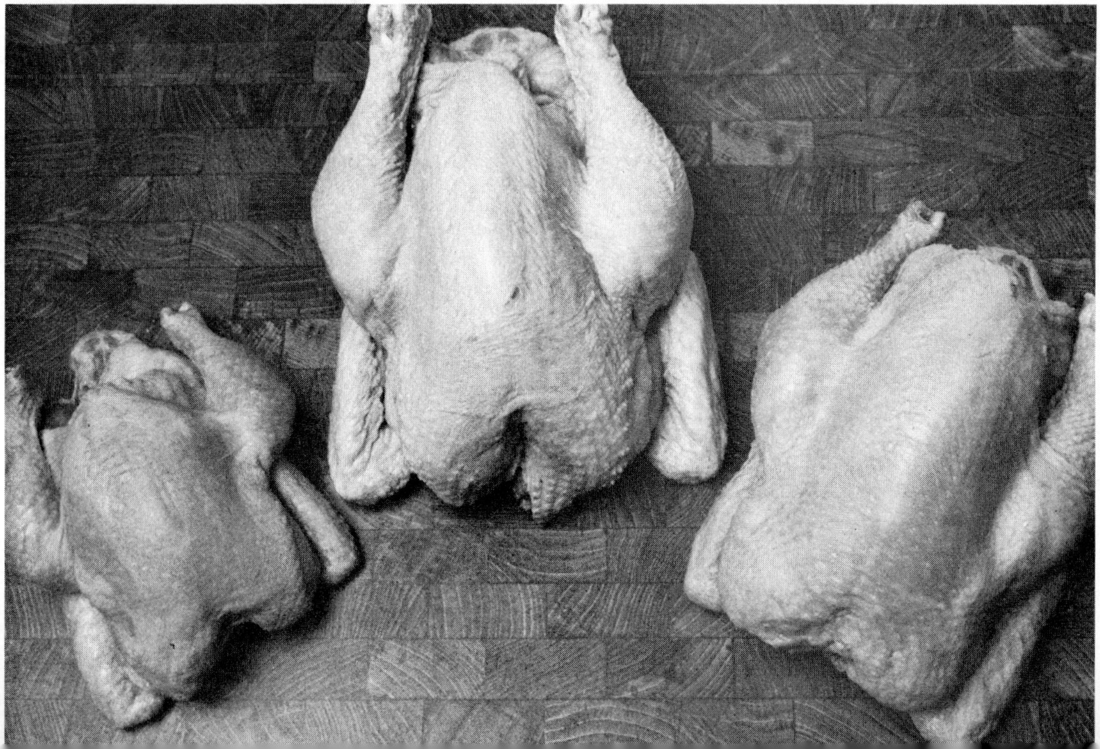

Stewing

Older birds may be tenderized by stewing — cooking slowly in water. The bird is cooked whole or in pieces, depending on its intended use. Place the bird in a heavy pot and barely cover with water. Simmer the bird for three to four hours, or until it is very tender.

A pressure cooker can save a great deal of time and energy. When water is heated under pressure, the temperature will go higher than boiling. While water boils at 212°F (100°C), under pressure it can go as high as 240°F (116°C). The higher temperature shortens the cooking time by about two-thirds. For instance, a stewing hen cooked under pressure will be tender in about one hour. It would normally take 2½ to 3½ hours to cook. Because of the shorter cooking time and the smaller amounts of water needed, the bird will retain more flavor.

Stewed chicken is seasoned with salt, pepper, and vegetables. A mixture of coarsely chopped vegetables is called a ***mirepoix*** (meer-PWA). It is used to season various types of meat.

Stewed chicken is sometimes served with dumplings and gravy. Or the meat may be removed from the bones and used to make salads, sandwiches, or casseroles. The stock in which the poultry was cooked should be saved and used as a base for soups or sauces.

CONVENIENCE FORMS OF POULTRY

Many convenience foods are made from turkey. Turkey ham, hot dogs, and patties are readily available. Turkey roll, made from all white or a mixture of white and dark meat is a popular convenience item.

For food service, turkey and chicken are available in exact portion sizes. They can also be purchased deboned or as chunks to use in many different recipes.

Completely cooked, frozen poultry entrees are also available. Turkey tetrazzini and chicken a la king are two popular ones. They need only be heated and served.

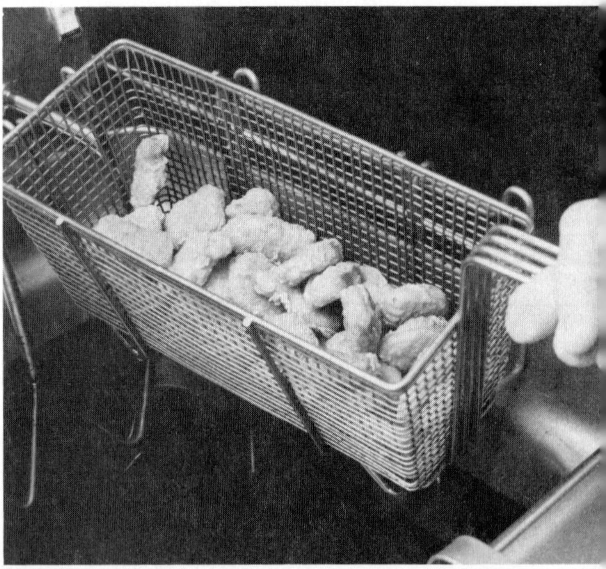

Pieces of chicken meat are often deep-fried and sold in food service establishments. They are popular and easy to prepare.

SUMMARY

There are four types of poultry — chickens, turkeys, ducks, and geese. The USDA grades poultry on its shape, amount of fat, cleanliness, and general condition. Poultry can be broiled, deep-fat fried, roasted, or oven fried. It can be served with stuffing, but the stuffing is generally cooked separately. Poultry is a popular food service item because it is nutritious, low in calories, and inexpensive.

chapter recap

CHECK YOUR KNOWLEDGE

1. What grades are given to poultry?
2. Explain how poultry should be thawed.
3. List the general steps for preparing poultry for roasting.
4. Where should the meat thermometer be placed when roasting a turkey?
5. What cooking methods are best for young broilers?
6. What cooking methods may be used for a mature hen?
7. How can you determine when poultry is well done and why is this important?
8. Explain why poultry is sometimes basted.
9. List the main ingredients in all stuffing.
10. What is a mirepoix?

EXTEND YOUR LEARNING

1. After reviewing Chapter 6, list three sanitary precautions that must be taken when preparing poultry.
2. Visit a poultry market or supermarket. Check what types of poultry available and in what forms. Make a chart listing each, the price per pound, and the method of cooking usually used with that type.
3. Check the meat section of a supermarket for cold cuts. Which are made from poultry? How does the price of these cold cuts compare with similar ones made from beef, pork, or veal?

"Ugh!" moaned Ruthann. "This next chapter is about fish. I hate fish! It's so smelly and slimy. I just hate to think about cooking it!"

Tony looked at her defensively. "The fish we caught this summer weren't smelly or slimy, were they Jim? I thought they tasted terrific!"

"You've got a problem, Ruthann," Jim added. "Maybe you smelled some bad fish when you were little and never forgot it. Besides, fresh fish aren't slimy at all!"

"I like fish better than steak!" Rosita joined in. "Especially rare steak! I don't see how you guys can eat raw meat like that!"

"You know," Jim responded, "I think it all depends on what you're used to. I never used to like lots of the foods that I love to eat now. I used to hate mushrooms, and now I wouldn't eat a pizza without them! Maybe once you try fish, you'll like it too!"

"Maybe so," Ruthann said. "But I'm not sure I could put fish on a pizza!"

"Seriously, Ruthann," Rosita said. "I bet if you try fish you'll like it just fine. We've all learned to like new foods because of this class."

chapter 14

fish and shellfish

Set your goals

When you complete the study of this chapter, you should be able to . . .

- Define and correctly use the vocabulary terms.
- Identify and select fish and shellfish.
- Prepare seafood for cooking.
- Practice correct storing, handling, and cooking procedures.

Build your vocabulary

breading
crustaceans
fillet
mollusks
poaching
seafood
shellfish
shucked
translucent

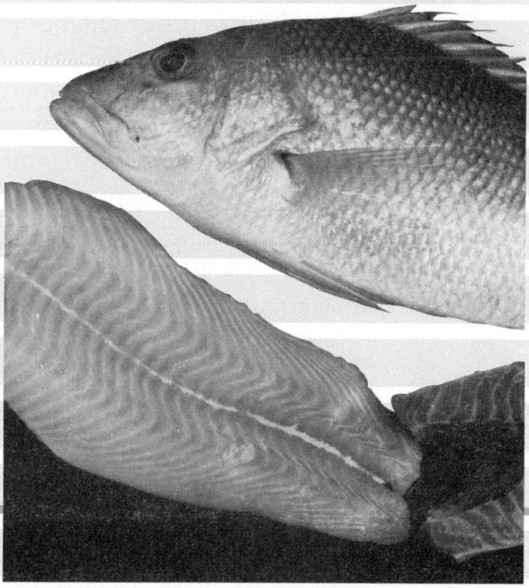

KINDS OF SEAFOOD

The term ***seafood*** includes any of the cold-blooded animals living in water which are used as food. Seafood may come from either freshwater or saltwater.

Seafood is a very popular food service item. It may be served as an appetizer, an entree, or a hearty salad. Like poultry, seafood is appreciated by diet-conscious customers because it is low in calories and fat. It is a source of high-quality protein and calcium, and is one of the few foods that is a natural source of iodine.

There are two main types of seafood — fish and shellfish. Fish have fins and a bony structure that is part of the spinal column. The bones of freshwater fish are numerous and fine. The bones of saltwater fish are larger and heavier than freshwater fish. Fish have no connective tissue. That means they cook quickly and, if cooked properly, are always tender. Some fish have more fat than others, but no fish is really fatty compared to beef, pork, or even poultry.

Shellfish have a hard, outer shell and no backbone or spinal column. The two types of shellfish are crustaceans or mollusks. ***Crustaceans*** have legs and segmented shells. Some have claws and feelers. Crabs and lobsters are crustaceans. ***Mollusks*** have a hard shell that opens and closes. Their bodies are undivided. Clams and oysters are mollusks.

SELECTING SEAFOOD

Seafood may be purchased fresh, frozen, canned, smoked, pickled, dried, and freeze-dried. A few years ago, cities far from a fresh supply of fish and shellfish depended upon canned or dried fish. Today, thanks to fast, refrigerated transportation, almost all parts of the country can enjoy the delicious flavor of fresh seafood.

Fish

Fortunately, it is easy to recognize if fish is fresh. Signs of freshness are shown in the chart below.

Fresh fish are prepared for market in several different forms as shown on page 213.

- **Whole**. Whole fish are sold just as taken from the water.
- **Dressed**. A dressed fish is whole with the internal organs and scales removed. The head, tail and fins, may or may not have been removed.
- **Steak**. Steaks are crosswise slices from a large, dressed fish.
- **Fillet**. The ***fillet*** is the side of fish, cut lengthwise away from the backbone.

Signs of Freshness in Fish

- Mild aroma.
- Firm flesh, elastic to the touch.
- Bright, full, clear eyes.
- Red gills, free from slime.
- Shiny skin with fresh color.

FISH PREPARED FOR MARKET

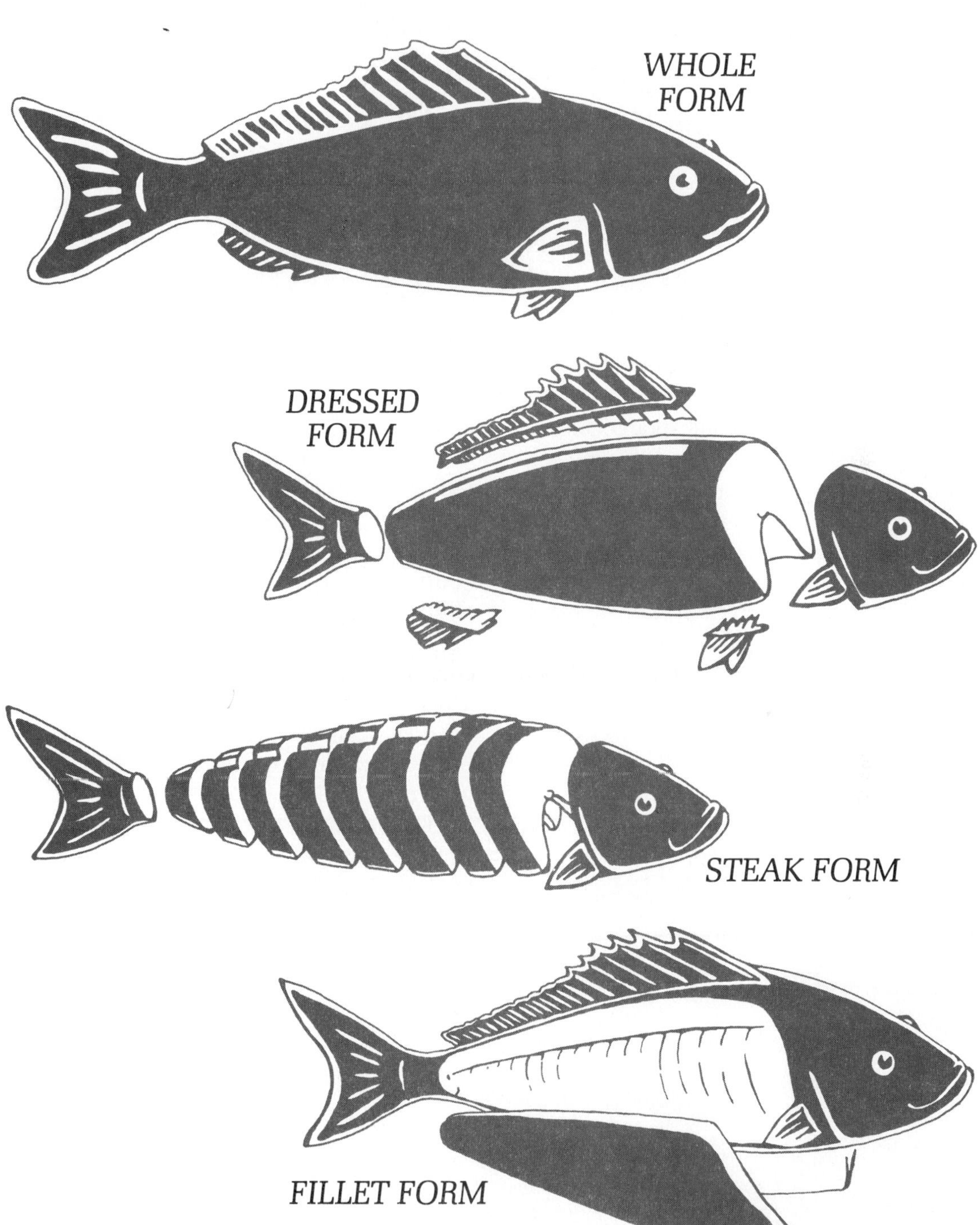

Shellfish

As noted previously, shellfish are identified by their hard, outer shell. Many varieties of shellfish are used by food service operations.

Shrimp

Shrimp are small animals within shells. They vary greatly in size and price. Large shrimp are much more expensive than small ones. Shrimp may be purchased fresh or frozen, raw or cooked. They may be sold in the shell or ***shucked*** — with the shell peeled off.

Shrimp have a black line along the back called a sand vein. Deveined shrimp are more expensive to buy because of the labor costs involved in removing the veins. Shrimp are always expensive, but ready-to-cook ones are a better value because of the labor cost involved in preparing them.

Like fish, fresh shrimp have a mild, pleasant odor. A strong odor means the shrimp are not as fresh as they should be. Raw shrimp are white or gray and ***translucent***. Translucent means that light can shine through, as it does through tissue paper or frosted glass. When cooked, they turn a beautiful pink. Shrimp are greatly prized because of their delicate taste and beautiful color.

Lobsters and Crabs

Lobsters are often called the king of shellfish because of their sweet, mild flavor. They also command a "royal" price. Two kinds of lobster are available on the market. Coldwater lobsters come from the cold North Atlantic. They are larger and have claws. The spiney lobster comes from the warm waters of the southern part of the Atlantic, from the Carribean Sea, and from the Gulf of Mexico.

Coldwater lobsters are purchased live and kept in a tank until chosen for preparation. Spiney lobsters are often cooked as soon as caught. Often only the lobster tail is sent to market. Both types of lobsters are gray-green when alive but turn a brilliant red when cooked. Lobster meat may also be purchased frozen or canned.

Crabs are also considered a great delicacy. They have a sweet taste and a delicate, pink color. There are four popular kinds of crabs. Blue crabs, the most common type, come from the Atlantic coast. Stone crabs are found in the Gulf of Mexico. Dungeness crabs come from the Pacific, and the king crab inhabits the icy waters of Alaska.

Crabs may be purchased alive or cooked. Like lobsters, they turn red when cooked. Canned or frozen crabmeat is often used in food service.

This oriental shrimp dish combines shrimp, fruit, nuts, and rice for a taste that is delightful.

Mollusks

Oysters, clams, and scallops are the most common mollusks. Oysters and clams are the soft animals living inside hard shells. Scallops are the muscle that opens and closes the scallop shell.

Oysters and clams may be purchased alive in the shell. Live, the shell should be tightly closed. If the shell is slightly open and does not close when touched, the animal is dead and unfit to eat. When served as an appetizer "on the half shell" they are opened just before serving.

Scallops are always marketed in the shucked form. They have a very sweet taste and are extremely tender. Bay scallops are popular in Florida. They are much smaller than the deep sea scallops. Scallops are sold either frozen or fresh.

Inspection and Grading

Only processed seafood is inspected by the federal government. The inspection comes under the USDI, the U.S. Department of the Interior. Inspection is voluntary, but only those businesses that process seafood under the continuous inspection of the USDI are permitted to use the fishery inspection emblem. The emblem confirms that the processed fish meet federal standards for wholesomeness.

Quality grades for processed fish and shellfish are similar to those used for poultry. Usually, only Grade A is found on the market.

The regulation and inspection of fresh fish is controlled by state and local laws.

Peach halves filled with scallops and garnished with bacon are ready for the broiler.

STORING SEAFOOD

All seafood is extremely perishable. Keep it loosely wrapped in the refrigerator until ready to be cooked. Store away from food such as butter and milk which may absorb its odor. Fresh seafood should be cooked within 24 hours of purchase.

Thaw frozen seafood in the refrigerator and cook promptly after defrosting. Remember, never refreeze seafood that has been thawed.

PREPARING SEAFOOD

Unless purchased directly from the fish boat, most fish will be pre-prepared, either dressed (internal organs and scales removed) or cut into steaks or fillets. Food service cooks order seafood pre-prepared for the type of recipe they will be using.

As seafood is cooked, the flesh loses its translucence. Seafood which is cooked until just done is tender and flavorful. It breaks into natural separations when touched with a fork. Remember, seafood cooks quickly. Overcooking makes it tough and dry.

Fish

Fish is a very versatile menu item. It may be cooked whole or in fillets and served as an entree. Fish is also used as an ingredient in a wide variety of recipes.

Fish have relatively little fat, but some contain more than others. Very lean fish such as tuna, halibut, ocean perch, and turbot are best when cooked by moist heat methods. Those with more fat such as salmon, herring, shad, and lake trout are best cooked by a dry heat method.

Broiling and Frying

Many fish may be broiled or fried. These methods are discussed in Unit 7.

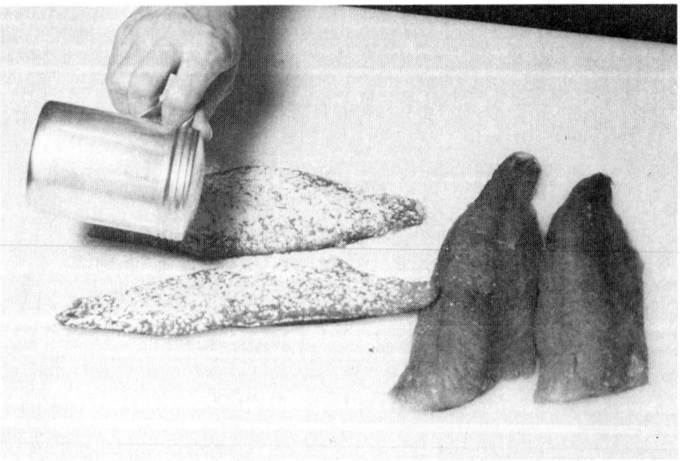

These fish fillets are being dredged with flour before frying.

Oven Frying

Oven frying produces a brown, crusty fish without actually frying in fat. The cooking process is very similar to that used for poultry. Dip the fish fillets in milk seasoned with salt and pepper and coat with bread crumbs, cracker crumbs, or rolled cornflakes. Butter a shallow baking dish and place the fish in it. The fish fillets should not touch each other. Bake at 450°F (230°C) until brown and flaky when tested with a fork — about 15 minutes.

Doesn't the high temperature toughen the fish since it is a protein food? Not in this case. The ***breading*** (the bread crumbs, cracker crumbs, or rolled cornflakes) protect the fish from the high heat. Because the fish is cooked only until done, it does not toughen.

Baking

Baking is a very simple cooking method. Place the fish in a greased baking dish and season as desired. Brush the fish with melted butter. Bake at 350°F (180°C) until the fish flakes easily. It will take from 25 to 40 minutes depending on the size of the fish.

A whole fish is delicious when stuffed with a seasoned bread stuffing before baking. The head and tail are frequently left on when the fish is to be stuffed.

These lobster tails were broiled in butter and lemon juice.

Poaching

Poaching is cooking in a small amount of simmering liquid. Place the fish in a frying pan and barely cover with liquid (often milk or water). The liquid may be seasoned as desired. Cover tightly and simmer 5 to 10 minutes until the fish flakes easily with a fork. A sauce may be made with the liquid and served over the fish.

If the fish to be poached is quite large, wrap it first in a fine, open-mesh cloth such as cheesecloth. The cloth will hold the fish together so it can be taken from the pan whole. Remove the cloth before serving.

Steaming

Steaming — cooking above simmering water — requires a special utensil called a fish steamer. It is a long, narrow pan with a tight-fitting cover and big enough to hold a six-pound, whole fish. It has a perforated rack to keep the fish out of the liquid.

Lightly grease the rack to keep the fish from sticking. Place the fish on the rack and lower into the pan. Add enough seasoned liquid to cover the bottom of the pan. Cover tightly. Place on top of the range or in the oven. Bring the water to a boil. Reduce heat and cook until fish flakes easily — 25 to 40 minutes, depending on the size of the fish.

Poached fish is often served with a creamy sauce.

Shellfish

Shellfish may also be prepared in several ways. Boiling and baking are the most popular methods. Some mollusks are eaten raw.

Shrimp

Shrimp are usually boiled either in the shell or already shucked. Either fresh or frozen shrimp may be used.

Bring enough water to a boil to barely cover the shrimp. Season as desired. Add fresh or thawed shrimp and bring the liquid to a boil again. Boil 8 to 10 minutes. When the shrimp are pink, they are done. Cool immediately. Save the cooking water as a base for soups and sauces.

Cooked shrimp may be iced and served as a cocktail or enjoyed in many other ways. One example is Shrimp Creole (KREE-ol), a mixture of shrimp and rich tomato sauce served on rice.

Lobsters and Crabs

Lobsters and crabs may be boiled, baked, stuffed, sauteed, or broiled. The meat may also be used for salads, sauces, and chowders, and is also served in sauces over rice.

The water to boil lobster or crab must be deep enough to totally cover the shellfish. Plunge the lobster or crab head first into the boiling water. Simmer for 10 to 12 minutes. Serve immediately with melted butter and lemon juice. If the seafood is to be used in other dishes, cool under cold running water before removing the meat.

Both lobster and crab are delicious served with specially seasoned sauces.

Mollusks

Oysters are often served raw as an appetizer. They can also be baked, stuffed, fried, poached, or made into a delicious stew.

Clams are sometimes served raw like oysters. The meat is also used in salads, mixed with seasoned bread crumbs, or made into the popular clam chowder.

Scallops are fried, prepared in cheese sauces, or broiled on a skewer.

This tasty oyster chowder is a filling meal on cold winter days.

Seasoning

Seafood has such a delicate flavor that it requires very little seasoning. The main ingredients used in seasoning seafood are butter to prevent drying, lemon juice, cheese, and salt and pepper.

CONVENIENCE FORMS OF FISH AND SHELLFISH

Because seafood spoils easily, it must be preserved for longer storage. Drying, smoking, and pickling of seafood have been used for centuries.

The advent of quick-freezing has made it possible to offer pre-prepared seafood in many different forms. All kinds of seafood are available already breaded and ready for frying. Fairly new on the market are mixtures of expensive shellfish, such as shrimp and crab and less expensive fish. The mixture is formed to resemble shrimp or crab legs. Such mixtures are popular because of their lower price.

Canned seafood was once the only seafood available to many inland regions of our country. Canned fish remains extremely popular as a recipe ingredient. Tuna, salmon, mackerel, and crabmeat are among the most well-known types of canned seafood.

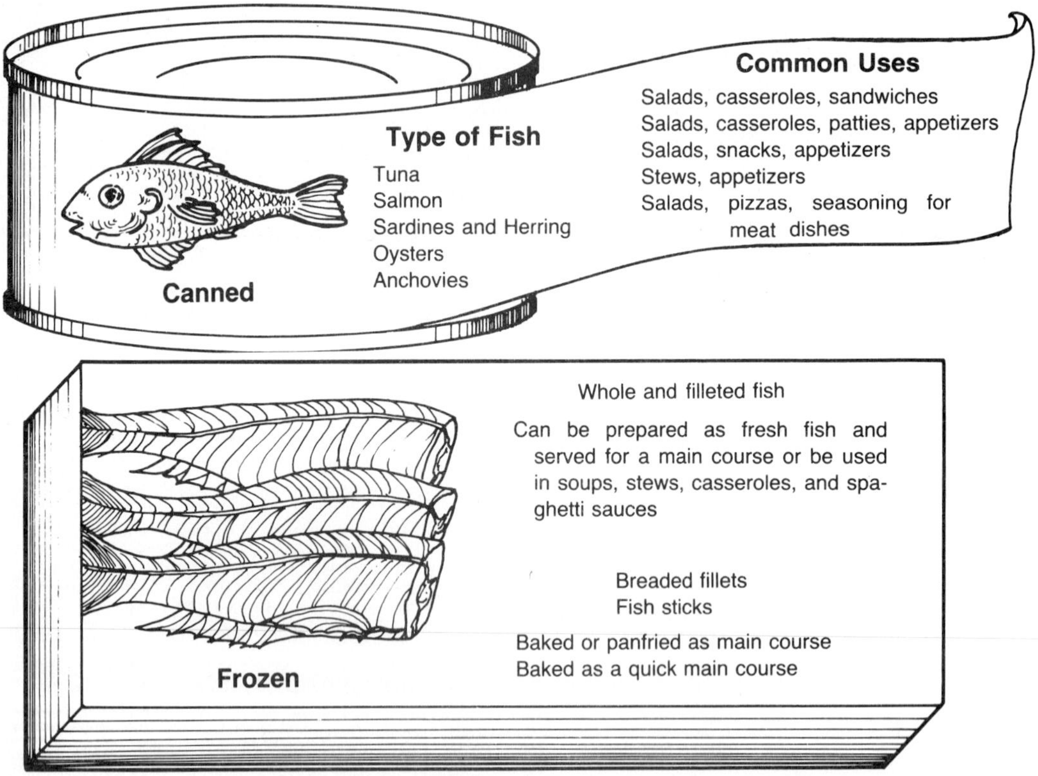

Type of Fish
Common Uses
Canned
Tuna
Salmon
Sardines and Herring
Oysters
Anchovies
Salads, casseroles, sandwiches
Salads, casseroles, patties, appetizers
Salads, snacks, appetizers
Stews, appetizers
Salads, pizzas, seasoning for meat dishes
Frozen
Whole and filleted fish
Can be prepared as fresh fish and served for a main course or be used in soups, stews, casseroles, and spaghetti sauces
Breaded fillets
Fish sticks
Baked or panfried as main course
Baked as a quick main course

Canned and frozen fish can save food preparation time. They are often combined with other foods such as pasta, rice, fruits, and vegetables to make delicious meals.

chapter recap

SUMMARY

Seafood is a term used to describe fish and shellfish. Both are popular food service items. Seafood is a versatile product. It can be used as an appetizer, an entree, or a salad ingredient. Because seafood is extremely perishable, it must be handled, stored, and prepared carefully. It should not be overcooked or its delicate taste and appearance will be destroyed. Fresh, frozen, and canned seafood are all used frequently in food service.

CHECK YOUR KNOWLEDGE

1. Describe the difference between fish and shellfish.

2. What governmental agency is responsible for checking the wholesomeness of fish and shellfish?

3. What grades of seafood are generally available?

4. List the signs of freshness in fish.

5. Briefly describe four of the methods of preparing fish.

6. Name the two types of shellfish.

7. How can fish be tested for doneness?

8. What happens to fish when it is overcooked?

9. Which shellfish are sometimes served raw?

10. List six forms of convenience seafood.

EXTEND YOUR LEARNING

1. Visit a supermarket and find as many convenience forms of seafood as possible. List the price of each and compare with the price of the same item fresh, if available. Make a chart to show the comparisons.

2. Select a fish recipe. Prepare it at home and ask your family to evaluate the product. Write a report on the response you received.

3. Visit a fish market and make a list of the fish and shellfish you are familiar with and those you are not. Research two you do not know and report to the class.

"What's your favorite vegetable?" Ruthann asked Jim as they walked toward class.

"Gosh, I can't think of any I really like except potatoes. French fried, of course," Jim answered.

Ruthann laughed, "When I was little, my mom would say, 'Ruthann, eat your carrots! They'll give you rosy cheeks!'"

"My mom always told me to eat my spinach so I'd have muscles like Popeye," replied Jim.

"Well, did you?" teased Ruthann as Jim held up his arm to show off his muscle. "Maybe there's something to all those old sayings. Carrots do contain lots of vitamin A and that does give you a smooth complexion and sparkling eyes."

"And spinach is high in iron and vitamin C," Jim added. "Too bad it doesn't work as fast for me as it did for Popeye! But sometimes vegetables can be so boring."

"But they don't have to be," Ruthann said. "My mom's vegetables always taste good. She says you have to time them just right so they don't get too soggy. I remember one time she fixed this really pretty platter with squash, cauliflower, onions, and mushrooms on it. She covered the whole thing with waxed paper and microwaved it. Those vegetables were really good!"

"Sounds okay if you like that kind of food." Jim sounded doubtful. "But you could never prepare vegetables that way in food service."

Ruthann was thoughtful. "I guess it's harder in restaurants, because you can't always serve the vegetables right away. It seems like a lot of restaurants don't try very hard to make their vegetables look or taste appealing. Let's ask Chef Robinson how we could do it."

chapter 15

vegetables

Set your goals

When you complete the study of this chapter, you should be able to . . .

- Define and correctly use the vocabulary terms.
- Identify and select a variety of vegetables.
- Correctly prepare fresh, frozen, canned, and dried vegetables using several methods.
- Store vegetables correctly.

Build your vocabulary

au gratin	produce
chlorophyll	pungent
deep-fat frying	sauté
du jour	scalloped
julienne	stir-fry
panfry	tubers

VEGETABLES IN THE MENU

A meal without vegetables would lose much of its appeal. Vegetables add beautiful colors, interesting flavors, and a variety of textures. They also contribute important vitamins and minerals to the diet.

In food service, the role of vegetables in the menu depends upon the operation. In schools, hospitals, and other institutions, vegetables have always played a key part in good nutrition. But some restaurants — especially in fast foods — limit vegetables to a leaf of lettuce and slice of tomato on a sandwich or french fried potatoes. That attitude is changing, however. Today, most restaurants know that well-prepared vegetables build profits as well as healthy bodies.

UNDERSTANDING VEGETABLES

Since there are dozens of different vegetables, it may seem impossible to remember how to prepare each. It's not difficult if you know that many vegetables are similar and require much the same cooking methods. Vegetables can be divided into groups by these similarities — by the part of the plant they come from, by color, by flavor, and by texture or moisture content.

Parts of the Plant

Vegetables come from the roots, leaves, stems, flowers, and seeds of plants. Some foods that are technically fruits are served as vegetables because they lack the sweet taste commonly associated with fruit. Tomatoes, green peppers, and eggplant are examples of these fruit-vegetables.

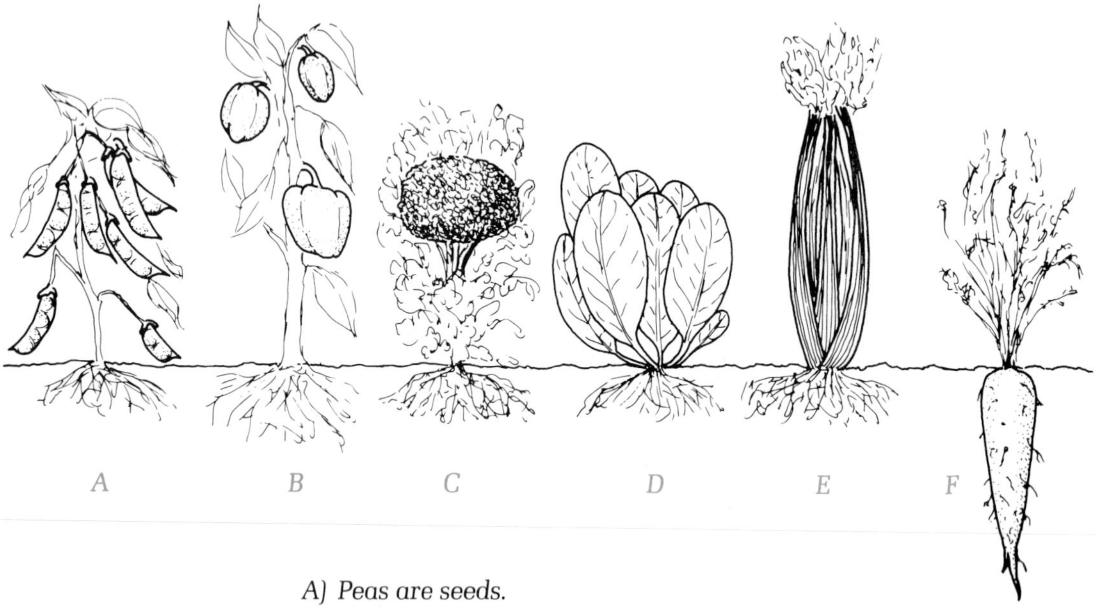

A) Peas are seeds.
B) Green peppers are the fruit of the plant.
C) Broccoli is the flower of the plant.
D) Spinach is a leaf.
E) Celery is the stem of the plant.
F) Carrots are roots.

Part of the Plant Eaten as Vegetable

Roots	Tubers	Bulbs	Flowers	Fruits	Leaves	Seeds	Stems and Shoots
Beets	Potatoes (white)	Garlic	Artichoke	Cucumber	Brussels Sprouts	Beans	Asparagus
Carrots		Leeks	Broccoli	Eggplant	Cabbage	Peas	Celery
Parsnips		Onions	Cauliflower	Okra	Chard	Corn	Chives
Potatoes (sweet)				Peppers	Lettuce		Fennel
Radishes				Pumpkin	Parsley		Rhubarb
Rutabagas				Squash	Spinach		
Turnips				Tomatoes	Greens		

The chart above shows the parts of the plant from which common vegetables come. The root vegetables may be actual roots like carrots and beets, or ***tubers*** (TOO-burrs), the thickened, fleshy portions of a root from which a new plant can grow. Potatoes, which are tubers, are starchy and filling. Some root vegetables are bulbs. Bulbs are round in shape and send roots down into the earth. Onions and garlic are examples of bulbs.

Color Families of Vegetables

Vegetables are sometimes grouped by color — white, yellow, red, or green. Here are some examples of vegetables in each color family:

- **White.** Cauliflower, potatoes, mushrooms, white turnips, and parsnips.
- **Yellow.** Carrots, pumpkins, sweet potatoes, corn, and rutabagas.
- **Red.** Beets, tomatoes, radishes, red cabbage, and red peppers.
- **Green.** Spinach, broccoli, peas, green beans, and green peppers.

Color is an important clue to the proper method of cooking. For instance, the green color in vegetables is caused by a substance called ***chlorophyll.*** Chlorophyll is easily destroyed by overcooking or by acid in the cooking water. However, the color of red vegetables is enhanced by the addition of an acid such as vinegar. Overcooking causes cauliflower to brown, but carrots turn a deeper orange when cooked. Preserving the lovely colors of vegetables is important since they add much to the appearance of a meal.

Color can also indicate the nutritive content of vegetables. For instance, yellow vegetables are usually high in vitamin A. Green vegetables are good sources of vitamin C and vitamin A. In general, the deeper the color, the higher the vitamin content.

The Flavor of Vegetables

Each vegetable has a characteristic flavor and aroma which makes it useful in food preparation. Some have strong flavors, others mild. You are probably familiar with the strong flavor and aroma of onions. They dominate the flavors of other foods cooked with them. Other strong-flavored vegetables include garlic, cabbage, cauliflower, broccoli, and turnips.

Mild-flavored vegetables contribute a delicate, but important flavor to food. For instance, mushrooms have a distinctive flavor that blends and adds a "touch of class" to chicken, fish, and other entrees.

The Texture of Vegetables

The texture of vegetables is closely connected to their moisture content. Celery and zucchini have a high moisture content and a crisp texture. They require little water for cooking and also have few calories.

Tubers, such as potatoes and some squash, are low-moisture vegetables. They have more calories and are more filling. They also require more water for cooking.

1. Cabbage
2. Celery
3. Asparagus
4. Cauliflower
5. Broccoli
6. Spinach
7. Iceberg Lettuce
8. Carrots
9. Radishes
10. Turnips
11. Pea Pods
12. Green Beans
13. Corn
14. Green Bell Peppers
15. Red Potatoes
16. Russet (Idaho) Potatoes
17. Acorn Squash
18. Red Tomato
19. Cucumbers
20. Bok Choy
21. Eggplant
22. Roma Tomatoes

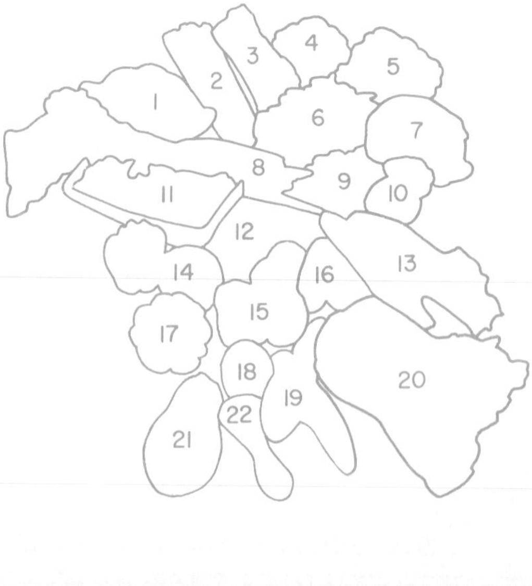

SELECTING VEGETABLES

Vegetables may be purchased in different forms — fresh, frozen, canned, or dried. Each is useful and has a definite place in food service.

Many restaurants take pride in preparing top-quality fresh vegetables. Their menus describe the choices in a way that stimulates customers' appetites and increases sales. "Garden fresh asparagus" or "glazed baby carrots" sounds more appealing than "vegetable ***du jour***" — vegetable of the day.

Fresh Vegetables

Of course, the vegetables must look and taste as good as their descriptions. That means careful selection and cooking. Here are some points to consider when choosing fresh vegetables:

- **Use.** Will the vegetable be served alone or as part of another dish? For instance, onions might be creamed and served separately, or chopped and added as flavoring to a meat dish. You need small, white onions for the first dish. For flavoring, large cooking onions can be used.
- **Color.** Bright color indicates freshness and quality.
- **Size and shape.** Vegetables that are much larger or smaller than usual or which have an odd shape will not have the best texture and flavor.
- **Condition.** Look for firm, crisp texture. Wilted leaves, soft spots, and decayed places indicate poor quality.

Quality Grades

Quality grades for fresh vegetables have been set by the USDA. They are designated by number. The top grade is No. 1.

Fresh vegetables are graded when they reach the market. Remember that fresh vegetables are perishable — they spoil easily. Careless handling may change the quality of a vegetable graded No. 1 in the morning to a much lower quality in the afternoon. But the vegetable will still carry the higher grade. Many food service operations buy regularly from the same ***produce*** (PRO-doos) vendors because they can count on good quality from them. (Produce refers to fresh fruits and vegetables.)

Food service establishments present vegetables in many different forms. The most visible use of fresh vegetables is on a salad bar.

Storing Fresh Vegetables

Most fresh vegetables lose quality quickly in storage. That is why only small amounts are purchased at a time. Not all vegetables have the same storage needs. Large food service operations often have several storage areas for fresh vegetables, each with a different temperature and humidity level. The chart below gives the best temperature and humidity for various vegetables. Small operations with limited storage store vegetables in the warmest area of the refrigerator and for shorter periods of time.

Remember these tips when storing fresh vegetables:

- Do not wash vegetables before storing unless they are very dirty.
- Store leafy vegetables in covered containers or plastic bags.
- Store tubers, roots, and bulb vegetables in a cool, dry place, off the floor. Do not refrigerate.

Frozen Vegetables

Frozen vegetables have several advantages for food service operations. They are closest to fresh in color, flavor, and nutrition. Unlike some fresh vegetables, they are available year-round and can be stored for months without losing quality. Pre-preparation work is already completed. It is also easy to predict the number of servings each package will yield. There is not waste as there is with fresh vegetables.

Storing Vegetables

Temperature and Humidity Guidelines

Temperature	0°F (18°C)	32°-40°F (0°-8°C)	40°-45°F (5°-8°C)	45°-50°F (8°-10°C)	Room Temperature
Humidity	**60-70%**	**85-95%**	**85-95%**	**75%**	**Varies**
Vegetables	All frozen vegetables	Asparagus Beets Cabbage Carrots Celery Corn Green onions Greens Parsley Radishes Turnips	Broccoli Cauliflower Green beans Green peas Green peppers Lettuce Tomatoes	Cucumbers Eggplant Okra Onions Potatoes Sweet potatoes Winter squash	Canned vegetables Dried vegetables Garlic

Quality Grades

Frozen vegetables are graded by the USDA as Grades A and B. There is no Grade C because only top quality vegetables are chosen for freezing. Grading is done by cooking a frozen sample of the vegetable according to the directions on the package. The cooked vegetable is graded for color, texture, and flavor.

Storing Frozen Vegetables

The high quality of frozen vegetables must be maintained through proper storage.

- Store vegetables at 0°F (−18°C) or colder in their original containers.
- Keep solidly frozen until ready to cook.
- Never refreeze vegetables after they have thawed.

Canned Vegetables

Canned vegetables are a convenience form of vegetables often used in food service. They are usually less expensive than fresh or frozen vegetables and easy to prepare. However, vegetables often lose color and flavor in the high heat used in the canning process. Not all vegetables are available in canned form.

Quality Grades

Canned vegetables are graded for quality much like frozen vegetables, grades A, B, and C. Grade A vegetables are the highest quality and the most expensive. Food buyers consider the operation's budget and quality standards, plus the intended use when deciding what grade to buy. For instance, the best restaurants order Grade A because they are very concerned about the appearance and attractiveness of the food. An institution, such as a school, is more concerned with providing the most nutrition for the least money. That buyer might order one of the lesser grades.

Food service buyers also purchase different grades of vegetables according to how they will be used. Grade A tomatoes are whole and uniform in size. If the tomatoes are to be used whole, Grade A would be ordered. Grade B might be used in a casserole. They are less colorful, have more watery juice, and vary in size. Grade C tomatoes are broken up in pieces and have paler, thinner juice. They are fine for soups or sauces.

Canned tomatoes are one of the most frequently used vegetables in the food service industry. The grade of tomato chosen depends on how it will be used.

Storing Canned Vegetables

Review the procedures for storing foods on pages 72-75. Although canned goods have a long storage life, they need proper care during storage.

Dried Vegetables

Dried vegetables such as dried beans and peas add protein to the diet at a low cost. They are often combined with a small amount of meat as an entree or used as a side dish. Chili, ham and beans, and split pea soup are popular menu items that use dried vegetables.

The market offers many different types of dried beans such as navy, kidney, pinto, soy, or lima. Peas are either green or yellow and usually split for easy cooking. Lentils are similar to dried yellow peas. Black-eyed peas are especially popular in the southern region of the United States.

Dried vegetables are graded as US No. 1, 2, and 3. US No. 1 dried vegetables are bright in color and uniform in size. There are no broken pieces, damaged seeds, or foreign objects such as sticks. Lower grades are poorer quality.

Not all dried vegetables are beans and peas. Dried potatoes are important in food service. They are most frequently mashed. Dried potatoes are also used in ***scalloped*** potatoes — potatoes cooked with a white sauce. ***Au gratin*** (oh GRAT-n) potatoes, made with a sauce and a lightly browned crust of bread crumbs and cheese, are also often made from dried potatoes. Other dried vegetables such as flaked onions, garlic, and parsley are used to add flavor to many dishes. Dried vegetables save preparation time, are easy to store, and are always available.

VEGETABLE PRE-PREPARATION

Fresh vegetables need some pre-preparation before cooking. Since vegetables grow close to the soil, they must be cleaned thoroughly before cooking. Remember, however, that some vitamins and minerals dissolve in water. That is why fresh vegetables are washed quickly under cold, running water, but not soaked.

Here are some additional pre-preparation guidelines:

- **Root and stem vegetables**. Scrub with a stiff brush. Remove any blemishes such as cuts, bruises, and the eyes of potatoes with a sharp knife. Most vitamins and minerals in potatoes are found either in the skin or directly underneath. If you must remove the skin, use a vegetable peeler to remove a very thin layer.

- **Stem vegetables**. Asparagus needs special attention because the stems have scales that sometimes catch dirt. Strip the scales from the stems and wash out the soil. Celery also may be very dirty. Scrub the stems with a stiff brush and trim any brown spots. Save coarse outer stems for soup.

- **Pod and seed vegetables**. Green beans are often dirty because they grow close to the ground. Place the beans in a colander and wash under cold water. Snap off the ends with a knife. Leave the beans whole or slice.

Peas need to be shucked (pods removed) and rinsed before cooking. If the peas are very young and tender, some of the pods may be sliced and cooked with the peas.

Fresh corn should be husked and the silk removed. Look for any damage to the kernels and remove with a sharp knife.

- **Flower vegetables**. Broccoli and cauliflower can harbor insects in their tightly closed buds. Soak in salted water for a short time to bring out any insects. Large broccoli stems should be split and, if tough, peeled.

- **Fruit-vegetables**. Tomatoes require very little pre-preparation. Wash thoroughly. Slice, quarter, or leave whole, depending upon the recipe.

Slice off the top of green peppers, remove the seeds and the pulpy interior. Slice into rings, strips, or dice as needed.

Eggplant turns brown quickly after slicing. Cut just before use and place the slices in water to which lemon juice has been added. The skin should be removed if it is tough.

Celery should always be cleaned with a stiff brush under running water. Any brown spots and coarse stems should be removed.

Lettuce is placed in a colander, thoroughly rinsed, and then left to drain before being used.

- **Leafy vegetables**. Spinach is frequently gritty with soil. Cut off the tough stems. Fill the sink with cold water and wash the greens by lifting them up and down in the water. Remove the greens and place in a colander. Drain the water from the sink and rinse any grit down the drain. Wash the spinach again, repeating the operation until no more grit can be felt in the sink after rinsing. Directions for cleaning other leafy vegetables were given in Chapter 10.

Pre-preparation also involves cutting food into smaller pieces. They may be sliced, diced, chopped, or cut ***julienne*** style, that is cut into narrow strips. Be sure to always cut vegetables into equal-sized pieces. The French knife and chopping board are used to cut vegetables into smaller pieces. Salad knives and paring knives are also used in vegetable preparation.

Many food service kitchens use large pieces of equipment to make vegetable pre-preparation more efficient. Food choppers, vertical cutters, food slicers, and blenders are used to cut vegetables into small pieces. Electric vegetable peelers can remove vegetable skins quickly. Blenders and mixers are used to make salad dressings, vegetable sauces, and mashed potatoes.

Canned and frozen vegetables need no pre-preparation. Dried vegetables such as peas and beans need to be soaked, usually overnight, to restore the water that was removed in drying.

PREPARING VEGETABLES

Vegetables can easily become mushy, tasteless, and lose color if not cooked correctly. Follow these principles of vegetable cookery:

- Use as little water as possible.
- Do not overcook.
- Cook in small batches as close to serving time as possible. Holding warm vegetables for serving causes loss of color and soggy texture.
- Suit the method of cooking to the color family and to the strength or mildness of flavor.

A salad maker is being used to shred this cabbage for cole slaw. This machine can slice, shred, or grate raw fruits and vegetables without tearing or mashing them.

Fresh Vegetables

Fresh vegetables may be prepared in a variety of ways. The method of cooking should be appropriate for the type of vegetable.

Boiling and Steaming

When boiling vegetables, always boil the water before adding the vegetables. For strong-flavored vegetables, use enough water to cover. For mild-flavored vegetables, use only enough water to cook. Cook strong-flavored vegetables, green vegetables, and white vegetables uncovered. Other vegetables may be cooked covered. When vegetables have finished cooking, drain the water and keep the vegetables warm for serving. Add the vegetable water to the stock pot for use in soups, sauces, and gravies.

With the development of compartment steamers, steaming vegetables has largely replaced boiling. The vegetables may be cooked in smaller quantities and the cooking time closely regulated. This gives higher quality vegetables. Review the use of the compartment steamer, page 134.

Baking

This is a favorite way of cooking some varieties of potatoes and squash. The use of the microwave oven makes it possible to have baked potatoes cooked to order. However, when a large number of baked potatoes are needed, the usual practice is to steam the potatoes until almost done. Then they are wrapped in foil. Just before serving, they are popped into a very hot oven to finish baking.

Idaho baking potatoes are large, oval potatoes noted for their white color and mealy texture. They are the most popular baking potato. These potatoes may also be baked in their skins until soft. Then the inside is scooped out and mashed with milk and seasonings. The mashed potato is heaped into each half potato shell and reheated in the microwave oven just before serving. These are called "stuffed baked" or "twice baked" potatoes.

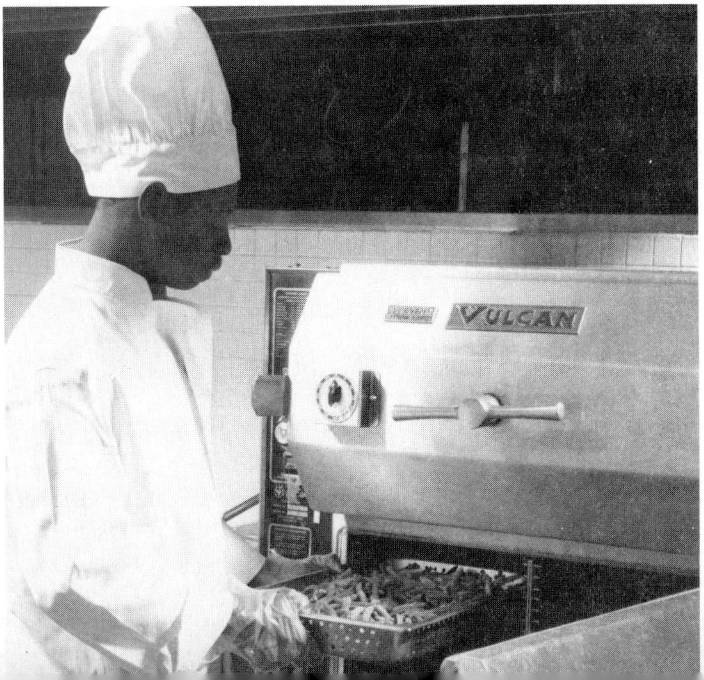

Green beans are being loaded into the compartment steamer. The beans will be steamed instead of boiled, therefore yielding a better quality vegetable dish.

Broiling

Occasionally, vegetables are broiled. This method is used mostly to brown or glaze partially cooked vegetables. Tomatoes, however, are broiled raw. Fresh mushrooms, either whole or sliced, may be broiled after brushing them with cooking oil.

Panfrying, Sautéing, and Stir-frying

To ***panfry***, use a small amount of oil in the bottom of the pan to coat the vegetables. Turn the vegetables just once after they brown on the bottom to avoid overcooking. Hash brown potatoes are prepared using this method.

To ***sauté*** (saw-TAY) or ***stir-fry***, pour a little oil or butter in the bottom of the pan. Add the chopped vegetables and flip or stir briskly until cooked. Sautéing is often a preliminary preparation step. You will often read in the recipe, "Sauté the chopped onions in the butter until golden brown."

Stir-frying is very similar to sautéing. However, in stir-frying, the vegetables are stirred, usually with spatulas, during cooking. The vegetables are considered done when tender-crisp, not soft. Stir-frying is a popular Oriental cooking technique. A combination of vegetables such as green peppers, celery, snow peas, and carrots are used in stir-fried dishes.

Deep-fat Frying

Vegetables are sometimes cooked by ***deep-fat frying*** — frying in enough fat to cover. For instance, a spear of broccoli might be dipped in batter and fried in deep fat. The most popular vegetables prepared this way are onion rings and potatoes. Specific directions for deep-fat frying are in Chapter 24.

Frozen Vegetables

Frozen vegetables, like fresh vegetables, are either broiled or steamed. Because freezing breaks down some of the structure of plants, frozen vegetables cook faster than fresh. Often there is enough water from the ice crystals on the frozen vegetables for cooking and no additional water is added. As the vegetables begin to cook, separate the pieces so the cooking will be even.

For convenience, many companies offer vegetables in sauces or interesting combinations. They are ready to cook and serve. Sometimes the vegetables are packaged in plastic bags that can be dropped into boiling water for cooking. Food service operations have been quick to adopt these innovations because they provide variety without added preparation.

Deep-fried vegetables are a common appetizer on many restaurant menus. Mushrooms, cauliflower, zucchini, onions, and green peppers are the vegetables most often prepared in this way.

Canned Vegetables

Since canned vegetables are already cooked, they need only be heated and seasoned. Drain the vegetables, putting the liquid from the can in a pan. Boil the liquid until there is just enough to heat the vegetables. Add the vegetables and heat with butter and seasoning. Do not overcook.

There are several ways to add interest to canned vegetables. Corn can be mixed with chopped pimiento and green pepper, or green beans with bacon bits and a sprinkle of browned, slivered almonds. Spinach is good with sliced, hard-cooked eggs and a dash of nutmeg.

Seasonings for Vegetables

Green Vegetables	Red Vegetables	White Vegetables	Yellow Vegetables
Asparagus	Beets	Cauliflower	Carrots
Chili powder	Cinnamon	Beau monde	Black pepper
Curry	Ginger	Parsley flakes	Onion flakes
White Pepper	Onion flakes	Sweet basil	Thyme leaves
Corn	Savory	White pepper	Summer squash
Nutmeg	Red Cabbage	Onions	Beau monde
Onion flakes	Black pepper	Curry	Cilantro
White pepper	Caraway seeds	Parsley flakes	Parsley flakes
Green beans	Tomatos	Sweet basil	
Mace	Black pepper	White pepper	
Onion flakes	Cumin		
White pepper	Garlic powder		
Green peas	Oregano		
Celery salt	Sweet basil		
Garlic powder			
Onion flakes			
Lima beans			
Allspice			
Black pepper			
Dry mustard			
Spinach			
Black pepper			
Nutmeg			
Onion powder			
Zucchini			
Beau monde			
Onion flakes			

Dried Vegetables

Many dried vegetables such as dried onions and garlic flakes are really used as seasonings. Some food service operations use dried potato products regularly.

Dried peas and beans require long cooking in a sauce or soup stock. In food service, canned baked beans are usually used and the cook adds a "secret" ingredient or ingredients to individualize them.

Seasoning Vegetables

The chart on page 235 shows suggested seasonings for various vegetables. Herbs and spices add flavor and aroma to food dishes. Care must be taken in the selection and use of seasonings. Many have a ***pungent*** (sharp) flavor and aroma. Always season with a light hand.

Vegetable Casseroles

Vegetable casseroles add variety to a menu. They are popular with customers. Baked beans and au gratin potatoes are examples of vegetable casseroles.

Sauces for Vegetables

Sauces are excellent flavor enhancers and are used frequently with vegetables. A sauce should be freshly made, have a light flavor and consistency, and should not be greasy.

Here are some sauce suggestions for vegetables:

- Cauliflower with hollandaise (a sauce with lemon, butter, and egg).
- Broccoli or asparagus with cheese sauce.
- Zucchini with tomato sauce.
- Green beans with browned butter sauce.
- Carrots with mint sauce.
- Beets with sweet-sour sauce.

✔ standards ✔

Cooked Vegetables

Appearance

✔ Cut in uniform pieces.

✔ Combination of vegetables and garnish is appropriate.

Color

✔ Bright, natural colors.

Flavor

✔ Full, natural flavor.

✔ Garnish, if any, complements flavor of vegetable.

Texture

✔ Just tender, not mushy.

Seasoning

✔ Does not dominate the flavor of the vegetable.

SUMMARY

Vegetables play an important part in most food service menus. Their wide variety of colors, textures, and flavors add interest to meals. They are excellent sources of vitamins and minerals. Vegetables may be prepared in many ways, but improper preparation can destroy nutrients and cause loss of texture, color, and flavor. Care must also be taken when storing vegetables, whether they are fresh, frozen, canned, or dried.

chapter recap

CHECK YOUR KNOWLEDGE

1. What is the role of vegetables in a food service menu?

2. List two vegetables from each of the following categories: root, bulb, flower, seed, leaf, stem, and fruit.

3. List three vegetables from each of the following color families: white, yellow, green, and red.

4. What gives green vegetables their color?

5. Name three rules to remember when storing fresh vegetables.

6. Why do food service buyers purchase different quality grades of canned vegetables?

7. List the basic pre-preparation steps that apply to all fresh vegetables.

8. What are some ways the nutritional content of vegetables can be preserved?

9. Name five methods that can be used to cook vegetables.

10. List three convenience forms of vegetables used in food service.

EXTEND YOUR LEARNING

1. Pressure cook three portions of fresh green beans. Cook the first portion for three minutes, the second portion for five minutes, and the third portion for ten minutes. Be sure to exhaust the steam and cool the vegetables immediately after each timing. Describe and rate the color, flavor, and texture of each portion. Prepare a written report of your findings.

2. Review the chart on storing vegetables. Then check each storage area in your classroom kitchen against the recommended temperatures in the chart. Make suggestions if you find problems.

"Jim, Tony, and David were at Jim's house one Saturday afternoon. They were trying to decide what to do that night.

"Let's see a movie," said David.

"No, there's nothing good on this week," answered Jim. "Maybe we could quick call some of the girls in our foods class and take them out to eat."

"When did you become a millionaire?" asked Tony. "Right now I'm not sure I have enough money to take myself out to eat, and you want me to pay for a girl too!"

"Well, everywhere in town can't be that expensive," said Jim. "Why don't we look at the newspaper ads for ideas for a cheap meal." He found the entertainment section of the newspaper.

"Here's one," said Tony, pointing. "All the spaghetti you can eat for $3.95. I could manage that."

"They wouldn't make a profit on you, either," said David. "I know how you like spaghetti!"

"The lasagna doesn't cost much there either," said Jim. "That's one dish I really love."

"How do you think they can sell food that cheap?" asked David.

"Pasta is an inexpensive food," said Tony. "It can be used to stretch a little meat or seafood a long way. It fills people up fast, too, so they don't eat as much as you'd think."

"How did you get to be such an expert on pasta, Tony?" Jim asked.

"Well, my Uncle Marco is a cook in an Italian restaurant. I once asked him why Italian restaurants were cheaper than ones that serve steak."

"This place sounds good to me," said David. "Let's see if we can find a date. We've left it till the last minute here."

"I hope Ruthann isn't busy," said Jim. "She really likes spaghetti.""

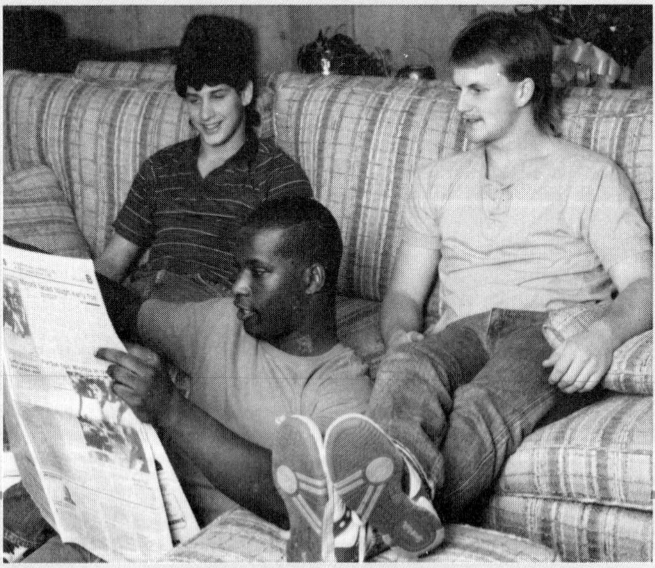

chapter 16

cereals, rice, and pasta

Set your goals

When you complete the study of this chapter, you should be able to . . .

- Define and correctly use the vocabulary terms.
- Identify various cereal, rice, and pasta products.
- Summarize the principles of starch cookery.
- Correctly prepare cereals, rice, and pasta.

Build your vocabulary

al dente	extenders
converted rice	parboiled rice
durum wheat	pasta

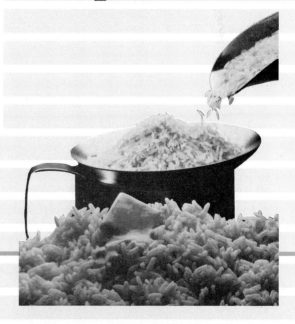

GRAIN PRODUCTS

Cereals, rice, and pasta are studied together because they have many similarities. First, they are all grain products. Grains include such familiar foods as wheat, corn, rice, barley, and oats. As grain products, they provide the body with similar nutrients. Grain products are basic foods throughout the world. They fill the body's need for heat and energy in an inexpensive way. When they are combined with small amounts of animal protein, such as meat or milk, they give the body the complete protein it needs. Grain products also provide a valuable source of iron and most B vitamins.

Grain products are all cooked similarly. That is because the main component of grain is starch. If you understand the principles of starch cookery, you can properly prepare any food in which starch is a main ingredient.

Starch helps thicken food because it can absorb liquid and swell. Heat speeds this process. Cooking grains causes this absorption and thickens the product. However, if cooked incorrectly, hard lumps of starch form. Have you ever eaten lumpy gravy or spaghetti that is all stuck together? If you follow the preparation directions in this chapter, you can avoid such problems.

CEREALS

To most people, "cereal" means beakfast foods. Cereals come in many forms. Cold cereals come ready-to-serve. Other cereals, such as oatmeal and grits, are cooked and served hot.

There are many other uses of cereals and cereal products in cooking. Here are some examples:

- Flour, made from ground grain, is the basic ingredient in baked products.
- Cereal products, such as cornstarch and flour, are used as thickeners for foods like puddings, sauces, and soups.
- Cereals and cereal products are used as ***extenders***. Extenders are inexpensive ingredients that are combined with more expensive foods to make them go farther. For example, bread crumbs or oatmeal are often used as an extender in meat loaf.

Cooking Cereal

Cooking improves the taste, flavor, and digestibility of cereals. Grains contain a hard, outer coating called bran. Sometimes this is removed during the manufacturing of the cereal product. If it has not been removed, cooking will soften it. The more bran, the longer it will take to cook the product. Follow these general directions for cooking cereal. Check the package directions for exact amounts and cooking times.

1. Measure the correct amount of water and salt. Bring to a boil. If milk is called for, be careful not to scorch it.
2. Measure the correct amount of cereal.
3. Stir coarse cereal directly into the boiling water, stirring all the time.

   Mix fine cereal with cold water before adding it to the hot liquid. The amount of cold water must be counted as part of the total water needed.

4. Reduce heat and cook until soft, stirring occasionally.
5. Serve immediately. If cereal must stand, cover tightly to prevent a scum from forming on the top.

RICE

Of all the grains, rice is used the most in entrees. It is often substituted for potatoes as an accompaniment for meat, fish, or poultry. Fried rice — a Chinese dish — is one example. Rice is also very useful as an extender for meat, poultry, or fish. Spanish Rice, Tuna and Rice Casserole, Rice Ring with Creamed Chicken, and Stuffed Green Peppers all use rice in this way. Because of its bland flavor, rice can also be used in soups and in desserts like rice pudding.

✓ standards ✓

Cooked Cereals

Appearance

✓ Does not look lumpy.

Flavor

✓ Flavorful, but not starchy.

Texture

✓ Moist, but not soupy.

✓ Free from lumps.

Chicken and rice is a popular dish that is very filling. The rice serves as an extender for the chicken, as well as a good accompaniment.

Kinds of Rice

Before processing, rice has an outer hull and a brown skin covering the starchy, white interior. Processing removes part or all of these coverings along with most of the vitamins and minerals. These are the various kinds of rice available:

- **Brown rice.** It still has the brown skin. It is more nutritious than other types, but takes longer to cook.
- **Polished rice.** The brown skin has been removed through buffing. Rice is graded according to the length of the grain. Long grain rice is considered top quality. It cooks easily and the grains do not stick together. The shorter-grained rices tend to become sticky when cooked. (This is an advantage when making a rice ring or pudding.) Polished or white rice is often used in food service because it is popular with customers.
- **Converted rice.** Rice that has been processed before polishing so the nutrients from the brown coating are driven into the kernel is called ***converted rice.*** Converted rice is more nutritious than polished rice, but more expensive. The kernels retain their shape well during cooking.
- **Parboiled rice.** Quick-cooking or precooked rice is also called ***parboiled rice.*** It has been partially cooked under pressure and then dried. The grains stay firm and separated. This rice is often used in food service because it cooks quickly and can be held for long periods before serving without becoming sticky.

Cooking Rice

Rice may be cooked in a variety of ways, but boiling and steaming are used most often. Rice should not be stirred during cooking.

Boiling

Follow these directions for boiling rice:

1. Place all ingredients in a heavy pot. Bring to a boil, stirring occasionally.
2. Cover, reduce heat to very low and cook without stirring for 20 minutes. All water should be absorbed and the rice should appear dry.
3. Test for doneness by tasting a grain. It should be soft.
4. Fluff with a fork to prevent steaming. Cover. Serve as soon as possible.

Steaming

These are the steps for steaming rice:

1. Bring the water to a boil. Combine all ingredients in a shallow steam pan. Place the pan in the steamer for the recommended time, usually 20 minutes for polished rice or 10 minutes for parboiled rice.
2. Test the rice for doneness.
3. Fluff the rice with a fork to allow steam to escape. Cover. Serve as soon as possible.

✓ standards ✓

Rice

Appearance

✓ Fluffy and dry.

Flavor

✓ Bland, mild, never starchy.

Texture

✓ Grains firm and separate.

✓ Tender.

PASTA

Pasta, an Italian word meaning "dough," is a term used for a variety of products ranging from spaghetti to noodles. ***Durum wheat*** is used to make flour for pasta. This type of wheat is very high in gluten, a protein found in wheat. (You will read more about gluten in Chapter 17.) Pasta made from durum wheat will not disintegrate, if cooked correctly. It will be tender but keep its shape.

In the United States, a pasta dish is usually the entree. In Italy, pasta is often served before the entree or as a side dish with the entree.

Kinds of Pasta

There are four general types of pasta. Each of these types has many, many variations known by Italian names. Most pastas are made by the same dough and differ mainly in shape. See the chart on page 244 for a description of various kinds of pastas.

Spaghetti is one of the most familiar forms of pasta. When a well-seasoned sauce is added, spaghetti makes a delightful meal.

Kinds of Pasta

Kind	Name	Description	Use
Flat	Mafalda Riccia	Flat, thin Flat, wide, curly edges	Salad; with sauce
Macaroni	Elbow Manicotti # 9 Ringli Straight	Curved, hollow tube Large, hollow tube Cut or uncut Slices of straight macaroni Hollow tubes	Salads; casseroles Stuffed With sauce; in casseroles Soups; salads Casseroles
Noodles (egg)	Broad Fettucine Fine	Variable width and length Wide, short Sliced finely	Casseroles Baked dishes Soups
Spaghetti	Fuselli Linguini Rotini Vermicelli	Curly Medium fine Spirals Very fine	Thick cream sauce Sauce and meat Sauce and meat Soups
Others	Alphabet Bows Seashells	Large and small Small Large	Soups Salads, casseroles, soups Salads, casseroles stuffing

Cooking Pasta

Pasta is always cooked by boiling. It may then be added to other ingredients for additional preparation or served as is. To boil pasta:

1. Bring water to a full boil. Add salt. Adding a bit of oil will help prevent sticking.
2. Add the pasta gradually, stirring all the time. Be careful not to break the strands of long spaghetti.
3. Boil macaroni 5-7 minutes, spaghetti and lasagna 6-8 minutes, and noodles 4-5 minutes.
4. Test for doneness. Pasta should be cooked ***al dente*** (an Italian term meaning "to the teeth"). When a small piece is chewed, it should be tender, but there should be a slight resistance to the teeth. Avoid overcooking.
5. Drain in a colander. Return the pasta to the pan and add butter or oil. Stir carefully to avoid breaking the pasta.

✔ standards ✔

Pasta

Appearance

✔ Retains original form.

Flavor

✔ Bland pleasant, never pasty.

Texture

✔ Tender but firm.

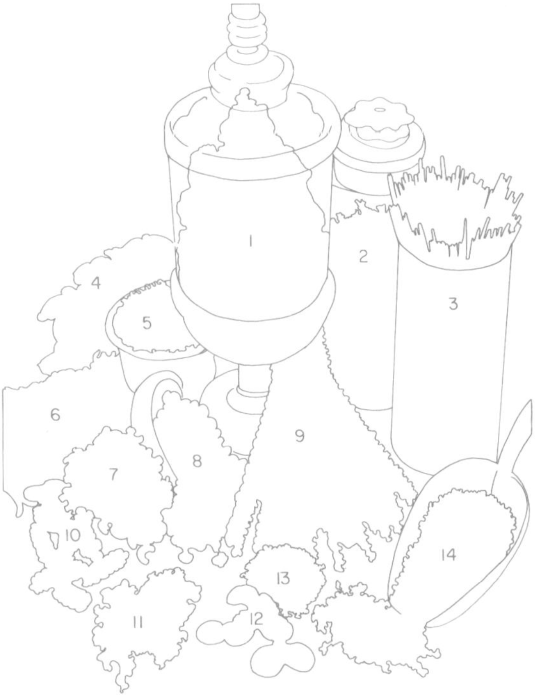

1. *Manicotti*
2. *Egg Noodles*
3. *Spaghetti*
4. *Large Shells*
5. *Kluski Egg Noodles*
6. *Cut Spaghetti*
7. *Elbow Macaroni*
8. *Small Shells*
9. *Fusilli*
10. *Robini*
11. *Curly Egg Noodles*
12. *Bows*
13. *Stars*
14. *Alphabets*

A PROFESSIONAL CHEF PREPARES LOBSTER SPINACH FETTUCINE

One-half cup of heavy cream is brought to a boil in a saucepan. The juice of half a lemon is added.

Fresh spinach is added. The mixture is cooked on high heat until the cream is reduced.

Precooked, herbed fettucine is added to the mixture.

The mixture is tossed in the pan, slightly above the flame.

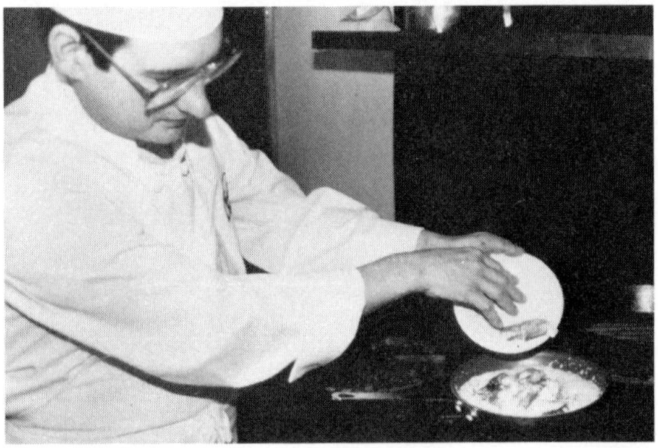

Precooked lobster meat is added.

The mixture is cooked until it thickens, tossing occasionally. When completed, the saucepan is removed from the heat. Parmesan cheese is added to the top of the mixture.

The finished product: Lobster Spinach Fettucine.

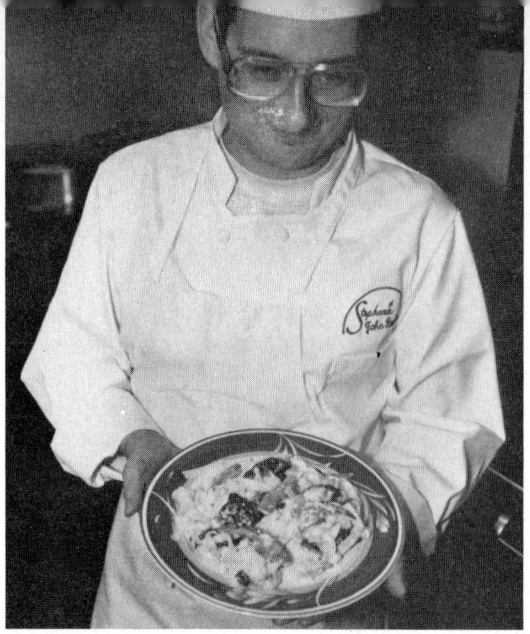

A proud chef presents his delicacy.

Pasta as the Entree

Although some pasta products may be chilled and used as a base for a salad, a sauce is usually added to pasta after boiling. Pasta dishes are a high profit entree in food service. A small amount of expensive meat and cheese adds color and flavor to inexpensive pastas. Popular dishes are made with each type.

The flat ribbon pasta such as lasagna is cooked, layered with cheese, meat, tomato sauce, and topped with Parmesan cheese. It is then baked. Many different cheeses, meats, and sauces may be used.

The hollow tubes such as macaroni are usually served with a cheese sauce or tomato and meat sauce. The larger tubes are stuffed with various mixtures, covered with a sauce, and baked in the oven.

The solid tubes such as spaghetti are often served Italian-style with tomato sauce and often meat. Spaghetti with white clam sauce is gaining popularity as an entree.

Noodles are often thought of as a soup ingredient, but they may also be fried and served in place of potatoes. Noodles are frequently combined in a casserole with seafood or poultry and a sauce. A noodle ring with creamed seafood or chicken is an attractive entree.

CARE AND STORAGE OF CEREALS, RICE, AND PASTA

These products keep well if properly stored. Be sure containers are tightly covered to keep out insects and rodents. Moisture can cause loss of flavor. Store cereals, rice, and pasta at room temperature.

Once these products are cooked, they must be kept warm until they are served. If not held properly, they can sour and become inedible. Refrigerate any leftovers promptly.

SUMMARY

Cereals, rice, and pasta are all inexpensive and versatile grain products. Although they are sometimes served plain, they combine well with other foods. Cereal grains are often used as breakfast foods. When finely ground, as in flour, cereals are used as thickeners and as a basic ingredient in baked products. Rice and pasta may be used in many ways in the menu, from salad to dessert. Special care must be taken to cook these products properly.

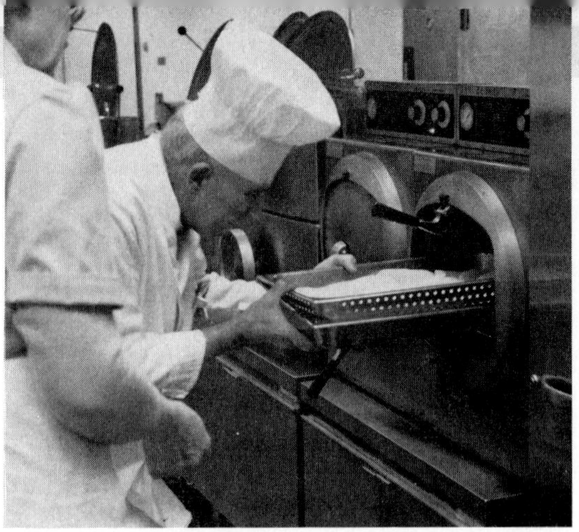

chapter recap

CHECK YOUR KNOWLEDGE

1. What are some familiar foods that come from grain?
2. For what nutrients are grain products a good source?
3. Name the main component of grain products.
4. Explain why some grain products are used as thickeners in cooking.
5. How can lumps be prevents when cooking cereal?
6. What are the four kinds of rice?
7. What kind of wheat is used to make pasta? Why?
8. Name four kinds of pasta.
9. Pasta should be cooked "al dente." What does this mean?
10. Give guidelines for storing pasta.

EXTEND YOUR LEARNING

1. Visit a supermarket and compare the price of ready-to-eat cereals and cereals that require cooking. Figure out the cost per serving of similar products.
2. Cook 1/2 cup each of converted rice, short-grain rice, and parboiled rice according to package instructions. Note differences in appearance, texture, and flavor. Write a brief summary of your conclusions.
3. Cook spaghetti according to package directions. Remove and test samples at 7, 10, and 15 minutes. Record your description of the texture of each sample. When was it "al dente?"

Unit 6

The Bake Station

Fragrant, hot breads, fancy cakes, homemade cookies, and specialty pies seem to draw everyone's attention. With just a few, simple ingredients, bakers produce creations which delight the food service customer.

In this unit you will learn the basic skills needed to work in the bake station. Products of the bake station include yeast breads, quick breads, cakes, cookies, pies, and pastries.

Although the ingredients in these delicious products are simple, the skills that produce them are not. In addition to skill, products of the bake station require a great deal of time. Imagine making 50 pies on a tight deadline. There's no time for mistakes!

Because of the long preparation time needed, much of the work in the bake station is done before other members of the professional cooking team report to work. It is cooler at that time of day and baking early ensures that all the baked goods will be ready when they are needed throughout the day.

Although many baked products appear to be freshly baked, they were probably prepared several days ahead of time and frozen. Some food service operations buy their baked products frozen, instead of preparing them from scratch. However, the term "homemade" on a menu certainly has customer appeal!

"Here, catch, Ruthann," called Jim, tossing her what looked like a golf ball.

"Hey, that's hard!" said Ruthann, catching it like a pro. "Oh, I know. It's a gluten ball. You did that experiment in the book."

"It's hard to believe," said Jim, "that soft, powdery, white flour could have anything so hard in it. When I washed out all the starch, I had a gluey, stretchy mess. Then when I baked it, it turned hard. It reminds me of the bread balls I used to make for fishing. When I tried it with cake flour, it didn't work at all. Chef Robinson said some kinds of wheat have lots of gluten, and others have hardly any at all."

Ruthann examined the ball. She said, "I remember when I was little, Mom used to make bread. She'd mix it and toss it on a board. Then she would knead it for ten minutes or so. Developing the strength of the flour, she said. When the time was up, she told me to stick my finger in it. If the hole popped right back, the dough was ready to rise. Now I know why the bread has to be kneaded. Do you know what? Now that Mom is working, Dad makes the bread."

"Why not?" said Jim. "I think it will be neat to learn how to make bread. What experiment did you do?"

"The effect of temperature on yeast," answered Ruthann. "Boiling water sure kills yeast flat. But in the jar with warm water and sugar in it, the yeast grew until it ran over."

"Like Chef Robinson says," Jim remarked, "yeast really is alive. Next week we get to make yeast rolls for the principal's dinner. Hope we get to eat some of them. Say, I'm hungry. Let's stop at the bakery and get a couple of those big raised doughnuts, the kind with the sticky tops. Okay?"

"Okay," said Ruthann. "But we'd better hurry or we'll miss our bus."

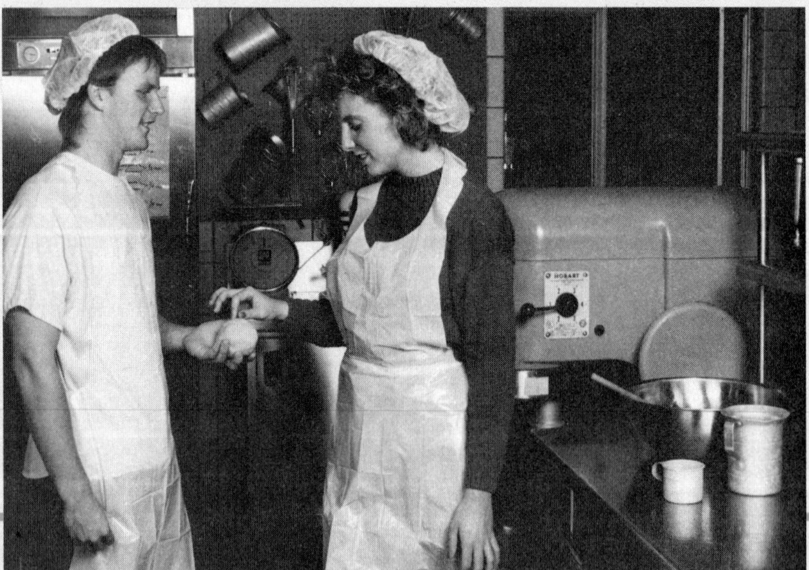

chapter 17

products of the bake station

Set your goals

When you complete the study of this chapter, you should be able to . . .

- Define and correctly use the vocabulary terms.
- Identify tools, and small equipment used in the bake station and demonstrate their use.
- Identify the functions of ingredients used in baking.

Build your vocabulary

bench
carousel oven
fermentation
gluten
hydrogenated shortening
leaveners
proofer
shortening

THE BAKE STATION

Because some food service operations lack space or experienced personnel, baked goods are ordered from commercial bakeries specializing in food service baking. However, the bake station or bakery can be very important to the success of the food service establishment. Many restaurants and institutions recognize that "homemade" cakes, pies, and breads add to the pleasure of the customer. Customers show their appreciation by return business.

The bake station is often set apart from the other stations. Because of the long preparation time needed, much of the work is done before the rest of the kitchen staff report for work. Production in the bake station does not rely on the work in other stations.

BAKING AND ITS PRODUCTS

The cooks of the bake station are called bakers or pastry cooks. They are responsible for turning out breads, cakes, cookies, and pastries. In some establishments, the bakers also prepare other desserts, such as custards, which are baked in the oven.

Breads

There are two basic types of breads — yeast breads and quick breads. Yeast breads are most familiar as bread for sandwiches, dinner rolls, and French or Italian bread. Many breakfast rolls are also yeast breads. Quick breads range from pancakes to biscuits and banana bread. Quick breads have a softer texture than yeast breads. As their name indicates, they can also be prepared more quickly.

Breads come in all shapes, sizes, and varieties. Rye, French, sourdough, white, sesame, raisin, pumpernickel, and white bread as well as cinnamon rolls, croissants, and dinner rolls are shown here.

Cakes

According to the dictionary, cake is a mixture of flour, sugar, eggs, milk, and flavoring which is baked in the oven. This hardly describes the types of cakes which are served daily to food service customers. Cakes are popular desserts in many operations.

Cookies

A cookie is a small, sweet cake. Cookies have more flour and fat, but less sugar, than cakes. There are thousands of varieties of cookies. However, in food service, only a few types are made. Cookies cut into shapes and decorated take too much time to make and bake. Bar cookies, baked in a pan, and cut into pieces are more economical. They are the type of cookie usually baked in food service.

Cakes come in many shapes and sizes. They are often decorated elaborately.

Pies and Pastries

Pies and other pastries such as cream puffs are made in the bake station. They consist of a crust and filling — usually either fruit or a flavored creamy filling.

EQUIPMENT OF THE BAKE STATION

Much of the equipment found in the bake station is similar to that in other stations. Other equipment is specialized and needed only for baking. Equipment found in many bake stations is described here. An operation with a large bakery may have more. A small operation may have less.

Tools

Many tools used for baking have already been described in Chapter 7. Some of these tools include spatulas, turners, spoons, and measuring cups and spoons, bowls, and baking pans. Other specialized baking tools are listed below:

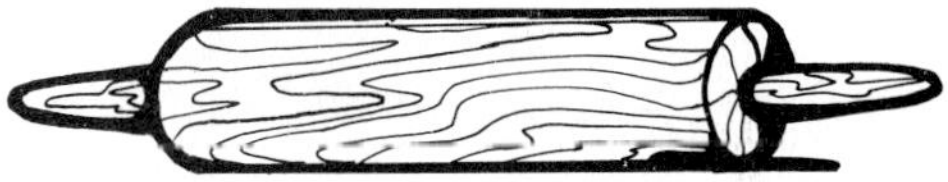

- **Rolling pin.** The rolling pin is used to roll out all kinds of items in the bake station. It is a cylinder made of wood with a steel rod fastened into handles at both ends. The best rolling pins have ball bearings for smooth rolling in any direction.

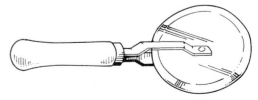

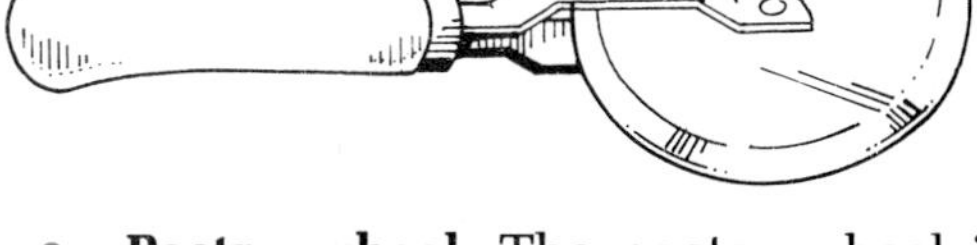

- **Pastry wheel.** The pastry wheel is used to cut rolled out dough, pastry, and pizza. It has a rotating cutter wheel on a handle.

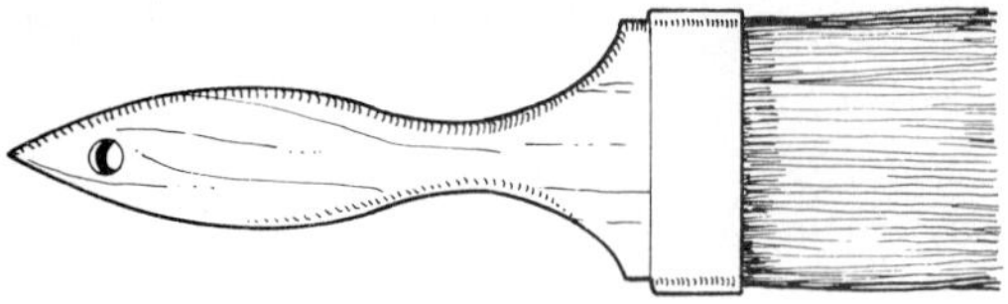

• **Pastry brush.** The pastry brush is used to brush melted butter or egg wash on items in the bakery. It is also used to spread thin icings. It is made of nylon bristles imbedded in a wood or plastic handle.

• **Pastry board.** The pastry board is sometimes called a cutting board. It is used as a base for rolling bread, cookie and pie doughs.

• **Bench brushes.** These brushes loosen flour from the table or the top of the dough.

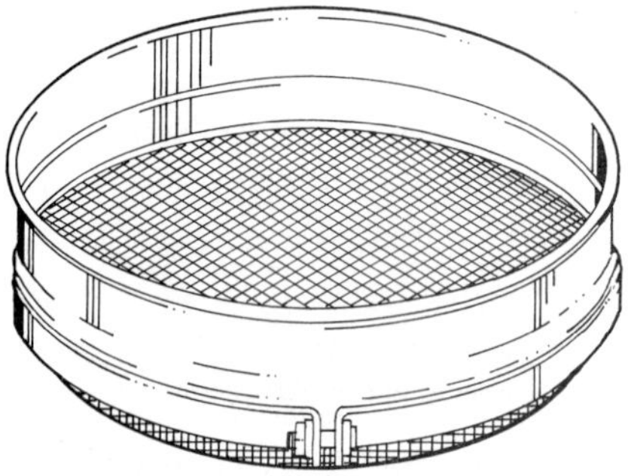

• **Flour sieve.** This is used to sift flour and to blend dry ingredients. It is usually a mesh screen supported in a round aluminum or stainless steel frame.

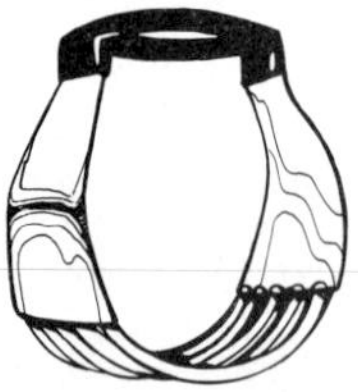

• **Pastry cutter.** A hand pastry cutter is used for blending shortening into flour when small amounts of pastry are being made. It is made of a set of curved wires imbedded in a handle.

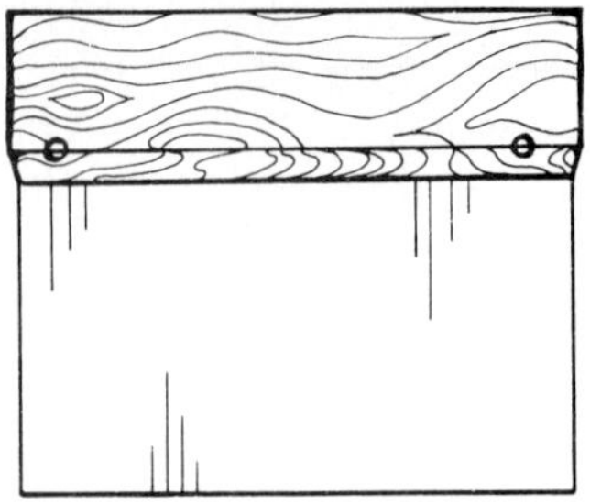

• **Bench knife** or **dough scraper.** This is used to scrape the dough from the table or to cut the dough into large chunks.

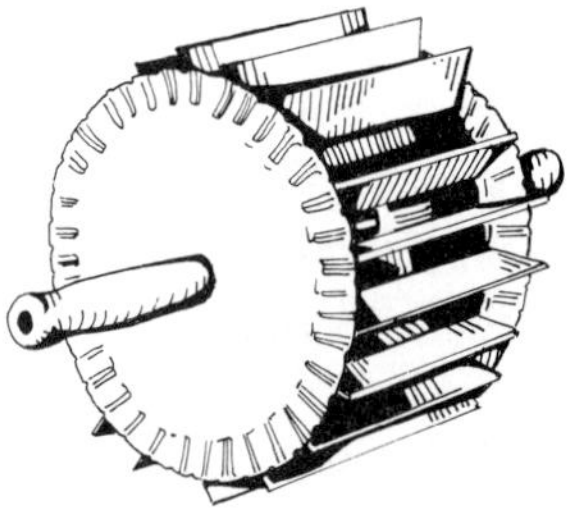

• **Bun dividers.** Bun dividers are cutters mounted on a roller with a handle. They are used for dividing the dough into equal portions.

• **Bun pan liners.** These liners are silicone-treated paper cut to fit the pan. The papers eliminate the need to grease the pan.

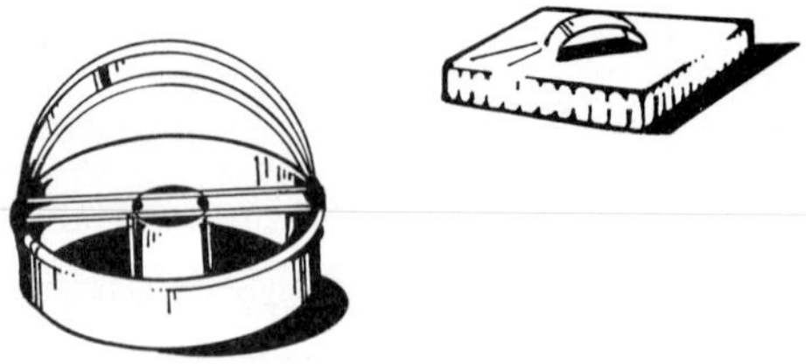

• **Cutters.** Cutters are individually shaped to cut doughnuts, biscuits, and cookies. In large bakeries, the shapes are mounted on a roller for quick cutting.

- **Bread pans.** Bread pans are usually made of tinned iron. Large bakeries use special bread straps to connect four to six bread pans. Some food service operations use small bread pans for baking miniature loaves to be served at individual tables.

Equipment

- **Mixers.** Mixers may be counter, bench, or floor models depending on the size needed. Mixers are described on page 124.

- **Ovens.** Conventional or stack ovens, described in Chapter 8, are used in the bake station. In large bakeries, the revolving tray or ***carousel oven*** is sometimes used. In this type of oven, trays revolve like seats on a Ferris wheel. As each tray reaches the long, narrow, oven door, the operator opens the door and places the food to be baked on the tray. The tray then moves up, and the next tray is filled. When all the trays are filled, they revolve until baking is completed. The trays are emptied in the order in which they were filled. Carousel ovens often produce steam during baking to make a very soft product.

- **Bench.** Bakers refer to their work table as a ***bench***. Many processes in the bake station take place on the bench.

- **Dough trough.** This is a large, oblong, stainless steel pan used for the rising of yeast dough. Smaller kitchens use a large bowl instead. (Note: "trough" is pronounced "tro" by professional bakers.)

- **Proofer.** A ***proofer*** is a cabinet with controlled warmth and high humidity. It is used for the final rising of yeast dough before baking.

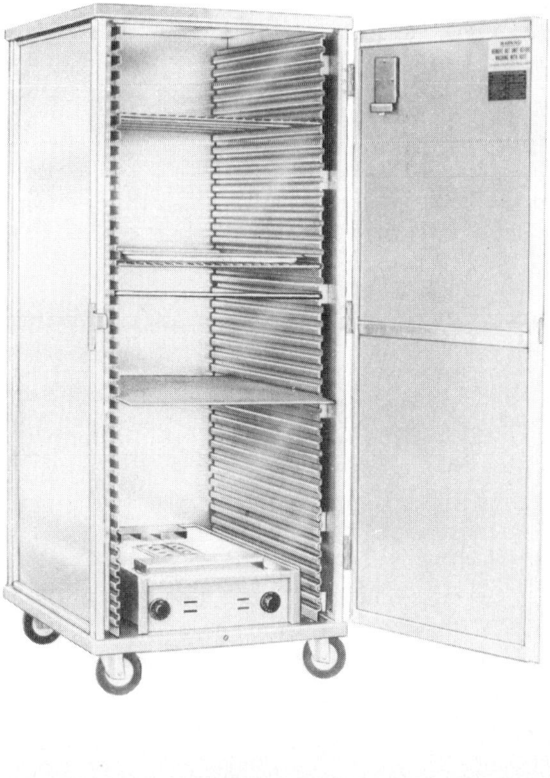

A proofer is sometimes used for short-term, nonrefrigerated storage. When used in this way, the proofer is not turned on.

INGREDIENTS

All products of the bake station have flour as a common ingredient. Flour may come from any of the grains, but in the United States the word "flour" means wheat flour.

Wheat Flour

There are two types of wheat flour used — white and whole wheat. Whole wheat flour is brown because it still contains the bran — the hard outer covering of the wheat kernel. White flour has been milled after the bran and the germ have been removed. The wheat germ is the part of the kernel from which a new plant grows. It contains oil, vitamins, and minerals. Wheat germ is removed because its oil interferes with the keeping qualities of the flour.

Gluten

When flour is mixed with water, a rough, rubbery, elastic substance known as ***gluten*** is formed. Gluten gives doughs the strength to hold gases produced by leavening agents.

Various flours are used for baking. The characteristics of each make it most suitable for making certain baked products. Some of the most common flour include:

- **Hard flour.** This has a high percentage of gluten. Hard flour is used in products with a firm texture such as bread and yeast rolls. It is often called bread flour.

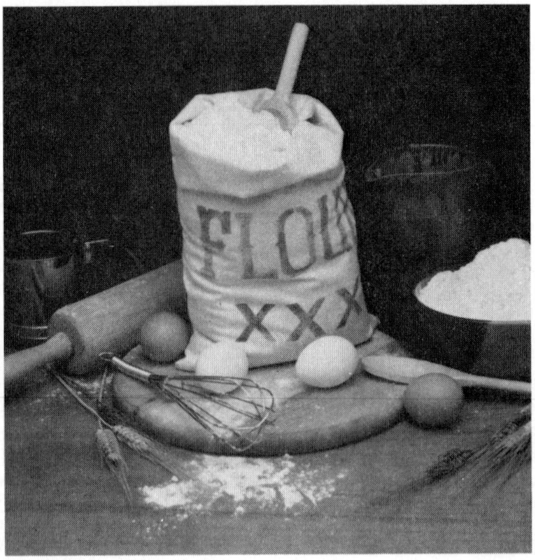

Flour is one of the most used ingredients in the food service industry.

Pie crusts require a soft, fine-grained flour. This yields a delicate, flaky crust.

- **Soft flour.** Soft flour has a very small amount of gluten. It is used for fine-grained products such as cakes and pastries. It is often called cake flour.

- **All-purpose flour.** This is a mixture of hard and soft flour. It can be used, as its name implies, for almost anything. It will make acceptable rolls, but the rolls will not be as firm as those made from hard flour. It will make acceptable cakes, but the cakes will not be as fine and velvety as those made with cake flour. It is often used for cookies and quick breads where a fine texture is not important.

Leaveners

Flour mixtures rise because of the activity of special chemicals, yeast, air, or steam. These are called ***leaveners***.

Chemical leaveners are baking powder and baking soda. Baking powder is a fine, white mixture of baking soda, an acid salt such as cream of tartar, and a starch. When liquid is added, the acid salt dissolves, reacting with the baking soda to form carbon dioxide gas. Heat speeds up this process. As the gas expands, it causes the product to rise.

Baking soda itself may be used as a leavener if the recipe calls for an acid such as buttermilk or vinegar. The chemical reaction is the same as with baking powder.

Yeast is a microscopic plant used as a leavener. It needs warmth, food, and moisture to grow. In doughs, the yeast feeds on the sugar and starch. As it grows it gives off carbon dioxide gas. The elastic gluten stretches causing the dough to rise. This process is called ***fermentation***. Yeast provides the characteristic flavor and aroma of yeast breads and rolls. Fresh yeast may be purchased, but most food service bakers use dry yeast. It is quicker and does not require refrigeration. The heat of baking kills the yeast, and the fermentation process stops.

Air expands when heated. Perhaps you remember this principle from science class. Air is incorporated in a number of ways. In baking, beaten eggs are often used as an ingredient. The beating mixes air with the eggs. When the dough or batter is baked, the trapped air helps the mixture rise. A cake mix is beaten for a certain number of minutes not only to be sure it is mixed, but also to beat in air. It makes a lighter cake.

Three of the most common leaveners are shown here.

Steam, generated when liquid is heated, also makes flour mixtures rise. Popovers are made from a very thin batter. They are baked in preheated baking pans in a very hot oven. The intense heat turns the water to steam, causing the batter to "pop". The outer part browns to a crisp crust, the steam escapes, leaving a large hole in the middle of the bun.

Most sweets produced in the bake station require shortening and sugar to be creamed together. The mixture is creamed until smooth.

Sugar

Sugar is the primary source of sweetening used in baking. The sugar adds flavor to baked products, makes them tender, and aids in browning. The following sweeteners are often used in the bake station:

- Granulated sugar is made of white crystals or granules. It is the most common type of sugar.

- Brown sugar contains light or dark brown granules, and is much more moist than granulated sugar. The darker the color of the sugar, the stronger the molasses flavor it has.

- Powdered or confectioners' sugar is made from granulated sugar ground to a fine powder. The fineness of the powder is designated by the number of Xs on the box. Powdered sugar can be sifted like flour, and it is used to make candies and icings.

- Syrup is a thick, sweet liquid. Syrups most often used in baking come from cane and corn plants. Molasses from cane sugar is used because of its distinctive flavor. Corn syrup is widely used in making frostings and icings. Honey is also used occasionally.

Shortening

When fats are used in baking, they are called ***shortening***. Although butter and margarine are used in baking, ***hydrogenated shortening*** is very common, especially in food service. Hydrogenated shortening is made from vegetable oil that has been specially processed to make it a white, fluffy solid. It is less expensive than butter or margarine, produces a lighter product, and requires no refrigeration.

Shortening is a necessary ingredient in most baked products. It contributes flavor, texture, and richness. As a product bakes, the fat melts to be replaced by gluten and starch. The slow melting prevents the gluten and starch from becoming compact and tough. Melting fat also makes biscuits and pastries flaky.

Milk

Baking requires milk in almost every product. Milk may be purchased in many different forms, fresh, evaporated, or dried. It may be sweet, buttermilk, whole milk, low-fat milk, or skimmed milk. Sweetened condensed milk is used in certain recipes.

Milk adds flavor, aids in keeping qualities, and improves the texture of baked products.

In food service, dried milk is often used in baking. It is easy to use, requires little storage space, and requires no refrigeration.

Eggs

Eggs add flavor, tenderness, and lightness to baked products. (You have just read that beaten eggs are leaveners.) Egg yolks add color and richness, making the products more attractive and tasty.

Eggs may be purchased fresh in the shell, fresh in liquid form, frozen, or dried. They may also be purchased as liquid whole eggs, yolks alone, or whites alone. The purchasing agent may even order a specified proportion of yolks to whites, if desired.

In the bake station, liquid fresh eggs are often used. These are eggs which have already been cracked and beaten smooth. Although they must be kept under refrigeration, they are easy to use and can be measured more accurately than fresh eggs in the shell.

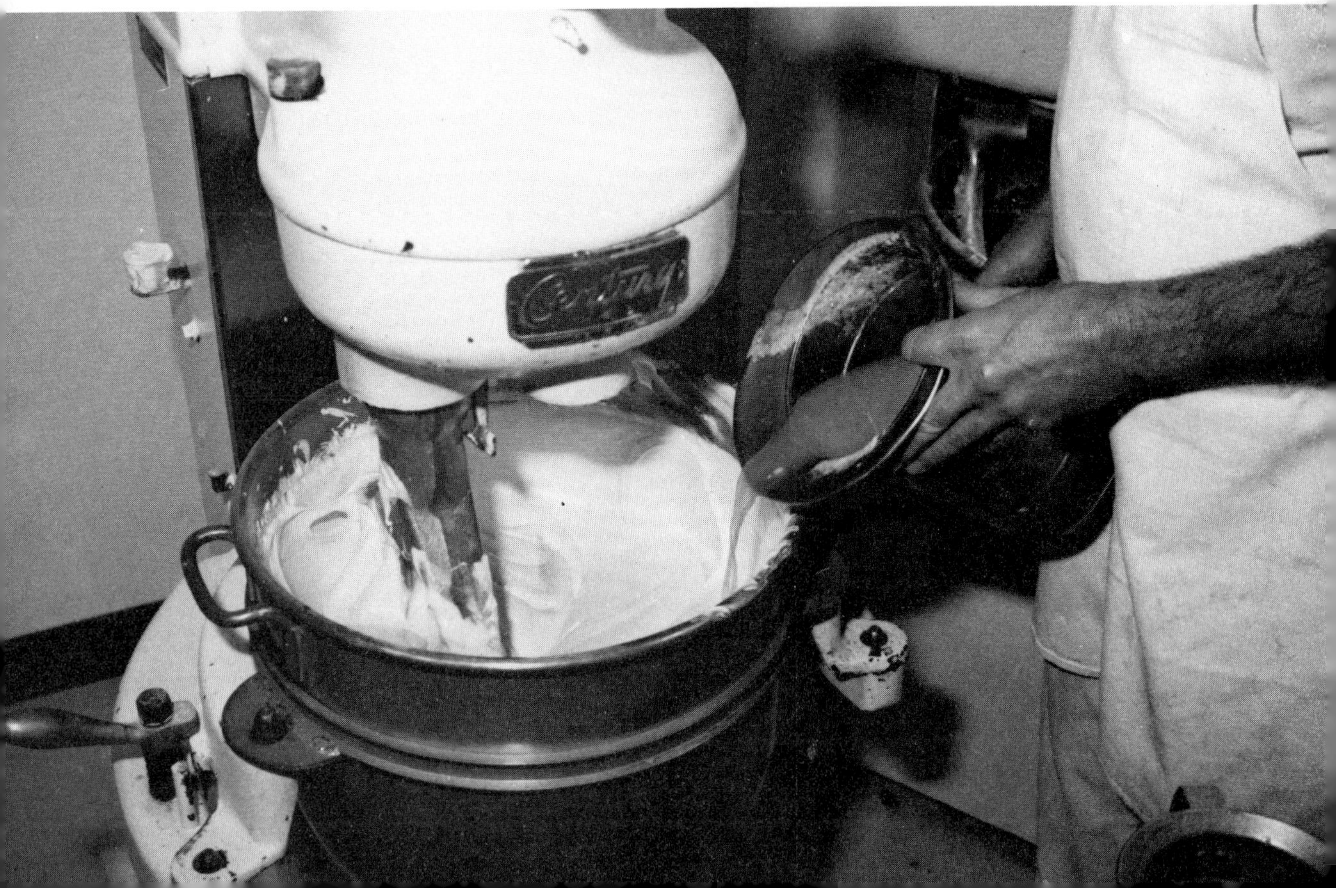

Eggs and milk are often added to a creamed mixture. This is done slowly to insure complete mixing of ingredients.

Salt, Flavorings and Spices

Salt is an essential substance in most baked products. In baking, it not only adds flavor, but also strengthens the gluten. Salt prevents yeast from growing too rapidly. Bread without salt has a coarse texture and becomes stale quickly. Bread with too much salt is firm, compact, and has an unpleasant taste.

Flavorings such as vanilla extract make the baked products much more tasty. Other extracts often used are lemon, almond, and rum. Chocolate and cocoa are also flavorings which can change the taste of a baked product.

Spices such as cinnamon, cloves, and nutmeg, or seeds such as poppy or sesame, are sometimes used in baking. They add flavor and a change of texture.

BAKING TEMPERATURES AND TIMES

In baking more than in any other process, control of time and temperature is absolutely essential. Products baked at too high a temperature will brown before the inside is baked. The crust will be cracked and the texture will be coarse. The product may even burn. If the temperature is too cool, the product will be compact with a colorless crust. This is especially true of cakes.

Be sure to preheat the oven. The oven must be at the correct temperature when the product is put in the oven. If it is not, the timing will not be correct.

Baking success depends on the baker. Ovens must be preheated to the correct temperature, timers must be set, and baked goods must be removed at the proper time.

Cinnamon, nutmeg, ginger, and allspice are often used in products of the bake station. Can you identify the spices pictured?

SUMMARY

The bake station is responsible for preparing breads, cakes, cookies, and pastries. Some specialized baking tools and utensils are used which are not found in other stations. Bake station products all use flour and frequently include leaveners, shortening, sugar, eggs, and flavorings. A good bake station can help insure the success of a food service operation.

chapter recap

CHECK YOUR KNOWLEDGE

1. Name four products of the bake station.
2. What is gluten?
3. Name four types of flour.
4. List four leaveners.
5. What type of sugar is used most often in baking?
6. Why is hydrogenated shortening preferred for baking?
7. What type of milk is most convenient to use when preparing baked goods?
8. Name the form of eggs used most often in the bake station.
9. What two factors must be controlled for successful baking?
10. What is preheating? Why is it necessary?

EXTEND YOUR LEARNING

1. Discuss the advantages and disadvantages of using commercially baked products in food service.
2. Assemble samples of each type of flour mentioned in the chapter. Place each in a bowl and label. Briefly describe the color, feel, and taste of each one. Then remove the labels and rearrange the bowls. Can you identify each correctly?
3. Some eggs are brown, others white. In the supermarket, compare the cost per dozen of both types. Find out if one is better or more nutritious than the other.

"Mmm, smell that bread!" Ruthann exclaimed as the school bus drove past Graf's Bakery. "They must have just taken it out of the oven!"

"Sure smells good!" Jim agreed. "It makes me hungry even though I've had breakfast. It smells almost as good as the bread we baked in class yesterday. Boy, that sure attracted a crowd. Kids were sticking their heads in our door begging for samples!"

"Did you see Mr. Jones come by?" Ruthann asked. "He said he could smell it all the way down in the front office!" Ruthann continued, "My dad bakes bread sometimes. He made some last Friday, and when Mom came home we just cut off big slices of that fresh bread and slathered on the butter. We were so full of bread, we hardly ate dinner."

"You know that real nice restaurant downtown — Summer's?" asked Jim. "They serve little loaves of hot, homemade bread on a wooden board with pots of butter to go with it. I'll bet that brings in the customers!"

"Have you ever been to Cynthia O'Day's?" asked Ruthann. "My Aunt Mary took me there last month. They serve hot cinnamon and orange rolls in a big, shiny pan with a round cover. We lifted the cover and took rolls right from the pan. I'd like to have that recipe!"

"Maybe Chef Robinson would have it," Jim suggested. "If he does, maybe we could bake those in class!"

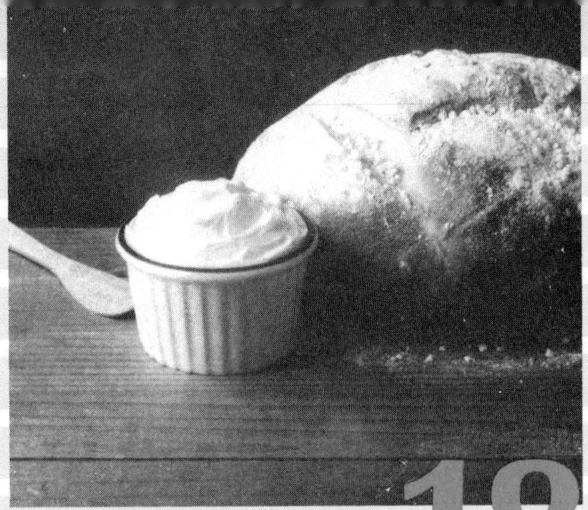

chapter 18

yeast breads and rolls

Set your goals

When you complete the study of this chapter, you should be able to . . .

- Define and correctly use the vocabulary terms.
- Describe the steps in mixing yeast doughs.
- Prepare and serve hard, soft, and sweet rolls of acceptable quality.
- Describe storage guidelines for yeast products.

Build your vocabulary

dough hook
egg wash
kneading
oven spring
panning
proofing
punched down
retarding
scaling

YEAST BREADS AND ROLLS IN FOOD SERVICE

If you could compare customer reaction to the food in two similar restaurants, you might see something like this. After the order is taken in Restaurant A, the waiter or waitress brings in a basket of cold rolls with butter and places them on the table. There is no reaction from the customers. In Restaurant B, the same scene takes place, but this time the customer is offered a basket of assorted hot rolls and butter. The basket is covered with a snowy white napkin. As the basket is uncovered, you would hear exclamations like this. "Oh, hot rolls. They look delicious!" Which restaurant is likely to have the most repeat business?

Bread

Few food service operations make the large loaves of bread used for sandwiches. Such bread is bought from commercial bakeries. But many restaurants have found it profitable to offer a small loaf of hot bread, served on a bread board with a sharp knife. Often softened garlic butter is offered with the bread. This small loaf is a welcome change from rolls, and customers seem to enjoy the novelty of cutting the bread.

Although such bread appears to be freshly baked, it was probably baked in quantity several days before and frozen. When it is reheated it gives all the pleasure of a freshly baked loaf. Some operations buy frozen dough ready to thaw and bake instead of preparing their own from scratch.

Although white bread is the most popular, many customers prefer whole wheat or rye bread if given a choice. Many food service operations now offer a variety of bread choices.

A variety of breads are often found on salad bars and buffet tables in food service establishments.

Rolls

Hard rolls, soft rolls, and sweet rolls are the most common types of rolls. All are popular with customers.

Hard rolls are made from the same dough as bread. They have a hard, crunchy crust and are usually served as dinner rolls.

Soft rolls are made from a slightly different type of dough. Eggs, plus more shortening and sugar, make a softer roll. Steam used during baking also gives the rolls a soft crust. Soft rolls may be served for breakfast, lunch, or dinner.

Sweet rolls are usually served at breakfast or along with soft rolls for lunch. They are made from a rich dough with extra shortening, sugar, and eggs. Sweet rolls often have a sweet filling and icing on top. They also are baked in an oven with steam so they will be very soft.

THE MIXING PROCESS

Although yeast doughs may be made by different methods, the one used most often in food service is described here. This method is used for bread and rolls, with only slight variations.

Preparing the Dough

Although yeast breads have the same basic ingredients, there are some differences depending upon the specific product being made. Bread and hard rolls, for example, need a high-gluten flour to give them their characteristic texture. Because they need less gluten, soft and sweet rolls are usually made from all-purpose flour. The lighter texture comes from varying the amounts of eggs, shortening, and sugar. The chart on page 266, compares the ingredient amounts used in hard, soft, and sweet rolls. Notice that eggs are used for soft and sweet rolls but not for hard rolls. Although some shortening and sugar are used in bread, a much higher proportion of these ingredients is used in soft and sweet rolls.

After kneading, this soft dough is rolled tightly and then cut and shaped into fancy rolls.

Comparison of Ingredients in Yeast Products

Ingredient	Hard Rolls	Soft Rolls	Sweet Rolls
Flour*	4 lb.	3½ lb.	3½ lb.
Sugar	½ oz.	4 oz.	6 oz.
Salt	¾ oz.	1 oz.	¾ oz.
Milk (nonfat)	4 oz.	4 oz.	2 oz.
Yeast	1¼ oz.	1 oz.	1 oz.
Water	1 qt.	1 qt.	2½ c.
Shortening	4 oz.	3½ oz.	5¼ oz.
Eggs	——	4 oz.	8 oz.
Flavoring	——	——	1 oz.

*Type varies.

Measuring

In baking, dry ingredients are always measured on the balance scale. Review the directions on page 55 for using one. And remember, accurate measurements are the foundation of successful baking.

Liquids such as milk, water, and eggs are often measured by volume. Follow the recipe directions.

Baking with Yeast

Yeast — the leavening agent used in these products — needs special handling. Temperature is the main factor in controlling yeast. Cold temperatures slow its growth and the dough rises too slowly. Hot temperatures, however, (above 140°F or 60°C) kill the yeast. Yeast needs a warm environment to grow properly and raise the dough.

Two methods are used to add the yeast to the other ingredients. The first consists of sprinkling the yeast on top of a mixture of warm water and sugar. The water should feel barely warm on the inside of your wrist or measure 105°-115°F (40°-45°C). Let the mixture stand about 10 minutes. it will become foamy as the yeast grows. Then it can be added to the other recipe ingredients.

In the second method, dry yeast is mixed with the flour. The liquid and fat in the recipe are heated to 120°-130°F (50°-55°C) and beaten into the flour-yeast mixture with the mixer.

Method of Mixing

When you first make yeast breads, it is helpful to mix the dough by hand rather than with a mixer. You get the "feel" of the dough and better understand the role of gluten. The method of mixing is the same. In one, you do the work. In the other, the mixer does the work. The chart on page 267 gives step-by-step directions for mixing hard rolls by hand and with a mixer. Directions for preparing soft and sweet rolls with a mixer are given in the chart on page 267. You can easily modify these for hand mixing.

Mixing Hard Rolls

By Hand	By Mixer
1. Place dry ingredients including shortening in mixer bowl. 2. Dissolve yeast in warm water. 3. Add water to dry ingredients and mix with spoon until smooth. Occasionally, scrape down bowl with rubber spatula. 4. Turn out on floured board and knead for 10 minutes. Add flour as needed to prevent sticking on board.	1. Place dry ingredients including shortening in mixer bowl. Using the paddle, mix on low speed for 2 minutes. 2. Dissolve yeast in warm water. 3. Change to dough hook. Add liquid to dry ingredients and mix on low speed until all the water is taken up by the dough. Occasionally, scrape down bowl with rubber spatula. 4. Increase to medium speed. Knead for 7 minutes.

Mixing Soft and Sweet Rolls (Using Mixer)

Soft Rolls	Sweet Rolls
1. Place dry ingredients including shortening in mixer bowl. Using paddle, mix on low speed for 2 minutes. 2. Dissolve yeast in warm water. 3. Beat eggs. Mix with water mixture. 4. Change to dough hook. Add wet ingredients to dry ingredients. Knead for 5 minutes. Scrape down occasionally with rubber spatula.	1. Place dry ingredients, except yeast in mixer bowl. Using paddle, mix on low speed for 2 minutes. 2. Add shortening to dry ingredients and mix for 2 minutes. 3. Beat eggs. Dissolve yeast in water and mix with eggs. 4. Change to dough hook. Add wet ingredients to dry ingredients. Knead for 5 minutes. Scrape down occasionally with rubber spatula.

Developing the Gluten

Kneading is a mixing process by which the dough is folded, pressed, and squeezed to strengthen the gluten strands. This may be done by hand or with a mixer that has a ***dough hook*** attachment. The dough hook is a hook-shaped beater. Yeast dough is very thick. If ordinary beaters were used, the dough would climb up the beaters. It might even cause the mixer to overheat and stop.

When the dough has been kneaded sufficiently, it will cling to the dough hook and clear the sides of the bowl. When pressed with the flat of the hand, the dough should hold the impression of the hand for a few seconds, then spring back. This means the gluten has been developed enough.

The time needed for kneading varies with the type of dough. Bread dough requires about ten minutes by hand or seven minutes with the mixer. Dough for soft rolls and sweet rolls needs a shorter kneading time because they do not have as firm a texture.

Several batches of yeast dough are being prepared for the dough trough.

Fermentation

Fermentation is the period when the yeast feeds on the starch and sugar, giving off carbon dioxide and causing the dough to rise. There are important factors to remember during this period.

Control of temperature is very important during the rising period. Remember that high temperature will kill the yeast. In large food service operations, the yeast dough is placed in the dough trough (rectangular, stainless steel pan) after kneading and rolled into a special fermentation room. The humidity in the room is controlled so the top of the dough cannot dry out and form a crust. Small food service operations do not have fermentation rooms. The dough is placed in a clean bowl. The top is lightly greased, and the bowl is covered. It is then set on the bench to rise. The warm temperature in the bake station will help the dough to rise.

For most recipes, the dough is allowed to rise until it is double its original size. If the dough rises more than that, the gluten strands become stretched and the dough collapses. This results in a poor quality product.

Sometimes bakers take advantage of the slower growth of yeast in cool temperatures. They prepare the dough in the evening then cover and refrigerate it. This is called ***retarding***. The yeast grows very slowly overnight because of the cold. In the morning, the baker removes the dough from the refrigerator. It can then be shaped as desired.

When the dough has risen the desired amount, it is ***punched down***. This means that the dough is folded and pressed to expel the cabon dioxide. A short rest period allows the gluten strands to relax and makes the dough easier to shape. The dough is kneaded slightly to work out any remaining bubbles of gas and is then ready for shaping.

Shaping

Portion control is as important in the bake station as in any other area of the food service kitchen. This process, known as ***scaling***, consists of dividing the dough into equal pieces of the correct size. This is usually done by cutting the dough with a dough scraper or bench knife and then weighing each piece to make sure it is the desired size. The recipe usually specifies the correct weight.

The next step is rounding. This means rolling each piece of dough with the flat of the hand to make a smooth, round ball.

Shaping Yeast Breads

Those golden, evenly-shaped loaves of bread don't just happen. Here is how they are shaped:

1. Sprinkle the bench with flour to keep the dough from sticking.
2. Roll a scaled piece of dough until it is the width of the loaf pan and double the length of the pan.
3. Fold the dough into thirds.
4. Seal the edges of dough by pressing them together with your fingers.
5. Reshape the loaf with your fingers, if necessary, to fit pan.

Shaping Yeast Rolls

Yeast rolls may be prepared in many interesting shapes.

1. Sprinkle the bench with flour to prevent sticking.
2. Roll the scaled pieces of dough to 1/4 in. (6 mm) thickness.
3. Shape as desired.

This bread dough has been scaled to size and is now being shaped for baking.

Shaping Sweet Rolls

Sweet rolls have a sweet filling or topping. An often used one is a mixture of nuts, cinnamon, and sugar.

1. Sprinkle the bench with flour to prevent the dough from sticking.
2. Roll the scaled piece of dough 1/4 in. (6 mm) thick and 9 in. wide.
3. Brush off excess flour with the bench brush. Brush with melted fat using pastry brush.
4. Sprinkle evenly with a mixture of sugar, cinnamon, and chopped nuts.
5. Roll the filling in lightly with a rolling pin.
6. Roll up the dough tightly. Cut into slices about 1 in. (2.5 cm) thick.
7. Place 2 in. (5 cm) apart on the bake pan. Brush with egg wash and proof until double in size.

Panning

Placing dough in pans for baking is called ***panning***. To prepare the pans, grease lightly with unsalted shortening. When placing rolls on the pan, remember that they will double in size. Place them well apart on the pan. Rolls are usually baked in a sheet pan or bun pan.

If a soft crust is desired, spread melted butter over the top of the loaves or rolls using a pastry brush. Many bakers paint an ***egg wash*** on top of sweet rolls before baking. An egg wash is a mixture of egg yolk and milk or water. It gives the top an attractive, shiny brown crust.

Proofing

Proofing is the final rising of the dough after shaping but before baking. It requires a warmer temperature than the original fermentation period. Commercial bakeries have a proofing cabinet with controlled humidity and warmth. In smaller bake stations, the pans are left on the bench or placed on top the oven and covered with a clean, damp cloth.

When the dough has doubled in size, it is ready to be baked. At this point the dough is very fragile. A sudden bump can cause it to fall. Be careful!

These biscuits are being panned and then stacked on a cart. When all the trays have been filled, they will be placed in the proofing cabinet.

Baking

First, preheat the oven. In the conventional oven, the shaped bread or rolls are usually baked first at 425°F (220°C) for ten minutes. The temperature is then reduced to 375°F (190°C) for the rest of the baking time. When large ovens are used, the oven is usually set at the lower temperature for the entire period. These ovens cannot cool off quickly enough to allow for a drop in temperature.

If there is a window in the oven, you will find it interesting to watch the baking process. However, avoid opening the oven door because cool air may cause the product to fall. At first, the rise will be so rapid you can almost see the product grow. This rapid rise is called ***oven spring***. When the starch has absorbed all the liquid and the gluten has coagulated, the structure becomes firm and browning occurs gradually.

This commercial oven holds five trays of biscuits at one time.

✓ standards ✓

Bread and Hard Rolls

Appearance

- ✓ Straight sides and well-rounded top.
- ✓ No large holes.

Color

- ✓ Top golden brown.
- ✓ Sides lighter brown.

Flavor

- ✓ Slightly yeasty, with sweet flavor.

Texture

- ✓ Thin crust may be tender or crunchy depending on type.
- ✓ Fine-grained, tender and moist.

On the Job

Making Soft Dinner Rolls

Assignment: Three workers are to make 100 cloverleaf dinner rolls. The yeast dough has been mixed and has completed rising. This assignment can be accomplished most efficiently by setting up a production line.

Check the Recipe

The dough is to be scaled into 3 lb. pieces. Each piece is then formed into a long roll. The roll is cut into small chunks that are made into balls, three for each cloverleaf roll.

Check Yourself

Before you begin work, make sure you are ready:

- Confine your hair with a hairnet, cap, or band.
- Wash your hands thoroughly.
- Put on a clean apron.
- Use plastic gloves for preparing the ingredients and assembling the rolls.

Assemble the Equipment

- Muffin tins for 100 rolls
- Portion scale
- Dough cutter
- Flour sieve or sifter
- Saucepan for melted butter
- Pastry brush

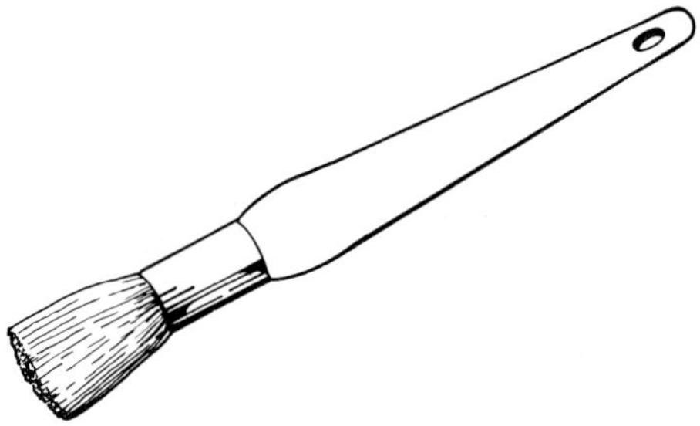

Follow this Procedure

Step 1. Place the dough and a portion scale at left end of counter. Next, place the dough cutter, flour sieve, and muffin tins.

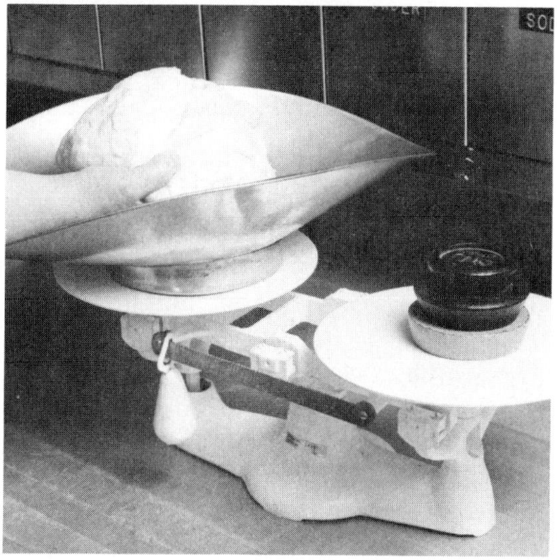

Step 2. Worker #1 scales 3 lb. pieces of dough and forms them into long rolls about 3 inches in diameter.

Step 3. ▲ Worker #2 cuts each long roll into small chunks and rolls each chunk into a ball with the flat of the hand.

Step 4. ▲ Worker #3 preheats the oven to 400°F. and places three balls in each muffin cup. Worker #3 then brushes each cloverleaf roll with melted butter. The muffin tins are then placed in the proofer.

Step 5. When the rolls have risen to the top of the tins, Worker #3 places them in the oven and bakes them for 20-25 minutes until golden brown.

standards

Soft Rolls

Appearance
- Size that is easy to eat.
- Interesting shape.

Color
- Smooth golden brown outside.
- Creamy yellow inside.

Flavor
- Slightly sweet, yeasty.
- Sweet rolls have sweet flavor.

Texture
- Thin, tender crust
- Fine-grained, tender and moist.

CARE AND STORAGE

When baked goods are done, use a hot pad to take the pans from the oven. Remove the products from the pan and place them on a rack away from drafts to cool. As soon as the rolls or loaves are completely cool, wrap in moisture-proof containers to keep them fresh. Hard rolls are not wrapped. Doing so would soften their crunchy crusts.

CONVENIENCE FORMS OF YEAST BREADS AND ROLLS

Like many other types of foods, yeast breads and rolls are available in convenience forms. Some operations use mixes for small loaves of breads, and hard, soft, and sweet rolls. The mixes are made to the specifications of the food service company. Only water needs to be added.

Other operations buy refrigerated yeast products already formed into loaves or rolls. The products can be baked to order so that customers can always have fresh, hot breads.

Frozen yeast products can also be purchased. They have the same advantages as the refrigerated products, but they take longer to defrost, proof, and bake.

These frozen Parker House rolls are just one of the many yeast products that can be purchased in convenience form.

SUMMARY

Homemade yeast breads and rolls often attract customers to a restaurant. Many people think yeast products are difficult to make. High quality products really depend on following recipe directions carefully. Two of the most important steps are adding the yeast and allowing it to ferment, and kneading to develop the gluten. Yeast dough is used for many different kinds of bread and rolls.

chapter recap

CHECK YOUR KNOWLEDGE

1. What ingredients are used in soft and sweet rolls that are not used in hard rolls?
2. What precautions must be observed when using yeast?
3. Why is a dough hook used when mixing yeast dough?
4. Why is bread kneaded?
5. What happens to yeast during fermentation?
6. What is retarding?
7. Name the first two steps used in shaping yeast dough.
8. What is an egg wash?
9. What is oven spring?
10. Name one convenience form of yeast bread.

EXTEND YOUR LEARNING

1. Visit a bakery. How many different shapes are there of soft rolls? Make diagrams for duplicating four of the shapes. When the class makes soft rolls, try out the new shapes.
2. In the supermarket, find as many convenience forms of yeast rolls as possible. (Look in the dairy case and frozen food section, as well as the bread section.) List each type along with the total price and the price per roll. Which type was most expensive? Which was least expensive?

"I'm sure glad we're learning about quick breads this week," remarked Ruthann. "Breakfast is my favorite meal of the day."

"What do quick breads have to do with breakfast?" asked Kim. "Aren't they just breads that don't take as long to cook?"

"Some of them are," answered Ruthann, "like banana bread. But there are other kinds of quick breads, and lots of them are served for breakfast."

"Like what?" Kim asked.

"I'll show you," Ruthann said. "Let's go look at that collection of menus Chef Robinson brought to class back when we were studying the menu. Here's one for the Red Rooster Restaurant. I've eaten breakfast there with my parents. Look, Kim, they have pancakes, waffles, and French toast. They are all quick breads."

"I love waffles!" Kim exclaimed. "Once I had some yummy waffles just smothered with fresh strawberries. Now I think I understand what quick breads are. They are any breads that don't have yeast in them. Is that right?"

"It sure is," Ruthann answered.

"Then," Kim went on, "that bakery where David works on weekends sells quick breads too. They sell muffins, popovers, and some delicious cinnamon biscuits besides yeast breads and doughnuts. I guess I just never thought of them as quick breads before."

"This is really starting to make me hungry," said Ruthann. "I'm glad class is starting in a few minutes. I can hardly wait to sample what we make today."

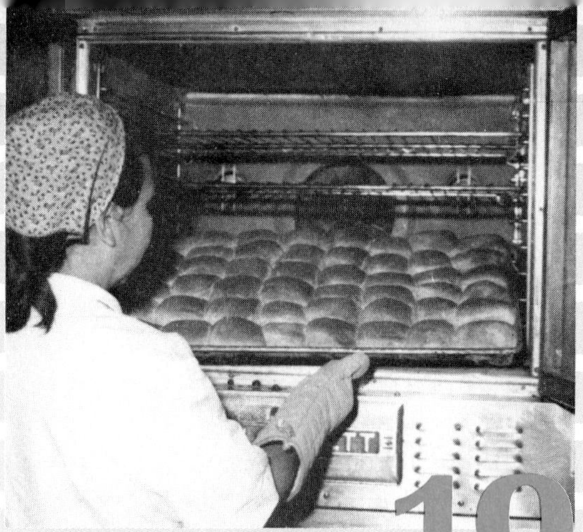

chapter 19

quick breads

Set your goals

When you complete the study of this chapter, you should be able to . . .

- Define and correctly use the vocabulary terms.
- Identify the basic ingredients used in quick breads and the purpose of each.
- Describe the three basic methods of mixing.
- Prepare a variety of quick breads.

Build your vocabulary

batter	crullers
cream	cut-in
crepes	fritters

KINDS OF QUICK BREADS

Quick bread is a term for many breads which mix easily and bake quickly. They are very different from yeast breads in flavor, texture, and keeping qualities. Quick breads are a popular addition to breakfast and lunch menus.

Quick breads may be generally divided into those baked in the oven, those baked on the griddle, and those fried in deep fat.

Ingredients

- **Flour.** Most quick breads, such as biscuits and muffins, are made with all-purpose flour. Hard or high-gluten flour would make a tough product. For corn bread or corn muffins, cornmeal is used in place of part of the flour. It cannot be used alone because corn contains no gluten.
- **Leaveners.** Quick breads are "quick" because they contain chemical leaveners which raise the bread as it is baked. Baking powder is often used, but so is baking soda in combination with sour milk or buttermilk.
- **Sweeteners.** Granulated sugar, brown sugar, and molasses are the most common sweeteners.
- **Eggs.** Most of the quick breads include eggs. Biscuits are the exception.
- **Shortening.** Shortening is a must for quick breads. In food service, hydrogenated shortenings are generally chosen.
- **Milk.** Milk is used in almost all quick breads. Sometimes, buttermilk or sour milk are specified.

Banana bread, muffins, biscuits, popovers, and cookies join yeast breads and pies in the bakery case.

Proportion of Flour to Liquid

Since the ingredients in quick breads are similar, how can there be so many varieties? The difference comes from the proportions of the ingredients and the methods of mixing and cooking. The amount of liquid in proportion to the flour makes the biggest difference. The mixtures for quick breads are classified according to these proportions. The thinner mixtures are called ***batters***. The thicker ones are called doughs.

Batters come in two general types — pour batters and drop batters. A pour batter can be poured from the mixing bowl or a pitcher. The usual proportions are one cup of liquid for every cup of flour, although some recipes have one or more eggs which add liquid and structure to the finished product. Pancakes, popovers, and waffles are made from pour batters.

Drop batters have a somewhat thicker consistency. They are too heavy to pour, but too sticky to handle with the fingers. Drop batters contain about one cup of liquid for two cups of flour. Cookies, muffins, and some biscuits are made from drop batters.

Soft doughs are stiff enough to handle and roll. The usual proportion is one cup of liquid to three cups of flour. Rolled biscuits, doughnuts, and some cookies are made from soft doughs.

Proportion of Shortening to Flour

The proportion of shortening to flour also affects the type of product. Biscuits have a flaky texture. This comes from a high proportion of shortening to flour. Biscuits have three tablespoons of shortening per cup of flour. Muffins have two tablespoons for the same amount of flour. See the chart below for a comparison of the proportion of ingredients to flour for biscuits, muffins, and breads.

Basic Ingredients for Biscuits, Muffins, and Breads

Ingredients	Biscuits	Muffins	Breads
Flour	2½ lb.	2½ lb.	2¼ lb.
Sugar	2 oz.	8 oz.	1 lb.
Shortening	1 lb.	1 lb.	10 oz.
Milk	3 cups	1 qt.	1 qt.
Baking powder	5 T.	4 T.	3 T.
Salt	1 T.	1 T.	1 T.
Eggs	——	4	8

Methods of Mixing

There are three methods of mixing flour mixtures other than yeast doughs. These are the biscuit method, dump or muffin method, and cream or cake method. These methods of mixing are compared in the chart.

The biscuit method of mixing produces a flaky texture desirable for such products as biscuits and pastry. When you pull a biscuit apart, it should separate into flaky layers. In this method, the dry ingredients are sifted together into a bowl. The fat is ***cut-in***. This means that the mixer with a pastry knife attachment is used to blend the shortening into the flour to make a mixture. (If your mixer does not have a pastry knife attachment, use the whip attachment or a dough hook.) Cutting in the shortening covers each small bit of shortening with flour. When the biscuit is baked, the shortening melts leaving the flour in soft flakes.

The dump or muffin method of mixing dumps the liquid ingredients mixed with the melted shortening into the sifted dry ingredients. After a quick mixing, the batter is ready for the oven.

The cake method is also called the creaming method. To ***cream*** means to beat the shortening and sugar together until the mixture if fluffy and very well combined. The beaten eggs are added to the creamed mixture. Then the dry ingredients are added alternately with the liquid. Creaming makes a very fine-textured product. Many quick breads are made by this method because of the desirable texture.

Muffin batter is being dropped into each cup of this lined muffin tin.

Basic Methods for Mixing Quick Breads

Pastry or Biscuit	Dump or Muffin	Creaming or Cake
1. Sift the flour, baking powder, and salt together in a mixer bowl.	1. Sift the flour, baking powder and salt together in a mixer bowl.	1. Cream the shortening and sugar together on medium speed, using the paddle.
2. Add the shortening. Cut it into the flour on low speed until the mixture is like coarse cornmeal.	2. Melt the shortening and mix with the milk.	2. Add eggs and mix for 5 minutes.
3. Add the liquid. Blend on low speed until a soft dough is formed.	3. Dump the milk into the dry ingredients.	3. Sift dry ingredients.
	4. Mix until dry ingredients are moistened. The mixture will be lumpy.	4. Add dry ingredients alternately with the milk to the creamed mixture. Begin and end with milk.

OVEN QUICK BREADS

Biscuits, muffins, and breads are baked in the oven. Biscuits and muffins are "basic" food items. Knowing how to prepare them will help in preparing other baked goods.

Biscuits

Biscuits are a light, flaky, quick bread usually baked in small rounds. Each biscuit has a flat top and is lightly browned. Baking powder is the usual leavener. See a recipe for Baking Powder Biscuits below.

Baking Powder Biscuits

Equipment: Sheet pans (18″x26″x1″), Baker's scale, Measuring spoons, Bench mixer, Paddle attachment, Quart measure, Hook attachment, Rolling pin, Biscuit cutter

Yield: 100 Biscuits
Temperature: 450°F

Ingredients	Amount	Method
Flour, all purpose	5 lb.	1. Preheat oven. Grease baking sheets.
Sugar	4 oz.	2. Blend dry ingredients in mixer.
Baking Powder	10 T.	3. Cut in shortening with dough hook. Mixture should look coarse like meal.
Salt	2 T.	4. Add milk. Mix into a soft dough.
Shortening	2 lb.	5. Knead dough on a floured surface for 5 minutes.
Milk	1½ qt.	6. Divide the dough into four pieces.
		7. Roll each piece into a ½ inch thickness.
		8. Cut with biscuit cutter.
		9. Place biscuits on baking sheets, with sides touching.
		10. Brush tops with milk. Let stand for 30 minutes.
		11. Bake 12-14 minutes, or until lightly brown on top.

Serving size: 2 biscuits

Cost per serving: ____________

✓ standards ✓

Biscuits

Appearance

- ✓ All same size and shape.
- ✓ Flat tops, straight sides.

Color

- ✓ Golden brown crust.

Flavor

- ✓ Pleasing, delicate.

Texture

- ✓ Tender, light, flaky.

The muffin on the left does not meet food service standards. The tunnels show it has been overmixed. Notice the muffin on the right does meet the standards.

Muffins

Muffins are made from a drop batter and baked in cup-shaped molds called muffin pans. See page 283 for a recipe for Plain Muffins.

✓ standards ✓

Muffins

Appearance

- ✓ Slightly rounded, bumpy tops.
- ✓ Uniform in size.

Color

- ✓ Golden brown.

Flavor

- ✓ Well-blended, nutlike.

Texture

- ✓ Even grain, tender, moist.
- ✓ Free from tunnels.

Plain Muffins

Equipment: Muffin tins, Baker's scale, Measuring spoons, Quart measure, Bench mixer, Paddle attachment, Bowl, Wire whip, Saucepan, Rubber Spatula, No. 20 scoop

Yield: 48 Muffins
Temperature: 400°F

Ingredients	Amount
Flour	2½ lb.
Sugar	8 oz.
Baking powder	5 T.
Salt	1 T.
Eggs	1 c.
Shortening	¾ lb.
Milk	1 qt.

Method

1. Preheat oven. Grease muffin pans.
2. Blend dry ingredients in mixer.
3. Beat eggs slightly with wire whip.
4. Melt shortening and cool.
5. Add cooled shortening to eggs. Blend in milk.
6. Dump wet ingredients into flour mixture.
7. Mix just enough to moisten dry ingredients. Batter should be lumpy.
8. Scoop batter into muffin tins with a No. 20 scoop.
9. Bake 20-25 minutes, or until the muffins are golden brown. When done, muffins will spring back if pressed lightly with a finger.

Serving size: 1 muffin

Cost per serving: ________________

Notice how uniform these muffins appear. This is the result of a standardized recipe.

This cook is filling an order for two short-stacks that has just been placed. Griddle breads, such as pancakes, cool quickly.

Loaves

Quick breads made into loaves are shaped like yeast breads but their texture, flavor, and aroma are very different. Quick loaves are often used for sweet, small sandwiches served with salads or instead of cookies.

GRIDDLE BREADS

Griddle breads are often called griddle cakes. Some, such as pancakes, are baked directly upon the griddle. Others, such as waffles, are baked on special equipment.

Pancakes

Pancakes are also called hot cakes and griddle cakes. A pancake is usually made from a thinner batter than hot cakes and griddle cakes. There are many different varieties of pancakes. Buttermilk pancakes, buckwheat cakes, and blueberry pancakes are some of the most popular. In some restaurants, pancakes are called simply a "stack." If the customer says, "Give me a stack," the waitress or waiter knows what is wanted — a stack of pancakes.

Pancakes and their cousins, waffles, are always served with syrup — maple, cane, honey, or berry syrup — and plenty of butter. Many customers like to order a side dish of grilled ham, sausage, or bacon.

Most food service operations make pancakes with a mix. It is premeasured, and all the cook has to do is add eggs and water.

✓ standards ✓

Pancakes

Appearance

- ✓ Flat, 5-6 in. (13-16 cm) in diameter.
- ✓ Circular shape.

Color

- ✓ Golden brown.

Flavor

- ✓ Varies with ingredients.

Texture

- ✓ Tender.
- ✓ Cooked through, but not dry.

A commercial crepe iron.

French Toast

French toast, a popular item on the breakfast menu, is easy to make. Bread, normally white, is dipped in a mixture of milk, eggs, and a little sugar. The mixture is usually flavored with vanilla. The bread is baked on a very hot griddle until golden brown on both sides. Serve French toast immediately with butter, syrup, honey, jam, or sugar.

Crepes

Crepes (KREPS) are very thin, French pancakes rolled with a filling. They are baked in a special crepe iron which can be turned to bake both sides. Because crepes are made from a very thin batter, they cook almost instantly. They are not browned like a pancake. When they can be removed in one piece from the iron, they are done.

Crepes have become very popular. Dessert crepes are served with a sweet filling and sweet sauce, usually fruit flavored. Crepes as the entree for luncheon are filled with a creamed meat such as chicken and served with a cream or cheese sauce.

BREADS FRIED IN DEEP FAT

Doughnuts, crullers, and fitters are products of deep-fat frying. ***Crullers*** are made from a soft dough rich in eggs. The dough is rolled, cut into strips, and twisted. After frying until golden brown, the crullers are sprinkled with sugar.

Fritters are made from a rich batter mixed with fruit or vegetables. The batter is dropped by spoonfuls into hot fat and fried until golden brown. Corn fritters and apple fritters are examples.

Because the flavor of these products comes not only from the ingredients in the dough but also from the hot fat, you need to understand the principles of frying in deep fat. Chapter 24 gives information on the fat or oil to use, the equipment needed, the method of cooking, and the care of the fat or oil after frying.

Doughnuts

There are two types of doughnuts — raised and cake. Raised doughnuts are made from a sweet yeast dough such as that described in Chapter 18. Cake doughnuts use baking powder or baking soda as the leavener.

safety tip . . .

Doughnuts are fried in fat heated to 375°F (190°C). Use extreme caution to avoid burns. Keep utensils dry to avoid spatters. Do not overload the fryer.

Convenience Foods

Mixes are commonly used in food service to speed preparation of quick breads. Many of the large food service chains order mixes made according to their own recipes. The mixes come premeasured. All the cook must do is add water or water and eggs and mix as specified on the package. You have probably used mixes in your own home for biscuits, pancakes, or muffins.

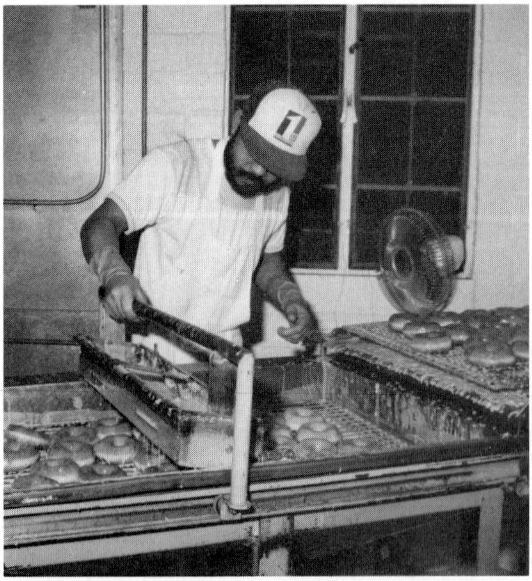

Doughnuts are prepared nearly 24 hours a day. They are a popular snack and breakfast food.

SUMMARY

Quick breads are breads which mix easily and bake quickly. They differ according to the proportion of ingredients used in them, the method of mixing, and the way they are baked. Quick breads are generally baked in the oven, cooked on a griddle, or fried in deep fat. Quick breads are an enjoyable addition to breakfast and lunch menus.

chapter recap

CHECK YOUR KNOWLEDGE

1. How do quick breads differ from yeast breads?

2. What type of flour is used for quick breads? Why?

3. Name two types of leaveners used in quick breads.

4. What causes the difference between pour batters, drop batters, and soft dough?

5. Name the three methods of mixing used in making quick breads.

6. What effect does the cut-in method of mixing have on the texture of biscuits?

7. Why are quick breads made with a different method of mixing than biscuits and muffins?

8. What are crepes?

9. Name three quick breads fried in deep fat.

10. What precaution must you observe when cooking with deep fat?

EXTEND YOUR LEARNING

1. Make a poster showing various types of quick breads. Identify each picture.

2. Check the price of a package of plain pancake mix. How many pancakes does it make? What is the cost per pancake? Figure out the cost per pancake using a recipe. How do they compare?

3. When you prepare biscuits, muffins, and quick loaves in class, set aside one of each. Compare their textures. What differences can you observe? What causes these differences?

"Jim poked his head into Ruthann's kitchen. "What's cooking?" he asked.

"Nothing yet," said Ruthann. "Today is Mom's birthday, and she loves angel food cake. Since we're studying cakes, she suggested I bake her one."

"I don't see any eggs," observed Jim.

"It's all in this box," said Ruthann. "After Chef Robinson told us how to make a truly great angel food cake, I chickened out and bought a mix. Let's see what's in the box."

"Two packets," said Jim. "They're labeled one and two. Packet one is the egg whites. You mix them with water. Packet two contains the flour and sugar. You fold that in after you beat the egg whites. Sounds simple."

"Before we start," said Ruthann, "I'd better turn on the oven."

"Do you have a tube pan?" asked Jim.

"I've got everything here," said Ruthann. "Until Chef Robinson explained it to us, I never knew why you needed a tube pan."

"This doesn't look much like egg whites," said Jim, pouring the contents of packet one into the bowl.

Ruthann stirred water into the bowl and turned on the mixer. The mixture began to fluff and look like egg whites. Soon it was very stiff. She removed the mixer and folded in the contents of packet two. "Doesn't it look yummy?" she asked.

Ruthann put the cake in the oven while Jim licked the bowl. "Mmm," he mumbled.

"I suppose I'll have to tell Mom I used a mix," said Ruthann. "You know," she continued, "my grandma remembers when cake mixes first came out. She said her friends argued for months about mixes. Most said they'd never use them. They preferred their family recipes. I'll bet they all use them now. What are you figuring on that pad?"

"Oh," Jim replied, "I'm just guessing at the cost of making this cake from scratch."

Ruthann looked at Jim in amazement. "I can't believe it! You hate math! You've really changed."

Jim grinned. "This course in food service has changed my mind about a lot of things.""

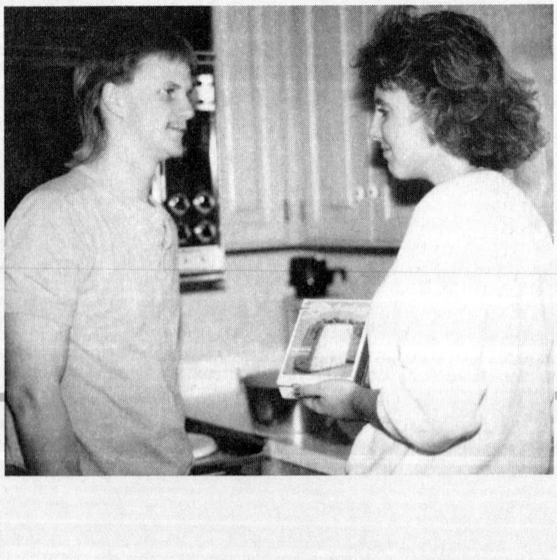

chapter 20

cakes and cookies

Set your goals

When you complete the study of this chapter, you should be able to . . .

- Define and correctly use the vocabulary terms.
- Identify from a recipe the type of cake.
- Demonstrate how to make cakes, frostings, fillings, and cookies.
- Explain the use of convenience forms of these products.

Build your vocabulary

conditioner
filling
foam cake
formula
frosting
high-ratio shortening
icing
pastry bag
sheet cake
shortened cake
tube pan

DESSERT FAVORITES

Cakes and cookies have been favorite desserts for centuries. Most people have a "sweet tooth." Desserts such as cakes and cookies seem to complete a meal and make it more satisfying.

Cakes are very delicate products. Their quality depends first of all on a correct recipe. A cake recipe is called a ***formula*** because it is very exact. Even a very small variation in the proportions of the ingredients can change the quality of the finished cake. Accurate measurement of each ingredient is vital. It is also important to follow the specific mixing directions in the recipe. Different types of cakes are mixed in different ways.

Each of these mouth-watering cakes resulted from careful measuring and mixing methods.

SHORTENED CAKES

A ***shortened cake*** is one made with shortening as a major ingredient. Originally, the shortening was always butter. No pastry cook would consider using anything else. Many people still call these cakes "butter" cakes even though hydrogenated shortening is almost always used instead of butter.

In the past, shortened cakes were always made by the creaming method. However, with the development of hydrogenated shortening, the simpler, blending method became popular. If you have studied the chapter on quick breads, you are already familiar with these two mixing methods.

In the creaming method, the shortening and sugar are first creamed to combine them and to add air. Next, the eggs and flavoring are added. Finally, the sifted dry ingredients are added alternately with the milk. Many pastry cooks still prefer the creaming method because it makes a fine-textured cake that is moist and tender.

The blending method — similar to the muffin method in quick breads — is faster. All the dry ingredients are placed in the mixing bowl. The eggs and liquid ingredients are put in the center of the dry ingredients. Then all the ingredients are mixed together. The blending method makes a high-volume cake. The chart on page 291 compares the steps followed for the creaming and blending methods.

Cakes mixed using the creaming method may contain butter or margarine instead of hydrogenated shortening. These cakes will not be as high as cakes containing hydrogenated shortening, but will have a richer, more buttery flavor. The recipe for Yellow Sheet Cake on page 292 uses the creaming method.

Cakes mixed by the blending method must use a special type of hydrogenated shortening called ***high-ratio shortening***. It can tolerate a higher proportion of sugar to shortening than other types of shortening.

A shortened cake may be baked in layers or as a ***sheet cake***. A sheet cake is a cake baked in a large, low-sided baking pan. Sheet cakes are often baked in institutions because they are easier to frost and serve. Layer cakes are more often made by restaurants because the appearance of the cake is more important.

This sheet cake was designed to celebrate America's birthday in a healthy way. Notice the flag's stripes are made of sliced strawberries and the whipped cream stars are laying on a field of fresh blueberries!

Methods of Mixing Shortened Cakes

Creaming Method	Blending Method
1. Cream sugar, shortening, and vanilla in mixer bowl, using the paddle on low speed. Cream 10 minutes. **2.** Add eggs and cream 5 minutes. **3.** Sift flour, baking powder, and salt together. **4.** Add alternately with the milk to the creamed mixture, beginning and ending with dry ingredients. Scrape down at least once. Mix about 3 minutes until well blended. **5.** Scale and pan in greased pans.	**1.** Sift flour, baking powder, and salt into mixer bowl. Add shortening. Blend on low speed with the paddle for 5 minutes. Scrape down at least once. **2.** Mix eggs, milk and vanilla. Add half the mixture to ingredients in mixer bowl. Blend on low speed for 3 minutes. Scrape down. **3.** Add sugar and blend for 3 minutes. Scrape down. **4.** Add remaining liquid and blend for 5 minutes, scraping down at least twice. **5.** Scale and pan in greased pans.

Yellow Sheet Cake

Equipment: Sheet pan (18″x26″x1″), Bench mixer, Whip attachment, Measuring cups, Rubber spatula, Baker's scale, Measuring spoons, Paddle attachment, Bowl, Sifter

Yield: 50 servings
Temperature: 350°F

Ingredients	Amount
Shortening	1 lb.
Sugar	2 lb.
Vanilla	1 T.
Eggs	8
Flour, cake	1 lb. 12 oz.
Baking powder	2 T.
Salt	2 t.
Milk	2½ c.

Method

1. Preheat oven. Grease and flour sheet pan.
2. Cream shortening, sugar, and vanilla for 5 minutes.
3. Add eggs one at a time, beating mixture for 1 minute after each addition.
4. Sift remaining dry ingredients.
5. Alternately add dry ingredients and milk to the creamed mixture. Using paddle, blend mixture after each addition. Scrape bowl frequently.
6. Beat mixture for 1 minute on medium speed.
7. Pour batter into sheet pan and spread evenly.
8. Bake for 35 minutes. Cake should spring back when lightly touched.

Serving size: One 4″ square

Cost per serving: ________________

FOAM CAKES

A ***foam cake*** is leavened by beaten egg whites. Beaten egg whites have air beaten into them which expands when heated, causing the cake to rise. The texture of foam cakes is very different from shortened cakes, but they are just as delicious. Angel food, sponge, and chiffon cakes are all foam cakes.

Angel Food Cakes

Angel food cakes are delicate, pure white cakes. Unlike shortened cakes, angel food cakes contain no chemical leaveners such as baking powder or baking soda. The air trapped in the beaten egg whites, which expands during baking, is the only leavener.

standards

Shortened Cakes

Appearance

- Flat top and smooth, delicate crust.

Color

- Golden brown crust (dark brown for chocolate cake).

Flavor

- Sweet, delicate flavor.

Texture

- Fine-grained, velvety.

standards

Foam Cakes

Appearance

- High, light cake.

Color

- Light brown crust.

Flavor

- Delicate and sweet (angel food).
- Egg and butter flavor (sponge).
- Sweet, with egg flavor (chiffon).

Texture

- Delicate, moist.

Angel food cakes contain fewer ingredients than shortened cakes. Only cake flour, granulated sugar, egg whites, salt, and vanilla or almond flavoring are used. Angel food cakes contain no shortening.

Angel food and shortened cakes also differ in the way they are baked. Angel food cakes are generally baked in an ungreased ***tube pan***. A tube pan is a large, round pan with a hollow tube in the center. This tube carries heat to the center of the batter. It also provides support for the cake. Angel food cake clings to the sides of the pan as it rises. That is why the pans are never greased.

Angel food cakes can be iced and decorated, or served right out of the pan. Their light texture and flavor make them a good option to heavier desserts.

Beating Egg Whites

In order to make angel food cakes, it is important to understand beaten egg whites. Unless the whites are beaten properly, the cakes will not rise well. Beaten egg whites are used in many dishes in cooking and baking.

If you are using fresh eggs, the first step is to separate the whites from the yolks. Eggs separate most easily when they are cold, but egg whites can be beaten to their highest volume when at room temperature. Be sure to allow time after separating for the egg whites to warm.

Be sure to separate the eggs one at a time into a small bowl. Then slip the egg white from the small bowl into the mixing bowl. This may seem like extra work, but there is a good reason for doing so. If even a small bit of yolk gets into the egg whites in the mixing bowl, they will not beat properly. By breaking each egg into the small bowl first, you can use the egg for another purpose if the yolk breaks. The whole mixing bowl of whites will not be ruined. When you separate eggs, be sure to save the half not used in the recipe (whites or yolks) for use in another dish.

Egg whites go through several stages as they are beaten. It is important to be able to recognize these different stages. Egg whites are usually beaten at high speed with the whip attachment on the mixer.

- **Foamy whites.** At this stage, the egg whites are bubbly and just starting to turn white. They have increased somewhat in volume.
- **Soft peaks.** The egg whites have become shiny and white and have reached full volume. When the whip attachment is removed, the whites stand up in peaks that bend over at the top.
- **Stiff peaks.** The egg whites are still white, shiny, and at full volume. However, the peaks now stand up straight.

Egg whites beaten beyond the stiff peaks stage become dry and begin to break apart. This causes them to lose air so baked products that contain overbeaten egg whites do not rise well.

Sometimes ingredients are added to the egg whites as they are beaten. Cream of tartar, for example, helps the whites retain their volume. Sugar and flavoring may also be added.

When beaten egg whites are combined with another mixture (such as dry ingredients), a folding motion is always used. To "fold in" means to gently mix with an over-and-over motion. This may be done with a mixer or by hand. Vigorous mixing would cause the egg whites to lose their air — and their leavening power.

Egg whites beaten to the stiff peak stage are often called for in cake recipes. Be careful not to overbeat, however. This can cause the cake not to rise properly.

Mixing Angel Food Cakes

The foam method of mixing is used for angel food cakes. Sponge and chiffon cakes are mixed in much the same way. Be sure to follow each step carefully.

1. Sift the flour and half the sugar together four times.
2. Place the egg whites in the mixer bowl. Using the whip attachment (if available), beat on high speed until foamy.
3. Add the cream of tartar and salt to the egg whites. Beat to stiff peaks.
4. Gradually add the remaining half of the sugar while continuing to beat.
5. Add the flavorings and blend. Remove the bowl from the mixer.
6. Fold in the flour-sugar mixture, a bit at a time. Continue until all the flour mixture disappears.
7. Scale as directed in the recipe and pour into ungreased tube pans. Bake as directed.

After baking, angel food cakes are cooled upside down in their pans. The pans have three "legs" on the top which support the pan during cooling. After the cakes are completely cool, they are removed by loosening with a spatula or knife and gently pulling the cake away from the pan.

Sponge Cakes

Sponge cakes are foam cakes which include both the whites and yolks of the egg. The air in the beaten eggs is the primary leavening agent. However, many recipes call for baking powder as well. Sponge cakes have a fine, yellow grain. They stay moist for a long time.

Sponge cakes usually contain whole eggs, sugar, hot milk, margarine, cake flour, baking powder, salt, and flavoring. They are baked in tube or loaf pans.

Mixing Sponge Cakes

Use a mixer with the whip attachment (if available) for mixing sponge cakes. All ingredients should be at room temperature.

1. Place the eggs and flavoring in the mixer bowl. Beat on high speed for 5 minutes.
2. Weigh and sift the sugar. Add gradually to the eggs while beating. Beat for 10 minutes, scraping down the bowl at least three times.
3. Heat the milk and the margarine until the margarine melts.
4. Sift together the flour, baking powder, and salt twice.
5. Reduce the mixer speed to low. Add the dry ingredients alternately with the milk to the egg mixture. Begin and end with the flour mixture.
6. Scale according to the recipe and pour into greased pans. Bake as directed.

Sponge cakes are very tender and fragile when warm. They are left in the pans until almost cooled. Then remove the cakes from their pans and finish cooling on racks.

Chiffon Cakes

Chiffon cakes are fairly new to the family of foam cakes. They use both egg yolks and whites, but the egg whites are beaten and added separately. Like angel food cakes, chiffon cakes are usually baked in tube pans and cooled upside down.

The ingredients for chiffon cakes include cake flour, sugar, baking powder, vegetable oil, separated eggs, and cream of tartar.

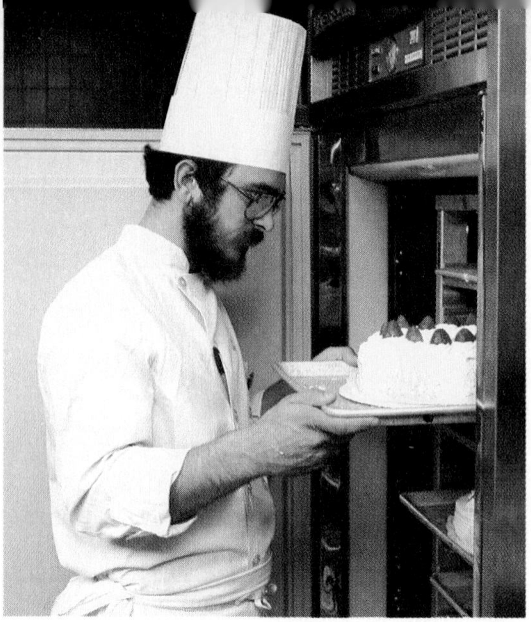

Chiffon cakes, although airy, contain high-calorie ingredients and are often frosted heavily. They are beautiful on the plate, yet not so attractive on the waistline.

Mixing Chiffon Cakes

For mixing, two mixer bowls are needed plus the paddle and whip attachments. If you do not have a commercial mixer, use regular beaters.

1. Sift the flour, half the sugar, the baking powder, and the salt into one bowl. Make a depression or well in the center of the flour mixture.
2. Add the following ingredients, in this order, to the well in the dry ingredients: oil, egg yolks, water, and vanilla. Mix, using the paddle attachment, on low speed until the ingredients are just blended.
3. Place the egg whites and cream of tartar in the second bowl. Using the whip attachment, beat on high speed until soft peaks form. Add the rest of the sugar gradually while continuing to beat. Beat until stiff peaks form.
4. Fold the flour mixture into the egg white mixture until well blended.
5. Scale the batter as directed in the recipe. Pour into ungreased pans. Bake as directed.

ICINGS, FROSTINGS, AND FILLINGS

To many people, a cake without a sweet topping is no kind of cake at all. To a pastry cook, an ***icing*** is a thin, pourable mixture of sugar and liquid. A ***frosting*** is a thick, fluffy, spreadable mixture. A ***filling*** is a sweet, moist mixture to hold the layers of a cake together. Often, the same mixture is used for frosting and filling a cake.

Icings and frostings may be cooked or uncooked. In this chapter you will study the preparation of only the uncooked variety. Many cooks believe they have the best flavor. The recipe for Chocolate Frosting on page 298 is typical of uncooked frostings.

Similar ingredients are used in icings, frostings, and fillings. However, many different variations are possible depending on which are used and in what proportion.

- **Sugar.** In uncooked icings and frostings, confectioner's or powdered sugar is always used. This type is very fine sugar.

Cake Baking Temperatures and Times

Cake	Temperature °F.	Temperature °C	Time
Shortened cakes			
Blended	375	190	See form of cake for time.
Creamed	350	177	
Chocolate	350	177	
Cupcakes	375	190	20 minutes
Layer cakes	See mixing method		25 minutes
Loaf cakes	350	177	45-60 minutes
Thick sheet cakes	350	177	35-40 minutes
Foam cakes			
Angel food	300-325	149-163	1 hour
Chiffon	300-325	149-163	1 hour
Sponge	350	177	25 minutes

The degree of fineness is specified by the number of Xs. 6X sugar is finer than 4X.

- **Egg whites.** Only the whites of eggs are used in uncooked icings or frostings. They must be fresh and free from odor. Egg whites contribute fluffiness and flavor.

- **Fats.** Butter gives the best flavor to uncooked icings and frostings, but it is expensive. Sometimes part butter and part hydrogenated shortening are used instead. Margarine may also be used as a butter substitute but it does not give as much volume as butter.

- **Milk.** Fresh milk, dry milk powder, evaporated milk, and cream all may be used in icings, frostings, and fillings. Be sure to use the type specified in the recipe.

- **Flavorings.** Chocolate is a favorite flavor for cake toppings. Real chocolate contains considerable fat and adds richness, thickness, and flavor. Extracts, such as vanilla, are used in most frostings and icings.

This food service worker is frosting the bottom layer of a three-layer cake. Notice that she is only putting frosting on top of the layer, and not on the sides. When the third layer is placed on top of the other two, she will frost the sides of the cake.

Chocolate Butter Frosting

Equipment: Bench mixer, Whip attachment, Baker's scale, Rubber spatula, Measuring cups, Paddle attachment, Measuring spoons, Double boiler

Yield: Frosts sheet cake (18″x25″x1″)

Ingredients	Amount	Method
Powdered sugar	1 lb. 10 oz.	1. Using the whip attachment, cream powdered sugar and butter for 5 minutes.
Butter	4 oz.	2. Turn off mixer and remove whip attachment. Scrape down bowl with rubber spatula.
Evaporated milk	¾ c.	3. Add milk. Using the paddle attachment, mix well.
Salt	¼ t.	4. Add salt and vanilla. Mix well.
Vanilla	1 t.	5. Melt chocolate in a double boiler.
Baking chocolate	5 oz.	6. Add chocolate. Beat frosting for 2 minutes on medium speed. Frosting should be fluffy.

Serving size: Frosting for one sheet cake **Cost per serving:** ____________

Icings

Icings are very easy to make and require few ingredients. A simple icing might contain only confectioner's sugar, flavoring, and a liquid. The liquid might be water, milk, or fruit juice.

Making the icing consists of mixing the liquid and the flavoring. Add the confectioner's sugar and beat until smooth.

This type of simple icing may be used on angel food cake, sponge cake, or cookies. It can also be used to seal the surface of shortened cakes before frosting.

Frostings

The most popular of the uncooked frostings is buttercream. It may be any flavor or color. It is also very simple to make.

Buttercream frosting consists of butter or margarine (or half butter and half hyodrogenated shortening), vanilla, and cream.

Using the whip attachment, cream the fat until light and fluffy. Cream in some of the sugar. Add the cream and vanilla. Then cream in the rest of the sugar. Beat until very light and fluffy.

Milk powder may be substituted for the cream. Cream it into the shortening before adding the sugar. Use water for the liquid, adding it slowly. If the water is added too quickly, the frosting may separate or become lumpy.

Frosting the Cake

Prepare the cake by trimming any uneven edges. Brush the cake lightly to remove any loose crumbs. If the cake is a layer cake, place the bottom layer, top side down, on the bench or plate. The filling is usually part of the frosting used to finish the cake. Spread it evenly on the bottom layer. Place the top layer over the filling, top side up. If you are using an icing under the frosting, spread it thinly over the cake and allow it to harden. The icing prevents the cake from crumbling as it is frosted.

The cake may be placed on a cake decorator's wheel for ease of frosting. The wheel can be turned as needed.

Frost the sides of the cake first. Holding the spatula parallel to the side, spread the frosting from the bottom to the top. Heap more frosting on top the cake and spread it evenly. Try to make the top as level as possible by building up the sides. Swirl the frosting on top to accent the fluffiness of the frosting.

Fillings

A soft, pudding-type filling may be used instead of frosting between the layers of a cake. It is often made from a pudding or pie filling mix.

Placing the finishing touches on a cake takes a steady hand and artistic eye.

Brownies

Equipment: Sheet pans (18″x26″x1″), Bench mixer, Whip attachment, Baker's scale, Measuring spoons, Bowls, Double boiler, Rubber spatula, Sifter, Cutting board, Chef's knife, Kitchen spoon, Paddle attachment

Yield: 70 Brownies
Temperature: 350°F

Ingredients	Amount
Butter	10 oz.
Sugar	2 lb. 8 oz.
Vanilla	1 T. 2 t.
Eggs	12
Baking chocolate	10 oz.
Flour, all-purpose	14 oz.
Baking powder	2 T.
Salt	1 t.
Chopped walnuts	1 lb. 8 oz.

Method

1. Preheat oven. Grease and flour sheet pans.
2. Cream butter, sugar, and vanilla thoroughly using whip attachment.
3. Add one egg at a time, creaming after each addition.
4. Melt chocolate in a double boiler over low heat, stirring constantly with a kitchen spoon.
5. Add chocolate to creamed mixture and mix well.
6. Sift together remaining dry ingredients.
7. Chop walnuts and stir into flour mixture.
8. Use paddle to stir the nut and flour mixture into creamed mixture.
9. Spread brownie mixture evenly in sheet pans.
10. Bake 35 minutes. Do not over bake.
11. Allow brownies to cool.
12. Cut into 2½″ squares.

Serving size: One 2½″ square

Cost per serving: ____________

COOKIES

Cookies are used frequently in some food service operations, not at all in others. Institutions such as schools make cookies often. They won't, however, show up on the menu of a fancy restaurant.

In some ways, cookies are like small cakes. The ingredients are similar, but the proportions are different. Cookies have a higher proportion of shortening and flour, but less sugar. Cakes are made from batters, but most cookies are made from doughs.

There are three basic types of cookies used in food service — bar, drop, and refrigerator. Each requires a different consistency of dough.

Notice the consistency of the brownie dough being poured into the sheet pan for baking.

Bar Cookies

Bar cookies are the most common type made in food service. They are delicious, but less time consuming to make than other types. The ingredients are mixed to form a soft dough that is spread in baking pans. After baking, each pan can be frosted, if desired, then quickly cut into serving-size bars.

Brownies are among the most popular bar cookies. See pages 302-303 for step-by-step directions.

✔ standards ✔

Bar Cookies

Appearance

- ✔ Even tops.
- ✔ Cut into equal-size pieces.

Color

- ✔ Lightly browned (dark brown if made with chocolate).

Texture

- ✔ Thin, tender crust.
- ✔ Moist, crumbly.

On the Job

Making Brownies

Assignment: Two workers are to prepare 140 brownies. After baking, the brownies are to be sprinkled with powdered sugar and cut into equal pieces.

Check the Recipe

The recipe for brownies is on page 300. You will need to adjust the yield from 70 to 140 brownies. (See page 52 to review this procedure.) Rewrite the list of ingredients with the new amounts for 140 servings. You will also need to determine the amount of powdered sugar needed.

Check Yourself

- Confine your hair with a hairnet, cap, or band.
- Wash your hands thoroughly.
- Put on a clean apron.
- Use plastic gloves for preparing the ingredients and making the brownies.

Assemble the Equipment

- Equipment indicated in the recipe

Prepare the Ingredients

- Ingredients indicated in the recipe
- Powdered sugar

Follow this Procedure

Step 1. Worker #1 greases pans and preheats the oven while Worker #2 assembles the equipment and ingredients.

Step 2. ▲ Worker #1 sifts flour, baking powder, and salt. Worker #2 melts chocolate in a double boiler over medium heat. Careful: chocolate burns very easily.

Step 3. Worker #1 places butter in mixer and creams on low speed.

Step 4. ▲ Worker #2 gradually adds sugar and vanilla to mixer, occasionally turning off the mixer to scrape down the bowl.

Step 5. Worker #1 adds the eggs one at a time, creaming after each addition.

Step 9. ▲ Working together, Workers #1 and #2 divide batter evenly between the pans. The mixer bowl is scraped and the batter spread evenly.

Step 10. Worker #1 places pans in the oven and sets the timer.

Step 11. While the brownies are baking, Worker #2 sifts the powdered sugar into a bowl.

Step 6. ▲ Worker #2 adds melted chocolate to creamed mixture, and mixes well.

Step 7. Worker #1 mixes nuts with flour and adds to creamed mixture gradually.

Step 8. Worker #2 turns off mixer and scrapes down bowl for final mixing of 1 minute on medium speed.

Step 12. ▲ When the brownies have cooled, Worker #2 sifts the powdered sugar over the top of each pan.

Step 13. Worker #1 cuts each pan of brownies into 70 equal pieces.

Drop Cookies

Some of the most popular cookies are drop cookies. If you like chocolate chip or oatmeal cookies, you may be familiar with home production methods of this type. Food service methods are not a great deal different. Of course, a much larger quantity is made at one time.

Drop cookies are made from a somewhat stiffer dough than bar cookies. The dough is often dropped by the spoonful onto baking sheets. For more precise portion size (and more predictable yield), a portion scoop may be used to measure the dough for each cookie.

Refrigerator Cookies

Refrigerator cookies are made from a very stiff dough. After mixing, the dough is formed into long rolls, wrapped, and refrigerated. Later, the rolls of dough are sliced and baked. You can see that refrigerator cookies require more labor than other types. One advantage is that the cookies can be baked as needed.

Refrigerator-type dough may also be formed into cookies with a ***pastry bag***. A pastry bag is a canvas or paper cone with changeable tips. The tips determine the shape of the finished cookies. Cookies made with a pastry bag are sometimes called "bagged cookies." The pastry bag is also used for decorating cakes and cookies with frostings.

CONVENIENCE FORMS

Convenience forms of cakes and cookies range from dry mixes to ready-to-serve items. The choice depends on the operation's budget, menu, work space, and its staff's skills.

Packaged cake mixes are usually used in food service. They contain all the dry ingredients needed for the cakes and usually include a ***conditioner***. A conditioner is a chemical which makes a moister, lighter cake. In mixes, the high ratio shortening and milk powder are already mixed with the dry ingredients. Any needed flavoring may be in the mix or in a special package to be added during the mixing process. The best mixes call for the addition of fresh eggs, water, and sometimes vegetable oil. Mixes make a very good cake, light and delicate. Large operations may order mixes made to their own specifications.

Mixes for cookies are also readily available. Like cake mixes, they need only the addition of liquid ingredients.

Some operations purchase frozen cookie dough. The dough is thawed, portioned, and baked. The thawed dough may be kept under refrigeration for several weeks and used as needed.

Operations which choose to purchase ready-to-serve cakes or cookies usually do so as a money-saving measure. This may eliminate the need for a bake station and workers to staff it. As with products baked on the premises, the quality can vary.

SUMMARY

Cakes and cookies have long been dessert favorites. There are two main types of cakes — shortened and foam. Because they use different leaveners, their textures are quite different. Cakes must be made using an exact formula to assure their quality. Bar cookies are the most common type of cookies made in food service. Many convenience form of cakes and cookies are used in food service operation to save time and labor.

chapter recap

CHECK YOUR KNOWLEDGE

1. Why are cake recipes called formulas?
2. What are the two main types of cakes?
3. What methods are used to mix shortened cakes?
4. What leavener is used in foam cakes?
5. Why are angel food cakes baked in a tube pan?
6. Name the stages egg whites go through as they are beaten.
7. What is the main difference between angel food cakes and sponge cakes?
8. Describe the differences between icings, frostings, and fillings.
9. What kind of cookies are used most often in food service? Why?
10. Name two convenience forms of cakes and cookies.

EXTEND YOUR LEARNING

1. Check the supermarket for the cost of a cake mix. Then find a similar recipe for a "made from scratch" cake. Calculate the most of the ingredients in the recipe. Also include an estimate for time to make both cakes. Calculate the cost of labor at minimum wage. Which cake is more expensive to produce? If you were a food service manager, which would you use?
2. Discuss the reasons only bar, drop, and refrigerator cookies are made in food service. Which would have the lowest labor costs?

"Jim was laughing as he joined Ruthann after class. "I made the flaky pie crust," he told her. "What kind did you make?"

"The mealy crust made with a paste," she answered. "What's so funny?"

"My pie crust," he answered. "The book says it should be round after rolling. Mine looked more like the map of Africa! Chef Robinson laughed too, when I showed him. He said I'd do better next time. I might even make North and South America!"

"Just so it turned out okay when it was baked," said Ruthann. "I think the paste method is easier to make and roll. Mine turned out pretty round. You had the hard kind to make."

"Did you see the mess Tony was in?" asked Jim. "He was making the same kind I was, but he thought it needed a little more water. Chef Robinson warned us about that, but Tony thought he knew best. He had a soggy mess, so he added more flour. It was so tough, he could hardly roll it out. Chef Robinson said to bake it anyway because we needed to see what happened when we didn't follow the recipe. I'll bet it will be one tough pie crust. Anyway, tomorrow we get to finish the lemon meringue pie. I love that pie! Next to apple, it's my favorite."

chapter 21

pies and pastries

Set your goals

When you complete the study of this chapter, you should be able to . . .

- Define and correctly use the vocabulary terms.
- Demonstrate proper piecrust preparation.
- Prepare a variety of pie fillings that meet acceptable standards.

Build your vocabulary

canvas liner	flute
crimp	meringue
docking	pastry flour
double pan	pie shell

PIECRUSTS

In a pie, the crust does more than just hold the filling. Its crisp, flaky texture and pleasing flavor add to the enjoyment of eating. A basic crust seems to go equally well with a main dish chicken pie, warm apple pie fragrant with cinnamon, or a tart lemon pie topped with meringue.

Perhaps pies are such popular items in food service because many people don't take the time to make them at home. Pastry crusts can be tricky to make. A crust that is dry, tough, or too salty spoils a pie. But food service cooks know that cooking is a science as well as an art. The standardized recipes they use call for special ingredients that help them make perfect crusts by the dozen. And if you follow the directions carefully, you will soon be able to do the same.

Of course, there are piecrusts that are not made of pastry. Graham cracker crusts are popular and some pies use cookie crusts. Even food service operations that serve pies regularly do not necessarily make their own from scratch. They may purchase frozen crusts or frozen pies or even ready-made pies that only need to be cut and served. But knowing the basics of making crusts and fillings will be an asset in food service work. It shows you have gone beyond the basics, that your knowledge of the food service kitchen is well-rounded.

The variety of pies offered at a bakery seems endless. A good food service worker knows how to make quantities of perfect crusts and delicious fillings.

Basic Pie Crust

Equipment: Bench mixer, Baker's scale, Measuring spoons, Rubber spatula, Paddle attachment, Quart measure, Portion scale

Yield: 8 double (9") pie crusts

Ingredients	Amount	Method
Flour, pastry Salt Shortening Water	4 lb. 3 T. 2 lb. 12 oz. 1 pt.	1. Place flour, salt, and shortening in mixer bowl. 2. Using the paddle attachment, mix on low speed until the flour and shortening form nut-like pieces. Do not overmix. 3. Stop the mixer and add the water all at once. 4. Turn the mixer on briefly to gather the dough together. Turn off immediately. 5. Scale the dough into 8 oz. portions for each crust. The top crusts may only require 6 oz. of dough. 6. Bake or refrigerate as the filling recipe directs.

Serving size: 8 oz. of dough

Cost per serving: ____________

Ingredients

Standard pastry piecrust requires only four ingredients — shortening, flour, salt, and water. These ingredients, however, must be carefully measured and mixed to form a tender, tasty crust.

In the home kitchen a variety of fats are used in making piecrust. Shortening, lard, and oil are all popular. But in food service, hydrogenated shortening is almost always the choice.

Two types of flour are suitable for piecrusts. Many cooks use all-purpose flour. However, the finest pastry chefs insist on ***pastry flour***. Pastry flour is low in gluten and makes a tender crust.

The last two ingredients, salt and water, are also important. Salt adds flavor to the crust. The water binds the other ingredients together to make a dough.

Equipment

When piecrusts are made in quantity, the mixer is usually used. For small amount (or beginners), the dough can be mixed by hand.

To make piecrust, you need measuring equipment, a sifter, pie pans, a rolling pin, and a pastry board with a ***canvas liner***. A canvas liner is a square of canvas which is placed over the pastry board. It helps keep dough from sticking to the board. If you mix the crust by hand, you will also need a bowl and a pastry cutter.

Mixing the Dough

The method of mixing makes a big difference in the texture of the finished piecrust. The crust may be flaky or mealy depending on the mixing method used. The chart at the right gives step-by-step directions for the flaky method and one of several mealy methods. Try both and compare the results.

In the flaky method, the shortening must be very cold when cut into the flour. Cold shortening can be cut into small, round pieces, as described in the chart. The shortening melts during baking creating soft flakes of pastry. The water added during mixing should be ice cold so the shortening does not warm up.

In the mealy method, cold shortening is also used. The blending of the water with part of the flour into a paste makes mixing in the shortening easier and quicker. The texture of the finished crust will be mealy rather than flaky. However, both methods produce tender crusts.

Pie Dough Mixing Methods

Flaky Method	Mealy Method
1. Measure the flour and salt into a bowl. **2.** Cut half the shortening into the flour until there are large lumps. **3.** Cut in the rest of the shortening until the mixture looks coarse. The lumps should be the size of small peas, each lump surrounded by flour. **4.** Blend in ice water until the flour has absorbed all the water. Do not overmix.	**1.** Divide the flour into two parts. The first part should be about five times the second. **2.** Cut all the shortening into the large portion of flour until it resembles coarse cornmeal. **3.** Add the second portion of flour to water and salt. Blend into a paste. **4.** Blend the paste into the first mixture until all the liquid is absorbed.

Panning the Dough

After the dough is mixed, knead it slightly. Then let it rest on the bench at least 30 minutes. This allows the gluten to relax and the moisture to spread evenly throughout the dough. The dough will be easier to roll out. Do not refrigerate the dough.

The next step is to shape and pan the dough. One-crust pies usually have a filling that is added after the bottom crust has been baked. The unfilled bottom crust is called a ***pie shell***. A two-crust pie consists of a bottom crust, a filling, and a top crust that are all baked together.

One-Crust Pies

These directions are for pie shells. If you are making a one-crust pie with a baked filling, follow the recipe for baking directions.

1. Scale the dough into 8 oz. (225 g) pieces. Each piece will make a 9 in. (23 cm) bottom crust. (For an 8 in. or 20 cm pie, divide the dough into 6 oz. or 170 g pieces.)
2. Lightly flour the pastry board or canvas liner and rolling pin.
3. Place the dough in the center of the board and form it into a round, flat circle.
4. Begin rolling from the center outward. Roll with light, firm strokes, giving the dough a quarter turn after each roll. Add flour to the board or liner if the dough begins to stick. Never roll back and forth on the dough, always from the center outward.
5. Continue rolling until the dough is about $^1/_8$ in. (3 mm) thick. Keep the shape round and the thickness even.
6. Fold the dough in half and carefully transfer it to the pie pan. Be careful not to stretch the dough as you fit it into the pan.
7. The edge of the crust is usually finished by fluting. To ***flute*** means to form an attractive, wavy edge around the rim of the pie pan. Trim the edge of the dough about 1/2 in. (1.3 cm) larger than the edge of the pan. Fold this extra dough under all the way around.
8. Pie shells tend to puff up during baking because there is no filling weighting them down. To avoid this, prick the dough all over the sides and bottom of the pan with a fork. This is called ***docking***. It allows the steam to escape so the crust will not puff up. Many bakers prefer to ***double pan*** by placing another pie pan of the same size inside the one with the dough. The weight of the pan holds the piecrust in shape.
9. When all the pie shells are panned, bake in a preheated 425°F (220°C) oven for 10-12 minutes, or until lightly browned.

Two-Crust Pies

Two-crust pies are made in much the same way as pie shells, but the filling and top crust are added before baking.

1. For each 9 in. (23 cm) pie, scale an 8 oz. (225 g) piece for the bottom crust and a 6 oz. (170 g) piece for the top crust. (For an 8 in. or 20 cm pie, scale a 6 oz. or 170 g piece for the bottom crust. For the top crust, use a 5 oz. or 140 g piece.)
2. Follow Steps 1 to 6 of the one-crust pie directions.
3. Fill the bottom crust with filling.
4. Roll out the top crust to a circle 1/8 in. (3 mm) thick and slightly larger than the top of the pie pan.
5. Fold the upper crust in half. Dock by making three cuts in the center of the fold. Place the top crust over the pie filling and unfold so the docking is in the center of the pie.

6. Trim the bottom crust even with the edge of the pan. Trim the top crust about ½ in. (1.3 cm) larger.
7. Moisten the top edge of the bottom crust with milk.
8. Fold the edge of the top crust under the bottom crust. Seal by fluting or crimping. To ***crimp*** means to press the edges of the piecrust together with a fork or special crimper tool. On a two-crust pie, fluting or crimping not only adds to the pie's appearance, but also seals in the filling.
9. Bake according to the recipe directions.

If the pie dough was scaled correctly, there should be very few scraps. Add any trimmings to fresh dough before adding the water and allowing it to rest. Pie dough that includes trimmings should always to used as a bottom crust because it will be tougher than fresh dough.

PIES WITH FRUIT FILLINGS

Pies with fruit fillings are usually two-crust pies. Apple and cherry fillings are most popular, but peach, apricot, and other fruits are also served frequently. In food service, frozen or canned fruits are usually used because they require little pre-preparation. Many operations use ready-prepared fillings which have been thickened. These are simply placed in the crust and baked.

If ready-prepared fillings are not used, the fruit must be thickened before baking. Otherwise the fruit juices would soak into the crust and make it soggy. Cornstarch is the most common thickener. It is tasteless and does not cause lumps if used correctly.

Preparing Fruit Fillings

Several different methods can be used to thicken and prepare fruit fillings. The two most common methods are explained here.

- **The hot juice method**. Canned and frozen fruit are usually prepared by the hot juice method. This method has several advantages. It eliminates the time-consuming preparation of fresh fruit. The amount of sugar can be measured exactly. The filling is thickened before it is put in the pie and does not shrink during baking. This method also allows the filling to be prepared ahead of time. The recipe for Apple Pie Filling on page 313 uses the hot juice method.
- **The fresh fruit method**. Clean and prepare the fruit. (Apples, for example, must be pared and sliced.) Combine the sugar, cornstarch, and flavorings and mix with the fruit. Some fruits, such as apples and peaches, darken when the inside of the fruit is exposed to the air. If the sliced fruit must stand more than a few minutes, soak it in a lemon juice solution until ready for use.

This food service worker is slicing apples for a two-crust apple pie using the fresh fruit method.

Apple Pie Filling

Equipment: Stock pot
Can opener
Baker's scale
Measuring spoons
Kitchen spoon
Measuring cups
Butter knife

Yield: Filling for 8 (9 inch) pies
Temperature: 400°F

Ingredients	Amount	Method
Apples, pie pack	2 #10 cans	1. Combine apples, sugar, salt, cinnamon, nutmeg, vanilla, and cornstarch in a stock pot.
Sugar	4 lb.	2. Heat the apple mixture to boiling. Stir constantly with a kitchen spoon.
Salt	2 t.	3. Add butter and stir until it melts.
Cinnamon	2 t.	4. Add lemon juice and stir.
Nutmeg	1 t.	5. Remove filling from heat and allow it to cool.
Vanilla	2 t.	6. Refrigerate until needed in a covered container.
Cornstarch	1 c.	7. Pour filling into 8 unbaked pie shells.
Butter	1/2 lb.	8. Dot with butter.
Lemon juice	1 c.	9. Moisten edge of bottom crust. Cover with top crusts.
		10. Seal edges. Trim off excess dough and flute edges.
		11. Perforate top crust generously.
		12. Bake about 45 minutes.

Serving size: Slice = 1/8 pie

Cost per serving: ____________

standards

Fruit Pies

Appearance

- Top crust slightly raised.
- Edges evenly crimped.

Color

- Top crust well-browned.

Flavor

- Filling sweet, but with slightly tart fruit taste.

Texture

- Bottom crust tender, never soggy.
- Juicy, but able to hold shape when piece is removed.

This coconut cream filling has been scaled into a pie crust for portion control.

PIES WITH SOFT FILLINGS

These may be some of your favorite pies. Coconut cream, pumpkin, lemon meringue and custard pies all have soft fillings.

When you make a pie with soft filling, follow the recipe directions carefully. Incorrect preparation can cause lumpy or grainy filling.

Look at the recipe for Lemon Meringue Pie on page 315. Note that the lemon juice is added after the filling is thickened. Lemon juice reacts with uncooked cornstarch and prevents it from thickening properly.

Chiffon Pies

Chiffon pies have a very light, delicate filling. They frequently are made with a graham cracker or nut crust. Beaten egg whites or whipped cream are folded into the filling to create the lighter or chiffon effect. Chiffon pies may be baked in the oven. More usually, gelatin is dissolved in the hot filling. After the filling has begun to gel, the whipped cream is folded in. The piecrust is immediately filled and refrigerated. A fluffy-type topping completes the picture of an unusually beautiful pie.

TOPPINGS

One-crust pies, especially cream and chiffon types, are usually served with fluffy topping. Toppings add both flavor and eye appeal.

Lemon Meringue Pie Filling

Equipment: Grater, Measuring cups, Bowl, Saucepan, Stock pot, Quart measure, Baker's scale, Measuring spoons, Wire whip, Kitchen spoon

Yield: Filling for 8 (9 inch) pies

Ingredients	Amount	Method
Water	$2\frac{1}{2}$ qt.	1. Grate the rinds of fresh lemons. Measure the gratings and set aside.
Sugar	4 lb.	2. Separate the egg yolks from the whites for the meringue. Set yolks aside in a stainless steel bowl.
Salt	2 t.	3. Melt the butter in a saucepan. Set aside.
Lemon gratings	$\frac{1}{2}$ c.	4. Pour $2\frac{1}{2}$ qt. of water, sugar, salt, and lemon gratings in a stock pot. Bring to a boil.
Egg yolks	16	5. Whip egg yolks slightly with a wire whip.
Cornstarch	12 oz.	6. Add 1 pt. of water and cornstarch to the egg yolks. Stir with a kitchen spoon until the starch dissolves.
Water	1 pt.	7. Slowly pour the starch-egg mixture into the boiling liquid, whipping vigorously with a wire whip until the filling thickens and clears.
Lemon juice	$2\frac{1}{2}$ c.	8. Add the lemon juice and melted butter to the filling. Stir with a kitchen spoon until thoroughly blended.
Butter	$\frac{1}{4}$ lb.	9. Remove filling from heat.
		10. Pour the filling into eight pre-baked pie shells. Let cool and top with meringue.

Serving size: Slice = $\frac{1}{8}$ pie

Cost per serving: ________________

standards

Pies with Soft Fillings

Appearance

- Evenly fluted edges on crust.
- Filling even and smooth.
- If meringue topping, meringue should be high and fill entire top of pie.

Color

- Crust lightly browned.
- If meringue topping, meringue should be lightly browned.

Flavor

- Creamy, flavor, never starchy.

Texture

- Tender bottom crust.
- Smooth, creamy filling, never gummy.

Pumpkin pies have a soft filling and are most often served during the fall and early winter as a holiday treat.

Lemon chiffon, coconut cream, custard, and chocolate cream are all pies with soft fillings.

Meringue

Equipment: Bench mixer
Measuring cups
Whip attachment
Measuring spoons
Baker's scale

Yield: Topping for 8 (9 inch) pies
Temperature: 350°F

Ingredients	Amount	Method
Egg whites Cream of tartar Sugar	2 c. 1½ t. 1 lb.	1. Using the whip attachment, beat the egg whites at high speed until they form soft peaks. 2. Gradually add half of the sugar with the mixer running. 3. Add cream of tartar and the remaining sugar gradually. 4. Continue to beat until the meringue forms stiff but moist peaks. 5. Swirl on top of pies and bake 12-15 min. until lightly browned.

Serving size: Topping for one pie **Cost per serving:** ________________

Meringue

Meringue (muh-RANG) is a fluffy mixture of beaten egg whites and sugar. It is heaped lightly on top the pie filling and swirled attractively. Be sure the meringue touches the edge of the crust all the way around. This will prevent it from shrinking away from the crust during baking, The recipe for Meringue above gives step-by-step directions for mixing and baking.

Whipped Toppings

Toppings are sometimes used on pies. The most common are whipped heavy cream, either freshly prepared or in ready-to-serve form.

Meringue adds a special finish to most any type of pie.

SUMMARY

Piecrust is a mixture of shortening, flour, salt, and water. These four ingredients combine into a crisp, flaky product that is equally good filled with meat, with fruit, or with a soft filling such as custard. Apple and lemon meringue are two of the most popular pies. When pie appears on a food service menu, it is sure to be a favorite.

chapter recap

CHECK YOUR KNOWLEDGE

1. In food service, what type of shortening is used for pie crusts?
2. What type of flour is best for piecrusts?
3. What causes the difference in texture between flaky and mealy piecrusts?
4. Why is ice water used when making flaky pie crust?
5. What is a canvas liner?
6. What is fluting?
7. Name two methods used to keep a single pie crust from puffing up during baking.
8. What should be done with pie dough scraps?
9. Why do bakers prefer the hot juice method over the fresh fruit method for fruit fillings?
10. In making lemon meringue pie, why is the lemon juice added after the filling is cooked?

EXTEND YOUR LEARNING

1. Visit a bakery shop in your area. List the number and kinds of pies which are available. Ask the sales person which is the most popular kind of pie. Bring your information to class.
2. Compare the cost of buying a ready-to-serve lemon meringue pie with making one. Calculate the cost of ingredients. Estimate the time it would take you to make the pie. Calculate labor costs at minimum wage. How do the costs compare?

Unit 7

Fast Food Techniques

It's hard to believe, but those familiar fast food chains have only been around since the 1950s. Why have they become so popular?

- More people are eating out more often.
- With busier working schedules, there is a demand for food that is served promptly.
- People are traveling more and eating at fast food chains because they guarantee the type, quality, and price of food.

Computers have been another reason for the quick development of fast food chains. They help managers keep track of inventory so cost control becomes easier. Most cash registers are now computerized. This allows sales to be checked as often as every 15 minutes. The manager can then plan the amount of food that is to be produced, yet keep waste to a minimum.

Of course, quickly prepared foods were available long before fast food chains. Many drug stores, for example, had lunch counters where a limited variety of food was cooked to order. Today, almost every restaurant utilizes some fast food techniques. For instance, many full-service restaurants have a short-order cook who prepares steaks, hamburgers, and other items to order.

This unit includes professional cooking techniques and foods that are often associated with fast food operations. However, grilling, broiling, and frying are not limited to fast foods. Neither are pizzas, Mexican foods, or beverages.

"Jim, Tony, and David were talking after school. It was a beautiful spring day, and they were discussing their summer plans.

Tony said, "I had a letter from my cousin Rick, the one who's a cook at Disney World. He said he's looking for a summer job for me there. Wouldn't that be great?"

"It sure would," said David. "Kim and I are thinking about getting jobs in fast foods. Chef Robinson said that's where the most jobs are. How about you, Jim?"

"I don't know," answered Jim. "I was talking to Ruthann and she wants a job in a hospital. She wants to be a dietitian when she graduates. As for me, I just haven't decided. Maybe fast foods is a good idea."

David said, "When I was visiting fast food restaurants last week for my extra credit project, I talked to one of the managers. He can't be more than 25, and he's already making a good salary. He started out grilling hamburgers. He said if you pay attention, work hard, and are serious about your job, you can move up fast."

"It's hard to believe," said Jim, "that fast foods have grown so quickly. When my dad was young there weren't fast food places like there are today."

"It's computers," interrupted Tony, "that make the difference. If I get a job at Disney World I hope I can learn more about them. They couldn't operate without computers there."

"You're right," exclaimed David. "The manager I talked to showed me the information he gets from computerized cash registers. He said he does most of his planning using computer data."

"I think you're right," said Jim, "but what I'd really like to be is a chef. I like to cook, and make food I cook look nice. I like to see people enjoying the food I cook. I'm going to look around more before I make a decision."

"Don't wait too long, Jim," advised Tony, "or the good jobs might all be taken.""

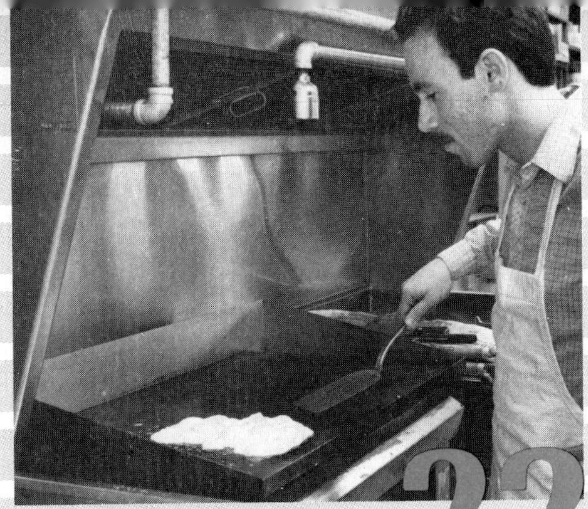

chapter 22

grilling

Set your goals

When you complete the study of this chapter, you should be able to . . .

- Define and correctly use the vocabulary terms.
- Correctly use and care for the griddle.
- Grill and assemble a hamburger using fast food techniques.
- Grill a variety of foods such as meats, fish, and eggs.

Build your vocabulary

assembly table	grilling
commissary	pumice stone
dressing	stoning
FIFO	warming cabinet

GRILLING

Grilling is a method of short-order cooking on a griddle. This method uses very little fat. The most typical and popular of all American foods — the hamburger — is usually grilled.

Hamburgers may be the best known grilled foods, but other short-order foods may also be grilled. Thin steaks and chops, small fish, eggs, sausages, bacon, and grilled sandwiches are just a few of the food that are often cooked by grilling. Although grilling is usually associated with fast foods, it is also used frequently in other food service operations to cook foods quickly.

Meat to be grilled must have natural fat, since very little fat is added in cooking. For instance, ground beef for hamburgers should have about 18 to 25 percent fat. This amount of fat seasons the meat, keeps the hamburgers juicy, and enhances their flavor. If the meat contains too much fat, the hamburgers will shrink too much during cooking.

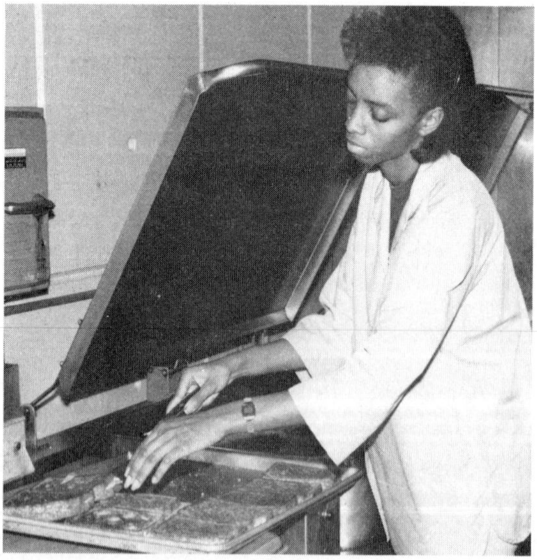

Being a short order cook requires concentration and good timing. Grilling foods to the same consistency requires practice.

Most meat products have sufficient fat for grilling. A light coating of grease is needed on the griddle to cook eggs, fish, and pancakes, and to grill sandwiches. This keeps the food from sticking to the griddle.

Salt and pepper are added after food is grilled. If added before, the salt causes smoking and interferes with browning.

Equipment

The griddle is a flat piece of highly polished metal with a drain to carry off excess grease. It may be a separate piece of equipment heated by gas or electricity, or it may be a built-in part of the range. Each section of the griddle can be heated separately so foods can be cooked at different temperatures at the same time.

A flexible, metal spatula or turner is needed to turn the food. It is also used to scrape food particles and excess grease from the griddle.

Many cooks like to keep an oil can containing vegetable oil near the griddle. Extra oil can be added as needed during grilling.

In food service, a ***pumice stone*** is needed to remove pieces of food stuck to the surface of the griddle. Pumice stone is a light, spongy rock which will clean the surface without scratching it. Review the information regarding the care of the griddle on page 131.

Using the Griddle

Grilling is a fast, simple method of cooking. Follow these general directions for use of the griddle:

1. Preheat the griddle to 325°-350°F (160°-180°C), or until a few drops of water sprinkled on the griddle sizzle and evaporate. Different foods may require different temperatures.
2. Check to see the surface of the griddle is free from food particles. Grease the surface lightly, if needed.
3. Place the food on the griddle and cook as directed.

HAMBURGERS IN FAST FOODS

Hamburgers are the mainstay of the fast food industry because they are most popular. The hamburger consists of the meat patty, the bun, and the dressing.

Ingredients

The ingredients used for hamburgers vary only slightly from one fast food chain to another. Those mentioned here are basic to most.

- **Patty**. The size, quality, and fat content of the hamburger patties are standardized within each fast food chain. The fat content is generally 20 to 25 percent. The patties are usually delivered fresh or frozen from the ***commissary*** — a food and supply warehouse that may be owned by the fast food chain. Patties come preportioned, that is divided into patties of a specified thickness and diameter. Preportioned patties save time and labor costs.

- **Bun**. Some fast food chains use local bakeries to supply the buns rather than shipping them from the commissary. The bakeries must follow exact specifications for bun height, weight, and diameter. The buns are presliced and may be plain or seeded. They must have a firm texture so they will not fall apart while the sandwich is being eaten. A few chains now offer whole wheat buns as an alternative to white ones.

- **Dressing**. The ***dressing*** is the extra garnish put on the hamburger in the bun to improve its appearance and to add flavor. Although different chains have different dressings, they usually include a slice of tomato, shredded lettuce, pickles, and onions. Ketchup and mustard are sometimes added as a dressing or they may be available in small packets so customers can add them if they wish.

The onions and tomatoes are freshly sliced each morning. The lettuce is shredded and refrigerated. In some chains, most dressing ingredients are delivered from the commissary ready for use. Mayonnaise is often used as a spread on the buns.

Method of Cooking

Many professional cooks look down on fast foods because fast food workers do not need a high degree of food service training. Standardization takes the art out of cooking. Workers are trained in only a few specialized cooking techniques and the use of fast food cooking equipment.

Perhaps you have noticed that some fast food chains promote broiled hamburgers, others grilled. Grilling carmelizes the slight amount of sugar present in the meat, adding to the flavor. However, some customers prefer the smoky flavor caused by the open flame of the broiler. Broiling techniques will be discussed in Chapter 23.

To cook hamburgers on a griddle, first prepare the griddle using the method described on pages 322-323. Then cook the hamburgers following these guidelines:

- Turn the meat often for even cooking. Do not pat or press the meat during grilling. This causes a loss of juice.
- Use a moderate grill temperature to prevent smoking.
- Scrape or pour off the excess fat as it accumulates. Griddles are equipped with grooves on the side to drain the fat off the surface of the cooking surface.
- Cook to the desired degree of doneness. Do not overcook or the meat will be dry.
- After using the griddle, wipe the surface with paper towels and clean off any stuck food particles with the pumice stone.

safety tip . . .

Every 24 hours the griddle should be cleaned by *stoning*. This means scrubbing the hot, well-oiled griddle with the pumice stone. After all the burned bits of food have been loosened, wipe the grill clean with paper towels. Empty and wash the grease drawer.

Notice how the hamburgers are lined up on the griddle. A metal spatula is used to turn the meat frequently.

After the hamburgers are grilled, they are placed in a bun and inserted in the ***warming cabinet***. The warming cabinet is a drawer heated by steam that keeps the cooked hamburgers and buns warm and moist until they are dressed.

Hamburgers in buns must not remain in the warming cabinet any longer than 10 minutes. After that time, the product loses quality quickly. Sandwiches not used within 10 minutes are an expensive waste because they must be thrown away.

Fast food workers learn to always follow a well-known rule of storage — "first in, first out." They call it ***FIFO*** and soon become used to that abbreviation. The hamburgers first put in the warming cabinet must be the first ones taken out for use.

Assembling the Hamburgers

Hamburger assembly is also standardized. Workers are trained to add certain amounts of dressing in a particular order. Although the type of dressings added is also standardized, customers may order the dressings they prefer on the hamburgers. Workers are trained to recognize the correct amount of dressing by appearance rather than by weight to save time.

In a typical fast food operation, the following procedure might be used to dress the burgers. The work takes place on the ***assembly table*** — a long, stainless steel counter.

1. The bottom slice of the bun is spread with mayonnaise.
2. The patty, lettuce, tomato slice, pickle slices, and onion are placed, in order, on top.
3. The top of the bun is added and the sandwich is securely wrapped or placed in a special box.

Each fast food chain gives its own special name to various types of hamburgers. Some sandwiches have two meat patties in a three-slice bun. Most operations also offer cheeseburgers. As a worker you must know the ingredients and the amount and type of dressing for each sandwich.

Serving

The completed sandwiches are placed on the warming shelf behind the serving counter. Infrared lamps keep the food warm.

There are definite rules for placing food on the warming shelf. Each type of sandwich or food is separated from the others. The sandwiches made first are placed closest to the customer service area. As with the warming cabinet, the sandwiches cannot stay on the warming shelf longer than 10 minutes. If they are not sold by that time, they must be discarded.

Without knowing how many sandwiches are likely to be sold at different times of the day, the manager would be unable to estimate needed protection. Of course, there are always surprises — perhaps a busload of people arrives or a sudden storm keeps customers away. Generally, though, during lunch and dinner hours sandwiches will be sold as fast as they can be made. The time between is the slack time. Then the manager must have enough sandwiches on hand to satisfy demand, but not so many as to cause waste.

GRILLING OTHER MEATS AND SEAFOOD

When grilling meats other than hamburgers, the same cooking method is followed. A slight coating of grease is needed on the griddle when cooking seafood or very lean meats.

Bacon, sausage, and pork chops are frequently grilled. Grilled ham is often served with eggs for breakfast or as an entree such as grilled ham with pineapple. Mixed grills such as shrimp and other seafood or lamb chops and mixed vegetables are other popular grilled entrees.

GRILLING EGGS

Grilling is often used for breakfast items such as fried or scrambled eggs. Eggs are cooked at lower temperatures. Set the griddle at 300°F (150°C).

Fried Eggs

To prepare fried eggs on the griddle, follow these steps:

1. Brush the surface of the griddle with oil and place a metal egg ring on it to keep the egg from spreading.
2. Crack an egg into the ring.
3. Cook about 2 minutes.
4. Test the egg white for firmness.
5. If the egg is to be served "over easy," slip off the egg ring and turn the egg carefully so the yolk does not break.
6. Cook a few seconds more to set the egg on the other side.

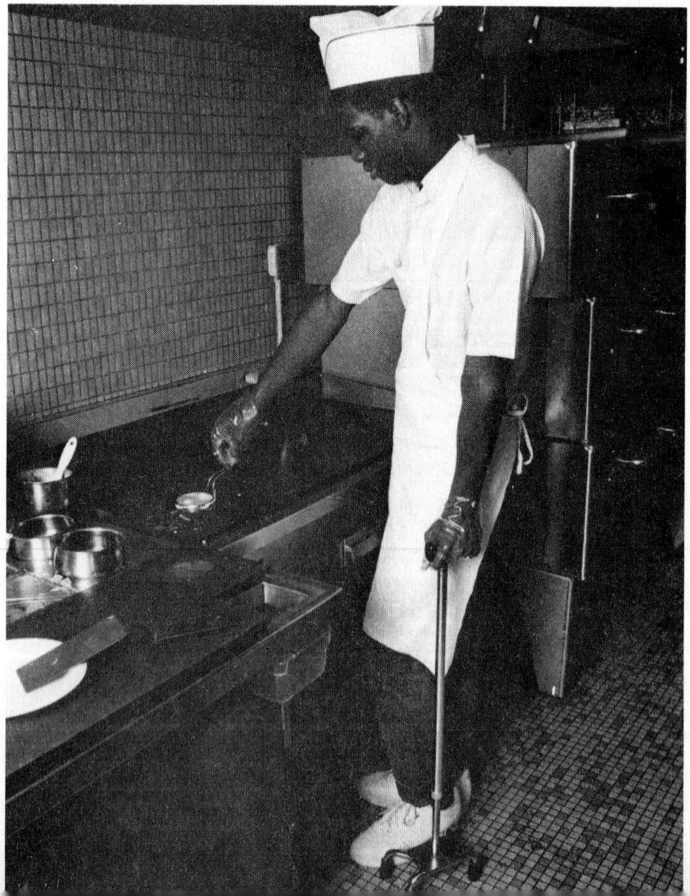

Fried eggs are often cooked in egg rings. The well-oiled griddle helps to cook the egg quickly without burning it.

Scrambled Eggs

Scrambled eggs may be cooked until soft and creamy or until firm and slightly browned. Sometimes the customer will request one way or the other. Follow these steps for making scrambled eggs on the griddle:

1. Beat fresh eggs slightly with salt, pepper, and one tablespoon of water for each egg.

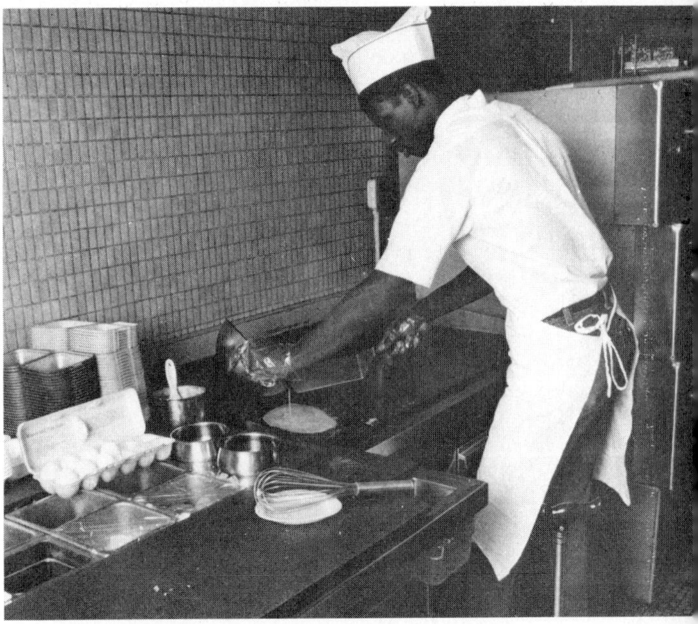

2. Pour the egg mixture on the lightly greased griddle.

3. Immediately turn the egg mixture with a flexible, metal turner and continue to turn until the mixture is cooked to the desired stage of doneness.

GRILLING OTHER FOODS

Several other kinds of food are often cooked on a griddle. Pancakes and French toast, described in Chapter 19, are grilled. Some hot sandwiches, especially the popular grilled cheese sandwich, are also cooked or heated on the griddle.

As you can see, meats are not the only food that can be grilled. This asparagus and onion combination will be a tasty complement to steak.

Fire safety is always on the minds of food service workers. However, the correct use of the griddle is a good time to review fire safety.

SUMMARY

Grilling is a cooking technique used to cook foods quickly. Foods are cooked on a griddle, a piece of flat metal over a heat source. Hamburgers are the most popular grilled food, especially in fast food operations. Other meats, seafood, eggs, and foods such as pancakes are also cooked by grilling.

chapter recap

CHECK YOUR KNOWLEDGE

1. Briefly explain what is meant by "grilling."

2. What percentage of fat should ground beef used for hamburgers have?

3. What is used to clean the surface of the griddle after use?

4. Where are the hamburger patties used by fast food chains made?

5. Name the three parts of fast food hamburgers.

6. What is the usual dressing on a hamburger?

7. What happens to the grease from the hamburger during grilling?

8. How long can a hamburger in the bun remain in the warming cabinet without loss of quality?

9. What is used on the griddle to keep an egg in a round shape during frying?

10. Name three other foods which are also grilled.

EXTEND YOUR LEARNING

1. Examine the griddle in your laboratory kitchen or in the school cafeteria. Locate the drain and grease cup. Can the sections of the griddle be heated separately? Can the amount of heat be controlled? Watch a demonstration on cleaning the griddle.

2. Write to three fast food companies that feature hamburgers. Ask them for information on the nutritional content of the food they sell. Report their answers to the class.

3. Discuss why so many fast food outlets have added food other than hamburgers to their menus.

"Never in my whole life," said Rosita, "have I eaten a piece or rare, bloody meat. I never intend to eat any. When Chef Robinson demonstrated broiling steaks and sliced the rare one, I was almost sick. I liked the well-done one."

Jim said, "I sank my teeth into a piece of that rare steak. It was really good — tender and tasty. My problem is that I can't afford a steak, ever!"

"That's right," said Tony. "Steak dinners are really expensive in a restaurant. But I'm with Rosita. I like them well done when I can afford one."

"Well, I liked the medium rare steak myself," Ruthann said. "It's tender and juicy, but not bloody. But to tell the truth, I think I could be a vegetarian. I can live without steak, but I really love vegetables. Besides, steak has all that bad cholesterol."

"Cholesterol?" asked Tony. "Why should I worry about that? I'm not going to have a heart attack."

Ruthann replied, "I guess that's what my dad would have said at your age. Just a few months ago, Dad had some chest pains. The doctor did lots of tests. One of them tested his blood cholesterol level. It was too high. So now Dad is on a low-fat diet — no whole milk, no cheese, no ice cream, no eggs, and beef only once a week. Now he's jogging, has lost weight, and looks and feels a lot better."

"Ruthann's right, of course," said Jim. "Even Chef Robinson pointed out the hidden fat in the marbling of the meat. Even hamburger has a lot of cholesterol. Maybe it's a good thing meat is so expensive. It wouldn't hurt any of us to watch what we eat a bit."

chapter 23

broiling

Set your goals

When you complete the study of this chapter, you should be able to . . .

- Define and correctly use the vocabulary terms.
- Identify foods suitable for broiling.
- Broil meats to the correct degree of doneness.
- Demonstrate proper care of the broiler.

Build your vocabulary

broiling	rare
grid marks	rib-eye
medium rare	well done

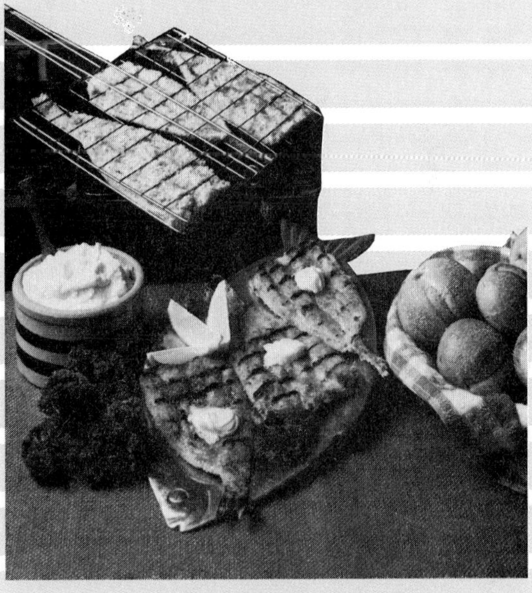

BROILING

In ***broiling***, food is placed on an open grid and is cooked by direct heat. (In an oven food is cooked by warmed air.) As the food is cooked, juices and melted fat drain off the food and fall through the grid.

Some broilers are run by gas or electricity. Others use charcoal. The heat may be above or below the food. Whichever method is used, broiling it is considered one of the finest ways to cook tender meats — especially beef.

In Chapter 12, you learned how to roast meat and cook it by the moist heat methods. Now you will study another of the dry heat methods. Broiling is used in both traditional restaurants and many fast food operations.

Ingredients

Broiling is a method used almost exclusively for meats. A few vegetables such as tomatoes and large mushrooms may also be broiled. Casseroles are sometimes slipped under the broiler for a few minutes to brown the top.

Vegetables and lean meat, poultry, and fish are usually coated with oil before broiling. This helps prevent the food from sticking and gives a better finished appearance. Seasonings (except salt) may also be added before broiling. If salt is added before cooking, it draws out the juices, leaving the food dry.

Beef

Look at the chart on page 187. Notice the cuts used for steaks. The most tender and expensive cuts are used for broiling. These include beef club, T-bone, porterhouse, tenderloin (filet) and the sirloin steaks. A few other cuts may also be broiled if tenderized first.

Ground beef patties are suitable for broiling since the grinding process breaks down the connective tissue and makes the meat tender. The best ground beef for broiling comes from the round, sirloin tip, or the chuck closest to the rib section.

Meat suitable for broiling must have considerable fat, not only on the outside, but all through the muscle. As you probably remember from studying meat, such meat is describe as being well marbled. The fat melts as the meat broils, browning the surface, helping to cook the meat, and keeping it juicy and flavorful.

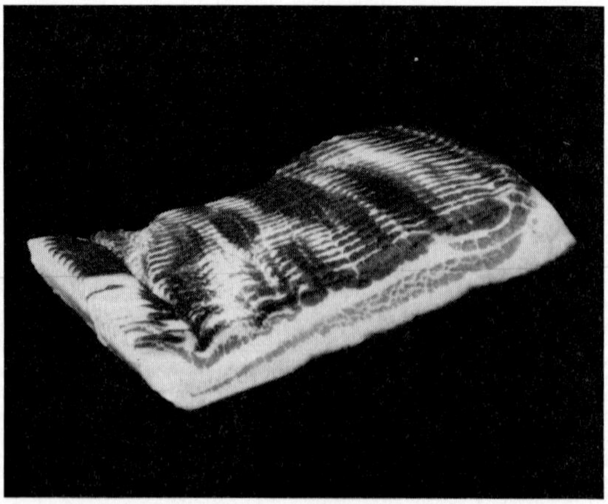

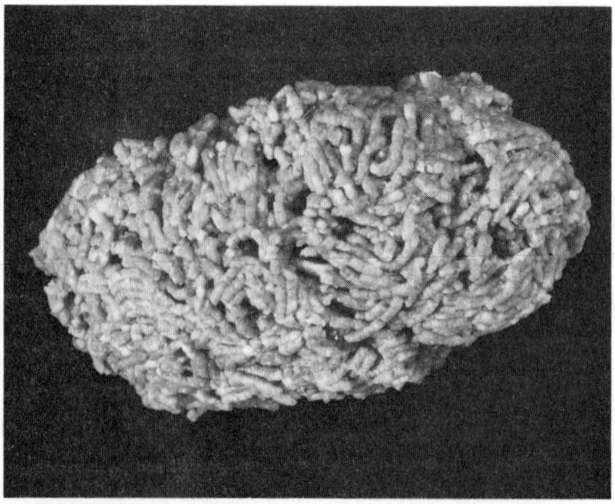

Both bacon and hamburger are excellent meats for broiling because they are well-marbled.

Veal, Lamb, and Pork

Veal is not broiled because it requires long, slow cooking. Since lamb is a young animal, most steaks and chops cut from a lamb can be broiled. Pork chops and ham steaks may also be broiled.

Poultry

Very young chickens and turkeys are suitable for broiling. Because they are quite small, they are halved or quartered for broiling. Young poultry has very little fat, so it is usually basted with melted butter or barbecue sauce. This keeps the meat from drying out and enhances the flavor.

Fish and Seafood

Although fish contain little fat, some have more fat than others. The less lean fish, such as salmon or trout, may be broiled successfully. Baste lean fish and seafood, like perch and cod, liberally with melted butter. This prevents drying out during cooking.

In a closed broiler food is placed on a rack-like surface. This is above a trough that catches the melted fat and juices.

Equipment

For broiling in the oven, a broiler pan is equipped with a rack to hold the food above the juices and fat. When broiling directly over the glowing coals, the meat is placed on the grid above the coals. The melting fat and juices drip on the hot coals below.

Use a long-handled fork to turn the meat as it cooks. If many pieces of meat are being cooked at once, a pan will be needed to hold them until they are ready to be served.

An infrared lamp is often used in food service to keep foods such as steaks hot until service. Microwave ovens are also used to reheat food quickly for service or to cook already browned rare steaks until well done.

Method of Cooking

Broiling is a simple method of cooking, and yet it requires judgment and experience to produce perfect results. As in all meat cookery, timing and temperature are the key to success.

Control of Temperature

In broiling, the temperature is controlled by the distance of the food from the source of heat. The thickness of the food determines what that distance should be. For instance, a thick piece of meat is placed farther from the heat so the outside will not brown too much before the inside reaches the desired doneness. A thinner piece of meat will be placed closer to the heat so it will brown before the center is overcooked.

Chicken needs to be placed farther away from the heat since it must be cooked well done. Fish, which cooks quickly, will be placed close to the heat source.

Timing

The amount of time needed for broiling depends on the degree of desired doneness. The timetable below shows the cooking time and distance from the heat for broiling meats.

These well-done steaks are one inch thick, therefore they were cooked two inches from the heat for 20 minutes.

Timetable for Broiling Meats

Cut of Meat	Thickness of Cut		Total Cooking Time (in minutes)			Distance from Heat	
	cm	in	Rare	Medium	Well done	cm	in
Beef steak	2.5	1	10	15	20	5	2
	3.8	1½	18	20	30	7.6	3
	5	2	25	35	40-50	10.2	4
Lamb Chops	2.5	1		15	20	5	2
	3.8	1½		20	30-35	7.6	3
Ham Slice, Smoked	2.5	1			16-20	7.6	3
Pork Chops	2.5	1			25-30	7.6	3
Bacon					4-5	5	2
Half Chickens					40-50	10.2	4

Degrees of Doneness

Broiled beef may be cooked rare, medium rare, well done, or any degree in between. Most customers who order beef are very particular about the degree of doneness. The broiler cook must learn to time cooking so that the exact desired degree of doneness is attained.

Sometimes, lamb is served rare or medium rare, but poultry and pork are always served well-done.

This is what to look for in determining the degree of doneness:

- **Rare**. When the heat has penetrated to the center of the meat but the center is very red and juicy, meat is considered ***rare***. When the meat is cut the juices will run red.
- **Medium rare**. In ***medium rare*** meat, the muscle has begun to coagulate from the heat, but the center is still very pink. When the meat is cut, the juices will still run red.
- **Well done**. In meat that is ***well done***, the center is gray-brown with no hint of pink. When cut, the juices are colorless.

Procedure for Broiling Meat and Poultry

1. Wipe off meat. If it is a steak, slash through the outside fat in several places to prevent the meat from curling.
2. Preheat the broiler. An electric unit should be radiating full heat. A charcoal broiler should have glowing, red coals with a dusting of gray ash.
3. Do not salt the meat before cooking. Salt delays the browning and causes loss of juices.
4. Brush oil lightly across both surfaces of the meat and place on the broiler rack.
5. Place the rack the correct distance from the heat.
6. Baste poultry frequently to prevent it from drying out.
7. Broil for half the estimated broiling time.
8. Turn the meat with the cooking fork. Be careful not to pierce the muscle since this will cause loss of juices.
9. Broil the other side.
10. Learn to test for doneness by pressing the meat lightly with your finger. The firmer the meat feels, the greater the degree of doneness. Continued practice will help you judge doneness easily.

Grid marks are dark lines on meat made by the hot rack. They are set as soon as the meat hits the grid or rack. Each time meat is turned, grid marks are formed. Meat with several sets of grid marks looks messy and unprofessional. Meat should only be turned once on each side, forming a crisscross pattern.

When cooking many steaks at the same time, a slight change of procedure is needed so the steaks can be served quickly and at the same time. Brown the steaks well ahead of time to the very rare stage. Place them in a single layer in a pan. Finish cooking to the desired degree of doneness just before serving time. This final cooking may also be done in the microwave oven.

Procedure for Fish

Fish requires some special precautions in broiling. Follow these rules:

1. Grease the broiler rack.
2. Brush the fish with oil.
3. Place the fish skin side down on rack.
4. Season the fish as desired. Sprinkle with paprika to assist in browning.
5. Place the rack about 2 in. (5 cm) from the source of heat for thin fish. Place thicker fish a bit farther away.
6. Do not turn thin fish. Turn thicker fish once.
7. Cook only until the flesh of the fish can be flaked with a fork. Overcooked fish is dry and tasteless.

Portioning

Because the size and thickness of meat can vary widely, preportioned meat is almost always used in food service. Preportioned means that the meat is ordered with the exact cut and weight specified. Buyers can specify the cut such as sirloin or club steaks, or halved or quartered chickens. That way, each customer's portion will be the same size.

BROILING HAMBURGERS FOR FAST FOODS

Some fast food chains broil the hamburgers instead of grilling them. The ingredients and the method of assembly and serving are much the same. The difference is in the equipment and method of cooking.

Equipment

Most fast food outlets serving broiled hamburgers use a conveyor-chain broiler. The conveyor chain broiler is divided into three parts. Two of the sections are used for broiling the patties. The third one toasts the buns. The food is placed on the broiler racks. The racks move through the broiler on conveyor belts at the correct speed to cook the burgers and toast the buns.

A new employee receives instructions on the operation of a conveyor-chain broiler.

Method of Cooking

About a half hour before opening time, the manager turns on the broiler. Several patties are broiled while the manager times them with a stop watch. When the heat is correct, the patty will pass through the broiler and be deposited in a basket at the end in the correct time and cooked to the correct degree of doneness.

Once the broiler has been checked, another worker takes over the process. A second worker stands at the other end of the broiler to place the cooked hamburgers in the toasted buns and then in the warming cabinet. From there, the burgers are treated just as the grilled hamburger sandwiches in Chapter 22. You may wish to review the direction for dressing and holding given there.

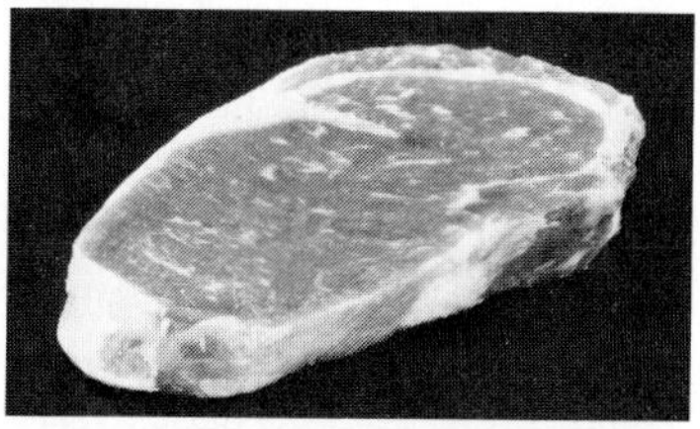
RIB-EYE STEAK

T-BONE STEAK

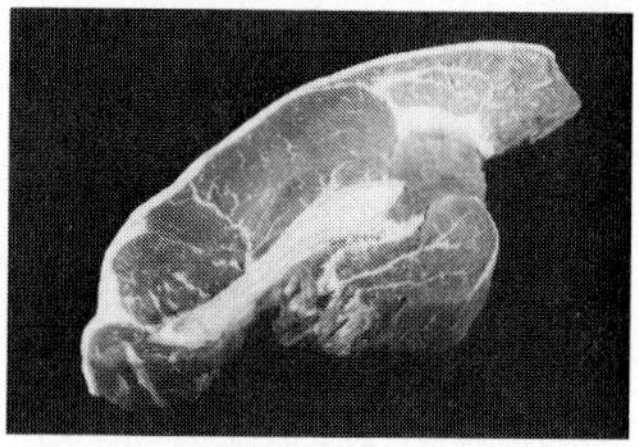
SIRLOIN STEAK

STEAKS FOR FAST FOODS

In response to customer demand for less expensive steak dinners, the fast food steak houses began. These lower-priced steak houses have become very popular.

Ingredients

Steak houses are different from the fast food outlets specializing in hamburgers. They usually offer complete steak dinners. Steaks are served sizzling hot on a hot platter with a baked potato or French fries. Some steak houses serve cole slaw as a salad, but many offer salad bars. Rolls and butter are almost always served. Other items such as desserts are available at an extra cost.

The Steaks

Fast food steak houses use less expensive, lower grade steaks. Remember that lower grades of meat are just as nutritious as choice or prime grades, but they are less tender and have much less fat. These steaks are usually tenderized to compensate for the lower grade. Steaks are purchased already tenderized and frozen.

Like hamburgers, the steaks must meet the operation's exact specifications. Rib-eye, T-bone, and sirloin are usually offered. The ***rib-eye*** is the muscle of the club steak which is cut from the rib section. Steaks for fast food outlets are often cut thinner so they give the appearance of a big steak. Chopped steak is also usually on the menu.

Equipment

Most steak houses broil the steaks. Some use a conveyor-chain broiler like the one used for broiled hamburgers. However, many steak houses prefer a long, open broiler. The customers enjoy choosing their steak and watching it being broiled.

The broiler cook will need the following small equipment: large salt and pepper shakers, tongs and a turner for turning steaks, and a wire grid brush, scraper, and brush for cleaning the broiler. Fireproof gloves are used to protect the broiler cook's hands from the hot fire.

An open broiler.

Method of Cooking

The broiler cook is responsible for thawing the steaks, broiling them, and cleaning the broiler at the end of the day.

Thawing the Steaks

Here is the way one steak house chain thaws their steaks. Other chains may vary their procedure somewhat, but all will be similar.

1. Remove the steaks from the boxes. Steaks are usually wrapped individually in plastic so they can be easily separated. The manager will tell you the estimated number of steaks that will be needed.
2. Separate the steaks according to type. Put the T-bones on one tray, the rib-eyes on another, the sirloins on the third, and the ground steaks on the fourth tray. Do not stack the trays. It will interfere with thawing. Place a paper marked with the time and date on top of each tray. Be sure all the steaks have been removed from the box.
3. Place the trays in the back of the walk-in refrigerator. Place the steaks leftover from the previous day in the front of the refrigerator so they will be used first. Remember the principle "first in, first out."
4. When steaks have thawed, remove their plastic wrapping. Place the steaks in the refrigerator near the broiler.

At the end of the day, return any unused steaks to the walk-in refrigerator. Place them in front so they will be used first the next day.

Broiling the Steaks

After the steaks have started thawing, the next job is to light the broiler. Most open broilers are in two sections. The first section, directly in front of the cook, is set at high heat — about 550°F (290°C). The back section is set at low heat — about 220°F (105°C).

While the broiler is heating, check to see that you have all small tools you will need. Once the broiler is ready, you will be too busy to stop and look for your tools.

Each fast food steak house has a definite system for placing the steaks on the broiler. The system must be followed so the cook will always know where a particular steak has been placed. The cook will also know the degree of doneness each steak has reached.

The hottest section of the broiler is used for browning. The cooler section is used for keeping the steak warm until it is ordered by the customer. After being ordered, the cook moves the right steak to the hot side again for finishing. Customers expect steaks to be the exact stage of doneness they have ordered. Only by following the system, can the cook be sure the order will be correct.

To broil a steak follow these directions:

1. Be sure the steak is completely thawed.
2. Place the steak on the broiler following the system you have learned. Never put several steaks on at the once and then spread them apart. This will form too many grid marks on the steaks.
3. Do not handle the steaks that are cooking. This causes loss of juices.
4. Turn the steaks when the blood seeps through the top side. Rare steaks are turned only once and have grid marks going only one way on each side. Well done steaks are turned three times and have grid marks at right angles to each other on both sides of the steak. This shows professionalism.
5. Season just before serving.
6. Put a "flag" on the steak to identify its degree of doneness.

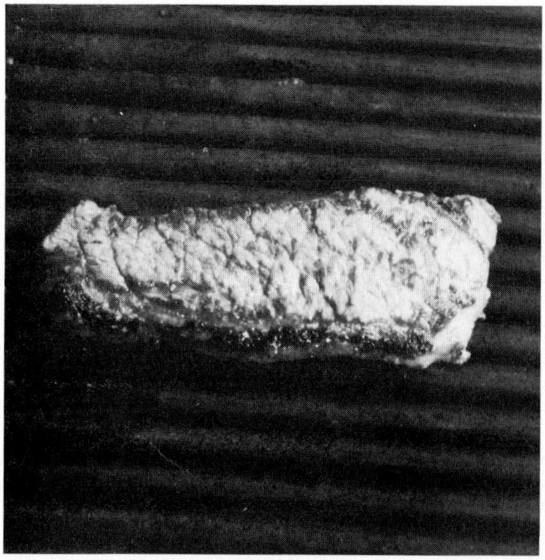

Broiled steak is delicious, especially when it is cooked over charcoal.

Care of the Broiler

While cooking, use the wire grid brush to scrape off any stuck bits of steak. Brush off the bits with the brush.

After the restaurant closes, clean the grids thoroughly with the wire scraper. Loosen any stuck pieces with the larger scraper. Finish with the wire brush and clean with a damp towel.

safety tip...

Sometimes the open broiler fire flares as the grease drips into the hot coals. A box of soda or salt should be on hand to smother the flames by sprinkling the soda or salt on the flare up.

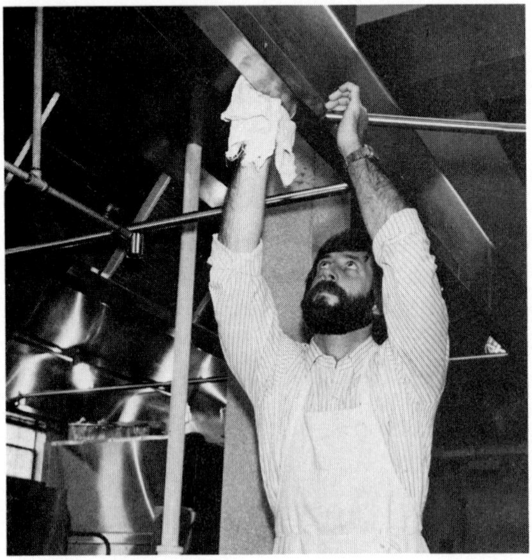

In addition to cleaning the broiler grids, someone also needs to clean the grease off of the smoke hoods, overhead grease traps, and moldings. This is a fire safety measure.

A large container full of baking soda should always be kept near the broiler.

SUMMARY

In broiling food is exposed directly to heat. The degree of doneness is determined by timing and by the distance the food is from the heat source. Poultry, fish, meat, and some vegetables are broiled. Steaks and hamburgers are broiled most frequently in fast food operations. Workers should use safety precautions and follow the procedures set up by their managers when broiling.

chapter recap

CHECK YOUR KNOWLEDGE

1. Name five cuts of meat that are suitable for broiling.

2. Why should meat that is broiled be well-marbled?

3. How can you prevent lean fish from drying out during broiling?

4. How can temperature be controlled during broiling?

5. Name three degrees of doneness for broiled beef.

6. What are grid marks?

7. What type of broiler is used in fast foods to cook hamburgers? To cook steaks?

8. What grade of steaks are usually served in fast food operations?

9. How does the broiler cook know the degree of doneness of each steak on the open broiler?

10. How are the grids of an open broiler cleaned at the end of the day?

EXTEND YOUR LEARNING

1. Discuss how the manager of a fast food restaurant specializing in broiled hamburgers knows how many hamburgers will be needed at any given time.

2. Check the meat section of a supermarket for the following types of steaks — sirloin, T bone, and tenderloin (filet). What is the price per pound of each? Which is the most expensive? Which has the most fat? Which seems to have the most bone in porportion to meat?

3. Make a chart of safety precautions to be observed when broiling.

"Jim and Ruthann had stopped for some fast food chicken and French fries on their way to a movie.

"Mmm," said Jim, "I sure do love these French fries, don't you? Next week I work in the frying station. I sure hope we learn how to make them. I tried them at home, but they burned, and the house was full of greasy smoke. Mom was mad about it."

"This is good chicken, too," said Ruthann. "This chicken doesn't taste greasy at all. Do you know how they get that coating on the outside?"

"According to the book," said Jim, "they put something on it called breading. We'll know more about it next week when we have a chance to try it out. David is the manager for that dinner we're putting on for our parents. Are your mom and dad coming? Mine have to work. Anyway, David says that chicken is a good buy right now. Maybe if I learn how to cook French fries at school, Mom will let me try them at home again."

"You know," said Ruthann, "almost anything tastes better if it's fried. Take this chicken, for instance. I like chicken any old way, but I like it fried the best."

"Me, too," said Jim, "but it makes a difference where you get it. I stopped in that place on the corner and bought a bucket of chicken for Dad. It was awful. There must have been something wrong with the fat. The chicken was greasy and had a strong taste. Dad took what was left back the next day. The manager said he was sorry. He had a new man frying the chicken, and maybe he used old grease or didn't clean out the fryer. Dad said he thought the fat was rancid."

"We made doughnuts last year in Home Ec," said Ruthann. "We had to use a thermometer to see if the fat was hot enough. Mrs. Kennedy said the doughnuts would be greasy if the fat wasn't hot enough. Maybe that's what was wrong with the chicken you bought."

"Maybe so," said Jim. "We had better read more about frying before that dinner next week. Whatever we make, we want it to be good.""

chapter 24

frying

Set your goals

When you complete the study of this chapter, you should be able to . . .

- Define and correctly use the vocabulary terms.
- Prepare sautéed, panfried, and stir-fried foods.
- Prepare deep-fried foods.
- Identify two fast food methods of preparing chicken.

Build your vocabulary

blanching	smoke point
breader-sifter	tartar sauce
dusting	tempering
fat absorption	wash
	wok

FRYING — A POPULAR COOKING TECHNIQUE

Frying — cooking in hot fat — is a technique used in virtually every food service operation. But it is fast food restaurants that use frying most often. A look at the characteristics of frying makes it easy to see why it adapts so well to fast foods:

- Food cooks quickly.
- A wide range of foods can be fried.
- Fried foods appeal to customers.

This chapter includes two different aspects of frying. First, it describes the various frying techniques including sautéing, panfrying, stir-frying, and deep-fat frying. It explains how these methods are used in many types of food service operations. The second part of the chapter tells how fast food operations specialize in frying techniques. You will learn the secrets these operations use to prepare delicious favorites in record time.

SAUTEING, PANFRYING, AND STIR-FRYING

These three techniques all involve cooking food in a small amount of fat. Vegetables are often sautéed, and sometimes meat or poultry. The food is cut into small, even pieces and cooked quickly in the hot fat. As the food cooks, it is flipped in the pan so every side is cooked. Sautéing is often used to brown and develop the flavor of foods before they are combined with other ingredients for additional cooking. Sautéing onions, for example, removes their "bite." Stew meat is browned to develop its flavor and color.

Panfrying is very similar. However, larger pieces of food are cooked. This means the food is cooked more slowly at a lower temperature and more fat is usually needed. Chicken, pork chops, fish, and potatoes are familiar panfried foods. Sometimes the words "sautéing" and "panfrying" are used to mean the same thing.

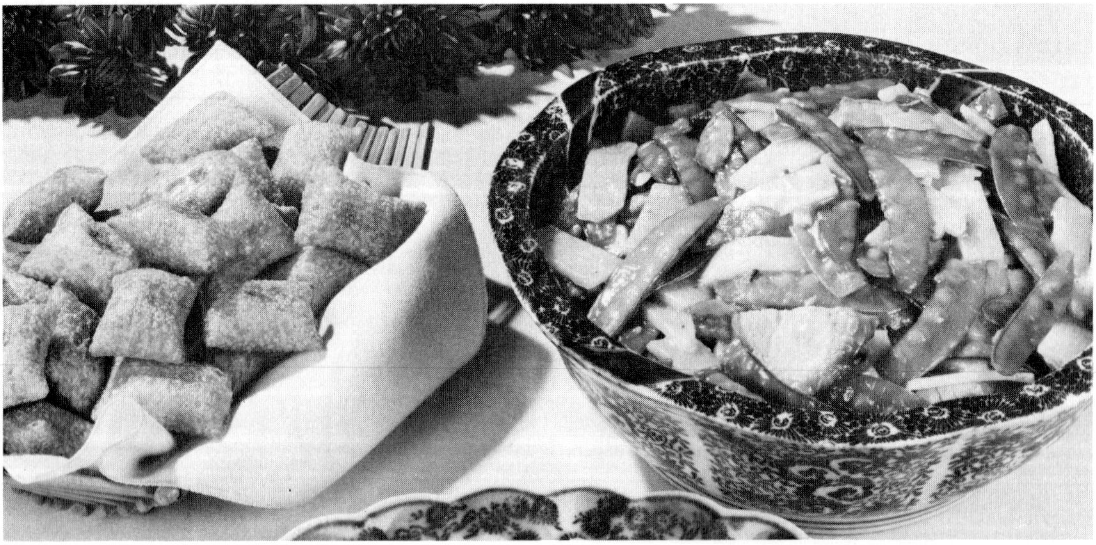

Chinese foods are often deep-fat fried or stir-fried.

Stir-frying is an Oriental cooking method that is suitable for many foods. It is very similar to sautéing. Food is cut in small pieces and cooked quickly in hot oil. A ***wok*** (WALK) — a special heavy pan with a rounded bottom and sloped sides — is usually used for stir-frying, but a heavy frying pan can also be used. The food is stirred as it cooks and is considered done when the vegetables reach the tender-crisp stage.

Equipment

A frying pan is needed for sautéing or panfrying. The frying pan should be of heavy gauge metal so that it retains the heat evenly with no hot spots. Frying pans come in many sizes to fit the amount of food to be cooked. A wok or heavy frying pan is used for stir-frying.

A turner is usually used to turn the ingredients as they fry. However, tongs or a cooking fork are better for larger pieces of food such as chicken and chops. For stir-frying, a slotted wooden paddle or spoon is the best choice.

Choice of Fat

A number of different fats an be used for frying. The choice depends on the food being cooked, the method of frying, and the taste desired.

For sautéing, butter is often used because many cooks believe it gives food the best flavor. Margarine is sometimes substituted because it is less expensive. However, both butter and margarine burn easily. The temperature must be kept fairly low. Shortening and oils, discussed on page 347, are also commonly used for sautéing.

Panfried foods vary in their need for additional fat. Foods like sausages have a high fat content and need little, if any, fat added to the pan. On the other hand, foods like potatoes require considerable additional fat. Oil or fat from bacon or ham may be used.

Oil is always used for stir-frying, occasionally combined with butter. Only a small amount is needed because foods are cooked very quickly.

Pre-Preparation

Some pre-preparation may be needed before sautéing, panfrying, or stir-frying. Sautéing usually takes the least pre-preparation time.

According to the recipe you are following, meats may need to be seasoned with salt and pepper and dredged in (coated with) flour. This helps in browning, protects the meat from the hot fat, and improves the flavor. If meat is to be stir-fried, it is cut into thin, equal pieces so that it will cook quickly. Larger pieces of meat are usually panfried.

Vegetables are cut into small pieces. If they are stir-fried, they should be cut into thin, even slices. The vegetables will cook quickly and the fat will be spread evenly throughout them.

Cooking Techniques

Check the chart on page 346 for step-by-step directions for sautéing, panfrying, and stir-frying food. Compare the differences and similarities in these three methods.

Sautéing

1. Use a sauté pan with sloping sides and heavy bottom, selecting the right size for the amount of food.
2. Slice, dice, or chop all vegetables according to directions in recipe.
3. Cuts of meat which are naturally tender and can be cooked quickly may be sautéed, such as calve's liver, veal chops or cutlets, beef tenderloin tips, and pork tenderloin.
4. Most chefs prefer butter for sautéing because of the flavor.

   To sauté vegetables
   - Place the specified amount of butter in pan and melt on medium heat.
   - When fat is hot, add ingredients to be sautéed.
   - Cook, stirring all the time, for about 5 minutes. Vegetables such as onions will become transparent and lightly browned. Be careful not to overcook mushrooms or they will shrivel.

   To sauté meat
   - Brown the meat rapidly on one side.
   - When the blood starts to seep to the surface, turn and brown the other side. Cook until golden brown. Sautéed meat is usually finished with some sort of sauce made with some of the fat and the browned bits in the sauté pan.

These onions have been sauteed. Green peppers and mushrooms are also frequently prepared in this way.

Panfrying Meat

1. Select small, tender, boneless meat, ¼ in. to ½ in. thick. (.6 mm to 1.3 cm)
2. Chill meat well. Meat at room temperature will cook through before it browns.
3. Oil meat lightly.
4. Heat frying pan to sizzling.
5. Brown quickly on one side. Turn and brown the other side.

Stir-Frying

1. A wok is needed to stir-fry successfully because it uses much less fat or oil.
2. Cut or dice all vegetables, meat, or other food to as nearly the same size and thickness as possible.
3. Place a small amount of oil in bottom of wok. Heat on high heat to sizzling.
4. Stir-fry longer cooking food first.
5. Add food.
6. Lift and stir food using a slotted spoon.
7. Cook only until crisp tender.
8. Lift out of oil and drain.

ORIENTAL STIR-FRY

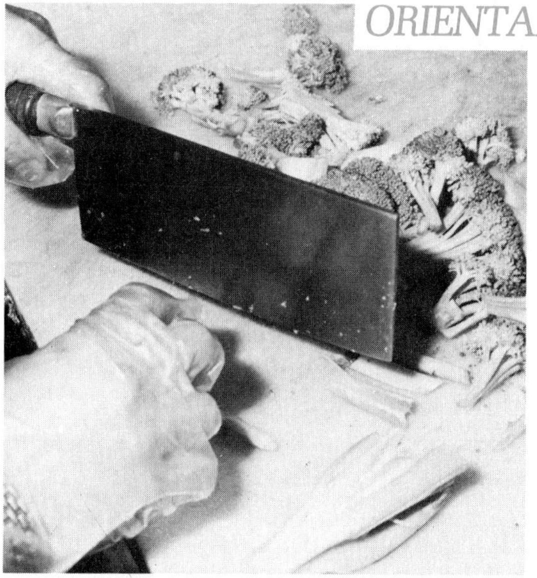

All the ingredients are chopped with a cleaver. Chinese cooks are very skilled with knives of various sizes.

The ingredients are placed in a wok containing hot fat and stirred occasionally.

The stir-fry is removed from the fat with a wire basket-like tool strainer that has a wooden handle.

Once the stir-fry has drained, it is placed on the serving platter. Stir-fry dishes containing vegetables are very tasty and nutritious.

Ingredients

Although fish, poultry, potatoes, and onions are the foods most often fried in deep-fat, the process also makes delicious dishes from leftover food. For instance, leftover chicken may be diced and mixed with a thick white sauce. The mixture is formed into patties or cones, rolled in cracker crumbs, and fried in deep-fat. These foods are called croquettes.

Fats for Deep-Fat Frying

Not all fats can be used in deep-fat frying. Fats must have special characteristics:

- **A high smoke point**. All fats have a temperature at which they disintegrate and smoke. This is known as the ***smoke point***.
- **Low moisture content**. Moisture in a fat causes spattering.
- **No flavor or odor**. The fat should not add any flavor or odor of its own.
- **Contain an antioxidant**. This is needed to retard spoilage. When fats and oils spoil they become rancid — they develop an unpleasant taste and smell.
- **Contain a stabilizer**. This helps prevent disintegration at high temperature.

Lard, vegetable, shortening, and vegetable oils are commonly used for deep-fat frying.

Lard is the fat from hogs. At one time, lard was the most commonly used fat for deep-fat frying. It has a naturally sweet taste that blends well with the flavor of food. It has a high smoke point. However, it turns rancid easily, requires refrigeration, and absorbs the flavor of the food being fried. Lard is sometimes blended with hydrogenated fat.

Hydrogenated vegetable shortening is a white, fluffy fat made from vegetable oils such as peanut, coconut, or cottonseed oil through a special process. Hydrogenated fats have no taste of their own. They have a high smoke point, do not turn rancid, and require no refrigeration. The flavor of food is not easily absorbed by these fats.

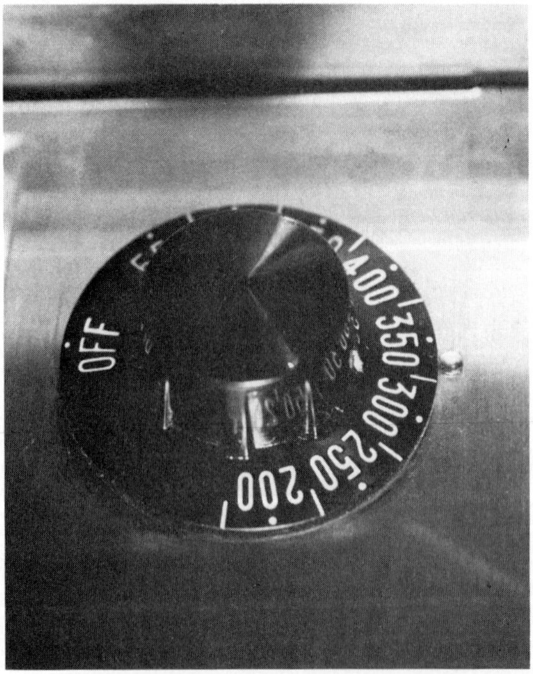

Correct temperature is very important when deep-fat frying. Fat that is too hot will smoke. Fat that is too cool will not cook foods quickly enough — resulting in grease-soaked food.

DEEP-FAT FRYING

Deep-fat frying means cooking food in larger amounts of hot fat. "French fried" is another name for deep-fat fried. Deep-fried foods are among the most popular on the menu. Fried chicken is second only to roast beef in popularity. Deep-fat frying adds flavor and variety to the menu and lends itself to quick service.

Vegetable oils are liquid at room temperature. They are probably used most often for deep-fat frying. They have all the advantages of the hydrogenated fats plus they are measured easily, readily available for use, and do not deteriorate readily under high heat. Vegetable oils have a very high smoke point. With proper care, they can be used over and over again. The chart below tells how to prolong the life of fat used for deep-fat frying.

Care of Fat

1. Heat fat only to required temperature. Overheating causes fat to decompose.
2. Fry only small amount of food at one time so that the temperature remains constant.
3. Remove floating particles as they accumulate so they do not burn.
4. Add fresh fat as needed during frying.
5. Turn off heat as soon as frying is completed.
6. Drain fat through fine strainer into clean container.
7. Wash fryer carefully so oil will not accumulate and become rancid.

Once this fat has cooled, it will be strained into a clean container. It can then be reused. The fryer must be cleaned to avoid fat buildup and sanitation problems.

Fat Absorption

A prime consideration in deep-fat frying is ***fat absorption*** — how much or how little of the fat enters the food. The flavor, appearance, and ease of digestion are directly related to the amount of fat absorbed by the food. There are several factors that affect fat absorption:

- **Quality and condition of the fat.** Rancid fat soaks into food more quickly.
- **Amount of cut surface.** Small and uneven pieces absorb more fat.
- **Type of food.** Soft and sweet foods absorb the most fat.
- **Length of cooking time.** The longer the cooking time, the more fat is absorbed. Cold fat and cold, wet food increase cooking time.
- **Temperature of the fat.** Different foods require different temperatures for proper cooking:

325°-375°F (160°-190°C) — for uncooked foods
325°-350°F (160°-180°C) — for blanching foods
375° (190°C) — for french fries and other partially cooked foods

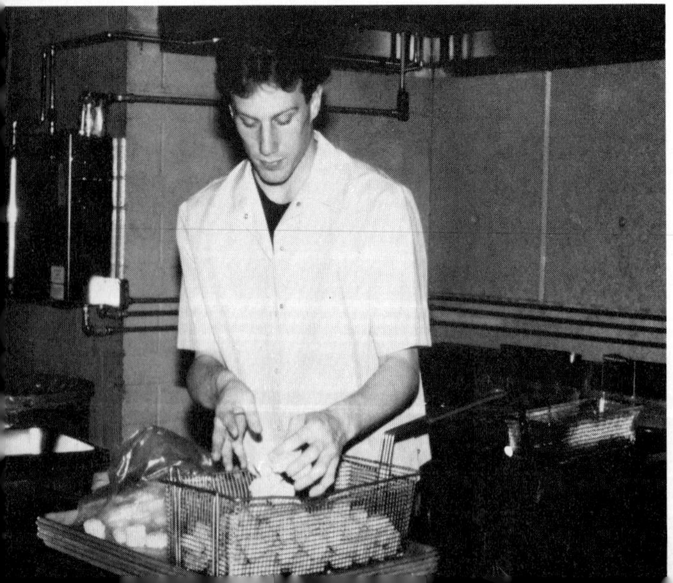

The potato nuggets being placed into this fryer basket will absorb a lot of fat due to their size.

Equipment

As described in Chapter 8, special equipment is essential for deep-fat frying. In food service, automatic deep-fat fryers are used. These may be heated by gas or electricity.

Fryers must be made of very heavy gauge metal to withstand high heat and insure even heating. They must be equipped with a basket to hold the food while it is cooking. A thermostat to control temperature and a timer for accurate cooking are also needed. You may wish to review the use, care, and cleaning guidelines on pages 132-133.

Pre-Preparation

Foods to be deep-fat fried usually need some pre-preparation. The two most common types of pre-preparation are blanching and breading.

Blanching

Blanching means partially cooking without browning. Some foods, like potatoes, take a long time to cook through. If fried at a high temperature, they become too brown on the outside before they are cooked in the center. To prevent this they are partially cooked at a lower temperature — blanched — then browned just before serving. Blanching also prevent potatoes from discoloring by sealing the cut surfaces.

Breading

Breading is coating a food with bread crumbs, cracker meal, or rolled cornflakes before frying in deep fat. Breading should have smooth, even texture and a delicate flavor. It should not contain salt because salt causes hot fat to decompose. Breading helps prevent fat absorption and forms a golden brown crust around the food. It also protects the food from the heat of the fat making a more tender and juicy product. Seafood, meats, croquettes, and onions are often breaded before frying.

There are three major steps in breading: coating with flour, dipping in a wash, and coating with the breading.

The ***wash*** is a liquid which helps the breading stick to the food. Usually, it is a mixture of beaten egg and milk.

Working from left to right, follow this procedure for breading:

1. Set up the assembly line as shown in the drawing.
2. Keep your right hand dry so that the breading will not build up on it and slow your work.
3. Pick up the food to be breaded with the left hand. Place it in the flour and coat it well. Shake off the excess flour. If more convenient, use a paper bag for this step. Put some flour in a paper bag, add a piece of the food to be breaded, and shake. Remove the item and continue until all the pieces are floured.
4. Using the left hand only, dip the floured food in the wash, wetting it thoroughly so there are no patches of dry flour. Proceed immediately to the next step.
5. Remove the food with the left hand and shake gently.
6. Still using the left hand, place the food in the breading and cover well.
7. With the right hand, press the breading into the food so it sticks to the food.
8. Bread again. Shake off any excess crumbs and place in the pan on the right.

To bread food, dip it first in flour, then in the wash, and finally in the breading. Breaded foods should be placed in a pan only one layer deep.

Breading may be done several hours before frying. Once food has been breaded, it must be refrigerated, or it may be frozen for future use.

Many foods can be purchased already breaded and ready to be deep-fat fried. They are widely used in food service. Management must decide if the quality and flavor of the food and the time saved are worth the extra cost of the prebreaded items.

Deep-Fat Frying Procedures

While deep-fat fryers vary somewhat in operation, all require the same general procedures:

1. Fill the fryer with at least 2 in. (5 cm) of fat or oil. Most fryers have a fill mark. Set the thermostat to the proper temperature and turn on the heat. This usually turns on an indicator light. When the correct temperature has been reached, the light will go off.
2. Bread items and place in the fry basket. Fill the basket about two-thirds full. Shake off the excess breading so it will not fall to the bottom of the fryer and burn.
3. Lower the basket into the hot fat. Some fryers do this automatically.
4. Fry until the food is golden brown. Do not overbrown. Some items will float to the top of the fat when done.
5. When the food is done, allow the basket to hang over the fryer for a few seconds so the excess fat drips back into the fryer. This helps to retain crispness.
6. Place the food on paper towels to absorb any additional excess fat.
7. Serve immediately or put under an infrared lamp to keep hot.

safety tip . . .

Do not leave hot fat unattended. If smoking occurs, reduce heat. If there is a fire, cover the fryer or pot and turn off the heat. Do not uncover until cool. Never put water on flaming fat.

This worker has filled one basket two-thirds full. Now she will continue to bread the chicken for the remaining two baskets while another worker begins the frying process.

FRIED CHICKEN IN FAST FOODS

Deep-fried chicken has always been famous in Southern cooking. About 25 years ago, Southern fried chicken was introduced to fast foods. It became very popular, and soon restaurants featuring the delicious chicken spread across the United States and into other countries as well.

Ingredients

Only a few ingredients are needed for Southern fried chicken. These include chicken, breading, wash, and shortening for frying.

- **Chicken**. The chickens must meet the exacting specifications of the fast food chain. The specifications vary among the chains, but usually the chickens must weigh between 2½ and 3 lbs. (1.1 and 1.4 kg). Each chicken must be divided into exact serving portions having about the same proportion of meat to bone. Only fresh chickens are purchased.
- **Breading**. In many fast food outlets, breading is made on the premises. In others, it is supplied from the commissary. The recipe for breading is often secret since the breading helps determine the flavor of the finished product.
- **Wash**. The wash is a thin mixture of milk powder, water, and egg. It helps the breading stick to the chicken.
- **Shortening**. This is made to the specifications set by the fast food chain. It is especially resistant to the continuous high heat of frying. Most chains use a solid hydrogenated fat instead of oil.

Equipment

Two pieces of equipment help speed fried chicken production in fast food outlets. These are the breader-sifter, and the pressure fryer.

- The ***breader-sifter*** is made of two stainless steel pans, one on top of the other. The bottom of the top pan is a mesh or sifter. The chicken is breaded in the top and then removed. The remaining breading is sifted to the bottom pan to be used again.
- Many operations use a pressure fryer rather than a conventional open fryer for chicken because food can be cooked at lower temperatures in the same amount of time. The pressure fryer has a fryer basket with shelves or tiers for holding the food to be fried. These tiers swing out for easy loading. The fryer's heavy lid clamps down, increasing the pressure inside the fryer as the fat heats. The fryer has a thermostat and a timer. The pressure in the fryer is automatically released when the cooking time is completed.

Many food service operations have to keep fried foods warm until the customer orders them. This manager is explaining the warming and serving procedure to a new employee.

FRIED CHICKEN COMING RIGHT UP!

The chicken is cut into pieces.

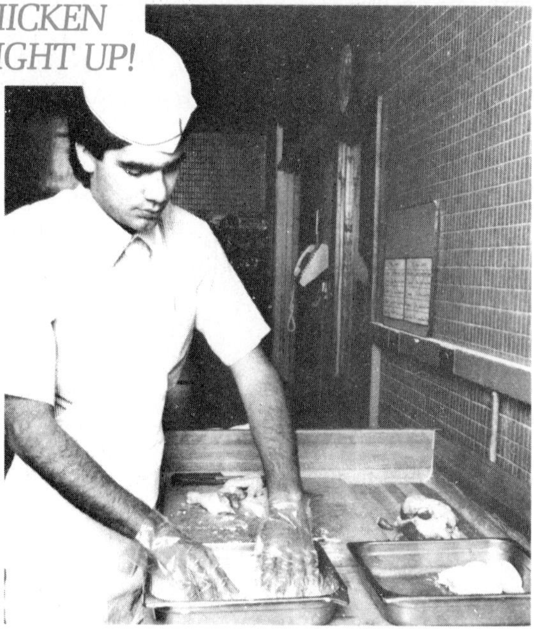

The legs and thighs are coated with a flour mixture.

The remaining pieces are coated and placed in a pan.

Each piece is shaken before being placed in the fryer basket.

Pieces are carefully placed so they cover the bottom of the basket.

The basket is lowered into the hot oil and cooked.

The fried chicken is lifted out of the draining fryer basket with tongs.

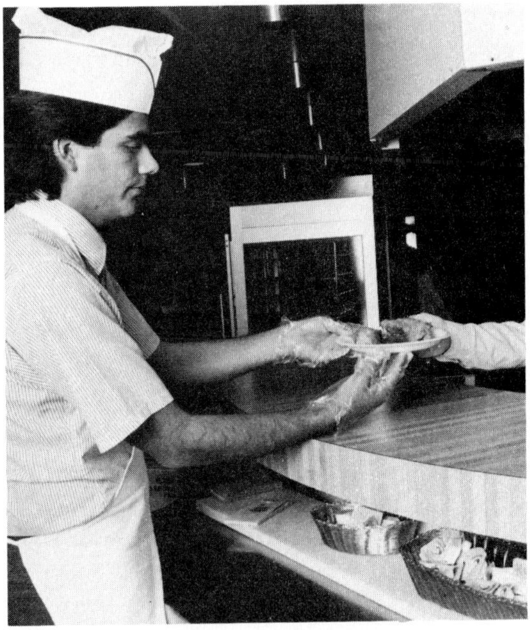

The chicken is garnished and served to the waiting customer.

Cooking Chicken for Fast Foods

There are two basic methods of deep-fat frying — open-frying and pressure frying. Some restaurants cook chicken using only one of these methods, while others offer customers more variety by using both methods.

Open-Fried Chicken

Open-fried chicken is fried in an open fryer. The frying procedures on page 351 of this chapter are used. Chicken fried in the open-fryer has a rough, crunchy crust.

To prepare the chicken, marinate (soak) it in a seasoned, acid mixture. Many restaurants use their own special acid mixture. However, good marinades may also be purchased. Marinating tenderizes the chicken, makes it juicier and more flavorful, and shortens the cooking time.

The marinade is drained from the chicken before it is breaded. Using the breader-sifter, the worker mixes the chicken with the breading mixture and shakes off the excess breading. The chicken is then dipped in the wash and rebreaded.

After again shaking off the excess breading, the chicken is placed in the fryer basket and lowered into the hot fat. It takes 12 minutes at 350°F (180°C) to fry the chicken to golden brown.

While the chicken is frying, the worker returns to the breader-sifter. During breading some of the wash becomes mixed with the breading and forms bread balls. By opening the dividers on the bottom of the pan, the bread balls are sifted out and discarded. Then, the breading material can be used again.

Pressure-Fried Chicken

Pressure-fried chicken is not marinated. It is dipped in the wash and then into the breading material. The seasoning of this breading is different from that used for open-frying. This is one of the differences that distinguishes the two types of chicken.

The worker shakes off the excess breading and places the chicken in the tiers of the basket. After the fryer is fully loaded, the tiers are closed and lowered into the pressure fryer. When the lid is clamped down, the pressure drives the temperature to 275°F (140°C). The chicken is usually fried for 12 minutes. Although the temperature is lower than that for open frying, the chicken cooks in the same time because the pressure drives the heat into the chicken.

The pressure is automatically released when the cooking time is up. Ventilating hoods over the fryers remove the steam.

After the cooking is completed, the worker lets the chicken drain for a few minutes. If it is to be served promptly, it is placed under infrared lamps. If it needs to be held longer than ten minutes, it should be placed in a warming cabinet.

A pressure fryer basket loaded with five tiers of chicken.

FRIED FISH

Fish and chips came to us from England. Chips are not potato chips, but are an English term for French fries. Fish and chips are carry-out food in England and are now popular here. Many hamburger chains have added fried fish sandwiches to their menus.

Ingredients

Fish sandwiches are composed of three parts, the fried fish, the bun, and the garnish or dressing.

- **Fish**. The fish must be a saltwater fish that holds its shape and does not have small, splintery bones. Ocean perch, pollock, and cod are often used, but cod is preferred. When caught and cleaned, the fish is pressed into blocks and frozen quickly. At the commissary, the blocks are cut into 2 oz. (55 g) portions for sandwiches.
- **Oil**. Oil is usually used for frying fish. It does not easily absorb odors or flavors.
- **Batter**. Fish is coated with a batter made from a mix.
- **Bun**. The bun is made to the same specifications as the buns for hamburgers.
- **Dressing**. ***Tartar sauce***, a mixture of mayonnaise, chopped pickles, onions, and other ingredients, is the traditional dressing for fish sandwiches. Some restaurants use a thick cheese sauce instead.

Equipment

Open fryers are used for deep-frying fish. Since fish fries so quickly, there is no need for pressure frying. Fish is not placed in a basket for frying because the batter would stick to the basket. The fish is fried directly in the fat and lifted out with a slotted spoon.

Cooking Fish for Fast Foods

In a fast food operation, the fish is removed from the freezer each morning and placed in a defrosting cabinet. Here the fish is brought from 0°F (–18°C) to 25°F (–4°C). It is still frozen but not frozen as hard. It is prepared for frying as follows:

1. The fish is marinated in a salty solution for a short time. This is called ***tempering***. It prepares the fish for the next step.
2. The next step is ***dusting*** — coating the fish lightly with cornmeal. The cornmeal helps the batter cling to the fish.
3. The fish is dipped in batter made from a mix. Allow excess batter to drip off the fish and back into the pan.
4. Fry at 350°F (180°C) until three corners float and the fish is lightly browned. Overcooking produces dry, tasteless fish.
5. Spread the bun top and bottom with tartar sauce or cheese sauce. Add the fish and any other garnishes specified. Wrap.
6. Place the sandwiches under infrared lamps to keep them at a steady 140°F (60°C), but never warmer. Fish sandwiches cannot be kept longer than 10 minutes before being sold.

FRIED OCEAN PERCH

The perch are filleted.

Each fillet is breaded and placed in a pan.

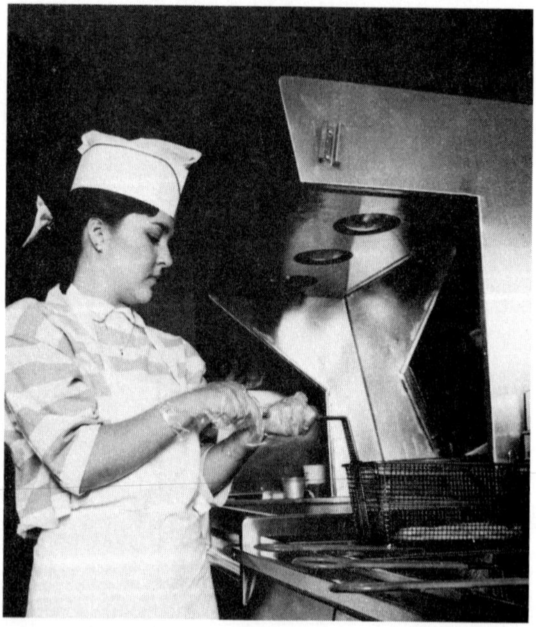

The fillets are placed in the bottom of the fryer basket and lowered into the hot oil.

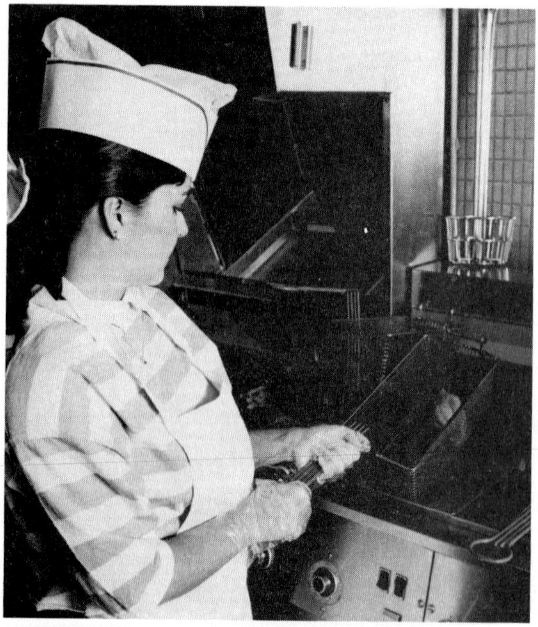

The deep-fried ocean perch are removed from the draining basket.

FRENCH FRIES AND FRIED ONIONS

Many people wouldn't consider a fast food meal complete without French fries. They are extremely popular with young and old alike.

In fast foods, the frying of potatoes and onions has become almost a science. Their quality is the same from batch to batch and is often higher than in many full-service restaurants.

This worker is pouring ready-to-use potatoes into the fryer basket.

Ingredients

- **Potatoes**. The potatoes are prepared in the commissary or purchased by the commissary ready-to-use. When delivered, the potatoes are blanched, frozen, and ready to cook. Idaho bakers are the preferred type of potato because of their mealy texture after frying.
- **Onions**. The onions are also breaded and frozen at the commissary. Large, sweet, Spanish onions make the best onion rings.
- **Shortening**. Any vegetable oil or fat may be used for frying. Some operations prefer a mixture of animal and vegetable fats. They believe the animal fat adds flavor.

Equipment

- **Fryer**. The open fryer described earlier in this chapter is used for French fries and onion rings.
- **Holding rack**. After the frying baskets are filled with the frozen potatoes, they are placed in the holding rack until they are fried.
- **Skimmer**. A skimmer is used to lift the onions from the hot fat. The excess fat drains through the holes in the skimmer.

The manager shows an employee how to place the fryer baskets on the holding rack.

Cooking Procedures for Fries and Onions

French fries and onion rings must be served freshly cooked for best quality. Most operations fry small amounts often during the day. Follow the general directions given here.

French Fries

1. Fill the frying baskets with the proper amount of frozen potatoes and place the baskets in the holding rack. If the potatoes are put out too soon, they will be limp when fried. Always follow the manager's production schedule.
2. Turn on the fryer and set the thermostat at 350°F (180°C). Automatic fryers have a light that shows while the fat is heating and turns off when it is the proper temperature.
3. Place a basket of potatoes in the lowering position on the fryer and immediately press the button to lower it.
4. Fryers usually have automatic timing. During frying, shake the basket occasionally so the potatoes do not stick together. When the cooking time is up, a buzzer sounds, and the basket of potatoes will come up out of the fat.
5. Let the potatoes drain for a few moments, then package them and place them on the warming shelf. Potatoes must be sold within 10 minutes or their quality deteriorates.

Fried Onion Rings

Because the breading would become soggy, onions are not allowed to defrost before cooking. They are not loaded into a basket because the breading would stick to it. Instead, they are fried directly in the hot fat and removed with a skimmer. They are usually packaged in small bags and placed on the warming shelf.

French fried onion rings accompany these vegetable kabobs. The kabobs consist of deep-fried mushrooms, lemon sections, steamed carrots and broccoli, and tomatoes.

SUMMARY

Frying is a popular cooking technique, especially in the fast food industry. Food is sometimes fried in a pan. Sautéing is an example of this. Most often, however, frying refers to deep-fat frying. Chicken, fish, French fries, and onions are breaded, then cooked in oil in a deep-fat fryer. If proper cooking techniques are used, a crisp coating over a tender product will result. This combination of textures makes fried food a popular menu choice.

chapter recap

CHECK YOUR KNOWLEDGE

1. How does sautéing differ from panfrying?
2. What is a wok?
3. Why are some foods panfried without fat?
4. Why is meat often dredged in flour before frying?
5. Give five qualities necessary for a fat that is used for deep-fat frying.
6. What is hydrogenated fat? Why is it often chosen for deep-fat frying?
7. Why is food breaded before deep-fat frying?
8. Name two types of deep-fat fryers.
9. Why is fish fried without using a basket?
10. What should you do if hot fat starts smoking?

EXTEND YOUR LEARNING

1. Have each person in the class survey 10 different people. Ask this question, "What is your favorite kind of chicken?" Write down the answers. In class, tabulate the results.
2. Discuss why less fat is needed for stir-frying than for panfrying.
3. Check the deep-fat fryer in your laboratory kitchen. Study the directions for use. Find and name the parts. What settings does the thermostat include? Is there a fill line?

"Rosita," asked Ruthann, "does your mother make her own tortillas?"

Rosita laughed. "She doesn't have the time. She buys them at the store just like you do. But I remember my grandmother making them. She'd pat the dough very thin and round and cook them on top of a charcoal grill. Then she would bring them to the table still hot, wrapped in a damp napkin. Mmm!"

"I remember the dietitian who visited our class talking about tortillas," said Ruthann. "She said most Mexican children have very good teeth but don't drink much milk. The nutritionists couldn't figure out where they were getting all the calcium. Then they discovered it came from tortillas."

"I remember now!" Rosita replied. "The corn is soaked in lime water to soften it before it's ground into meal. The corn soaked up the calcium from the lime!"

Jim joined their conversation. "I don't know too much about lime, but I do know that Mexican food tastes great."

"And it isn't very expensive to fix either," Rosita added.

"Say, I've got a great idea!" said Jim. "We've been trying to come up with a menu for the Advisory Council dinner next month. How about planning a Mexican fiesta? It would be great food and still not break our budget!"

"That sounds terrific!" replied Ruthann. "We could decorate the tables with centerpieces that reflect our theme. Let's suggest it to the rest of the class!"

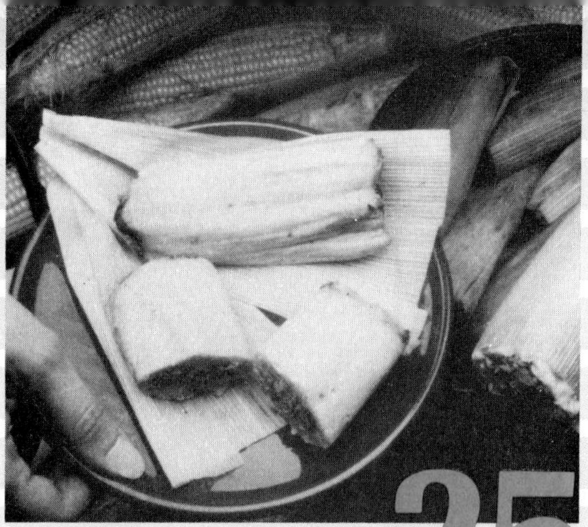

chapter 25

pizza and mexican foods

Set your goals

When you complete the study of this chapter, you should be able to . . .

- Define and correctly use the vocabulary terms.
- Identify common pizza variations and prepare pizzas that meet standards of excellence.
- Prepare a variety of Mexican foods.
- Identify seasonings used in Mexican foods.

Build your vocabulary

burritos	peel
dusting powder	refried beans
enchiladas	sheeter
food release	staging
masa harina	tacos
nachos	tamales

ETHNIC FOODS ARE POPULAR FAVORITES

Pizza and Mexican foods are not really "fast foods" since they must be assembled and baked to order. They have, however, become popular alternatives to hamburgers and fried chicken. In fact, they are so common, they are seldom considered ethnic dishes.

Pizza, tacos, and enchiladas are served everywhere, but they do vary a bit from place to place. The pizza sauces are made from different recipes. The tacos served in Indiana are likely to be milder than those served in Texas. Nationwide chain outlets have minimized such differences. Remember, most chains aim for a consistent product in every operation. They have built distinctive types of buildings. They have developed techniques to shorten preparation time and improve quality control.

There are also many restaurants specializing in these foods that do not belong to a chain. These independent operations cater to the taste of their customers.

In this chapter, you will learn how pizzas and Mexican foods are prepared in the large chains. Once you know these basics, it will be easy to adapt to the differences in a particular operation.

PIZZA

Pizza came to the United States from Naples, Italy. The original pizza was thick crusted with a coating of tomato sauce, cheese, and sometimes a bit of meat. However, pizza has now been Americanized. The crust is often crisp and thin and more sauce, cheese, and toppings are used.

Pizzas may be any size. Very small ones are served as appetizers. Many operations offer a small "pizza for one" at lunchtime. Large pizzas serve 12 persons or more.

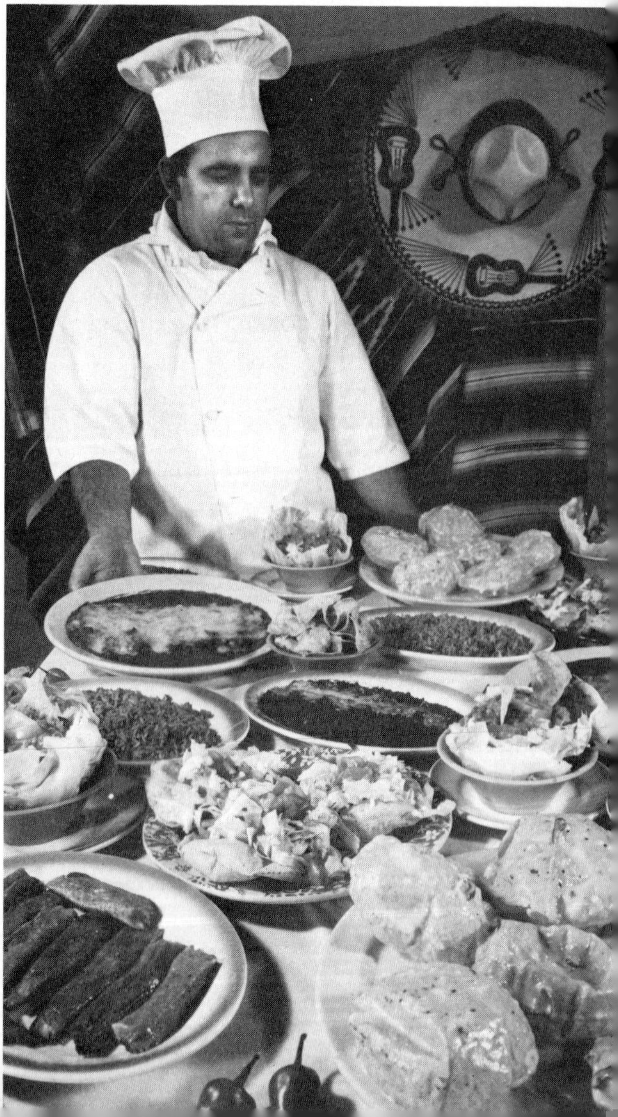

These Mexican dishes were prepared in a restaurant that specializes in Mexican foods.

Ingredients

A pizza has four basic parts, the crust, the sauce, the cheese, and the topping.

The crust is made from a yeast dough. A thick crust is made from a high gluten flour, but a thin crust is made from all-purpose flour. Some operations use olive oil to add real Italian flavor and soften the crust during baking. Others substitute less expensive oils.

Most sauces are made from tomato sauce, tomato paste (a very thick puree of tomatoes), and seasonings such as oregano, onions, and garlic. In chain restaurants, the sauce is often prepared in a commissary — the company supply store — and delivered to the outlet. It usually comes in cans containing the tomato sauce and tomato paste. The seasonings are packaged separately and mixed with the tomato sauce and paste in the restaurant kitchen. The type and proportions of the seasonings is often secret.

Either mozzarella or cheddar cheese is used on pizza. Mozzarella is preferred, but since it is more expensive, cheddar is sometimes substituted. The cheese is sliced or grated. It may be purchased locally or delivered from the commissary.

Pizza toppings vary widely. Some operations give specific topping choices, while others allow the customer to choose the toppings. Ground beef, pork, pepperoni, and Italian sausage are the most popular meat toppings. Sometimes chicken, shrimp, or anchovies are used.

Other popular toppings include onions, mushrooms, green peppers, and black olives. There are almost endless topping combinations.

Equipment

Special equipment helps make pizzas quickly and efficiently. Operatons which do not specialize in pizza often lack some of this specialized equipment.

- A vertical mixer for mixing the dough.
- A ***sheeter*** — a machine for automatically rolling and cutting the dough. The dough is passed between the two rollers of the sheeter and is cut to fit the pizza pans. The sheeter can be used only for thin crusts. A rolling pin is used to roll the dough if a sheeter is not available.
- Pizza pans for baking. Pizza pans are round with shallow sides. They come in various sizes.
- Ladles for measuring the sauce.

Franco uses a ladle to measure and spread the sauce from his special recipe on a pizza crust.

- Ovens for baking the pizzas. Most pizza restaurants use deck ovens with heavy bottoms called hearths. Some very large outlets may have a traveling convection oven. The pizza travels on a conveyor belt as it bakes, somewhat similar to the conveyor chain broiler described in Chapter 23. It may be divided into three sections, each with its own door and speed of travel. One section can be set for thin crusted pizzas, the middle section for thick crusted pizzas, and the third section for pizzas with heavy topping.
- A wooden paddle with a long handle called a ***peel*** to remove the pizza from the oven.
- Special gloves to protect the hands from the heat of the oven.
- A divider to cut the pizza evenly into servings.
- An oven brush to remove crumbs from the oven.

Method of Preparation

In making pizza, each of the four parts — the crust, sauce, cheese, and topping — must be considered. All affect the quality of the finished dish.

The Crust

Since the crust is a yeast bread, it is important to follow the guidelines for baking with yeast. You may wish to review Chapter 18.

Look at the recipe for making Thin, Crisp Pizza Crust on page 368. It uses water, yeast, oil, salt, and flour. After the ingredients are mixed, the dough rises at room temperature. Portions of the dough are scaled and either rolled automatically in the sheeter or by hand with a rolling pin. The rolled crust is placed on a pizza pan which has been sprayed with ***food release*** — a mixture of vegetable oil, alcohol, and lecithin — to keep the dough from sticking to it.

A wooden peel is used to place the pizza in the oven, as well as to remove it.

Thick pizza crust is made somewhat differently. It does not contain the oil which makes the thin crust tender and crispy. Proportions of flour and water are different. After mixing, thick pizza crust is scaled and refrigerated in an oiled, covered container. When needed, portions are removed and spread by hand in a pizza pan which has been sprayed with food release. The dough is allowed to rise about 20 minutes.

Scaling Dough, Sauce, and Cheese for Pizza

Thin, Crisp Crust			
Pizza Size	**Dough**	**Sauce**	**Cheese**
Very Small (2 in.)	3¾ oz.	½ c.	2 oz.
Small (8 in.)	6 oz.	⅔ c.	3 oz.
Medium (12 in.)	9¼ oz.	¾ c. + 2 T.	5 oz.
Large (18 in.)	13 oz.	1 c. + 2 T.	7 oz.
Thick, Chewy Crust			
Pizza Size	**Dough**	**Sauce**	**Cheese**
Very Small (2 in.)	6 oz.	5 T.	2¼ oz.
Small (8 in.)	9½ oz.	½ c.	3½ oz.
Medium (12 in.)	16 oz.	¾ c.	6 oz.
Large (18 in.)	21 oz.	1 c.	8 oz.

These two large thick-crust pizzas require approximately 42 oz. of dough!

Thin, Crisp Pizza Crust

Equipment: Bench mixer, Quart measure, Measuring spoons, Rubber spatula, Measuring cups, Baker's scale, Paddle attachment, Bowls, Bowl covers, Dough Cutter, Portion scale, Rolling Pin, 12 pizza pans (12″)

Yield: 12 pizza crusts (12″ diameter)

Ingredients	Amount	Method
Warm water (105°F)	1 qt.	1. Pour the warm water into bowl of bench mixer.
Yeast	2 T.	2. Sprinkle yeast on top of water. Stir with rubber spatula for about 2 min.
Oil	½ c.	3. Add oil and salt. Mix for 1 min.
Salt	¼ c.	4. Add flour. Using paddle attachment, mix on low speed for 3 min.
Flour	8 lbs.	5. Remove dough and place in lightly oiled bowls. Cover and let rise at room temperature for 6 hrs.
		6. Scale 13 oz. portions using dough cutter.
		7. Roll out each portion and place in pizza pan.

Serving size: 1 pizza crust

Cost per serving: ____________

A good pizza sauce requires a lot of chopped ingredients.

The Sauce

Although pizza sauce is often purchased, the sauce is very easy to prepare. Try the recipe for freshly prepared Pizza Sauce below. To develop the full flavor of the ingredients, the sauce should be stored in the refrigerator at least four hours before using.

Purchased pizza sauce needs the seasonings added before use. In fast foods, the seasonings supplied with the sauce have been precooked to speed the flavor release. If regular seasonings are used instead, the sauce should be cooked for an hour to develop the flavor.

Measure the sauce for each pizza using a ladle of the correct size. Spread the sauce on the unbaked crust.

Pizza Sauce

Equipment: Cheesecloth, String, Measuring spoons, Cutting board, Chef's knife, Can opener, Stock pot, Measuring cups, Kitchen spoon, China cap or blender

Yield: 1 gallon

Ingredients	Amount	Method
Thyme	2 t.	1. Cut a square of cheesecloth and a length of string.
Basil	2 t.	2. Measure and place the thyme, basil and oregano in the center of the cheesecloth.
Oregano	2 t.	3. Tie cheesecloth (Bouquet Garni) with string. Set aside.
Onion	1 c.	4. Chop onions, celery, green peppers and garlic.
Celery	4 stalks	5. Mix all ingredients in a stock pot.
Green pepper	1 c.	6. Simmer 3-4 hours.
Garlic cloves	4	7. Remove Bouquet Garni. Stir well with a kitchen spoon.
Tomato sauce	1 #10 can	8. Force sauce through a china cap or process in a blender.
Sugar	¼ c.	9. Adjust seasoning to taste.
Salt	1 T.	10. Refrigerate until needed in a covered container.
Pepper	1 T.	

Serving size: ⅔ cup per pizza

Cost per serving: ____________

The Cheese

The cheese is usually sent from the commissary already sliced or grated. If cheese does not come from a commissary, kitchen workers may need to grate or slice it. Keep it refrigerated until it is needed. The amount of cheese to be placed on the pizza is specified by the company. Cheese is expensive and should not be wasted. Place the cheese on top the sauce, but do not cover the bare edge of the crust with cheese. Most fast food operations will specify the exact way the cheese should be spread on the sauce.

The Topping

Each company or operation also specifies the exact amount of toppings used and the order for placing them on the pizza. This is part of cost control as well as quality control. Directions must be followed exactly. For instance:

- The sausage is presliced, and a certain number of slices are placed on the pizza in a precise order.
- Vegetables such as mushrooms and peppers are sliced on the premises and arranged as specified.
- The ground meat and cheese has been portioned so each pizza has exactly the same amount of each.
- If extra cheese or meat is ordered by the customer, a set amount is added and an extra charge is made.
- ***Dusting powder*** is a prepared mixture of oregano and Parmesan cheese. It is lightly dusted on the pizza just before baking to add flavor and finish.

✓ standards ✓

Pizza

Appearance

✓ Pleasing proportion of crust to sauce, cheese, and topping.

✓ Pieces of topping cut in appropriate sizes.

Color

✓ Crust well-browned.

✓ Interesting combination of colors in sauce and toppings.

Flavor

✓ Fresh.

✓ Hot, tasty.

Texture

✓ Crust crispy or chewy, depending on type used.

Baking

The deck oven is used most often for baking pizza although a conventional oven can be used. If you are baking several pizzas at the same time, place the larger pizzas at the back of the oven. The smaller pizzas will bake faster and should be placed in front for easy removal.

Sometimes the pizzas will form bubbles in the crust as they cook, especially those with thin crusts. After five minutes of baking, check for bubbles using the cutter and spread the ingredients gently over the bubbles so they do not show. Check again for bubbles after seven minutes.

Pizza is done when:

- The crust is lightly browned.
- The cheese is no longer runny.
- The top is well cooked.

Cooking time will vary from 8 to 15 minutes depending upon the size of the pizza, the thickness of the crust, the amount of topping and the number of pizzas baking at the same time.

Most beginners tend to overcook the pizzas, making them too dry. There is a specific time when the pizza should be removed from the oven. Experience will help you determine that time.

Staging

Staging means allowing the baked pizza to sit on top of the oven for about 30 seconds before cutting. Staging allows the pizza to set so it can be cut more easily.

Serving

The pizza is usually cut into pie-shaped pieces. The pizza cutter is a saw-toothed wheel set in a handle. A divider is used as a guide for the pizza cutter so each piece is the same size. The individual pizzas are not divided. Small pizzas are cut into four sections, the medium ones into eight, and large into eight or twelve sections. Pizzas should be served as soon as they are cut, as their quality deteriorates rapidly.

This pizza has been cut into 10 pie-shaped pieces. You can tell it was staged because the pieces cut easily.

MEXICAN FOODS

Mexican foods are widely served in both fast food and full-service restaurants. They are colorful, have exciting flavors, and are easy to make. They are also highly nutritious and yet inexpensive. Although Mexican food has the reputation of being hot and spicy, it does not have to be. The seasoning can be adapted to taste. Mexican food was not devised for delicate tastes. The flavor is always robust, distinctive, and delicious.

Seasonings

Although Mexican cooking uses many of the same herbs and spices as other cuisines, there are some that distinguish the food as Mexican.

- Cilantro, sometimes called Chinese parsley, is the Mexican word for fresh coriander. Cilantro is very aromatic and flavorful. No other herb can be substituted for it.

- Comino is a herb also known as cumin. It is sold with the seeds either whole or ground. The whole seeds have much stronger flavor than the ground seeds. Comino is the dominant flavor in chili powder.

safety tip . . .

When handling hot chilies, wear rubber gloves. Be very careful not to rub your eyes or any unprotected skin areas.

- Chilies are known as peppers in the United States. Chilies may be very hot, very mild, or any stage in between. Anyone cooking Mexican food must know about chilies. The chart tells about common types of chilies.

Types of Chilies

Type	Name	Appearance	Flavor
Fresh	Jalapeno	Small, medium to dark green with a rounded, tapered end	Hot
	Poblano or Passilla	Small, very dark green	Medium hot
	Serrano	Similar to jalapeno	Very hot
Dried	Ancho	Dark red, wrinkled	Hot
	Chipotle	Dried jalapeno	Hot, smoked
Mild	Bell	Bright green or red	Mild, sweet
	Pimiento	Orange, red	Mild
	Banana	Yellow	Mild

Chile Sauces

Do not confuse these with American chili sauce. These Mexican chile sauces may be made fresh or purchased in the can. The chile sauces are served alongside Mexican food in case you want a "hotter" flavor. The red sauce, salsa roja, is more mild than the green sauce, salsa verde.

Tortillas

Tortillas are the standard Mexican flat bread. In Mexico and in the Mexican-American communities they are sometimes made by hand. For food service, ready-made tortillas are purchased. They are sealed in plastic for freshness and refrigerated. Tortillas may be served soft and hot as a hot bread. They are also used as the foundation for many dishes. Tortillas fried in hot oil until crisp are called tostados (toh-STAD-dohs). If the crisp tostados are broken into pieces, they are called tortila chips.

There are two types of tortillas, corn and wheat tortillas:

- Corn tortillas are made from a finely ground corn flour called ***masa harina***. They are about 6 in. (15 cm) in diameter. Corn tortillas are the most popular type.

- Wheat flour tortillas are about 8 in. (20 cm) in diameter. They are softer, whiter, and blander. They are especially popular in chicken dishes.

Tortillas are already cooked when purchased, but they must be reheated for use. Cold tortillas will crack when rolled. Be careful not to reheat them longer than necessary to soften and warm them. They become hard and brittle very quickly. To reheat tortillas, use one of these methods:

- Place tortillas one at a time on hot griddle or heavy frying pan. Cook on one side about 30 seconds and turn. Do not brown. Place immediately in a tightly covered dish or wrap tightly in foil to keep them hot.

- Wrap tortillas in foil or in a clean, damp cloth. Place in preheated 350°F (180°C) oven for about 15 minutes. Keep wrapped until used.

- Wrap tortillas in damp towel or plastic wrap. Heat in a microwave ovenfor $1\frac{1}{2}$ minutes.

Both corn and flour tortillas are used in food service. These corn tortillas will be used to make enchiladas.

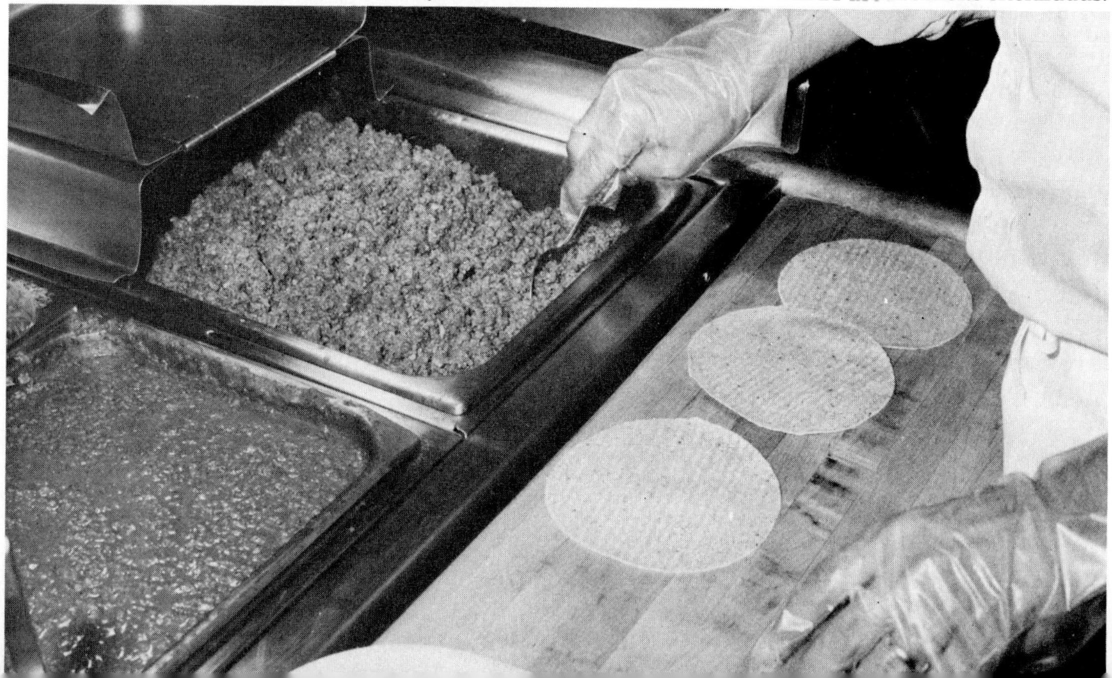

Tacos

The most popular and well known Mexican food is undoubtedly the ***taco***. Taco really means "snack," and that is the way Mexican eat them. The outside is a warm, soft tortilla. A filling is placed in the center of the tortilla, and it is rolled and eaten.

Like the pizza, the original taco has been Americanized. Tacos are often fried crisp and folded into a half-moon shape. Filling is added between the two sides of the half-moon. Sauce and garnishes are added before serving.

Ingredients

There are many variations in tacos. Any of the four parts — the filling, the sauce, and the garnish — may be varied.

- **Taco shell**. Taco shells are usually made from corn tortillas. The shell is purchased already shaped as a half-moon. The shell is fried quickly in deep fat and then filled. Some operations offer wheat flour tortillas.
- **Filling**. The filling consists of any hot, cooked, shredded or ground meat that is seasoned with taco sauce.
- **Sauce**. Each taco chain has its own sauce recipe to make its tacos taste different from others. The sauces have a tomato base and are seasoned with chili powder, salt, onions, and other seasonings. The sauce mixed with the meat is usually mild, but hot sauces are served alongside for those who like tacos hot and spicy.
- **Garnish**. Shredded lettuce, chopped tomatoes, shredded cheese, chopped green onions, and chopped avocado are the most popular garnishes.

Service

In some restaurants, customers may order the filling and garnish and make their own tacos. In fast food operations, the taco shells are filled and garnished in the kitchen. Usually, three tacos make a serving.

Nachos

Nachos are freshly fried corn tortilla chips served with a bowl of melted cheese. Soft cheeses such as Monterey Jack or Longhorn cheeses are preferred because they melt easily and do not become stringy unless melted at too high a temperature. The cheese is usually mixed with finely chopped mild or hot chilies.

In fast foods, the melted cheese is placed over the nachos before serving. Customers must separate the cheesy nachos to eat them, rather than dip them into a bowl of melted cheese.

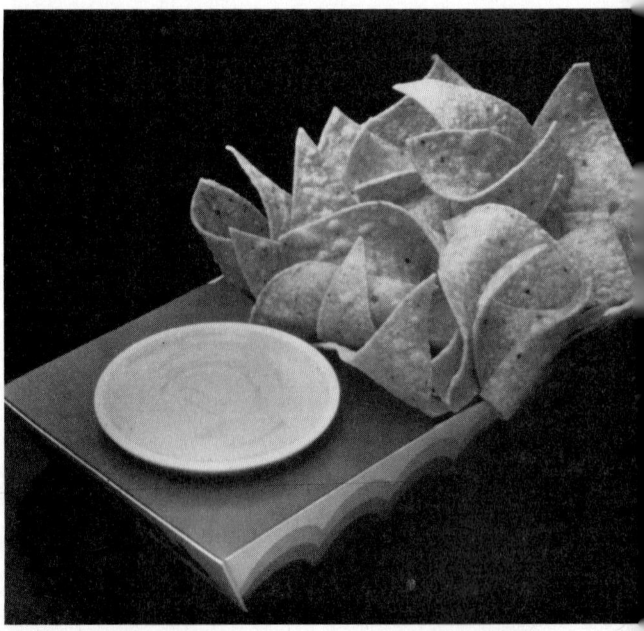

Nachos are a favorite snack. They can be eaten plain, with melted cheese, or with chilie-filled cheeses.

Burritos

Burritos (burr-EE-toes) are wheat flour tortillas rolled around a filling. In some restaurants, the tortillas are served wrapped in a steamy towel along with a variety of fillings and the sauce on the side. Guacamole (a sauce made from avocado) and sour cream are often served with burritos.

Enchiladas

Enchiladas (en-chi-LAH-dahs) are a favorite dinner food in Mexican restaurants. They are soft, fried tortillas rolled around a variety of fillings and baked with a sauce. Other Mexican foods may be as good, but none can compare with the infinite variety of enchiladas.

Refried beans, burritos, and tacos are all favorite Mexican foods. Cheese, sauce, and onions are three ingredients they have in common.

Enchiladas Con Queso
(Enchiladas with Cheese)

Equipment: Cutting board, Chef's knife, Portion scale, Bowls, Large frying pan, Measuring cups, Rubber spatula, Kitchen spoon, Quart Measure, Measuring spoons, Slotted spoon, 4 Baking pans (13″x9″x2″)

Yield: 48 enchiladas
Temperature: 350°F

Ingredients	Amount	Method
Oil	1 c.	1. Chop onion and garlic.
Onion	2 lb.	2. Place oil, onion, and garlic in a large frying pan. Cook on medium heat for 5 minutes.
Garlic	8 cloves	3. Add broth, tomatoes, and seasoning (Option: Brown the ground beef, drain, and add to sauce.)
Broth, chicken or beef	1 qt.	4. Simmer 1 hour.
Tomatoes, #2½ cans	1	5. Dip each tortilla into sauce. Remove quickly and drain slightly. Stack.
Chili powder	⅓ c.	6. Spread a small amount of sauce in the bottom of each baking pan.
Salt	1 T. 1 t.	7. Spoon 2 T. of cheese onto each tortilla. Roll tightly.
Whole comino seeds	¼ c.	8. Place 12 tortillas (seam side down) in each baking dish.
Oregano	⅛ c.	9. Spoon remaining sauce over enchiladas.
Ground beef (optional)	3 lb.	10. Sprinkle with remaining cheese.
Corn tortillas	48	11. Bake 15 minutes, until cheese is melted.
Cheddar or Monterey Jack Cheese	3 lb.	

Serving size: 2 enchiladas

Cost per serving: ________________

Ingredients

Enchiladas are made from either corn or flour tortillas, a filling, a sauce, and a garnish. Each kind of enchilada calls for different ingredients in the filling and sauce. Beef, pork, cheese, chicken, and ground beef, and sausage called chorizos are just a few of the many varieties available. Sometimes ***refried beans*** are used. Refried beans are cooked dried beans which have been recooked in fat such as bacon or ham drippings. A recipe for Enchiladas with Cheese is on page 376.

Method of Preparation

Follow the recipe directions for preparing the filling and sauce desired. Then follow these steps for assembling the dish:

1. Since the tortillas are rolled with the filling in them, they must be warmed to prevent cracking. Traditionally, the tortillas are dipped in the sauce and then fried. It is neater and easier to fry the tortillas very briefly on both sides first. Do not brown. Stack the tortillas, and cover with a damp towel to keep them warm.
2. Spread a small amount of the sauce on the bottom of the pan.
3. Dip a tortilla from the stack in the remaining sauce and place it flat on a board.
4. Spoon the correct amount of filling on the tortilla. The filling should be warm, but not hot.
5. To roll the enchilada, roll as tightly as possible, and place with the seam side down in a baking pan.
6. Continue filling and rolling the enchiladas. Place them close together so they are touching in the pan.
7. When the pan is filled with the enchiladas, ladle the thick sauce over the top using a ladle. The enchiladas should be completely covered with the sauce so they do not dry out during baking.
8. Enchiladas are more attractive if garnished before baking. Shredded cheese, chopped onions, or sliced olives, enhance the flavor and add appeal.
9. Bake at 350°F (180°C) for about 20 minutes or as specified in the recipe.
10. After baking, a fresh garnish such as chopped parsley or cilantro or sliced avocadoes may be added.

Enchiladas are often served with a salad for a well-balanced, nutritious, and attractive meal. Three enchiladas are considered a normal serving.

The correct amount of filling is placed in the center of each corn tortilla.

Each enchilada is rolled as tightly as possible.

Each enchilada is then placed on the serving plate.

A thick meat sauce is ladled over the top of the enchiladas.

Shredded cheese, chopped onions, and sliced olives are added.

A scoop of sour cream on the side adds the finishing touch.

Tamales

Tamales (tah-MAH-lees) are a rather unusual dish. They consist of a meat filling covered with corn tortilla dough in a wrapping of corn husks. Tamales are cooked by steaming.

The tamales are formed in layers. Clean, soaked corn husks specially processed for this use make up the outer layer. Spread a layer of masa dough over them, leaving some husk showing on all edges. Next, spread the filling over the masa dough. The filling often includes beef, pork, or chicken mixed with taco sauce and cheese. Then fold the tamales into neat packages with the corn husks on the outside. Steam the tamales in a steamer or in a roasting pan on a rack. They usually cook 45 minutes to one hour and are done when the masa dough is completely cooked.

Tamales are served in the corn husks. A sauce is often provided to add as desired. After cooking, tamales may be frozen. They can be reheated by steaming without thawing.

Tamales are served in many specialty restaurants. They can also be purchased frozen or in cans.

FRIED TORTILLA SHELLS

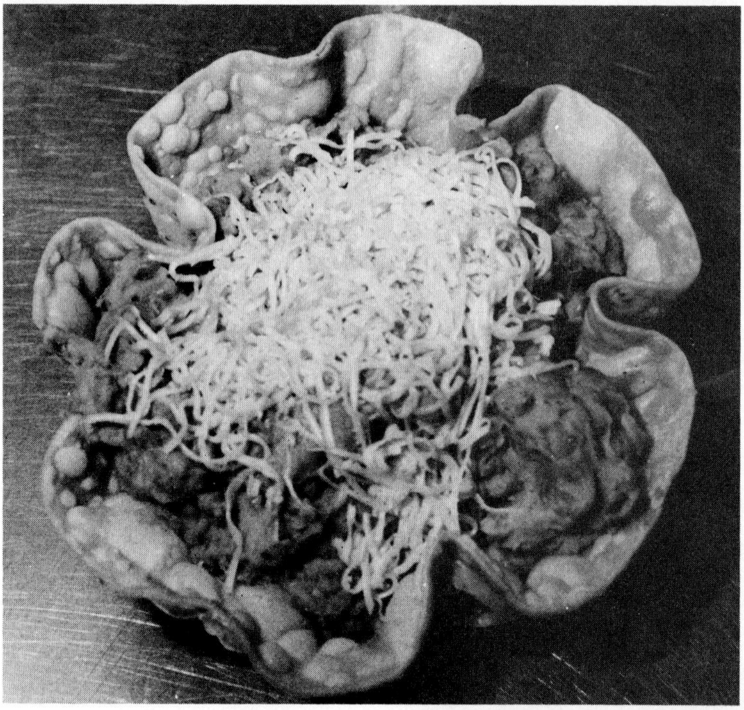

Fried tortilla shells are often filled with refried beans or salads. In addition to being attractive serving dishes for food, the crispy shells can be eaten.

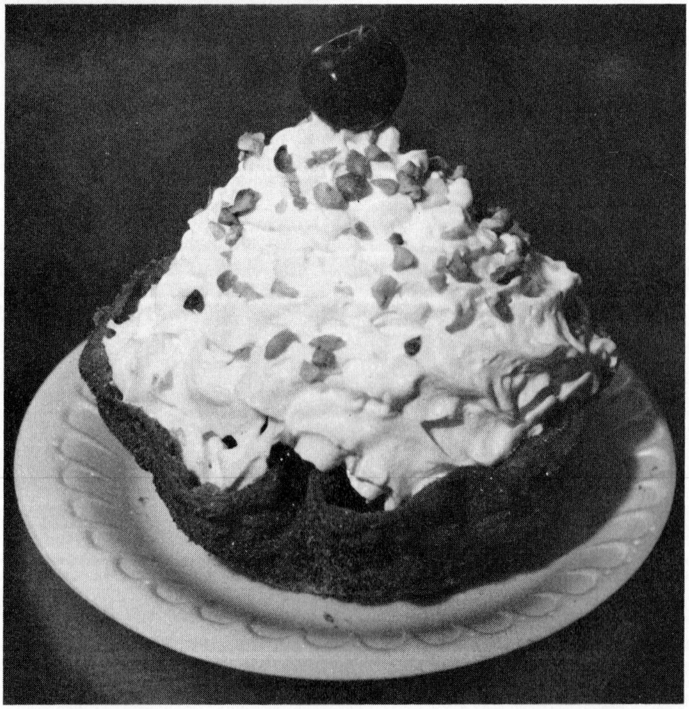

This shell was dipped in cinnamon and sugar right after it was fried. It makes a pretty dish for this sundae, and tastes great too!

chapter recap

SUMMARY

Many foods originally developed in other countries are now popular in America. Pizza and Mexican foods are popular alternatives to hamburgers and other fast foods. Countless varieties of pizza are available. Mexican foods are both nutritious and inexpensive. They are known for their robust flavor that comes from distinctive seasonings.

CHECK YOUR KNOWLEDGE

1. What are the four parts of a pizza?
2. What kind of leavening is used in pizza dough?
3. What is a peel used for in pizza baking?
4. What are the two types of pizza crust?
5. What factors affect the cooking time for pizza?
6. Name three seasonings which are commonly used in Mexican cooking.
7. Name one hot and one mild type of Mexican chilis.
8. What are the two types of tortillas?
9. Name two Mexican dishes that use tortillas.
10. What are nachos?

EXTEND YOUR LEARNING

1. Compare the nutritional value of a slice of pizza to a hamburger in a bun. Which provides the best nutrition for the calories? Back up your choice.
2. Use your library to find out how Mexican use native products in their cooking. Write a brief report.
3. Have each person in the class ask ten different people which they would prefer for lunch — tacos, a slice of pizza, or a hamburger. Bring your results to class and tabulate the totals. Discuss possible reasons for the results.

"Jim, Ruthann, and Kim were examining the job assignment list on the bulletin board outside their classroom.

"Ugh!" said Jim. "Here it is the last week of school, and look what jobs I'm stuck with — cleanup and beverages. Why can't I do something important?"

"Cleanup is important, Jim," said Ruthann. "Remember when I got sick last Thanksgiving at the church supper? That wouldn't have happened if the cutting board had been sanitized."

"Beverages are important, too, Jim," Kim added. "Your whole meal can be ruined if your drink tastes bad. Maybe you don't like coffee, but lots of people do. I was in the bakery last week. They sell coffee with their doughnuts and rolls. A man was really telling off the clerk. He said the coffee tasted like dishwater."

"That's right, Kim," said Ruthann. "I like coffee sometimes, if it's hot and strong."

"Well, I don't drink coffee," said Jim, "so why should I have to know how to make it?"

"Everyone in food service should know about all kinds of beverages, Jim," Kim said. "Maybe you don't think coffee is important to you, but it is to others. They feel about coffee the way you feel about chocolate shakes. How would you like to be served a watery, warm shake with not enough chocolate in it?"

"Okay, okay!" exclaimed Jim. "I get your point, girls. Now I can see that Chef Robinson just saved the best jobs till last for me. He probably knew he could count on a great worker like me to get the foods lab shiny for the summer — and make great coffee for the teachers so they won't be too grouchy during finals week.""

chapter 26

beverages

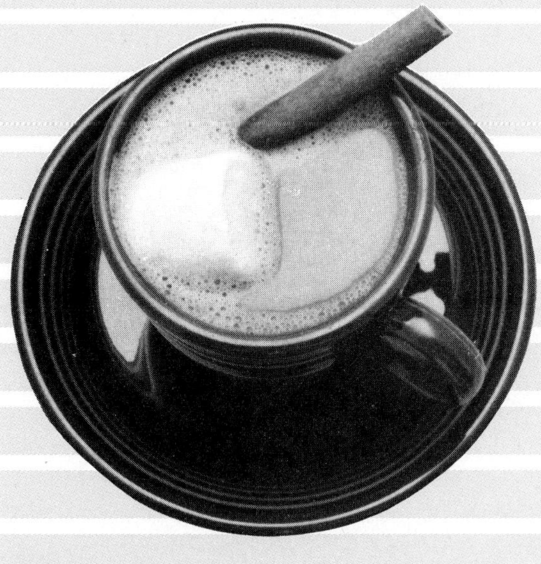

Set your goals

When you complete the study of this chapter, you should be able to . . .

- Define and correctly use the vocabulary terms.
- Prepare coffee in an automatic drip coffee maker.
- List the steps in the preparation of hot tea and iced tea.
- Correctly fill milkshakes and soft drinks.

Build your vocabulary

brewed	orange pekoe
caffeine	pasteurization
homogenized	seat line
milk stone	urn

TYPES OF BEVERAGES

A beverage is a drink. Strictly speaking, water is a beverage since it is a drink. But in food service, a beverage usually means a hot drink, such as coffee or tea, or a cold drink, like soft drinks and milk shakes. All food service operations serve beverages, but they are especially important in fast food establishments. Other operations serve beverages mainly with meals, but fast food chains also sell them frequently as a snack.

COFFEE

Beverage service is important in food service because it can make or break a meal. A cup of hot, delicious coffee adds a final touch to a meal, but a cup of lukewarm or bitter coffee can ruin a meal. For this reason, beverage service is a frequent cause of customer complaint.

In the United States, coffee is the most popular beverage. In fact, the phrase "have a cup of coffee" is an offer of hospitality. Breaks in business routines are commonly called "coffee breaks."

Coffee — the symbol of American hospitality.

Coffee comes from roasted and ground coffee beans. The flavor and aroma of coffee depends upon the kind of coffee beans, the country from which they came, and the roasting process. Most ready-to-use coffees sold in the United States are blends of different beans. People vary in their preference for coffee taste. Some like it very rich and full-bodied, but others prefer a light taste. A food service operation chooses a blend that pleases the majority of its customers.

Once coffee is ground, it loses its aroma and flavor very quickly if exposed to the air. That is why coffee purchased in the store is vacuum packed, usually in cans. (Vacuum means that the air has been removed from the container.) However, cans are expensive. Most food service operations buy freshly ground coffee in airtight bags. Because freshness is essential for high quality coffee, it is used up within a day or two after the bag is opened.

Coffee contains a substance called ***caffeine***. Caffeine gives coffee its stimulating or energizing effect. It also keeps some people awake. Many people enjoy coffee but not its stimulating effect. That is why most operations also offer decaffeinated coffee — coffee which has the caffeine removed.

Within the past twenty years, instant coffee has won acceptance because it is easy to use. However, most customers prefer "real," freshly made coffee. Many food service operations make fresh regular coffee. When decaffeinated coffee is requested, however, it is served as a small packet of instant coffee with a pot of hot water. This practice annoys many customers. The best operations brew both regular and decaffeinated coffee.

Equipment

Only two types of coffee makers are commonly used in food service operatons.

- **Urn**. An ***urn*** is a large coffee maker with a faucet for removing the coffee. The fully automatic urn is used in food service only when large quantities of coffee are needed at one time.
- **Automatic drip coffee makers**. These are the most popular equipment for making fresh coffee in small amounts. The water drips from the top container, through the finely ground coffee in a filter in the center, and into the pot below.

Preparing Coffee

Coffee is ***brewed***. This means that the flavor of the ground coffee is extracted by hot water. Anyone working in food service should learn how to make a good cup of coffee. Coffee should be clear, fragrant, hot, and have a fully developed flavor.

Follow these rules to make quality coffee:

- Use only clean equipment. Coffee contains several oily substances which enhance its flavor. These oils can build up in the coffee-making equipment. If the coffee maker is not cleaned thoroughly after use, the coffee will develop a bitter, unpleasant taste. The chart on page 386 tells how to clean coffee makers.

- Use only fresh coffee. These same oily substances become rancid with age, causing coffee to lose its flavor and aroma. Coffee grounds cannot be reused.

- Select the correct coffee for the type of equipment. Coffee comes in different grinds, from coarse to fine. The choice of grind depends on the equipment used. A coarse grind is used for coffee made in an urn. Filtered coffee uses a very fine grind. Coffee manufacturers specify on the coffee label the type of equipment the coffee suits.

- Weigh or measure the amount of coffee needed, if necessary. In food service, most coffee is purchased premeasured for specific coffee makers. This eliminates mistakes.

- Most coffee makers have a measurement line for the amount of water to be added. Use it.

An automatic drip coffee maker.

• Many coffee makers are automatic and will turn off when the coffee is done. If the coffee maker is not automatic, brewing must be timed carefully. Underbrewed coffee is weak and watery. Overbrewed coffee is bitter and has a muddy appearance.

• Hold brewed coffee for only a short time. As coffee brews, the escaping steam carries the aroma of the coffee into the air. The flavor and aroma continue to develop for about ten minutes. From then on the flavor and fragrance of the coffee gradually decrease. For this reason, most food service operations prefer to make coffee in small amounts in automatic drip coffee makers.

Cleaning Coffee Makers

Automatic Drip Coffee Makers	Coffee Urns
1. Clean coffee decanters after each use using warm water.	**1.** Brush inside walls thoroughly each day using hot water.
2. Throw away filters.	**2.** Rinse with hot water until water comes out clear.
3. Clean warming plates with damp cloth and dry.	**3.** Rinse inside of cover.
	4. Unscrew glass gauge, brush, and rinse.
	5. Remove and clean faucet.
	6. Place several gallons of fresh water in urn. Leave cover slightly ajar.
	7. Empty urn in morning before making fresh coffee.

Serving Coffee

Coffee is served with sugar and cream. In food service, artificial sweetener in small packages is placed with the packages of sugar in the sugar bowl. In elegant restaurants, cream is still served in pitchers, but in most of food service, packets of coffee creamer or individual containers of cream are used. Fast food operations usually serve coffee in foam cups with lids. This allows customers to take their coffee with them if they wish.

TEA

Tea comes from the leaves of the tea bush grown in the Orient. Both green and black teas are used in food service. They both come from the same bush. The difference is the way they are processed.

In the Orient, the mild flavor of green tea is preferred. This type of tea is usually served with Oriental foods. In processing the tea leaves for black tea, the leaves are fermented. They are spread on trays outdoors in humid weather. Black tea is preferred in the United States and England because it is stronger in flavor. Of the black teas, ***orange pekoe*** is the highest quality since it is made from the young, tender, top leaves.

Tea may be purchased loose by weight on in convenient packets or bags for individual service. These small bags are used frequently in food service. Tea is also available in an instant form which is sometimes used to make iced tea.

Equipment

Tea may be made in either a pot or in the cup. A china pot is considered the most elegant way to serve tea, but a stainless steel pot which holds two cups of water is generally used in food service. A second, slightly smaller pot to hold extra hot water is desirable.

Preparing Tea

To brew tea, the tea leaves are soaked in near-boiling water for a short time to extract the flavor and fragrance. Tea is simple to prepare. However, a good cup of tea is hard to find, even in fine restaurants.

Good tea has a few, simple requirements — high quality tea, fresh boiling water, and a preheated pot and cup. To make tea, follow these rules:

- Rinse the pot with boiling water.
- Place the tea bag in the pot and fill with boiling water.
- Preheat the cup by rinsing with boiling water.
- Serve immediately.

Serving Tea

The common practice in food service is to place the tea bag on a saucer with the cup and carry it to the customer with a pot of hot water. This results in a lukewarm, flavorless cup of tea, and often an unhappy customer. Using the rules just described greatly improves this beverage. Tea is served with sugar, lemon, or milk as the customer desires.

ICED TEA AND COFFEE

During the summer months, iced tea and coffee are popular. Although they can be made simply by pouring strong, hot tea or coffee over ice, instant coffee and tea are commonly used. This saves ice since the beverage is already cool when it is poured over ice. The instant form also makes a clearer, more sparkling beverage.

A commercial iced tea brewer.

MILK

Milk is a popular beverage that is also very nutritious. It is one of the best sources of calcium and furnishes many other minerals and vitamins.

Fresh milk has a delicate, sweet flavor. Its creamy texture and color please adults and children alike.

Milk Standards

Because milk is an animal product and can easily become contaminated, special procedures are needed in processing. The composition, production, and processing of milk are strictly regulated by law. Legal standards for milk are set and enforced by the U.S. Public Health Service and also by state and local regulations. Dairy farms are inspected to make sure that the cows are clean and healthy and the milking equipment is sanitary.

Pasteurization

For the safety of customers, all milk served in food service must be pasteurized. ***Pasteurization*** is the process of heating milk in approved equipment to 161°F (75°C) and holding it there for 30 seconds. This is called flash pasteurization. The treatment does not change the taste of the milk, but is a safety measure. Pasteurization kills any disease-causing bacteria in the milk.

Milk as a Beverage

There are several kinds of milk commonly served as a beverage. You are probably familiar with most of them.

- **Whole milk**. Whole milk contains all the natural butterfat found in milk. Although the requirement for the percentage of butterfat varies, 3.5 percent butterfat is the accepted standard. Whole milk is usually

Milk is a very nutritious beverage.

homogenized — treated mechanically so the butterfat is scattered in very fine globules throughout the milk. They cannot rise to the top and form cream.

- **Low-fat milk**. Within the past few years, low-fat milk has gained popularity because it is lower in calories and cholesterol than whole milk. This is a result of the removal of much of the butterfat from the milk.
- **Skim milk**. All the butterfat is removed from skim milk. This makes it very low in calories and cholesterol.
- **Chocolate milk**. To be called "chocolate milk" the beverage must meet the same standards as whole milk. "Chocolate drink" may contain no milk at all.
- **Buttermilk**. This milk is slightly fermented, somewhat acid, and sharp in taste. Cultured buttermilk, the only type sold in food service, is made from skim milk which has been soured by adding microorganisms. These microorganisms are called a culture. Flakes of butter are added to buttermilk to improve its appearance.

Serving Milk

Milk should always be served very cold. In some communities the law requires that milk be served to the customer in the original container. In other places, individual servings are drawn from large milk dispensers.

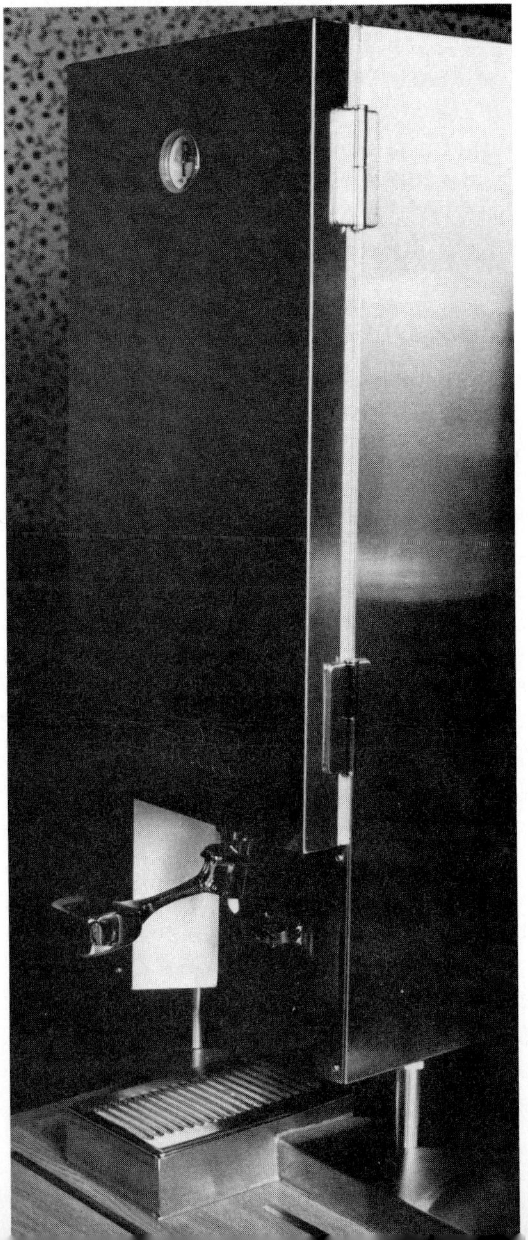

A commercial milk dispenser.

COCOA AND CHOCOLATE

The flavor of chocolate is popular all over the world. Chocolate blends well with milk to make many delicious drinks which can be served hot or chilled. Hot cocoa is especially popular as a breakfast beverage or late evening snack.

Ingredients

Cocoa and chocolate come from the bean of the cocoa tree which grows in Central and South America. The beans are processed, roasted, and ground into a paste from which the various forms of chocolate are made.

Pure chocolate contains about 50 percent fat or cocoa butter. Most beverages are made from cocoa rather than chocolate beause the large amount of fat in chocolate makes it unsuitable for beverage making.

Cocoa contains not less than 22 percent cocoa butter by government standards. Dutch process cocoa has been specially treated to develop a darker color, a milder flavor, and a smoother beverage.

Instant cocoa contains Dutch process cocoa, sugar, flavorings, milk powder, and lecithin. Lecithin is a product of soybeans that adds body and smoothness to the beverage. The mix blends instantly with cold or hot water and is used almost exclusively in food service. It is packaged in small amounts that make one cup of cocoa.

MILK SHAKES

Milk shakes have long been a favorite as a beverage. They are a special favorite in fast food outlets. A recent survey showed that half of those eating in fast food outlets preferred milk shakes as a beverage. In fast foods, milk shakes have been standardized and are instantly available. The old-time mixer is no longer needed. They are prepared in an automatic dispenser.

Ingredients

The ingredients in a milk shake are simple — milk, ice cream, and flavoring. Some fast food chains use a milk substitute in place of the milk and ice cream. (These beverages are commonly called "shakes" instead of "milk shakes".) Vanilla, chocolate, and strawberry are the most familiar milkshake flavors.

The thickness of ready-made dispenser milkshakes is not due to any large amount of ice cream. A stabilizer is added to increase the thickness and make the foam stable.

Milk is one of the basic ingredients of a milk shake. Milk substitutes can also be used. Here milk is being poured into an automatic milk shake dispenser.

Equipment

Fast food operations use an automatic dispenser that can dispense several flavors of shakes. In the newest type, the operator selects the flavor, pushes a button, and holds the cup under the serving spout. The machine automatically ejects the right amount of flavor syrup into the cup as it is being filled. It takes only about six or seven seconds to make a shake.

Preparing Milk Shakes

The key to quality of dispenser milk shakes lies in following the manufacturer's directions exactly. Be especially careful to follow the daily start-up procedure outlined in the instruction manual. Also follow these tips:

- When the machine is ready for use, draw a sample shake. Test for consistency. Most machines have a control to adjust the thickness.
- Check for flavor and color by drawing a sample shake of each flavor. Adjust the amount of syrup to the desired flavor and color.
- Make sure you use the specified cup size.
- Lift the lever all the way up so the cup will fill quickly.

This cup is being filled to the seat line with milk shake. Seat lines are a part of standardization and cost control.

- Fill to the ***seat line***. Close to the top of each cup is a mark called the seat line. This mark is used to make sure all shakes will be the same size.

Some restaurants cap each cup and mark the flavor on the cap with a grease pencil. Follow your supervisor's instructions.

Care of Milk and Milk Shake Dispensers

Milk stone is a deposit that forms inside any piece of equipment used with dairy products. It harbors bacteria and must be removed each night. Following the manufacturer's instructions, dismantle the dispenser. Clean thoroughly with a special milk stone remover. Rinse with cool water. Recharge the dispenser the next morning.

Soft Drinks

Restaurants may use glasses to serve soft drinks, but most fast food outlets offer soft drinks in paper cups. In filling cups for soft drinks from a dispenser, follow these tips:

- Fill the cup exactly half full with crushed ice unless the customer requests otherwise.
- Tilt the cup while dispensing to reduce the amount of foam.
- Cover with a lid and, if instructed, mark the flavor on the lid with a grease pencil.

The size of the cup tells this cashier how much to charge for the soft drink.

SUMMARY

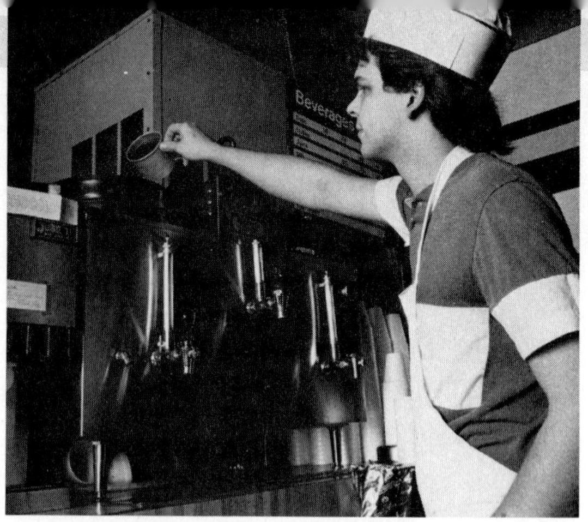

The importance of beverages in food service can easily be overlooked. Beverages which are poorly prepared or served can ruin a meal. Coffee, tea, milk, soft drinks, and milk shakes are the most common food service beverages. Each has its own equipment and standards for excellence. Food service workers should know how to operate and clean beverage equipment. They should also know how to serve beverages in a way that is satisfying to their customers.

chapter recap

CHECK YOUR KNOWLEDGE

1. What is a beverage?
2. How is ground coffee packaged for food service?
3. What is caffeine?
4. Why should brewed coffee be served promptly?
5. What is required when making a good cup of tea?
6. Why is milk pasteurized?
7. Name three types of milk served as a beverage.
8. Why are beverages made of cocoa rather than chocolate?
9. What is added to milk shakes to make them thick?
10. What is milk stone?

EXTEND YOUR LEARNING

1. Compare coffee made by the automatic drip method with instant coffee. Rate each on color, flavor, and aroma.
2. Make a pot of orange pekoe tea using the directions in this chapter. Make a second cup by pouring the hot water into the cup and letting it sit a few minutes. Then put in a tea bag of orange pekoe tea into the cup. Compare for flavor, aroma, color, and temperature.
3. Buy a chocolate shake from a fast food outlet. Make a chocolate milk shake using chocolate flavoring, ice cream and milk. Compare the results.

Unit 8

Beginning a Career in Food Service

Now that you have mastered the basics of food service, it is time to look to the future. You have studied nutrition, management, small and large equipment, the pantry station, the hot stations, and the bakery, as well as fast foods. But what's the next step?

This unit will help you to look at all the options — additional education, part-time work, and full-time work. You will learn how to find a job by gathering and organizing information, getting a social security number, and developing a personal fact sheet. You will also learn how to fill out an application properly. Interviews will also be discussed since they are the deciding factor in getting a job. You must dress and act appropriately for a job interview.

However, a professional cook's future does not end there. You also need to learn how to adjust to your new job, as well as your co-workers. Then, you will be on your way to becoming part of a professional cooking team.

This unit will help you put all of your knowledge to use by gaining some work experience in food service. But don't forget that moving up the career ladder requires you to continue learning about the food service trade. You have now completed the first step, but there is much more to learn.

"At the end of the school year, Jim, Ruthann, Rosita, Kim, David, and Tony were discussing their food service teacher.

Tony said, "Chef Robinson is different from most teachers. Maybe it's because he's actually earned his living in food service. Today he was telling us about jobs in food service, but he didn't tell us just the good parts. He told us about the other parts too — like bad hours, night work, and the poor pay."

"I liked the way he showed us there are lots of food service jobs besides cooking," said Kim. "I think I might like a job in the storeroom now that I've learned to run the computer."

"That's not for me," said Rosita. "I like to be out where I can meet people. I'd like to be a waitress, or a hostess who also runs a cash register."

"I'm like you, Rosita," Tony exclaimed. "I like people too. After all I've learned about cooking and menus and cost control, I want to have my own restaurant. I can just see myself shaking hands with all my customers."

"I'm still thinking about working in a hospital," Ruthann said. "I've visited the community college. They have some good courses there. It should help me decide if I really want to be a dietitian."

David said, "I've really learned a lot from this class. I'm taking the advanced course next semester. If I do that, my boss at the bakery said he'd hire me full-time as a baker."

Jim commented, "We've all taken the same class this year, and all have different ideas about what we want to do. I've decided to take all the food service classes I can. I really like it! Maybe I'll even go to college or one of those special schools for cooks. No more quitting school for me. Just wait, in a few years I'll be Chef James!"

"Have you ever changed!" exclaimed David. "What happened to the job at Sizzling Sam's and all that money in your pocket?"

"I still want money," said Jim, "but now I'm willing to wait and have a career, instead of just taking any kind of job. After all, if I'm going to work for the rest of my life, I might as well enjoy it!""

chapter 27

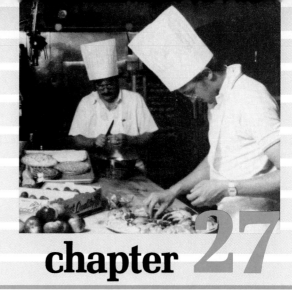

look to the future

Set your goals

When you complete the study of this chapter, you should be able to . . .

- Define and correctly use the vocabulary terms.
- Identify ways to find out about job openings.
- Prepare a personal fact sheet.
- Complete a job application.
- Identify dos and don'ts for interviews.

Build your vocabulary

advisory council
classified section
employment agencies
interview
job application
references
social security number
supervisor

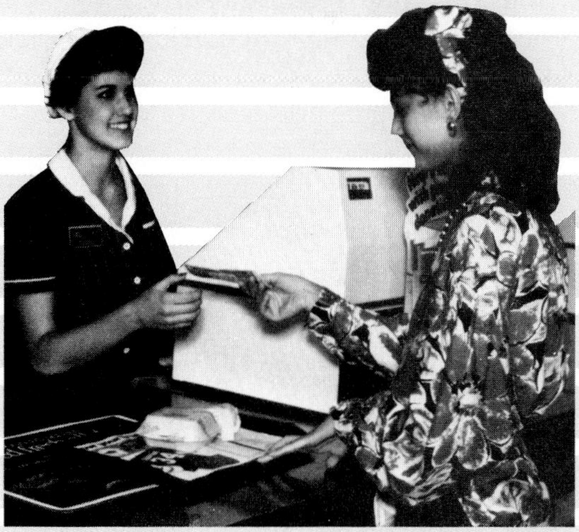

WHAT'S NEXT?

During this class, you have studied about the food service industry and learned many cooking skills. If you have decided on a career in food service, you may be asking, "What's my next step?" The answer depends on you. You have several options:

- **Additional education**. This course only gave you a start on what you need to know in food service. You have had a taste of several different jobs. While it is still possible to work your way up to the top in a food service operation, you will advance more quickly with additional education. Does your school offer more advanced classes? Is there a vocational school or community college in your area with a food service program. If you would like to be a manager or registered dietitian, consider a four-year college program.

Many people who start to work full-time after graduation later wish they had taken more classes. If you are unsure, consider going to school and working part-time.

- **Part-time work**. Part-time work is usually easy to find in food service. If you are going to school, you can probably find a job during some of the hours you are not in class.

A job gives you practical experience in a real food service operation. You will learn to use different equipment, develop new skills, and see how you cope with the pressures of the job.

- **Full-time work**. After graduation many students choose full-time work. This daily work experience helps them learn new skills quickly. With a regular paycheck, they begin a more independent life.

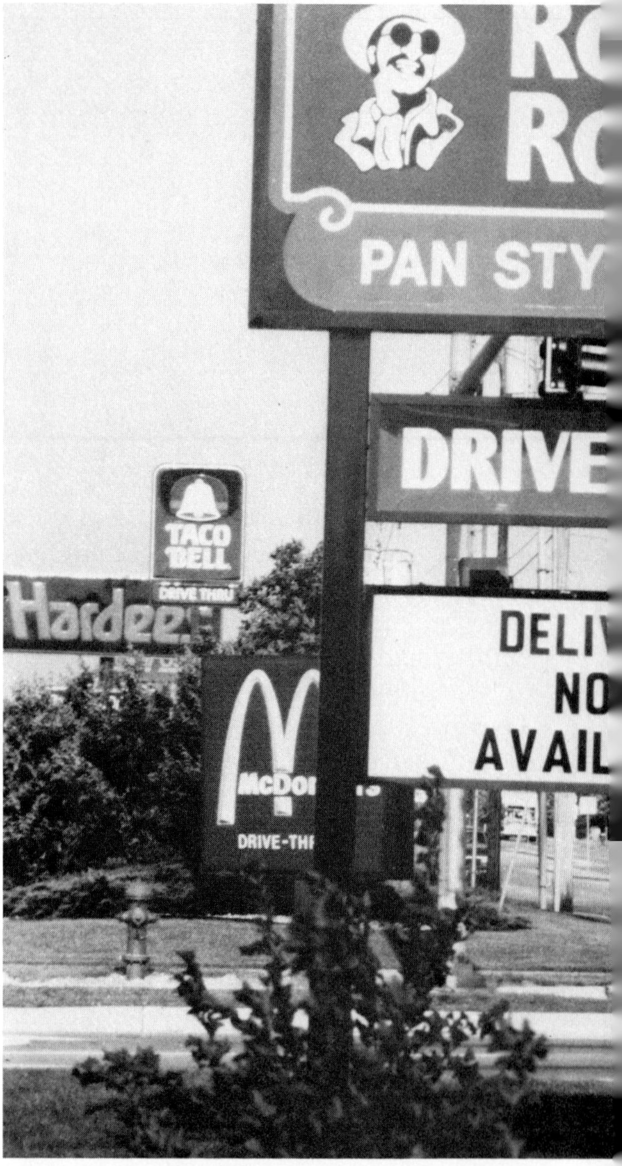

Fast food establishments provide many part-time and full-time work opportunities. Fast food is a good place to get some food service experience. They train most employees on-the-job which does not require additional education past high school.

FINDING A JOB

You are more likely to find a job if you know how to look for one. Knowledge, planning, and organization pay off.

Begin by reviewing what you know about yourself. What are your interests? Do you know your strengths and weaknesses, your abilities and aptitudes. (You may wish to reread Chapter 1.) Add to this information what you have learned about yourself in this class. What areas of food service particularly interest you?

It is important to remember that most first jobs in food service are beginning-level jobs. Without experience, you will not be hired as a supervisor or manager. Instead, you may be offered a job cleaning off tables or chopping vegetables. That's a start even if you really want to become a pastry chef. Once you have experience and show that you work hard no matter what the job, you can move up to something better.

Finding Job Openings

The first step to getting a job is finding out where there are job openings. Here are some good sources of information:

- **Personal contacts**. Do you have a friend or relative who works in food service? These people are personal contacts. They can tell you about job openings. If they know you are a good worker, they may be willing to recommend you for a job. You can make other personal contacts on your own by visiting food service operations and meeting people who work there.
- **Newspaper advertisements**. Check the ***classified section*** in the newspaper. This lists job openings under the heading "Help Wanted." The jobs are listed alphabetically. There are usually more in the Sunday paper than during the week.

  An ad will tell you the type of job available, the experience or training needed, and often the working hours and wage offered. Ads usually contain abbreviations to keep them short. The chart on page 398 shows some of the abbreviations commonly used in ads.
- **Your teacher**. Ask your teacher about possible job openings. Most food service teachers work with an ***advisory council*** — a group of men and women from the community who work in food service. Advisory council members often help students in the food service program find jobs where they can gain experience.
- **The vocational counselor**. Most high schools have a vocational counselor. The counselor keeps in contact with employers and employment agencies. Check to see if your vocational counselor knows of job openings in food service.
- **Employment agencies**. Cities and large towns have ***employment agencies***, both private and public. Employment agencies are in the business of matching employers who have job opening with people who need jobs. Private employment agencies charge a fee for finding you a job — usually a percentage of your pay for a number of weeks. State employment agencies are free. Check you phone book under "Employment" for the address of the one nearest you.
- **Area businesses**. You can also use the telephone book to make a list of food service operations in your area. Look in the advertisements section. Besides looking under "Food," try other titles like "Nursing Homes," "Hospitals," and "Schools." These places usually need food service workers, too.

Understanding Want Ad Abbreviations

aft	=	afternoon(s)	min wage	=	minimum wage
appl	=	applicant	morn	=	morning(s)
appt	=	appointment	nec	=	necessary
asst	=	assistant	nego	=	negotiable
avail	=	available	oppor	=	opportunity
ben	=	benefits (such as insurance)	pd	=	paid
bgn	=	beginning	pos	=	position
empl	=	employment	pref	=	preferred
eve	=	evening(s)	pt or PT	=	part-time
exc	=	excellent	qual	=	qualified or qualifications
exp	=	experience	refs	=	references
ft or FT	=	full-time	req	=	required
hrly	=	hourly (paid by the hour)	sal	=	salary
hrs	=	hours	temp	=	temporary
HS	=	high school education needed	wk	=	week
immed	=	immediate	wtr	=	waiter
incl	=	included	wtrss	=	waitress
mgr	=	manager	yrs	=	years

Organizing Your Information

The more organized you are, the more likely you are to find a job. When you talk to many people it is easy to mix up names or forget about a job lead. Organized people also make a better impression when they apply for a job.

Job Lead Cards

Invest in a package of small index cards when you begin you job search. Use these to record information about job leads. The card on this page shows one way to record this information.

front

Appointment — Tuesday 4:00 p.m.
Ruby Holt
(personnel manager)
Burger Village
4601 Long Street
Journal Star (Sat. 9/18)

back

Small company — only 30 workers in restaurant — they serve fast food — all workers are between 17-22 — they do hire part-time and holiday help.

FOOD SERVICE TRAINING

*Working as a **caterer's helper** provides excellent training in food preparation and presentation.*

*Being a **broiler chef's assistant** offers opportunities for advancement in the professional kitchen.*

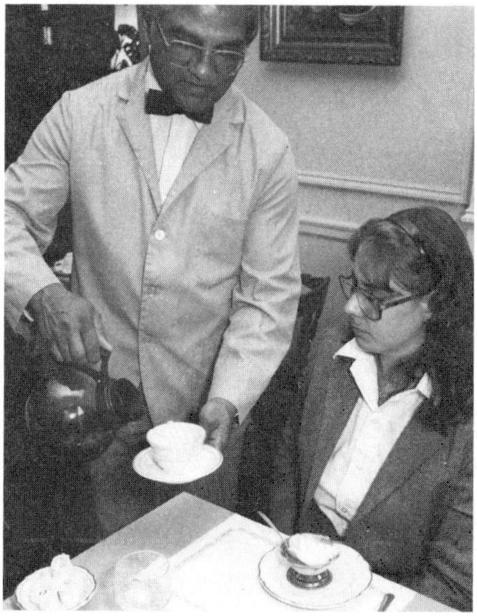

*Beginning your work experience as a **waiter** can open many doors in the food service industry.*

*A **beverage counter worker** learns to meet the public in addition to becoming an expert in beverage preparation.*

***Training under a pastry chef** offers you opportunities to move up the career ladder.*

*An **assistant salad cook** learns preparation techniques that will enable him to work in many areas of the kitchen.*

Personal Information

Before you apply for any job, you need to write down the information that an employer may ask about you. For almost every job, you will be asked to fill out a ***job application*** — a form that asks personal information. Those who must borrow a phone book to look up addresses or don't know the city of their birth, make a poor impression.

Getting a Social Security Number

In the United States, every worker must have a ***social security number***. Employers must deduct money from your paycheck and send it to the government with your name and number. When you retire, or are disabled, you receive money each month from the social security fund.

If you do not already have a social security card, get an application from the nearest social security office. You can find the address in the telephone book. Your school vocational counselor may also have applications.

Making a Personal Fact Sheet

A personal fact sheet contains the information about yourself that you have collected and organized on paper. A personal fact sheet is mainly for your own use, but you may also give it to prospective employers. You should make the sheet neat and easy to read. A typed sheet makes the best impression. Here are some tips on what your personal fact sheet should contain.

1. Your name, address (including zip code), and telephone number.
2. Social security number.
3. Date and place of birth
4. Age, height, and weight
5. Education and training. Your most recent school experience goes first, then you work backwards. Include the name of each school, complete address, and the dates you were there.
6. Job experience, if any. Again, begin with the most recent. List the names of the places you worked, addresses, dates, and kinds of jobs held.
7. Interests and activities. List your hobbies, sports, clubs, and other activities.
8. Honors or awards you have received.
9. References. People who know you well and are willing to recommend you for a job are called ***references***. Your teacher, for example, might be willing to be a reference for you. Be sure to ask a person's permission before listing his or her name as a reference. Include your references names, addresses, and telephone numbers. Usually, no more than three references are needed.

Look at the sample personal fact sheet on page 401. Can you identify each of the parts?

PERSONAL FACT SHEET

Name Purcell (Last) Patricia (First) Jane (Middle) Soc. Sec. # 597-01-9987

Address 1230 Lake Avenue (Street) Peoria (City) FL (State) 39812 (Zip Code)

Telephone Number 904-692-9337 Date of Birth 12-04-72

Emergency Number 904-692-4593 Age 16 Sex F Height 5'5"

Education:

Grammar School Mims Elementary (Name) Jacksonville (City) IL (State)

Middle or Junior High Dell Junior High (Name) Peoria (City) FL (State)

High School Central High School (Name) Peoria (City) FL (State)

Work Experience:

Job	Employer	Address	Telephone
Cashier	Ms. Traci Morse	900 Lawndale, Peoria	691-0511
Babysitter	Mrs. John Ford	207 Riverside, Peoria	692-7553
NA			

Interests and Activities:

Track, cooking, swimming, aerobics, and reading. Member of the Central High Track Team and Serviteens

Honors and Awards:

Crisco Award, 1987; Third Place, Math and Science Fair, 1986; Member of the All County Track Team, 1986.

References:

Name Ms. Traci Morse Position Manager of Dale's Delicatessen

Address 900 Lawndale, Peoria, FL Telephone 691-0511

Name Mr. and Mrs. John Ford Position Neighbors

Address 207 Riverside, Peoria, FL Telephone 692-7553

Name Mr. Larry Baker Position Food Service Teacher

Address Central High School, Peoria, FL Telephone 691-0702

APPLYING FOR A JOB

Once you know where there are job openings, you need to formally apply for the jobs which interest you. It is best to make an appointment ahead of time. Be sure not to call during the busiest times of the day.

The Application Form

By taking your personal fact sheet with you, you will have most of the information you need to fill out an application. Employers use application forms to find out about you. They also look to see whether the form was filled out neatly, completely, and correctly. Misspelled words and other mistakes make a poor impression.

The Interview

The employer usually chooses those with the best applications for an ***interview***. An interview is simply a face-to-face meeting that allows the employer to meet you and ask you questions. Interviews help employers decide who is the best person for the job.

Remember that the employer's first impression of you comes from your appearance. Everything about you should look neat, clean, and businesslike.

Your attitude is as important as your appearance. Do your homework before you go to the interview. In other words, know something about the place you are applying — the type of food served, what jobs are available. Be pleasant, interested, and excited about the job.

Here are some tips for interviews:

- Arrive early for the appointment.
- Never take a friend or family member with you.
- Listen to the questions and state your answers clearly.
- Sit erect and look the interviewer in the eye.
- Show your interest and willingness to cooperate.
- Be courteous and thank the person when the interview is over.

It is important to dress appropriately for an interview. Your appearance and facial expressions make a lasting impression on the employer.

FOOD SERVICE CAREERS

After working as a chef for many years, this gentleman decided to share his culinary talents with students at a vocational-technical center. ***Culinary experts who enter teaching*** *offer their students some rare educational training.*

An ***executive chef's*** *duties include planning menus, ordering food, keeping records, interviewing, and overseeing the operation of the kitchen. It takes many years to gain the experience needed to become an executive chef.*

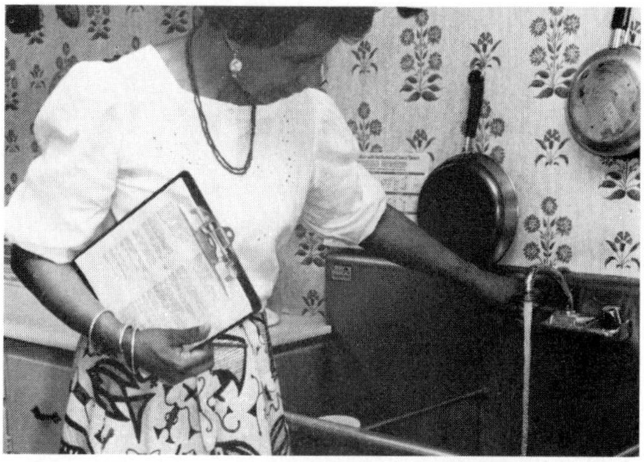

Being a ***health inspector*** *requires that you take special courses in safety and sanitation at the college level. This type of detective work requires knowledge of health codes and standards.*

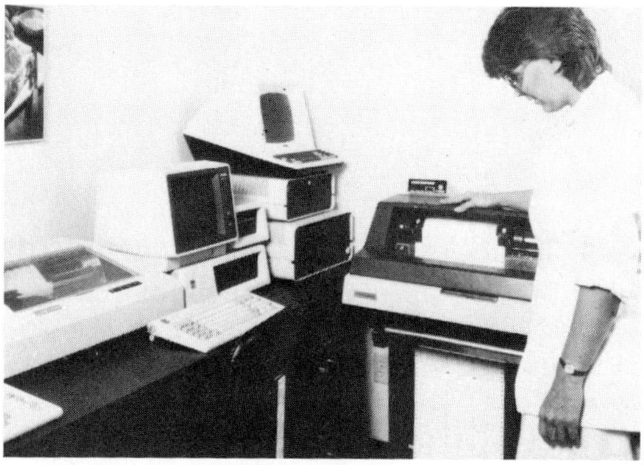

Dietitians *are trained in nutrition. They attend four years of college and take an examination to become registered. Computers are used by dietitians who work in hospitals and other institutional settings.*

The ***chef rotisseur*** *(ro-tee-SUR), also known as the broiler chef, oversees all meat and poultry preparation. This chef has specialized in the preparation of meat and poultry dishes. It takes dedication and much experience to be a broiler chef.*

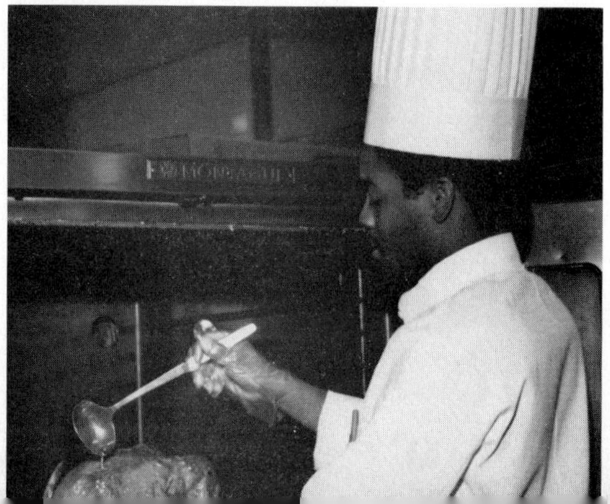

A ***chef saucier*** *(sos-cee-EH) checks on the progress of a stew. He prepares all of the sauces, in addition to overseeing the preparation of fish dishes, stews, and hot appetizers. The chef saucier is often the head chef.*

SUCCEEDING ON THE JOB

You have gotten a job and are about to start. How can you increase your chances of success?

As a new employee, you will be introduced to the person to whom you will be responsible. This person is usually called your ***supervisor***. Your supervisor will probably assign another worker to help you for a few days so you learn quickly to fit into the team.

Your supervisor is important to your success. It is your supervisor who is responsible for your on-the-job training, for helping you learn the skills you need for your job.

Listen carefully and make every effort to learn quickly. Be sure to follow the instructions you are given accurately. You may find it helpful to keep a small notepad and pencil in your pocket so you can write down things you might forget. Ask questions, but do not make a nuisance of yourself.

The training you have already received in class will help you on your job. Remember, though, that every operation does not do things exactly the same way. Do your tasks the way your supervisor tells you even if it is different from what you learned in class.

Take you job assignment seriously. Time is an important resource. Do not waste it. Check yourself often to be sure you have covered all the details, completed all the steps. Your supervisor will be impressed with the quality of your work as well as the interest you show in your job. In order to move up the career ladder, you should continue to learn all you can about the food service trade. You have now completed the first step, but there is much more to learn.

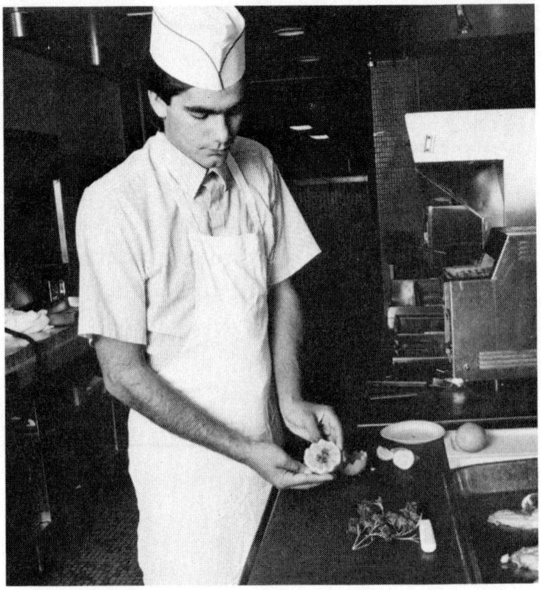

This pantry worker takes pride in his lemon garnishes. Skill development is very important in food service.

A fast food worker knows how to greet the public. Smiles and a positive attitude are essential for success in the food service industry.

SUMMARY

If you are considering a food service career, you must decide between additional education and looking for work. Your job search may include reading want ads and contacting friends, counselors, employment agencies, and businesses. Before applying for a job, you should have a social security number, a list of personal information, and references. A neat appearance, efficiency, and an attitude of responsibility are traits that will help you advance in your career.

chapter recap

CHECK YOUR KNOWLEDGE

1. What types of additional education are available for food service?

2. What are the advantages of a part-time job?

3. What are three good sources of information on job openings?

4. What is an advisory council?

5. What do you need to help you fill out a job application quickly and correctly?

6. What document must each person have before beginning work?

7. What are references?

8. List five tips for a successful interview.

9. Who are you responsible to on the job and why?

10. What traits will help you advance in a food service job?

EXTEND YOUR LEARNING

1. Prepare a personal fact sheet using the one on page 401 as an example.

2. Using the want-ad section in the newspaper, look for job openings in food sevice. Make a list of openings that includes some full-time and some part-time jobs. Write a letter of inquiry about the job that interests you most.

3. In small groups, write mini-plays showing the wrong and right way to act at a job interview. Perform the plays for the class.

glossary

advisory council A group of men and women from the community who work in food service and help plan the school food service program.

a la carte (AH-la-CART) Food offered with a separate price for each food item on the menu.

al dente An Italian term meaning tender, but with a slight resistence when chewed. Pasta is cooked al dente.

assembly table A long, stainless steel counter leading to the serving area on which foods are put together.

au gratin (oh GRAT-n) Made with a sauce and crust of bread crumbs and cheese.

back of the house In food service, the part of the operation out of sight of the customer.

bacteria Simple one-celled microorganisms.

balance scale A device made of two platforms connected by a bar; used to measure ingredients by weight.

basting Spooning cooking juices over meat or poultry as it cooks.

batter A thin, pourable flour mixture.

bench A baker's work table.

binder An ingredient which holds ingredients together.

blanching Partially cooking a food without browning it as a preliminary step before final cooking.

body The main part of a salad.

botulism A type of food poisoning which can easily cause death.

breader-sifter Tool used for breading food and for breading ingredients before reuse.

breading Coating of bread crumbs, cracker crumbs, or rolled corn flakes covering fish or poultry before frying.

brewed Having the flavor extracted by water, as in coffee or tea.

broiling Cooking done by exposing food directly to a heat source.

burritos (burr-EE-toes) Flour tortillas rolled around one or more fillings.

caffeine A stimulating substance often found in coffee.

calories A measurement of the amount of energy produced when food is burned by the body.

canape (CAN-a-PAY) A small, eye-appealing sandwich served before the first course, usually at dinner.

canvas liner A square of canvas which is placed over the pastry board to keep dough from sticking to the board.

carbohydrates Nutrients found in starches and sugars which provide most of the body's energy.

carousel oven Oven with revolving trays used for baking.

caterers People who specialize in preparing food which will be served elsewhere.

chlorophyll A substance which gives plants their green color.

classified section The part of a newspaper which advertises job openings.

clip-on Card or paper listing daily food specials which are clipped onto the menu.

club sandwich A decker sandwich made with ham and turkey.

coagulation The process of becoming firm, as protein does when heated.

commissary A food and supply warehouse often owned by a fast food chain.

compartment steamer A cabinet which cooks food quickly through the use of circulating steam.

conditioner A chemical additive which makes a higher, moister cake.

conduct (con-DUKT) The ability to transfer heat.

congealed salads Gelatin salads.

connective tissue The white, stringy substance that binds muscle fibers together.

consistency The degree of thickness and smoothness of a product, such as salad dressing.

contaminate To make food dirty or harmful to eat.

convection oven An oven which uses a fan to circulate hot air over food.

convenience food Any partially prepared food item that simplifies preparation.

converted rice Rice processed before polishing to drive the nutrients from the coating into the kernel.

cream 1. *verb* To beat shortening and sugar together until the mixture is fluffy and very well combined. 2. *noun* The part of milk which is highest in butterfat.

crepes (CREPS) Very thin pancakes rolled around a filling.

crimp To press the edges of pie crust together with a fork or a crimper.
crullers Soft dough that is rolled, cut into strips, twisted, and deep-fried.
cuisine (Kwee-ZEEN) A particular style of cooking, often relating to a country or region.
crustaceans Shellfish with legs and segmented shells.
cured Meat treated with ingredients to give it a distinctive flavor and retard spoilage.
cut-in To combine fat with flour until small pieces of fat are covered with flour.
cycle menu Menu offering different food item daily for a set period of time.

deck oven An oven with a series of stacked baking shelves, each with its own door and temperature control.
deep-fat frying Frying food in enough fat to cover it.
desired yield The amount of food you need a recipe to make.
disjointed Cut into pieces for cooking and serving.
docking Making small holes or slits in pie crust to allow steam to escape.
double pan To cook a pie shell between two pie pans of the same size so it will keep its shape.
dough hook A hook-shaped beater used on a mixer to knead yeast dough.
dredged Coated with seasoned flour before cooking.
dressing Garnishes added to hamburgers.
du jour Phrase meaning "of the day" as in "soup du jour" — soup of the day.
durum wheat A type of wheat high in gluten, a protein.
dusting Coating meat or fish lightly with flour or cornmeal.
dusting powder A mixture of oregano and Parmesan cheese used as a finish on pizza.

egg wash A mixture of egg yolk and milk or water brushed on bread and rolls before cooking.
employment agencies Businesses which match employers with people who need jobs.
emulsion A mixture of liquids which do not separate from each other.
enchiladas (en-chi-LAH-dahs) Soft tortillas rolled around fillings and baked with a sauce.
entree (AHN-tray) The main course of a meal.
equipment Small or large appliances. Also used to mean tools, utensils, and appliances.
equivalents Amounts that are equal, but expressed in different ways.
extenders Inexpensive ingredients combined with more expensive foods to make them go farther.

fabricated cuts Cuts of meat which have been trimmed and cut to a specific serving size.
fat absorption Saturation of foods with fat during deep-fat frying.
fat-soluble vitamins Vitamins stored in body fat.
fermentation Process in which yeast feeds on starch and sugar, giving off carbon dioxide, and causing dough to rise.
FIFO Abbreviation for "first in, first out," the rule of storage where the oldest supplies are used first.
fillet In fish, a lengthwise cut from the side of the fish.
filling A sweet, moist mixture used to hold layers of a cake together.
first aid On-the-spot treatment of injuries until medical help arrives.
fixed menu A menu which offers the same foods every day.
flammable Materials that catch fire easily.
flat top range A cooking appliance which has burners under a solid top.
flavor enhancer An ingredient added to a dish to develop the taste.
flute To form a decorative edge around a pie crust.
foam cake A cake which rises because of the air trapped in beaten egg whites.
food release A mixture of vegetable oil, alcohol, and lecithin sprayed on pans to keep food from sticking.
forecasting The act of projecting information, such as the number of meals to be served on a given day.
formula A recipe, particularly for a baked product.
fricassee (frik-a-SEE) To serve meat or poultry in its own gravy.
fritters Rich batter that is dropped by spoonfuls into hot fat.
front of the house In food service, the areas of the establishment seen by customers.
frosting A thick, fluffy, spreadable mixture used on cakes and other desserts.

game In cooking, wild birds used as food.
garnish An edible decoration that brings color or flavor to a dish.
gauge The thickness of metal.
gel A jelly-like solid.
giblets The edible internal organs of poultry.
gluten The protein found in flour.

grading Officially determining the quality of a food product.

griddle top range A cooking appliance with a smooth top. Foods such as eggs and pancakes are cooked directly on the top.

grid marks Dark lines on meat made by a hot broiling rack or grid.

grilling A method of short-order cooking on a griddle.

grind The finished shape of a knife edge.

hazard Any risk or danger.

high-ratio shortening A special type of hydrogenated shortening which can tolerate having a higher proportion of sugar added to it than other shortenings.

homogenized Milk that has been treated to scatter the butterfat throughout the milk.

hor d'oeuvres (or-DURVS) Small bits of tasty food served before dinner or with cocktails.

hydrogenated shortening Vegetable oil processed into a fluffy, white solid.

icing A thin, pourable mixture of sugar and water used on cakes and other desserts.

institutions Public or charitable establishments, such as schools, hospitals, and nursing homes.

internal temperature The temperature in the middle of food, such as meat.

interview A meeting in which an employer questions a job applicant. This helps the employer to choose the best person for the job.

inventory An itemized list of stock on hand in storage areas.

invoice Itemized list of goods and prices accompanying a supply delivery.

job application A form giving personal information filled out by someone applying for a job.

julienne Cut into narrow strips.

kneading A mixture process by which dough is folded, pressed and squeezed to strengthen the gluten strands.

leaveners Chemicals, yeast, air, or steam which help flour mixtures rise.

management Controlling and directing in order to get a job done correctly and within the allotted time.

marbling Small flecks of fat found throughout meat.

marinating Using acid liquids to break down the connective tissue of meat.

mark up The cost of operating a business, expressed in terms of a percentage, added to food costs to determine the selling price.

masa harina Finely ground corn flour used to make tortillas.

medium rare Degree of doneness in meat in which the center of the meat is still pink.

menu The food choices offered at each meal.

metabolism The process of turning food into energy inside the body.

meringue A fluffy mixture of beaten egg whites and sugar.

microorganisms Living cells so small that they can be seen only with a microscope.

milk stone A hard deposit that forms inside any equipment used with dairy products.

mirepoix (meer-PWA) A mixture of coarsely chopped vegetable used to season meat.

mise en place (mees-en-PLASS) To organize equipment and ingredients completely before starting to cook.

mollusks Shellfish with undivided bodies and a hard shell that opens and closes.

nachos Crisp tortillas dipped in or covered with mixture of melted cheese and chilies.

nonprofit Food service operations which must cover costs but do not need to make a profit to stay in business.

nutrients The chemicals the body needs which are supplied by food.

nutrition The study of food and the way the body uses it.

open-faced sandwich Sandwich made of one piece of bread topped with a filling and garnish.

open top range A cooking appliance with open burners on top.

orange pekoe The highest quality black tea.

original yield The amount of food a recipe makes.

oven spring The rapid rise of yeast dough at the beginning of the baking process.

overhead broiler A self-contained unit with a warming oven above a broiler grid and another oven or storage beneath it.

panfry A method of frying larger pieces of food using enough oil to coat the pan.

panning Placing dough in pans for baking.

parboiled rice Rice partially cooked under pressure and then dried.

pasta A variety of products, such as spaghetti and noodles, made from durum wheat flour.
pasteurization The process of heating milk to kill harmful bacteria.
pastry bag A cone made of canvas with changeable tips used to make bagged cookies and to make frosting decorations.
pastry flour A low-gluten flour often used to make pie crust.
peel A wooden paddle with a long handle used to remove pizza from the oven.
pie shell An unfilled piecrust.
pilot light A flame which burns continuously and lights the burner when the control is turned.
pita bread Thin, soft yeast bread that forms a pocket when baked. Also called pocket bread.
plating The placing and arrangement of food on a plate.
poaching Cooking in a small amount of simmering liquid.
pocket bread A thin, soft yeast bread that forms a pocket when baked. Also called pita bread.
portion control The use of strict measurement to achieve equal serving sizes.
portion scale A small scale that can weigh amounts up to one pound.
precosting Figuring the cost of each ingredient used in a standard recipe.
pre-preparation Getting foods ready to cook.
produce (PRO-doos) Fresh fruits and vegetables.
production line An efficient, assembly-line technique for preparing food.
production schedule A form filled out by the head cook in each station specifying the tasks to be completed.
proofer A cabinet with controlled heat and humidity used for yeast dough rising.
proofing Final rising of yeast dough.
protein The nutrient essential for growth, repair, and maintenance of the body.
pumice stone Light, spongy rock that will clean a griddle without scratching it.
punched down Dough is pressed and folded to release the carbon dioxide built up during rising.
pungent Having a strong, sharp flavor and aroma.
purchase order A form the buyer fills out for the delivery of a certain product.
purees Thick, sieved ingredients often used as a base for soup.

rare Degree of doneness in meat in which the center is heated but still very red and juicy.
RDA The Recommended Daily Allowances — a chart that estimates how much of each major nutrient a person of a given age and sex needs daily.
references People who know you well and are willing to recommend you for a job.
refried beans Cooked, dried beans which have been recooked in fat.
registered dietitian A professional who is trained in nutrition.
requisitions Written orders for food, are used within the operation to withdraw supplies from the storeroom.
retarding Refrigerating yeast dough before it rises to slow the growth of the yeast.
rib-eye A type of steak cut from the muscle of the club steak.

salamander A smaller broiler usually located above a range or other cooking unit.
salmonella (sal-mu-NELL-uh) A bacteria found in many raw foods which can cause illness if not killed by cooking.
sanitation The science of maintaining a clean and germ-free environment for food production.
sanitize To clean with a product that kills all microorganisms.
sauté (saw-TAY) A preliminary cooking step in which food is cooked in a small amount of fat and stirred frequently.
scaling Dividing dough into equal pieces by cutting and weighing it.
scalloped Cooked with a white sauce, as in scalloped potatoes.
scoring Cutting the long fibers of meat horizontally and vertically with shallow gashes in order to tenderize it.
seafood Cold-blooded animals living in water which are used for food.
seat line Mark on cup which shows how full it should be.
serrated Having saw-like notches on the edge.
shaved Sliced extremely thin, as in meats for sandwiches.
sheet cake A cake baked in a large, low-sided baking pan.
sheeter A machine that automatically rolls and cuts thin crust pizza dough.
shellfish Seafood with a hard, outer shell and no backbone or spinal column.
shortened cake Cake made with shortening as a main ingredient.
shortening Fats used in baking and cooking.
short-order cook Person in charge of preparing quick foods.

shucked Having the shell peeled off — as in shellfish.

skewers Long, stainless steel pins used to hold food together during cooking.

smoke point The temperature at which fat disintegrates and smokes.

social security number A number you must have in order to work. It enables social security payments made by you and your employer to be credited to your account.

specifications A detailed statement of the standards required by the purchaser of an item.

spread A thin coating of butter, margarine, or mayonnaise used on bread.

spring scale A device for measuring ingredients. When the ingredient is placed on the scale, the weight is shown on a dial.

staging Allowing the baked pizza to sit on top of the oven for a short time before cutting.

standardized recipe A recipe giving exact directions about ingredient amounts and preparation methods.

staph A type of harmful bacteria caused by human beings that can contaminate food.

steam-jacketed kettle A large, round appliance with a container inside for food. Live steam circulates between the outside and inner container, cooking the food.

sterilizing Killing all microorganisms.

stir-fry An Oriental cooking technique in which food is fried quickly in hot oil until tender-crisp.

stock rotation Putting new products behind or under supplies of the same product so that older products will be used first.

stoning Cleaning a grill by scrubbing with pumice stone.

supervisor The person to whom a worker is directly responsible.

table d'hôte (TAHB-lah-DOTE) A complete meal offered at a fixed price.

tacos Corn tortillas filled with meat, vegetables, etc.

tamales Meat mixture wrapped in tortilla dough and corn husks and then steamed.

tang The part of a knife blade that is attached to the handle.

tartar sauce A mixture of mayonnaise, chopped pickles, onions, and other ingredients often used as a garnish for fish.

teamwork Working together for a common purpose.

tempered Steel that is heat-treated so that it is very hard, yet still flexible.

tempering Marinating fish in a salty solution.

tent cards Cards listing daily food specials which are folded to stand up on a table.

thermostats Devices which keep the temperature of a piece of equipment exactly where you need it.

time management Judging the time needed to prepare and cook food and using time in the most effective way.

time schedule A written schedule specifying in the correct sequence the time needed for food preparation.

tools Hand-held items used for food preparation, cooking, and serving.

tortillas (tor-TEE-yahs) Round, Mexican flat breads made with corn or wheat flour.

toxins Poisonous substances.

translucent Allowing light to shine through.

truss To tie the wings and legs of poultry close to the body.

tube pan A type of cake pan which is large, round, and has a hollow tube in the center.

tubers (TOO-burrs) Thickened, fleshy portions of a root from which a new plant can grow. Some vegetables are tubers.

underliner The part of a salad put on the plate first. Often called the base.

urn A large coffee maker.

vendor A seller of a product.

volume The amount of space taken up by anything.

warming cabinet Drawer heated by steam used to keep sandwiches such as hamburgers warm until dressing is added.

wash A liquid which helps breading stick to food. It is usually made of beaten egg and milk.

water-soluble vitamins Vitamins which are not stored in the body.

well done Degree of doneness in meat in which the center is gray-brown.

wholesale cuts The large sections of meat into which a carcass is divided.

wok (WALK) Heavy pan with rounded bottom and sloped sides which is often used for stir-frying.

work flow The movement of work in an orderly manner so that it can be done most efficiently.

work simplification Doing a job in the easiest, simplest and quickest way possible.

work station A specific work area where a particular kind of food is prepared or a specific job is done.

yield The number of servings a recipe will provide if it is followed exactly.

index